58

D1275999

THE TRANSFORMING POWER OF AFFECT

THE

TRANSFORMING

POWER

OF AFFECT

A Model for Accelerated Change

DIANA FOSHA, Ph.D.

BASIC BOOKS

A MEMBER OF THE PERSEUS BOOKS GROUP

Published by Basic Books,
A Member of the Perseus Books Group

D. Fosha & M. I. Slowiaczek, (1997) Techniques to accelerate dynamic psychotherapy, *American Journal of Psychotherapy,* 51(2): 229–251, adapted with permission of the Association for the Advancement of Psychotherapy.

D. Fosha, (1995) Technique and taboo in three short-term dynamic psychotherapies, *Journal of Psychotherapy Practice and Research,* 4(4): 297–318, adapted with permission of the *Journal of Psychotherapy Practice and Research.*

Designed by Martin Lubin Graphic Design

A catalog record for this book is available from the Library of Congress.

ISBN-10: 0-465-09567-4   ISBN-13: 978-0-465-09567-4

To my three amazing graces,
MARTY, MOLLY, AND ZOE

*... he understood this, too:
that accident ruled every corner
of the universe except the chambers
of the human heart.*

DAVID GUTERSON, *Snow Falling on Cedars*

CONTENTS

ACKNOWLEDGMENTS

The affective model of change is a dyadic model of transformation. I wish to take this space to honor my own formative and transformative others.

D. W. Winnicott and Habib Davanloo have been essential sources of influence. Like so many others who became entranced with his work, I have had a profound relationship with Winnicott, albeit in transitional space, which is probably where most lasting teaching and learning takes place. My other mentor has been Habib Davanloo: once exposed to the effectiveness, intense experience, and relentless authenticity of his work, I was hooked; my life has not been the same since. Though I am sure that much of what follows is unrecognizable to him, I know that none of it would exist without his unique work.

David Malan was the source of my first short-term dynamic psychotherapy epiphany. His exhilaratingly aggressive hypothesizing and active intervention took nothing away from psychodynamic psychotherapy; if anything, they seemed to make it more muscular. His courageous, empirically based plainspeaking has been a beacon of clarity and integrity.

At the Doctoral Program in Clinical Psychology of the City University of New York, Steve Ellman, Gilbert Voyat, and Paul Wachtel demonstrated through teaching and personal example that clinical work and intellectual rigor are not only compatible but deeply potentiating. Paul Wachtel was instrumental in articulating what I was beginning to suspect: that there could be a disjunction between psychoanalytic theory and psychoanalytic practice. I have greatly appreciated his implicit mentoring and explicit friendship over the years.

My own teaching, more than anything else, has sharpened my thinking and forced me to face blind spots, imprecision, and inconsistencies: my students in the CUNY Doctoral Program in Clinical Psychology, the Bellevue Hospital Psychology Internship Program, the AET Institute, and currently Adelphi University's Derner Institute have spurred me to keep refining what I have to say.

I am grateful to my patients for having allowed me to have an impact and for giving me their trust and engagement; I feel privileged to have been a partner in and witness to amazing journeys and moving transformations.

I have been blessed with wonderful colleagues and friends. The Montreal swamp rats, Paul Rosenberg (West), William Alder, and, most especially, Bob Okin, were essential to survival in the early days: French dinners, shared angst, and good talk made our struggles the stuff of lively interaction rather than lonely despair. Michael Alpert's generosity and commitment to fostering communication and community have been indispensable to the evolution of the experiential STDPs in the 1990s; most exceptional, perhaps, has been his steadfast willingness to push the envelope (and, when called for, to change envelopes).

Isabel Sklar has been a solid source of support, companionship, empathy, strength, and learning: her videotapes reveal the depth of her willingness to give to her patients. Patricia Coughlin Della Selva and Michael Laikin have taught me more than they probably know: despite some ideological differences, the videotaped evidence of the effectiveness of their work has led me to emphasize the importance of authenticity in therapeutic stance above and beyond the demands of any particular model. Jane Marke's capacity to distill complex matters to their essence and come up with a clear, concrete course of action has never ceased to amaze me: she has been a valuable friend and a most helpful colleague.

Three gifted clinicians, Mabel Quinones, Maria Slowiaczek, and Peggy Spier, joined me in grappling with the paradigm shift pivotal to the development of accelerated-experiential dynamic psychotherapy in an environment of support, affirmation, and challenge. The three chapters in this book on strategies of intervention build on the work Maria Slowiaczek and I did together on what became our 1997 paper on AEDP techniques—the product of two consciousnesses forging coordination while seeking to preserve authenticity.

Leigh McCullough was a wonderful midwife, right there when I was in acute labor prior to the birth of AEDP. I was able to appreciate at first hand what a wonderful therapist she is, warm and present, and how active her intelligence. I was lucky to benefit from her wonderful skills and friendship at a moment that turned out to be pivotal. As a colleague, her work, enthusiasm, and unpretentious honesty have been an inspiration.

To my conversations with Peter Costello, I owe a far greater piece than the text formally acknowledges of my conceptualization of the role of communication in the complete processing of core affect and of the role of therapist as trusted companion (à la Bowlby). And I thank

Jenna Osiason, with whom I have met under the guise of supervision every Monday for an hour over the past four years, for sharing her luminous clinical work and for her empathic friendship as we have struggled with how best to help patients and think about what we were doing.

I want to thank also the following colleagues and supervisees who have shared their clinical work through videotape with courage, openness, and commitment to advancing the cause of effective psychotherapy. I cannot express how much I have learned from them: William Alder, Michael Alpert, Alanne Baerson, Harold Been, Joe Celentano, Peter Costello, Patricia Coughlin Della Selva, Habib Davanloo, David Davis, Cathy Duca, Karen Ezra, Brenda Forte, Dawn Fried, Sarah Hardesty, Allyson Hentel, Allen Kalpin, Gabrielle Kaminetsky, Yael Kapeliuk, Lisa Kentgen, Michael Laikin, Frances Leon, Harold Lifschutz, Jeffrey Magnavita, David Malan, Jane Marke, Leigh McCullough, Eileen McElroy, Robert Okin, Jenna Osiason, Ferruccio Osimo, Claire Owen, Mabel Quinones, Paul Rosenberg, Tewfik Said, Steven Sandler, Connie Seligman, Isabel Sklar, Maria Slowiaczek, Peggy Spier, Vincent Stephens, Dawn Baird Taylor, Margaret Tompsett, Manuel Trujillo, Gil Tunnell, Janet Waterhouse, Susan Westelle, Jason Worschel, and Christ Zois.

Over the years, Dina Copelman, Eydie Kwart, Marie Rudden, Jim Stoeri, and Jack and Pat Heidenry have been a joy to have as friends.

My editor at Basic Books, Cindy Hyden, has been a wonderful resource. To paraphrase what Wilbur says of Charlotte in *Charlotte's Web:* she is in a class by herself. It is not often that someone comes along who is a true friend and a good editor. She has been both. The editorial process has at times felt like therapy, with Cindy making her way through the thicket of verbiage to get to the core, bring it out, and let it shine. Thank you.

Alex Bloom, Martin Lubin, and Michael Wilde all gave me the best of their unsentimental minds. It was particularly gratifying to earn their appreciation and eventually elicit personal elaborations and associations in the margins of the text they were helping me transform. To the degree that the book is not leaner and meaner, it is not for their lack of trying. Martin Lubin, this time in his role of live-in graphic designer, elegantly designed and typeset every page as well as the jacket.

My parents, both writers (my father a playwright, my mother a theater critic), chose to leave Romania to come to New York, relinquishing a culture that, for better or worse, was resonantly theirs so that I could grow up in a richer and less restrictive one. I deeply admire the intrepid energy and unquestioning devotion to achievement and to moving forward of my mother, Madeline Fosha; my father, Harry Fosha, role-modeled creativity, playfulness, humor, and devotion to writing for its own sake. I hope that their sacrifice is honored by what has come of it, though nothing can make up for what they have lost. The irony is that their wrenching personal experiences led them to insist that whatever I choose to do be practical and not language-dependent. Well, they tried: some things are in the blood.

It is a source of great sadness to me that I didn't get to share more adventures with my first true other, my grandfather, Artur Focsaner. One terrible fall evening when I was in first grade and learning how to write a capital E in script seemed truly beyond me, he understood the importance of accessing an altogether different self-other emotion-configuration: good pals, we walked through Bucharest, had grown-up stuff to eat and drink, imbibed the fragrant night air; of course by the time we got back home, way past bedtime, capital E in script was a piece of cake. That was my first AEDP experience. I miss, too, my mother-in-law, Sophie Lubin, and regret that she did not live to see her granddaughters.

In the life that I have co-authored, I have been extraordinarily blessed with three transforming others: my husband, Martin Lubin, and my daughters, Molly Sophia and Zoe Ariel Lubin-Fosha. Marty has both held me and given me a lot of space to roam and wander: his holding, with its objective edge informed by his irrepressible humor, has made me feel safer than I could have ever imagined. Though no one is fonder of words than he, his presence and his actions are gifts beyond words.

Molly has been miraculously blessed with empathy from infancy. It is a joy to behold her unfolding journey as she becomes more gorgeously herself every day. My thanks to her for being such a great friend, though I do wish she wouldn't beat me at Spit all the time. Zoe's free spirit and undaunted originality are sources of endless awe and inspiration. May she continue her inner directedness, and remain unscarred by the world. I thank her for gracing my life with her presence; if, however, her putting on her shoes in the morning required less active intervention, I would not be brokenhearted. I wouldn't have been able to write large parts of the chapter on the healing affects were it not for how they have affected me, and effected their transformational magic.

THE TRAJECTORY OF THE AFFECTIVE MODEL OF CHANGE

The patient on the videotape was an intelligent, good-looking man whose life was in such disrepair that corrosive despair lay just beneath his sarcastic, vague, aloof façade. The interviewing clinician, Habib Davanloo, was direct in his first question: "Could you tell me what seems to be the problem that you want to get help for it [*sic*]?" Making no eye contact and staring at the ceiling instead, the patient replied, "Uh, no, not exactly. I only have some hazy idea of what might be the problem ... I'm not even sure whether those difficulties are a normal part of being a human being ..." The interviewer challenged his vagueness, but the patient went on: "What I'm trying to say that umm, it becomes a more plausible thing, with a more plausible cause, when you realize ... I have a problem with commitment. ... But don't forget that of course it took me many many years to realize that I had a problem there. I mean, I've been plodding in the dark for almost as long as I've been alive. Which brings up another point, maybe I have a problem with feelings" (Davanloo, 1990, pp. 9–10). With terms like *schizoid* and *fragile* swirling in my mind, I felt I was watching someone whose treatment, *if* the therapist was skilled, would take years and years. Yet after two hours of intensive and at times outright confrontational interaction with a relentless therapist, the patient's life story emerged with startling coherence and poignancy; his eyes clear and his gaze direct, the patient had raged and wept, and he was transformed.[1]

A THERAPY IN SEARCH OF A THEORY

Nothing in my fine training in psychoanalytic psychotherapy prepared me for that kind of effectiveness. I had to learn to do what I had witnessed. Shortly thereafter, I began my training with Davanloo. Over time, and many personal and professional transformations later, the

[1] The case of the German architect (Davanloo, 1990, pp. 1–45).

affective model of change, and accelerated experiential-dynamic psychotherapy (AEDP), the therapy approach it informs, emerged and evolved.

The affective model of change would never be without the short-term dynamic psychotherapy (STDP) experience. The stance and techniques detailed in the second part of this book are not a natural outgrowth of the theoretical model, but rather a spur to it. Here, clinical experience shaped theory: knowing the power of core affect to transform the self, I knew what had to be explained. Part 1, therefore, aims to provide a conceptual foundation for affect-driven transformation experienced within an emotionally connected dyad.

Working with Davanloo, I learned firsthand about the power of the visceral experience of emotion. In watching his extraordinary—and unique—clinical work, I saw the possibility of profound, substantive, and lasting change occurring rapidly. I realized that assumptions about the fragility of patients often are rationalizations for ineffective technique. Fragility should not be assumed, nor used to inhibit clinical action: it is a clinical assessment to be made in the course of—not prior to—dynamic interaction with the patient. At last I came to understand that patients (that is, all of us), being products of invariably less than perfect caregiving, can tolerate remarkably odd situations and make the best of what is offered, provided they sense that something authentic and valuable is to be had; thus, automatic constraints on therapeutic expression are fundamentally unnecessary—even counterproductive. Patients and psychic phenomena prove quite robust; for the well-trained clinician, the danger of ineffectiveness and avoided action looms much larger than the danger of damage from direct intervention.

A return to process notes and one-and-one supervision became impossible after immersion in Davanloo's exposure method of clinical training: taboos were being broken left and right. No more inner sanctum of the psychotherapy session; the video camera was there. No more cozy privacy of one-on-one supervision; the group was there. No more self-protection of process notes: the work was out there, on tape, not filtered through the categories of my perception, figures of my speech, or idiosyncrasies of my style. Excruciating as the exposure was, exhilaration was the other side of the coin: I felt seen. Finally, one could truly learn.

Over time, however, it became increasingly clear that Davanloo's method of engagement through aggression was suited to his way of making contact, but not to mine. Furthermore, while a powerful method in fact was being employed, it was not sufficiently articulated, and there was no mechanism for its transmission except from master to disciple. The psychodynamic framework that informed Davanloo's STDP—a received drive-superego theory—did not do justice to the radical nature and transformative impact of the phenomena that it so reliably elicited.

As the STDP movement burgeoned, my growing unease was shared by colleagues with similar training (Alpert, 1992). Our struggle was to preserve the essence of Davanloo's therapeutic effectiveness—that is, the power of visceral experience and the capacity to get to it quickly, from the initial moments of the first encounter with the patient—while evolving a more user-friendly mode of relating, to hold the deep affect work. Gradually, a switch occurred from radical challenge and pressure to radical empathy and emotional engagement through attunement, resonance, affect sharing, affirmation, and self-disclosure. (See the Appendix for the evolution of the empathic stance as it recounts the family history of the experiential STDPs.) Relating through a stance characterized by "a radical acceptance of the patient" (Osiason, 1995) also yielded access to core affective phenomena—but it revealed new anxieties, for patients *and* therapists: only with an emotionally engaged therapist can the terrors of love, affirmation, and feeling good truly be discerned.

Now it was time to evolve a metapsychology to account theoretically for the empirical power of working with affect from an emotionally engaged stance and to articulate the phenomena in which transformational processes are rooted. The mission of this book is to elucidate both. Insofar as the clinical experience has shaped the creation of the theory, the why precedes the what and the how.

Freud inferred developmental theory from the pathological phenomena he observed in the consulting room; clinical psychoanalysis is masterly and unrivaled at explaining stasis, but not so when it comes to change. In contradistinction, the work of analytically informed attachment theorists and clinical developmentalists investigating mother-infant interaction is thoroughly change-oriented. The parallels between the affective model of change and both attachment theory and moment-to-moment mother-infant interaction are uncanny—and so persuasive that attention to the phenomena of attachment and *moment-to-moment fluctuations in mutual affective coordination* follow an introduction to affect in these pages by way of foundation for the sections on therapeutic technique.

THE AFFECTIVE
MODEL OF CHANGE
AND ACCELERATED
EXPERIENTIAL–DYNAMIC
PSYCHOTHERAPY

The power of affect to transform is enormous. Unlike other change processes, it is not gradual and cumulative, but intense and rapid—even more so when harnessed to the depth and thoroughness of psychodynamic work. This clinical fact shaped the development of the affective model of change, which identifies and makes sense of the power of affect and puts it to work in an affirming therapeutic relationship. Similarly, the attachment process, though operating within a completely different time frame, is also greatly mutative: who we are reflects the history of our relational bonds from infancy on. By synergistically linking emotion and attachment, the explosive transformational power of affect can be harnessed through a relational process and put to maximal and lasting therapeutic use. The task of this book is to elucidate an affective theory of change, a clinical stance, and a series of techniques to reliably bring this about. The operative question is, How can the therapist evoke a relational environment in which the transformational power of affective experience can contribute to the emergence and development of the patient's essential self?

Affect and attachment are the persistent, pervasive, preoccupying issues of daily experience; they infuse all we do with a characteristic phenomenological texture and quality. We manage and respond to matters of affect and attachment throughout our lives. This is what makes a therapy focused on such matters potentially so transformative: it reaches into the very texture of our experiencing, where emotional life is lived.

So much pathology is the result of anxiety and shame and aloneness (which potentiates fear and shame) and the resulting lack of access to emotional resources. The aim of AEDP is to reverse the process. Traditional psychoanalysis is very good at tracking the re-creation of childhood experiences in everyday adult life and in the transference; this is an important activity, particularly in understanding the nature of the genesis of defenses. In the affective model of change, however, the focus is on unlocking affect, giving the patient the chance to ride the deep river of affect and create new experiences based on the use of previously unavailable resources. The affective model is healing-centered and privileges healing forces: adaptive strivings and deep motivation for change. Through connection and unlocking, the nature of emotional information processing is altered toward therapeutic aims.

The synergy of attachment and affect results in the establishment of safety, a corresponding reduction in anxiety, and in turn a mitigation of the need for defenses, promoting and permitting access to core affects and their explosive healing properties. Experience is paramount. The single most important and defining aspect of the therapy is that it is experiential: the clinical phenomena are not inferred, referred to, interpreted, or only talked about: they are *experienced* by the patient. The experience of vital affects in the context of an attached relationship is the primary agent of emotional transformation, in life and—a fortiori—in treatment.

Without relational support, intense affects can become toxic instead of promoting optimal functioning and well-being. When attachment figures cannot support the individual so that he feels safe in feeling his feelings, affective experiences can threaten to overwhelm the integrity of self and relationships; when faced alone, they can be unbearable. The individual, painfully aware of the inadequacy of his own resources but determined to survive, comes up with protective strategies to defend against emotional experience. Yet defensive measures, while adaptive in the short run, eventually lead to the kind of psychic suffering that brings patients to seek help: the individual is robbed of a powerful source of growth, and his personality reflects it. Here is the seed of psychopathology: when reliance on defenses against emotional experience becomes chronic as a result of the failure of the emotional environment to provide support, psychic development goes off course. Thus, aloneness in the face of overwhelming affective experience plays a major role in the development of psychopathology.

The patient comes to treatment having reached the end of his rope. Yet coming reflects hope; the potential for emotional and relational responsiveness in a facilitating environment always remains alive. The very making of an appointment with a total stranger to deal with the greatest intimacies and vulnerabilities of one's life is an act of profound faith. The aim of affect-centered therapy is to harness the patient's adaptive potential and massive resources for healing, all of which have been waiting for the right facilitating environment to emerge. As the psychic equilibrium shifts toward health, the distorted solutions (i.e., defense mechanisms) rooted in environments that failed to support the individual's growth can be abandoned.

We seek to highlight the willingness to risk and trust that coexists with the patient's suffering and despair, demoralization, and defeat. Strongly aware of the repetition of pathology-generating patterns, we seek a new beginning by affirming the life force within and charting a new course—specifically, undoing the environment's affect-facilitating failure and catalyzing the experience of the mutative power of healing affects. Just as the patient's potential for healing is emphasized, so too is the power of the therapist (i.e., rooted in an understanding of the power of the other) to be effective, contribute to the course of therapy, and make an impact. Specific strategies of intervention empower the therapist to access and process core affective experiences; it is these techniques, together with an emotionally engaged therapeutic stance, that are the principal identifying features of the affective model of change.

TRAJECTORY
OF THE BOOK

Chapter 1 articulates a model of affect and its transformational powers fundamentally rooted in a relational matrix. Informed by emotion theory, the clinically based construct of *core affect* is articulated and developed here: expression and communication to an open, receptive other are integral aspects of its full experience, ultimately leading to a transformation of the self. By making communication an intrinsic aspect of the full experiential cycle of processing an emotion, affective and relational elements are revealed to be organically linked within the core phenomena under consideration here.

Chapters 2 and 3 locate the specifically relational underpinnings of the affective model of change in the work of psychoanalytically oriented developmentalists and attachment theorists. Viewing that work through the lens of affect introduces the construct of *affective competence* (the capacity to feel and deal while relating) in both infant and caregiver—including the emergence of adaptive efforts, however pathological, to maintain attachment ties. The discussion affectively reframes the constructs of the good-enough caregiver (mother or therapist), the internal working model, and the reflective self function, to ascertain what constitutes optimal (in terms of promoting security and resilience) dyadic interaction. In the internalization of ways of relating unique to each dyad are the seeds of both pathology and healing—the intergenerational transmission of pathology and the motivation for reparation—that pervades moment-to-moment living, even after traumas. A major aspect of affective competence is responsiveness to these self-righting tendencies, for reparation is a crucial force in the organization of the experience of both dyadic partners. The expectation of the possibility of repair is at the heart of establishing states of mutual affective coordination that are at the foundation of securely attached relationships.

Chapter 4 addresses psychopathology as the product of a compromised capacity to process affect. A pivotal notion is the pathogenic force of aloneness (the undoing of aloneness which is at the very center of the psychotherapeutic process). The discussion traces the pathogenic sequence that leads to chronic reliance on defenses—an adaptation-driven tactic that restricts functioning even as it affords the individual some measure of safety, self-integrity, and affectively coordinated connection.

Chapter 5 is a change of pace—a closely annotated therapeutic vignette—that brings to life the concepts in the preceding discussion and puts into play the clinical tools that will follow. Explicitly using her own reflective self function to bypass the patient's relationship-avoidant defenses, the therapist discloses how the patient exists in her heart and mind and seeks to elicit the patient's experience of the therapist's affective involvement.

The elements of the affective model of change are now in place. The rest of the book is devoted to operationalizing it.

Chapter 6 introduces the two modes of being, self-at-worst and self-at-best, reifying them in three representational schemas for categorizing the moment-to-moment shift of the clinical material and processing the impact of every intervention. The reciprocity among these schemas contributes to understanding the patient's dynamics intrapsychically (*triangle of conflict*), relationally (*self–other–emotion triangle*), and historically, over time (*triangle of comparisons*). The introduction of the self–other–emotion triangle allows the therapist to clearly ground the experiential affect work (triangle of conflict) and the historic-dynamic work (triangle of comparisons) in a relational matrix, where self, other, self-other interaction and emotion are contingent and inextricably intertwined.

Chapter 7 is devoted to the phenomenological description of core affective experience (characterized by the absence of defense and aversive signal affects, and by its capacity to engender state transformations) and to distinguishing it from other kinds of emotion-laden experiences. Whereas the preceding chapter differentiates mental contents according to their psychodynamic functions, this chapter codifies emotional phenomena to guide therapists through otherwise unmapped terrain. The concept of *core state* is introduced: a state of deep openness, self-attunement, and other-receptivity in which deep therapeutic work can take place. The realm of core affective experience is further enlarged to include *self experiences* (feeling true, real) and *relational affective phenomena* (closeness, being in sync), in addition to *categorical emotions* (e.g., fear, disgust, anger, joy, sadness).

Chapter 8 discusses the *healing affects*—universal core affects and states that arise in the wake of therapeutic, or deeply positive, experiences. These include self experiences of pride and competence and relational experiences of love, gratitude, and feeling moved. When healing affects are focused on and experientially elaborated, the adaptive action tendencies that characterize the ensuing state transformations are of enormous benefit to the patient. The therapist at these moments emerges as a paradigm of the patient's experience of the *true other*, the dyadic experiential counterpart of the true self.

Chapter 9 resumes case work, illustrating how all concepts are put to use in the conduct of an initial interview that culminates in a psychodynamic formulation by patient and therapist jointly, and demonstrates fluid application of tools and techniques, including representational schemas and a clear sense of what is and is not core affective experience.

The next three chapters identify strategies of intervention or engagement: each shows a different way to facilitate the experience of core affect, promote relational openness, and minimize the impact of defenses and aversive inhibiting affects, such as anxiety and shame.

Chapter 10 considers *relational strategies:* how to deepen the developing intimacy between patient and therapist—which here is front and center, not background holding environment—by focusing on it, and how to derive maximum therapeutic mileage from it.

Chapter 11 explores the *restructuring interventions,* which involve more traditional psychodynamic ways of working with patterned aspects of the patient's functioning, but the conversation is approached from an empathic perspective, and it explicitly enlists and enhances the patient's awareness and contribution.

Chapter 12 turns to the *experiential-affective interventions,* toward reaping the full transformational power of affect. These strategies of intervention specify different ways in which the facilitation, processing, deepening, and working through of heightened affective states can be used to best therapeutic purposes. Case vignettes indicate just how to work though the dark affective waters to support the patient's achievement of mastery and not loss of control as the individual accesses the depths, and to affirm that he is not bearing the experience alone this time.

The last chapter presents, fittingly, another extended case. If the vignette in chapter 5 shows relational work with deep affect, and the vignette in chapter 9 emphasizes the construction of a psychodynamically coherent narrative to help the patient make sense of his overwhelmingly confusing experience, this one takes place largely in the experiential domain. Patient and therapist ride two major affect waves that at the end of the session put the patient on shores quite different from those she started out on; not only is her experience of herself transformed, but so are her perspectives and her sense of the resources with which she will continue the journey.

PART I

Theoretical Foundations

CHAPTER 1

AFFECT AND TRANSFORMATION

Affect is the most fundamental element of the mind and brain. Like the physical elements of gravity, wind and lightning, emotion has force and direction.

GARFIELD, 1995, P. XI

The most important human relationships are those that are transformational. Affect plays a key role in such relationships, and core affect is at the very center of the model because it is fundamentally linked to the experience of one's essential, authentic self.

To live a full and connected life in the face of difficulty and even tragedy requires the capacity to feel and make use of our emotional experience. So much of the alienation from and fraying of family and social life that lead individuals to seek therapy can be traced to the terror of affect. People disconnect from their emotional experience, afraid of being overwhelmed, humiliated, or revealed as inadequate by the force of feelings, only to pay the price later in depression, isolation, and anxiety. If affect-laden experiences can be made less frightening in the therapeutic environment—that is, if patients can be helped to feel safe enough to feel—then they can reap profound benefits, for within core affective states are powerful adaptive forces and processes with tremendous therapeutic potential.

THE NATURE OF AFFECT

Affect is conceptualized as a wired-in, adaptive, expressive, communicative aspect of human experience (Bowlby, 1980; Damasio, 1994, 1999; Darwin, 1872; Ekman & Davidson, 1994; Goleman, 1995; Greenberg, Rice, & Elliott, 1993; James, 1902; Lazarus, 1991; Nathanson, 1992; Tomkins, 1962,

1963). Affects mediate the interaction between the individual and his emotional environment; they are sources of information and personal meaning, and underlie experiences of authenticity and liveliness.

Affect is a multifaceted phenomenon, grounded in the neurophysicality of our experience: each facet reveals a complex aspect of the individual's experience of self, other, and the relationship between them. Biological and psychological, innate and learned, sensory and motor, information-processing and meaning-generating, experiential and expressive strands of experience all join in influencing how affect is construed and how it operates. Affect is an important motivator and organizer of human behavior. Emotional expression has been shown to play a primary role in both self-regulation (organizing infants' responses to environmental stimuli, for instance) and the regulation of the experience of others, as in the way affective signals direct the actions of caregivers (Beebe & Lachmann, 1988, 1997; Stern, 1985; Tronick, 1989).

Subjectively, the experience of affect is what makes us feel alive, real, and authentic, what allows us to be spontaneous, and what gives meaning to our lives. Individuals lacking affective access as a result of neurophysiological damage (to the prefrontal cortex) not only lead lives robbed of color and texture, they also lose access to the kind of information that gives life meaning. Their interpersonal functioning is impaired as well as their judgment, decision making, and other complex executive functions: the very sense of self is disrupted (Damasio, 1994; Schore, 1994), and so is the sense of other.

Similar impairments occur when the individual's capacity to handle and benefit from his affective experience becomes restricted as a result of psychological trauma (Herman, 1982). Psychological impairment is very much related to difficulties in the efficient processing of emotions, without which people become deprived of important sources of information (Damasio, 1994), adaptive action tendencies (Darwin, 1872; Frijda, 1986; Greenberg & Safran, 1987; McCullough Vaillant, 1997), and internal liveliness and spontaneity (Ferenczi, 1931, 1933; Winnicott, 1949, 1960). Finally, without deep affect, there can be no deep relating.

Core Affect

All major works on emotion (cf. Darwin. 1872; Ekman, 1984; Lazarus, 1991; Tomkins, 1962, 1963) emphasize the way in which emotion serves the individual's adaptation. While their focus may be more on cognition or communication, or development or physiology, it is clear that however construed, emotion is fundamental to a person's optimal being.

Equally noteworthy, from the perspective of a clinical psychotherapy practice, are the myriad efforts people make to mute, sabotage, and reduce the impact—the powerful, transforming impact—of emotions in their lives. Clearly, emotions can transform for good and bad, and psychic maneuvers designed to block access to their experience and expression are also powerful forces to contend with. Day-to-day clinical work reveals many ways in which people cut themselves off from the wellsprings of adaptation; the therapeutic work consists of helping them be nourished once again by emotional experiences, and includes understanding precisely why emotions had to go underground, be shunted off to the side or consigned to oblivion in the first place.

The view of affect proposed here is from a distinctly clinical perspective. The term *core affect* has been chosen simply to refer to that which is vital and spontaneous and comes to the fore when efforts to inhibit spontaneity (i.e., defensive strategies) are not in operation. The aim of this work is to help clinicians effectively counteract the forces against experience (defenses), allay fears that fuel those forces (anxiety, helplessness, and shame, e.g.), and harness the power of core affective experience so that it can enrich and improve the individual's life. The facilitation of core affect enhances the patient's adaptation and helps him gain access to inner resources necessary to meet his unique needs, specifications, and life agenda.

Core affect, or more precisely, *core affective experience*, refers to our emotional responses when we do not try to mask, block, distort, or severely mute them. Defining aspects of the experience of core affect include: a subjective, personally elaborated experience; some change in bodily state; and the release of an adaptive tendency toward some expressive action, known as an *adaptive action tendency* here defined by Goleman (1995) broadly and psychologically: "each emotion offers a distinctive readiness to act; each points us in a direction that has worked well to handle the recurrent challenges of human life" (p. 4). Core affect certainly includes categorical emotions such as fear, sadness, joy, and anger, but it also includes self and relational affective experiences: *categorical emotions* are the self's reactions to events; *self affective experiences,* however, are the self's reading of the self, and *relational affective experiences* are the self's reading of the emotional status of the relationship (discussed in detail in chapter 7). When accessed, the core affective phenomena activate deep transformational processes. (See chapters 6 and 7 for the distinction between these and other affectively laden experiences that are not mutative.) The defining feature of core affect is that it has the power to engender a potentially healing state transformation when experienced in the absence of defenses and such blocking emotions as anxiety and shame.[1] As James (1902) said, intense emotions seldom leave things as they found them, and this applies to the body, the self, and the relationship: they are all transformed in the wake of core affective experience.

Core affect is at the interface between affect conceived clinically and as conceived by emotion theory. Emotion theorists (e.g., Darwin, 1872; Ekman, 1984; Ekman & Davidson, 1984; Frijda, 1986, 1988; Lazarus, 1991) and now neuroscientists (e.g., Damasio, 1994, 1999; LeDoux, 1996) consider emotion vital to optimal adaptation and functioning. Emotion theory integrates its perspective with "a biological and evolutionary perspective on emotion and regards emotion as a biologically wired-in form of information about the self in interaction with the environment" (Safran & Segal, 1990, p. 57). The work of emotion theorists describes how emotions function within our overall design: how they operate when we operate as we are meant to. Clinically, however, we know full well what deviations we take from that organismic agenda; rarely do the affects of everyday life appear in pure form. The affective model of change links the clinical experiential world with emotion theory and allows the former to benefit from the latter—in the realm of core affect.

A NOTE ON TERMINOLOGY AND USAGE

Overall, *affect* and *emotion* are used interchangeably; *categorical emotions* refer to those distinct universal emotions such as fear, anger, joy, and sadness, with their characteristic physiological signatures and wired-in adaptive action tendencies. *Core affective experience* (or *core affect*, for short) refers to all aspects of emotional life experienced directly and viscerally, in the absence of defenses and anxiety—including, but not necessarily limited to, categorical emotions and self and relational affective experiences (described in chapter 7).

---

[1] A neuroscientific analogue can be found in a study mentioned by Damasio (1994) comparing brain activity and neuromusculature involved in a spontaneously emerging "true" smile (core affect) and a willed false or social smile: "the true smile is controlled from limbic cortices and probably uses basal ganglia for its expression" (pp. 140–41). According to Damasio, Duchenne, a contemporary of Darwin's, "determined that a smile of real joy required the combined involuntary contraction of two muscles, the zygomatic major and the orbicularis oculi. He discovered further that the latter muscle could be moved only involuntarily," and he called the involuntary activators of the orbicularis oculi "the sweet emotions of the soul" (Damasio, 1994, p. 142).

What Core Affect Is and Isn't

Chapters 6 and 7 discuss in detail the features of core affect and how to distinguish it from other types of clinical material, especially from other affectively laden experiences that are not mutative. When experienced in the absence of defense and signal affects such as anxiety and shame, for instance, core affect can engender a potentially healing state transformation; its very experience has a physical signature. Experiences marked by blocked emotional access (in contrast to core affective experiences, defined by their mutative nature) have the quality of "going around in circles," "not going anywhere," or "being stuck."

Not everything that follows "I feel ..." statements is necessarily core affect: "I feel like a bagel this morning" is most definitely not core affect (nor is it affect in any meaningful way). Yet neither is the declaration, "I feel sad" or "I am angry" sufficient for us to conclude that we are dealing with core affect; for that there needs to be a congruent visceral component—a visceral or motoric *oomph*—some sense of inner stirring that accompanies the verbal expression. Disembodied utterances never reflect core affective states; in one way or another, the body is involved.

Phenomena of Transformations and Facilitating Conditions

A psychotherapy informed by the affective model of change aims, through stance and techniques, to facilitate the emergence and processing of core affective phenomena and the transformational processes they unleash. When facades fade and fears are soothed, core affect comes to the fore of experiencing. A large part of the technical concerns of this book are devoted to just how that felicitous state is most efficiently and reliably brought about—and how to make use of those moments when core affective experience, spontaneously and ready-made, presents itself.

Within the therapeutic relationship, powerful affect contributes to the metamorphoses of the self: in the context of a dyadic relationship, it is the central agent responsible for therapeutic change. The therapeutic situation, however, is not the only one to elicit affect and harness its transformational power. The description and understanding of affective dynamics has gained immeasurably from the examination of four other contexts where similar affective phenomena and processes of transformation are explored:

1. Darwin (1872) understood emotion to be deeply rooted in the body, refined and shaped over eons and wired-in, vital to the survival of species. He was the first to systematically articulate the phenomenology and core dynamics of the categorical emotions. By looking across species, ages, and cultures, Darwin eliminated the variance contributed by culturally acquired display rules (Ekman & Friesen, 1969) and reached the invariant universal emotions.

2. The clinical developmentalists (Beebe & Lachmann, 1994; Emde, 1988; Sroufe, 1995; Stern, 1985; Tronick, 1989) are immersed in the rapidly changing world of the baby, who is developing in the context of emotionally charged interactions with his caregivers. The caregiver-child relationship, like the therapy relationship, involves rapidly evolving changes with long-term impact, where the fate of dyadic affective communication will be reflected in the affective processing characteristic of the individual. As Bowlby (1991) suggests, what cannot be communicated to the (m)other cannot be communicated to the self. This analogue is the inspiration for the examination in chapters 2 and 3 of attachment theory through the lens of affect.

3. Person's (1988) work on romantic passion and the state of being in love essentially addresses the nature of core affective experience, the processes that lead to individual metamorphosis, and the dynamics that characterize it:

> Romantic love offers not just the excitement of the moment but the possibility for dramatic change in the self. It is in fact an agent of change. ... Romantic love takes on meaning and provides a subjective sense of liberation only insofar as it creates a flexibility in personality that allows a breakthrough of internal psychological barriers and taboos. ... It creates a flux in personality, the possibility for change, and the impetus to begin new phases of life and undertake new endeavors. As such, it can be seen as a paradigm for any significant realignment of personality and values. (P. 23)

4. The luminous work of William James (1902) has focused on yet another dyadic relationship of transformation, that between the religious individual and God. The phenomena described in testimonials of religious conversion and other religious experiences are not markedly different from those that are characteristic of individuals' profound therapeutic experiences of lasting impact.

What do having religious faith, being in love, being cared for, and species survival have in common with powerful psychotherapy? Emerging in such different contexts, the similarity of the accounts of phenomena and processes lends credence to their being deep invariants of transformative emotional experience uncovered in a variety of settings through diverse methods. By examining deep-seated convergences, despite such phenotypic divergence, it becomes possible to distill the essence of conditions required to foster the transformational power of affect.

The primacy of survival, bonding, love, and faith ultimately precludes the ascendancy of defenses—and getting past defenses is a primary element of the affective model of change. So is the power of the bond (discussed in the chapters on attachment) and the safety it creates; through connection, anxieties—those fears that make us shrink and withdraw rather than emerge and be expansive—are allayed, thereby eliminating the other critical barrier to the experiencing and subsequent harnessing of the power of basic emotion.

CORE AFFECT:
CENTRAL AGENT OF CHANGE

> Emotional occasions . . . are extremely potent in precipitating mental rearrangements. The sudden and explosive ways in which love, jealousy, guilt, fear, remorse, or anger can seize upon one are known to everybody. Hope, happiness, security, resolve . . . can be equally explosive. And emotions that come in this explosive way seldom leave things as they found them. (James, 1902, p. 198)

While personality is shaped by experiences with attachment figures over time, it is also shaped by intense emotional experiences of often short duration. William James explored the power of intense emotions to lead to lasting transformations of the personality almost a century before Beebe and Lachmann (1994) focused on the potential of heightened affective moments to effect change as a consequence of the state transformations they engender. Unlike other developmentally based models that address slow change processes over time, affect-centered models of change deal with rapid transformations. Both types of change can have lasting impact. In choosing affect as the medium in which to work, more gradual processes, once fully invested with the affective charge they might otherwise only implicitly posses, can be brought into the realm of more rapid change.

Emotion theorists and researchers (e.g., Darwin, 1872; James, 1902; Nathanson, 1992; Tomkins, 1962, 1963) note that the potential for transformation inheres in the very essence of emotions and is an almost invariable by-product of intense affective experience. By facilitating access to just such experience, accelerated experiential-dynamic psychotherapy (AEDP) aims to harness its mutative power. Defenses and anxiety are at a minimum when the patient is in the state of deep and genuine visceral experiencing, so affective change takes hold rapidly, as compared with the incremental change characteristic of developmental models. To paraphrase Deep Throat in *All the President's Men*, we need to "follow the affect."

Viscerally experiencing deep emotion within the therapeutic relationship helps the patient master a vital psychological process with profound implications for his life. *The visceral experience of deep affect involves a state transformation* (Beebe & Lachmann, 1994). In this altered state, the therapy goes faster, deeper, better: the patient has a subjective sense of "truth" and a heightened sense of authenticity and vitality; very often, so does the therapist (Fosha & Osiason, 1996). Whenever we are outside this state, our therapeutic activities are aimed at getting us back there. Therapeutic results are amplified by new self-perceptions and a freeing of emotional resources. Eventually, as patients also experience themselves as strong, effective, and resourceful rather than weak and helpless, their emotional and relational repertoire expands exponentially.

A state transformation can be achieved through accessing either of two types of core affective experiences: *core emotions* and a *core state*. *Core emotions,* such as anger, joy, sadness, fear, and disgust (i.e., categorical emotions), are in a class by themselves. They are primary in the sense that they are universal, wired-in organismic responses, present if not actually from birth, from early in life. Core emotions are deep-rooted, bodily responses with sensorimotor and visceral correlates. Many of these emotions have their own specific physiology and arousal pattern (Ekman, 1983; Zajonc, 1985), as well as their own set of characteristic dynamics (Darwin, 1872; Nathanson, 1992, 1996; Tomkins, 1962, 1963). The bodily correlates of these emotions are highly salient and an integral aspect of how we experience them.

The core state, a concept introduced and elaborated herein, refers to an altered state of openness and contact, where the individual is deeply in touch with essential aspects of his own experience. The core state is the internal affective holding environment generated by the self. In this state, core affective experience is intense, deeply felt, unequivocal, and declarative; sensation is heightened, imagery is vivid, pressure of speech is absent, and the material moves easily. Effortless focus and concentration also are features of the core state. Relating is deep and clear, as self-attunement and other-receptivity easily coexist. Communications are marked by a subjective sense of certainty, and often by remarkable eloquence. Whether or not the material is new, it feels as if it is happening for the first time. Both therapist and patient have the subjective experience of purity, depth, and "truth."

In conclusion, the affective model of change is a dyadic model whereby core affect in relationship is the central vehicle of change. Its concerns are (a) the power of phenomena to transcend blocks and barriers, (b) how the dyad constructs safety and alleviates anxiety, and (c) how the experience of the transformation itself leads to further adaptive transformation in never-ending cycles. Thus core affect, the dyad, and transformation—with anxiety and defense as obstacles to be overcome—are the elements of the affective model of change.

WHY DOES THE EXPERIENCE OF CORE AFFECT HEAL?

▼ The experience of core affect is healing in and of itself. Even when the affects are painful and frightening, the patient experiences increased aliveness and meaning.

▼ Experiencing emotions so long feared confers a sense of mastery. Overcoming what has previously been overwhelming, confronting what one has been avoiding, is empowering.

▼ The visceral experience of affects brings access to new resources, renewed energy, and an adaptive repertoire of behaviors, collectively referred to as *adaptive action tendencies*. (Many of these cluster around specific emotions, as a result of which they are accessed more readily: the ability to fully experience anger, for example, often leads to renewed strength, assertiveness, and the determination to stand up in defense of one's rights.)

▼ Affect is often a royal road to the unconscious. Deep experiencing unlocks deeper experiencing, and through it, entire realms of previously unavailable material (e.g, memories, fantasies, and states with their accompanying anxieties, defenses, and psychic pains can be worked through).

A HOLDING ENVIRONMENT
OF THEIR OWN

To work their transformational magic, affects require the regulation of a reasonably intact self or relational holding environment. Affects develop in the transitional space between self and other. There, they gain meaning and texture through being reflected by the self's other and enriched by complementary response. Seeing one's affects thus mirrored outside oneself deepens their resonance and multiplies their associations; they become more alive and differentiated. Sharing affect with an other enlarges the emotional repertoire of an individual even as it supports him so that he is not overwhelmed by experiencing it.

In the affective sharing process, the individual is not alone with frightening and intense feelings; rather, by allowing resonances and layers of personal meaning to develop and be discovered through communication, tendrils of new meaning sprout, articulating previously undifferentiated aspects of self experience. Through the sharing of affect, there is also the opportunity to achieve a coordinated state with the other (Tronick, 1989), which is the set goal of the attachment system (Costello, 2000) and a major aspect of the therapeutic alliance (Safran & Segal, 1990). Fully experienced and relationally elaborated affect makes it clear how an authentic self and deep relational connection are not only not conflicting, but can, through cycles of resonant responding, greatly enhance one another. Through the process of affective resonance, core affect can simultaneously foster authenticity and intimacy.

Affective experiences between self and other eventually become internalized and reflected in the individual's psychic structure, in the form of something akin to an internal affective holding environment.

THE COMPLETE PROCESSING OF
CORE AFFECT AND THE AFFECTIVE
MODEL OF CHANGE

Being aware of, in touch with, and being able to express emotions help the individual access biologically adaptive information that can assist him in negotiating his life (Greenberg & Safran, 1987). As "central aspects of biological regulation, [emotions] provide the bridge between rational and non-rational processes, between cortical and subcortical structures"

(Damasio, 1994, p. 128). In addition to the phylogenetically honed adaptive capacities residing within the categorical emotions (most familiarly the activation of the fight-flight response), emotion has the potential to confer on the individual more idiosyncratic advantages—no less important for being so—rooted in the essence of his being singularly who he is. Thus core affective experience is not only adaptive but also crucial in actualizing the self's unique existential agenda.

In the most profound way, affect is how the individual stays in touch with himself and with his own take on the world; it is also how he communicates to others that essential information about himself. When the "information" he communicates is genuine and true (subjectively equivalent to *core*), and when the response of the other is equally so, the opportunity for true emotional growth is occasioned.

What are the constituent elements of a full experience of core affect, and how do these enhance the individual's adaptation? The cycle that gets evoked by core affective experience involves attention, appraisal, experience, expression, motivation, communication, and mutual coordination. Through such complete processing of affective experience—that is, with no barriers to its intrapsychic experiencing, (adaptive) expression, communication, and ensuing coordination of state with the other—the experiencer of the emotions gets to a new place, fostering what Person (1988) describes as the "flux in personality, the possibility for change, and the impetus to begin new phases of life and undertake new endeavors" (p. 23).

Core affect is both an intrapsychic and interpersonal phenomenon ultimately linked to self- and mutual regulation and state coordination. Emotion to which the other is intrinsic is a key aspect of the affective model of change. To reap the full transformational benefits of core affective experience, its complete processing optimally culminates in communication with a receptive, open other.

Attention

Emotion automatically shifts our focus: it heightens our attention to certain concerns, allowing others to fade into the background. It serves as "a compelling signal that something of significance is occurring. It also motivates subsequent activity, which is organized around this significant occurrence. The person is, in effect, pressed to attend to and deal with a new encounter whose adaptational salience created the new reaction in the first place" (Lazarus, 1991, p. 17).

Tomkins (1970) describes the amplifying function of affect: "Affect either makes good things better or bad things worse ... by adding a special analogic quality that is intensely rewarding or punishing" (pp. 147–48). Affect and the attention it brings set the stage for the salience of heightened affective experiences: emotion is motivating and opens up new possibilities, creates new configurations, new directions, and new goals—and new goals organize new events.

Appraisal

Appraisal is an information-processing, intrapsychic aspect of the operation of core affect; it shows how the impact of the environment registers on the self and how emotion informs motivation. Emotions tell the individual how he is related to what is going on in a situation. Without access to emotion, it is not possible to understand another person's intentionality (Costello, 2000). Emotion reflects the self's appraisal of the environment in a way that lets the individual know what he himself thinks, so to speak, and thus informs his adaptive action tendencies, an important aspect of core affect to be further discussed.

Core affect communicates to the self about the other and to the other about the self. "No other concept in psychology is as richly revealing [as emotion] of the way an individual relates to life and the specifics of the physical and social environment" (Lazarus, 1991, p. 7). The appraisal discussed here is not only the purely physiologically based appraisal rooted in subcortical responses (LeDoux, 1996) of emotion, but a refined, relationally informed appraisal of the meaningfulness of a situation for the individual—replete with personal ramifications and reverberations, assessing the situation in terms of its potential for fulfilling or thwarting the self's essential agenda (Slavin & Kriegman, 1998).

Visceral Experience and the Body

Visceral experience is the center point of the cycle of core affect, the indispensable element of the affective model of change. The capacity to experience core affect directly and deeply is what everything else depends on, and is what the strategies of intervention of AEDP aim to reliably facilitate in patients. If access to core affective experience is blocked or distorted, then all the other stages of the cycle are equally compromised. This is the hallmark of the affective model of change and where it becomes differentiated from both academic (i.e., nonclinical) emotion theory and other psychodynamic (i.e., nonexperiential) treatments. Until visceral access to core affective experience can be obtained, all clinical efforts remain focused on the removal or bypassing of the affect block.

THE PHYSICAL LOCALIZATION OF EMOTIONS

In visceral experiencing, we also have the link with the body, the physical home of the self. There is a profoundly physical experience to the emotions (as in "lump in the throat," "heavy heart," or "my blood was boiling"). Even when we deal with nonspecific quiescent core states—where there is no specific emotion, but instead, say, an overall feeling of calm and relaxation—there is a specific landscape of the body feeling (Damasio, 1994, 1999) that is a physical correlative of the affective state. Different body landscapes manifest themselves not only in different subjective experiences for the individual, but also in different rates and patterns of speech, different access to internal experience, as well as different qualities of concentration, attention, and relating.

By rooting the contents of the mind in bodily sensations, psychic experience becomes rooted in viscera, taking on muscle and sinew, definition and force, solidity and reality. Similarly, by making the experience of the body the object of the mind, the limits attached to the finite body dissolve when the body is experientially apprehended: internal space bounded by our skin becomes the objective correlative of internal psychic space. Thus, ever-unfolding experience acquires physical reality, and the physical finiteness of the body is transcended, given the endless possibilities for further experiential unfolding.

Expression

As Damasio (1994) points out, "the etymology of the word nicely suggests an external direction, from the body: emotion signifies literally 'movement out'" (p. 139). Somehow the full experience of emotion depends on its expression (its being put out), and in that way involves both motion (back to the body) and communication (out to the other). *Expression* of affect deepens the *experience* of affect. Access to the entire range of affective experience is easier when emotions are expressed than when they are experienced purely internally. If the function of emotion is the amplification of what is important (Tomkins, 1970), then expression is further amplifying—a meta-amplification—fully engaging emotional, verbal, sensory, and motoric aspects of the affective experience.

As core affect is communicated, externalized, it becomes further transformed: an intrapsychic experience is projected outward on the screen of interpersonal space where both patient and therapist together watch it unfold (and each also watches separately). Once it leaves the insulating privacy of internal psychic space through its being expressed, core affective experience *then becomes part of external reality, to which the self can then react.* While losing partial subjectivity and gaining partial objectivity and reality, once expressed, core affective experience can be examined and apprehended in the light of day. In keeping with newly defined challenges, a course of action—emotional action, that is—can evolve. With core affects out there, particularly painful, feared, and frightening core affects, they become challenges in the external environment with which the self must deal. These challenges kick into gear the next wave of adaptive action tendencies, that complex web of perceptual, cognitive, emotional coping responses that will be considered next.

Motivation: Adaptive Action Tendencies Released by the Core Affects

> All emotions are, in essence, impulses to act, the instant plans that evolution has instilled in us. ... That emotions lead to actions is most obvious in watching animals or children; it is only in "civilized" adults we so often find the great anomaly in the animal kingdom, emotions—root impulses to act—divorced from obvious reaction. ... With new methods to peer into the body and brain, researchers are discovering more physiological details of how each emotion prepares the body for a different kind of response. (Goleman, 1995, p. 6)

Each core affective experience is associated with an "expressive impulse" (Lazarus, 1991, p. 272) or with a specific action disposition (Safran & Segal, 1990, p. 57) with "a distinctive readiness to act" (Goleman, 1995, p. 4).

> Specific emotional states are thus linked with specific action dispositions. Anger, for example, occurs in response to an event experienced as an assault and is associated with actions which are self-protective and retaliative. Fear is evoked by events appraised as dangerous and is linked to hypervigilance and flight. Love is linked to affiliative behaviors. The core of emotional experience thus consists of organized expressive-motor acts associated with behavioral systems that are biologically wired-in through a process of natural selection. (Safran & Segal, 1990, p. 57)

Adaptive action tendencies, the coping responses and resources released by the full experience of core affect, reflect the individual's new responses given his access to new information—about himself, the other, and the situation—that was not accessible to him prior to the full experience of the emotion. One patient, for example, had never mourned the death of his father when he was a young child. Only after he fully grieved at his loss did he realize that emotional denial of his father's death (and holding on to him through identification, experiencing himself as "deadened") had resulted in his putting his life on hold for more than two decades. He determined that he needed to say good-bye to his father by going to his grave, and that only after that would he truly be able to move on and live his own life. By gaining access to his emotional truth, the individual paradoxically recovers what he never before has had. The quality of emotional truth is simultaneously what one has always known and breathtaking newness (Bollas, 1987, 1989; James, 1902; Person, 1988).[2]

Given that the relationship to the other is an intrinsic aspect of the affective model of change, as is the focus on self experience, two new terms are introduced. *Adaptive relational tendencies* are expressed in the disposition to connect and achieve mutually coordinated states that mediate processes of attachment, mutuality, and intimacy, thus serving the self's relational agenda. *Adaptive self action tendencies* serve the self's unique agenda by assuming attitudes and actions that foster self-actualization: this often comes in the form of becoming aware of the nature of one's basic needs (Greenberg, Rice, & Elliott, 1993) and acting in ways conducive to fulfilling those needs.

The therapeutic process, through progressive refocusings, illustrates how emotion externalized through expression serves adaptation via the activation of successive waves of adaptive action tendencies. The patient, for instance, relates an incident about his wife. "So how did you feel about that?" the therapist asks. In one way, the therapist's intervention demonstrates her staying with, deepening, articulating, and elaborating the patient's experience. Yet beyond that, the dyadic process of transformation already has begun seamlessly: with this simple question, the therapeutic process is off and running. What both therapist and patient examine together has changed from a description of an event to a depiction of the patient's experience of it; unfolding in a relational context, experiences evolve, and through deepening and articulation, change is brought about.

---

[2] Bollas (1987) evocatively captures this paradox in his analysis of the *unthought known*.

Communication and Mutual Coordination

Bowlby (1991) states, "The principal function of emotion is one of communication—namely, the communication, both to the self and to others, of the current motivational state of the individual" (p. 294). For Darwin (1872), as for Bowlby, the important function of emotional expression is communication among individuals. Emotions show others what particular emotional or motivational state one is in; implicit is the motivation to do something intrinsically related to a specific emotion—to act on it. Darwin viewed humans as having an evolved sympathy for others, thus being enormously affected by the response of others; he believed that humans evolved to be responsive to the effect that their communication has on other humans.

EXPRESSION FOR COMMUNICATION:

THE AFFECTIVE COMMUNICATION SYSTEM

Why is it more effective to say something to somebody than merely to think it and feel it, even if the other does little more than listen? Why should it make such an enormous difference to communicate something to another person? In expression—*and reception by the other*—the full cycle of processing core affect is complete. In communicating affective experience, the discovery that an other is ready to receive the formerly unthinkable and previously unbearable creates an enlarging, endless universe. In the realm of core affective experience, the difference between aloneness and the sense of being integrated in the mainstream of mutuality—community—is created by the act of affective communication with one other person, who is open and interested.

Communication implies a dialogue; it makes possible the coordination of affective states and depends on both the other and the other's state (Costello, 2000). It is possible to have a full experience of core affect and yet keep it inside, to oneself, if the other is not receptive. When the emotional dialogue is reciprocal, however, each partner is further transformed and also transforms the other. Reciprocal transformative communication articulates the essence of the affective model of change.

Reaching a state of affective coordination with an other releases adaptive relational tendencies (the *affective competence* to be discussed in chapters 2 and 3) that foster further development of the relationship, deepen the bond, promote intimacy and closeness, and within it, deeper knowledge of the other and the self. Security of attachment is enhanced, strengthening exploration and psychic resilience, confirming that, in this view of core affect, it takes two to tango. Reaching coordinated core affect states and the subsequent release of adaptive relational tendencies depends on the receptivity and openness of the other: it is of fundamental importance that the therapist be affectively competent, neither overwhelmed by the emotion—the patient's or hers—nor hostile to it. Here lie major implications for the AEDP therapist's stance.

THERAPEUTIC STANCE AND THE AFFECTIVE MODEL OF CHANGE

...nobody sees essence who can't face limitation.
Louise Gluck, *Circe's Power*

The essence of the therapeutic presence in the affective model of change is being inside the patient's world as an other, and the patient's feeling it and knowing it. In the presence of such a presence, the patient's world unfolds. This presence—equal parts knowing and wanting to know, being there and wanting to be there—makes it possible for people to talk to someone else about parts of themselves that are painful and hidden and frightened and frightening and dangerous and disorganizing. Empathy, which involves a process of attunement both to core affective experience and to what makes it scary, painful, or exhilarating for the patient, requires the therapist's immersion in the patient's world so as to articulate tacit experience (Gendlin, 1991; Safran & Segal, 1990).

The therapist's stance is informed by an understanding of the affective phenomena of empathy, affect contagion, affective attunement and resonance, and the reaching of coordinated state (Gold, 1996; Stern, 1985; Tronick, 1989). Through affective resonance, sharing, and empathy, the therapist's affective response to the patient's experience serves to amplify the patient's affective experience. For instance, the therapist's being moved by an aspect of the patient's experience that others previously had met with indifference or contempt, having caused the patient to dismiss it as inconsequential or unworthy, is an extraordinarily powerful way of unlocking a patient's awareness of and grief about the suffering he has undergone. This is a stance, a presence, a way of being that is both inside and outside the person: the therapist becomes truly transitional, in Winnicott's sense. Or as Mann and Goldman (1982) say about the impact of feeling deeply understood:

> [T]he patient feels as if someone is *beside him and inside him* and is offering to remain there to help. The fact that the therapist reaches in so deeply without being frightened, depressed, or disgusted, and is offering to remain there for the purpose of helping, arouses in the patient feelings of gratitude and trust that hark back to the earliest of human experiences. (P. 36, italics added)

Being right next to the person so intimately, so tenderly, so closely, with so much feeling, melts resistance. The patient finds himself wanting to speak, wanting to share, finding and naturally coming upon essential parts of the self previously hidden from the world as well as from himself.

> Because of the therapist's early activity ... and confidence that the patient can be helped, the patient develops an attitude of trust of an intensity that one does not ordinarily see so quickly in other treatment modalities. ... [I]t should be emphasized that the ego has not suspended judgment in the establishment of this trust. It participates and sees a realistic basis for this trust, for the therapist has accurately and clearly stated the patient's lifelong affective problem. (Mann & Goldman, 1982, p. 49)

The disastrous experience of aloneness—unwilled, unwanted, dreaded aloneness (as opposed to sought-after, willed, restorative aloneness)—and the pathology-creating anxiety that accompanies it numb the mind and necessarily render huge regions of self inaccessible. It is important to reiterate that fear-fostering aloneness arises in response to the unresponsiveness and unavailability of the other when the self is in need (Bowlby, 1991). When the other is receptive to emotional communication, however, aloneness as a pathogenic agent is eliminated.

When development proceeds in a good-enough way, empathy, compassion, altruism, pride, generosity, and joy are as much part and parcel of our makeup as are self-interest and aggression. When our capacity to feel deeply is intact, we can tap into those deep organismic resources. In other words, the noble emotions are as wired-in as the base ones, and must be so in therapy as in life. These are natural psychic attributes and forces; only when optimal development goes off track are these attributes impaired, defective, distorted, or largely absent. In a healthy individual we should find capacity for connectedness and for independence, pleasure in himself and pleasure in others, self-concern and caring for and about others, empathy and compassion, and the ability to both give and take.

We have evolved into a highly social species with well-differentiated interpersonal affective interactions that are crucial to emotional survival in a textured world of object relations; these are the relationally adaptive core affective experiences. If the lexicon of positive experiences is impoverished, if theoretical thinking about them is not differentiated, and if therapeutic constructs for representing and conceptualizing change and positive motivational forces and healing emotional experiences are inadequate, then *therapists* will not be able to guide patients in exploring this internal and interpersonal terrain. Lack of differentiation of constructs should not be equated with lack of phenomena. This is the field of investigation that Beebe and Emde and Stern and Tronick are pioneering. We are in the process of developing the microscope that will allow us to describe microorganisms: we know they are there, their investigation is in progress, yet we do not possess a fully differentiated taxonomy. The following chapters, it is hoped, will further the development of the lexicon of core affective experiences to include both positive affective experiences and relational experiences.

SUMMARY

The process of development through intense interactions with others leads one, through successive metamorphoses, to an ever-evolving authentic self. Through the process of resonance and coordination, returning to the bedrock of personal internal experience and that which marks the patient's inner experience as pure and true, and by fostering access and facilitating core affect, the patient's authenticity grows and solidifies. Encouraged to be as authentic as he can possibly be, with an other who is as authentic as she can possibly be (through the therapist's own contact with core affective experience), the patient sheds the layers of skin calloused by inauthentic, affect-phobic interactions. Through successive metamorphoses, the experience of the true self becomes increasingly easier to access. The voice of the true self is found and grows strong; when this happens, as one patient said, it's like "the sound of a flute in a brass band."

Core affect is the marker and catalyst at all stages of the process: in and of itself a powerful agent of transformation, it is also a marker of state and a means of profound communication to the other about one's own state; it is a source of information about oneself for oneself and for the other. Finally, core affect is the vehicle by which the coordination between self and other takes place, so that each can become the transformational vehicle of the other. In the affective model of change, it is ultimately the therapist who, through deep engagement and affect-facilitation, becomes the object the self of the patient uses to transform itself into its new avatar—that is, into its increasingly essential and authentic version.

For the philosophically and conceptually minded, it should be noted that the true self is an experiential construct, and not a structural or a reified one. There is no such thing as a true or essential self; we all have a multiplicity of selves, and then some. There is, however, such a thing as the in-the-moment *experience* of one's true or essential self, and it is precisely this experience of authenticity that is the object of the quest. In the moment, directly experienced, the essential self knows what's right and true.

CHAPTER 2

ATTACHMENT THROUGH THE LENS OF AFFECT

Many of the most intense emotions arise during the formation, the maintenance, the disruption and the renewal of attachment relationships. ... Because such emotions are usually a reflection of the state of a person's affectional bonds, the psychology and psychopathology of emotion is found to be in large part the psychology and psychopathology of affectional bonds.

BOWLBY 1980, P. 60

Attachment, as both phenomenon and construct, refers to the fundamental human need to form close affectional bonds; it is at the foundation of our psychological life. Like affect, attachment operates on many levels: it is as meaningful from the across-the-ages perspective of evolutionary biology as it is from the moment-to-moment clinical endeavor devoted to understanding the subtlest fluctuations of the human mind. Bowlby (1980) believed that the psychology and psychopathology of emotion is largely the psychology and psychopathology of affectional bonds. This chapter and the next will explore the therapeutic implications of this idea.

Attachment theory and the affective model of change are conceptually resonant: both understand personality structure as the result of coping strategies, that is, defenses against painful emotional experience and relational loss. These strategies kick in when the individual's environment is not optimally facilitating, which results in interference with the individual's capacity to make the most of his emotional resources.

The prominence of defense as a strategy to minimize fear and emotional pain is a common feature of both attachment theory and the psychodynamically based affective model of change. As a secure relationship that provides the safety required for the individual to explore is a feature of attachment; so too is it an essential aspect of the affective model of change. Relational safety promotes exploration, which in AEDP translates into the willingness to experientially immerse oneself in the core affective phenomena so crucial to deep therapeutic change.

ATTACHMENT, CAREGIVING, AND EXPLORATION IN ATTACHMENT THEORY AND AEDP

Attachment theory (Ainsworth et al., 1978; Bowlby, 1973, 1980, 1982) is concerned with elucidating how the quality of the child-caregiver bond affects the development of the child. Attachment is what results when the more vulnerable member of the dyad bonds with an other, a "preferred individual, who is usually conceived as stronger and/or wiser" (Bowlby, 1977, p. 203). The stronger/wiser other also bonds with him; it is a mutually regulated yet highly asymmetrical relationship. Where bidirectionality of influence operates, each simultaneously affects and is affected by the other (Beebe & Lachmann, 1988; Beebe, Lachmann, & Jaffe, 1997; Emde, 1981; Tronick, 1989, 1998).

As defined by Bowlby (1982), attachment comprises three behavioral systems that operate in us, serving optimal adaptation throughout life: the *attachment behavioral system*, whose primary function is protective; the *caregiving* or *parenting behavioral system*, whose primary function is facilitative; and the *exploratory behavioral system*, whose primary function is to promote learning about the environment (Ainsworth et al., 1978).

The Attachment Behavioral System and Its Affective Marker, the Safety Feeling

Bowlby (1982) proposed that for the child the attachment bond with a protective adult figure is a primary mechanism for the maintenance and regulation of safety. The caregiver needs to serve as a secure base (Ainsworth et al., 1978) and is crucial in promoting the child's experience of safety and allaying his fear. Fear plays a crucial role: it activates attachment behaviors and curtails exploration. Through the attachment bond, the child benefits from his own and his caregiver's resources, and he is not alone with whatever dangers he might be required to handle. The attachment system is active "from the cradle to the grave ... when a person is distressed, ill or afraid" (Bowlby, 1977, p. 203); for the child, "attachment behaviour is activated especially by ... *the mother being or appearing to be inaccessible*" (Bowlby, 1988, p. 3; italics added). "The security of the base depends on its availability, sensitivity, responsiveness, and helpfulness ... Bowlby suggests that the term alarm be reserved for fear in the face of the initial stimulus, and that anxiety be reserved for the fear of the inaccessibility or non-responsiveness of the caregiver" (Costello, 2000). The caregiver's "inaccessibility or non-responsiveness" becomes the primary danger in the child's emotional world, and anxiety regarding "the inaccessibility or non-responsiveness of the caregiver" becomes the driving force of the attachment system and the resulting organization of the personality.

Through proximity to the caregiver (i.e., physical nearness as well as emotional closeness), what otherwise would be unbearable anxiety and fear are kept at bay; instead, the child experiences a *safety feeling* (Sandler, 1960; Joffe & Sandler, 1965): "It is clear that ... the presence of the object is a condition for a state of well-being" (Joffe & Sandler, 1965, p. 399). The safety feeling—a true *sense* of well-being, and not just the absence of anxiety (Sandler, 1960)—is the experiential correlate of secure attachment: it is an internal state with visceral, sensory, and psychological aspects, experientially manifested in feeling relaxed, at ease, calm, and confident to take on new challenges. When the safety feeling prevails, the individual is at his best; somewhat akin to the practicing stage toddler, the world is his oyster. Whereas the safety feeling is the experiential correlate of secure attachment, the freedom to explore the world is the behavioral consequence of being *and* feeling safe.

The Caregiving Behavioral System

The counterpart of the attachment behavioral system is the equally wired-in, natural parenting function or caregiving behavioral system. It refers to the actions a parent or caregiver engages in to restore herself as a secure base (Ainsworth et al., 1978) for the child, responding to vulnerability with protectiveness and caretaking (Bowlby, 1988, 1991; Costello, 2000; George & Solomon, 1999; Shane, Shane & Gales, 1997).

The caregiving system creates the environment within which attachment and exploration operate: it is the holding environment in action (Costello, 2000).

> [P]arenting behaviour … is … ready to develop along certain lines when conditions elicit it. That means that in the ordinary course of events, the parent of a baby experiences a strong urge to behave in certain typical sorts of way, for example, to cradle the infant, to soothe him when he cries, to keep him warm, protected and fed. … Parenting behaviour, as I see it, has strong biological roots, which accounts for the strong emotions associated with it. (Bowlby, 1988, pp. 4–5)

Parenting fulfills many needs *for the caregiver*, among them loving and feeling loved, needed, and useful. Having a positive impact on another is a core existential experience of the self. Just as the phenomenon of attachment is not limited to children, however, by no means is the parenting function limited to the adults formally designated as caregivers. Empathy and caring responsiveness are present in young children from very early on (e.g., Zahn-Waxler & Radke-Yarrow, 1982; Radke-Yarrow, Zahn-Waxler, & Chapman,1983); they also are present in patients toward therapists, and it is crucial that these responses be registered, welcomed, and acknowledged.

The Exploratory System
and Its Affective Markers,
Joy, Exhilaration, Exuberance, and Pride

In conditions of safety, other primary motivations, such as the urge to explore, satisfy curiosity, and desire new experiences (Lachmann & Beebe, 1992; Tomkins, 1962) can emerge. No longer overwhelmed by fear, the child can explore his world and acquire new learning by mastering new situations, thereby augmenting his adaptive resources. Engaging these pursuits with curiosity and zest, the individual experiences a sense of effectiveness and competence (White, 1959, 1960), accompanied by joy, exhilaration, exuberance, and pride (Emde, 1988; Kissen, 1995). These positive affects are the affective markers of the exploratory behavioral system.

The AEDP therapist's goal, therefore, is to "establish trust and facilitate a safe environment from the get go" (Fosha & Slowiaczek, 1997) to promote relational safety and enhance emotional exploration. The safer the patient feels in the relationship with the therapist, the more he will be willing to relinquish growth-inhibiting defenses and risk new ways of feeling and interacting. The experience, processing, and expressing of deep affective experience—including new emotions and emotions previously feared to be unendurable—is the AEDP realm in which the exploratory system manifests itself.

Wachtel (1993) noted that anxiety is at the core of the psychodynamic understanding of psychopathology. As in attachment theory, *the anxiety–safety dimension is a fundamental coordinate for the affective model of change.* Central to both is the tenet that contact with the attachment figure counteracts anxiety, whereas the experience of aloneness exacerbates it. The experience of aloneness in the face of what is experienced as psychically dangerous is at the core of AEDP's understanding of psychopathogenesis, just as the feeling of safety is at the core of its understanding of resilience and optimal psychological health. In treatment—as in attachment situations that go well—the goal is to counteract pathogenic aloneness by establishing a safety-engendering therapist-patient relationship based on the availability and responsiveness of the therapist. The conditions of anxiety leading to the exclusion of large areas of self experience are thereby countered—those responsible for the psychopathology that brings the patient to treatment. According to Bowlby (1988), the role of the therapist is

> to provide the patient with a secure base from which he can explore the various unhappy and painful aspects of his life, past and present, many of which he finds difficult or perhaps impossible to think about and reconsider without a trusted companion to provide support, encouragement, sympathy, and, on occasion, guidance. … This … not infrequently requires that the therapist sanction his patient to consider as possibilities ideas and feelings about his parents that he has hitherto regarded as unimaginable and unthinkable. In doing so, a patient may find himself moved by strong emotions … many of which he finds frightening, and/or alien and unacceptable. (Pp. 138–39)

When previously disallowed experiences can be explored, the patient becomes better able to deal with them within himself, and life-shrinking anxiety dissolves. The resulting openness between patient and therapist, and also within the patient (Bowlby, 1991), deepens trust, strengthens connection, and increases self-confidence, making possible even greater risk-taking (i.e., new learning) in the future. The threshold at which situations are experienced as dangerous gets higher and the individual's repertoire of experiences and responses gains depth and versatility.

The therapeutic work is twofold: the relational, thus safety-promoting work (the little-step-by-little-step process), which includes support, validation, encouragement, and so on; and the exploratory work (the core affect–releasing process), whereby the individual has the opportunity to expand his emotional world, countering the constriction brought about by anxiety-driven functioning. Both try to provide "the conditions which make it possible for the True Self to come into its own" (Winnicott, 1960, pp. 142–43).

AEDP's model of therapeutic presence and action also has its roots in the caregiving behavioral system of attachment. The emphasis is on "being there," promoting safety, being a "trusted companion" (Bowlby, 1973, 1988) in exploratory journeys and in an essential way, seeking to counter anxiety-fueling isolation. Caregiving responsiveness "is ready to develop along certain lines when conditions elicit it" (Bowlby, 1988, pp. 4–5), and AEDP is built on the premise that responsiveness to the patient's needs and willingness to help are key elements of its therapeutic stance. Our patients' suffering elicits caregiving responses in us. The ethos of AEDP is to use and develop these biologically based urges. Like a talent that has to be nurtured and trained for its full potential to be realized, so natural caregiving responses to suffering have to be nurtured and trained for them to evolve into the skilled responses that constitute therapeutic caregiving.

The therapist seeks not only to promote the patient's safety but also accompany him on his affective exploratory journey. Just as the attuned parent puts an object before the child in a way that allows the child to experience his finding of the object as his own discovery (Winnicott, 1963a), so the therapist can at times guide the patient toward exploring emotional regions that might otherwise remain uncharted, allowing the unfolding of self experience.

The stance that emerges from such aims is a radical departure from therapeutic neutrality. Analytic theory has always grounded its understanding of the patient-therapist relationship in the early parent-child relationship. Yet analytic focus traditionally has been on the repetition in the transference of the psychopathogenic aspects of the relationship. By grounding the therapeutic relationship in attachment, the focus instead is on transposing relational conditions conducive to the patient's optimal safety, exploration, and growth.

REPRESENTATIONAL PROCESSES: THE INTERNAL WORKING MODEL AND THE REFLECTIVE SELF FUNCTION

The Internal Working Model

On the basis of repeated caregiving experiences that "start during the first year of life, and are repeated almost daily throughout childhood and adolescence" (Bowlby, 1980, p. 55), the attachment relationship becomes represented and internalized: the individual forms an *internal working model of relationships* in which the self is represented in dynamic relation to a specific caregiving other. For example, the repeated experience of crying followed by being soothed "leads to the expectation that distress will be met by reassurance and comforting" (Fonagy et al., 1995, pp. 234–35); note the nod to affect: "Integrated with, and perhaps integrating, … these expectations are the emotional experiences associated with these interactions" (Fonagy et al., 1995, pp. 234–35). The internal working model guides the individual's regulation of his own experience, exploratory behavior, and relationship to the attachment figure. Eventually, it also guides the individual's caregiving toward his own children. Attachment shapes development through its structuring internal representations of self and other in interaction; manifested in patterns of attachment, these internal representations provide the basis for understanding how the relational handling of affective experience shapes personality and functioning.

Positive, secure attachment experiences lead to an internal working model that represents "an unconscious belief system into which early experiences are integrated and that, under favorable conditions, reflects *the individual's confidence in the significant other's availability, understanding and responsiveness*" (Fonagy et al., 1995, p. 234, italics added). In such an internal working model, one that characterizes secure attachment, the other is represented as responsive and reliable and the self as worthy of being protected and responded to.

Just as the feeling of safety has its origins in a secure attachment relationship with an available and responsive caregiver (Bowlby, 1988; Sandler, 1960), similarly anxiety and the defense mechanisms to which anxiety gives rise have *their* origins in an attachment relationship with an unavailable or unresponsive caregiver. Defensive exclusion (Bowlby, 1980) becomes a major strategy both to restore the availability and responsiveness of the caregiver and to reinstate a state of mutual affective coordination (Tronick, 1989) with her. The caregiver's anxiety has a major role: to maintain a relationship where she is in responsive contact with him, the child excludes all aspects of his experience that his caregiver cannot tolerate, hoping to preclude her turning away from and becoming unavailable to him. The child thus sacrifices the fullness of his reality, relationships, and affective inner life. The success of the strategy is reflected in the achievement of what Main (1995) calls *secondary felt security,* which characterizes the child's experience of functioning based on the internal working model that grows out of a particular interaction with a caregiver. Felt security is a powerful force that maintains such patterns.

Eventually there comes to be an isomorphism (Costello, 2000) between what is communicated to the mother and what can be communicated to the self (Bowlby, 1991). That which becomes off-limits in the communication with the caregiver eventually becomes off-limits for the person to experience and consider—even in the privacy of his inner life. The mechanism of defensive exclusion, instituted to deal with alarm and fear of relational loss, becomes encapsulated in the individual's defensive structure: it is reflected in the internal working model and becomes manifest in the individual's patterns of attachment (Bowlby, 1980).

What is radical in this formulation, and pivotal to the model of affective change informing AEDP, is how powerful the effect of the *other* is conceptualized to be for the development of the self: the very sense of security that underlies our autonomy, exploration, individuated growth, and so on, is rooted in a belief about the other, growing out of one's experiences with that other, based on the other's *actual* availability, understanding, and responsiveness. When we find ourselves in the role of *other*—as parents, significant others, or therapists—we have enormous opportunities to make an impact.

The notion of defense as a strategy used to maintain relational closeness (Bowlby, 1980; Main, 1995) is the counterpart of AEDP's notion of defense as a strategy used to compensate for the failure of the affect-facilitating environment. In both, defenses come to the fore to deal with the anxiety produced by the failure of the attachment figure to help the individual feel safe in his dealings with the internal and external worlds. Contingent on the availability or unavailability of the caregiver, the individual's actions will be aimed at either conservative safety restoration (i.e., deployment of defensive/protective strategies), when the caregiver is unavailable or unresponsive, or growth-enhancing, self-expanding exploration of the world (inner and outer), when the caregiver is available and responsive and the child feels safe.

Defense As Response to Failure of the Environment

The patterns of attachment of children are classified (Ainsworth et al., 1978) based on the behavior they exhibit in the Strange Situation paradigm.[1] In secure attachment, fear and anxiety are kept at bay as a result of reliable, responsive caregiving; in insecure attachment styles, fear and anxiety are kept at bay through reliance on defense mechanisms. Disorganized attachment, however, reflects the breakthrough of fear that rends the fabric of security as a consequence of the failure of defense mechanisms sufficiently strong to compensate for the disintegration of the caregiver's capacity to protect.

Key to the distinction between secure and insecure patterns of attachment is the notion of defense as an attempt to counter the fracturing anxiety generated by the caregiver's failure to provide responsive, helpful caregiving, which is incorporated in the individual's internal working model and reflected in his patterns of attachment (Bowlby, 1980). Defensive processes, organized coping responses aimed at minimizing the experience of distress, function protectively, but not without untoward consequences. Degree of defense in relationships and functioning in the world becomes the nodal distinction between resilience and increased vulnerability for developing psychopathology—specifically in the form of personality patterns characterized by insecure internal working models.

Secure attachment is a strong protective factor against the development of psychopathology; specifically, it is a protective factor against being adversely affected by trauma (Alexander et al., 1995, in Eagle, 1996). Conversely, insecure attachment lowers the threshold for the

---

[1] In the Strange Situation paradigm, child and caregiver play together for a while in a room filled with appealing toys. After a while, the caregiver leaves the child alone with a friendly stranger (i.e., the experimenter). After about three minutes, the caregiver returns. She and the child play together again for a while. Then, both the caregiver and the experimenter leave, and the child is left alone for three minutes, after which time the caregiver returns for good. The distressing features of the situation include the unfamiliarity of the room, the introduction to a stranger, and two three-minute separations from the parent—and the experience of aloneness itself.

development of psychopathology (Coates, 1998; Dozier, Stovall, & Albus, 1999; Urban et al., 1991). Finally, as we would intuitively expect, trauma and loss interfere with the establishment of secure attachment (Lyons-Ruth & Jacobvitz, 1999; Main & Hesse, 1990). Secure attachment promotes optimal development (Coates, 1998; Erickson, Sroufe & Egeland, 1985; Urban et al., 1991).

Affective Competence

From the vantage point of the affective model of change, attachment theory concerns both the relational processing of intense affective experiences and the long-term consequences of internalizing the dyadic handling of such experiences. Affect plays as major a role in the evolution of attachment patterns as in the transformational processes of therapy. *Affective competence*—feeling and dealing while relating—introduces a way to reframe how internal working models reflect the dyadic handling of emotional experiences.

Affective competence involves being able to feel and process emotions for optimal functioning while maintaining the integrity of self and the safety-providing relationship (i.e., attachment). Both *feeling but not dealing* (being overwhelmed with feeling and unable to cope) and *dealing but not feeling* (to "go on automatic," eradicating feelings in order to cope) are products of defensive strategies. Closeness is achieved at the cost of either compromised external functioning (resistant pattern of attachment) or loss of internal suppleness and aliveness (avoidant pattern of attachment).

The attachment categories reflect different types of affective competence: they represent distinct relational strategies for handling intense affective experiences. In secure attachment, healthy relational handling of affect based on flexible strategies results in rich affective experience. In insecure attachment, two defensive solutions arise in response to the emotional environment's failure to be affect-facilitating. In the disorganized/disoriented pattern of attachment, defensive strategies fail to maintain psychic cohesion by keeping fear at bay.

SECURE ATTACHMENT

Feeling and dealing while relating. The securely attached child is able to experience his feelings of separation and reunion and is not overwhelmed by them; they enhance the strength of the attachment bond, contributing to his resilience. Faced with separation, he cries, protests, and loses interest in play. Reunited with his mother, he can be soothed by her; calm again, he resumes his enthusiastic exploratory play.

INSECURE ATTACHMENT

Feeling but not dealing. The insecure, resistant child, who cannot let go relationally and cannot modulate his own affects, cries at separation from the mother but fails to be soothed by reunion with her; he continues to whimper and cling, and does not resume play. The relational maintenance costs the child his independent functioning and exploration of the environment. The problem here is not too much affect, but rather too much *anxiety* mixed in with affect, stirred up by the caregiver's unpredictable reliability. The whimpering and crying of the resistant child is a long way from the experience of inconsolable grief (a core affect evoked by loss); instead it is a mixture of grief, anxiety, and the defensive exclusion of anger that might unduly threaten the attachment relationship. Here, regressive defenses use certain affects to defend against other, more anxiety-laden affects. Here also is defensive exclusion: exploration and independent functioning are eliminated from the child's emotional lexicon, as are affects that would disrupt the attachment relationship. The resistant attachment style sets the stage for the emotionality (not *core* emotion) that interferes with, rather than informs, optimal functioning.

Dealing but not feeling. The insecure, avoidant child sacrifices his affective life in order to function. Throughout, his play uninterrupted, he exhibits neither distress at separation nor joy at reunion, *as if* he were indifferent to the caretaker's goings and comings. Physiological monitoring, however, shows him to be as aroused by the vicissitudes of attachment as his more expressive counterparts (Cassidy, 1994). It would be interesting to see if the play of the avoidant children could be differentiated from the play of securely attached children along the dimension of zest and joyfulness. At work here is a Faustian defensive strategy whereby the relationship is maintained through minimizing its importance and suppressing its emotional charge—but such emotional suppression (i.e., not feeling) predisposes the child to future problems. Emotional suppression is thus related to minimal relational engagement, for feeling and relating are intertwined. The avoidant attachment style sets the stage for future isolation, alienation, emotional impoverishment, and at best, a brittle consolidation of self.

Not feeling and not dealing. In disorganized/disoriented attachment, the momentary emotional loss of the parent—while physically present—as well as the contagion of fear and confusion that gets transmitted from parent to child (Main, 1995; Main & Hesse, 1990) produces intense anxiety and overwhelming affect; their combination leads to a split in consciousness that produces disorganization. The attachment bond itself is threatened. Its vulnerability to disruption, even if short-lived, heightens the danger the child experiences and leaves him feeling terrifyingly alone. The affects here—predominantly fear—rupture the organization of cognition and behavior and fragment the integrity of self. Disorganized attachment shows the devastating effects of the failure of the relationship to provide even the most rudimentary assistance with fear abatement. Instead, the very relationship with the caregiver, who is alternately experienced as frightened and frightening (Main, 1995), augments the child's fear response, fertilizing the soil in which dissociation and splitting of personality become the only viable strategies to prevent even more pervasive psychic disintegration in the face of danger. In response to the trauma of the holding environment breaking down, the behavior of the disorganized children is the psychic equivalent of the body's going into shock.

The Reflective Self Function

The *reflective self function* (Fonagy et al., 1991) refers to the capacity to conceive of the wishes, intentions, and actions of others in terms of mental states, including being able to experience the responses of others as reflecting *their* experience, an experience different from one's own. The reflective self function reveals that the child has a theory of mind, both of his own mind and of the mind of the other. As Eagle (1995) describes it, it is "the stance one takes later in life toward one's early experiences." Coates (1998) sees the reflective self function as the capacity to have a mind of one's own and to hold the other in mind:

> One recognizes one's own state of mind as such; one is aware of one's own beliefs and intentional preferences. Implied in this is the possibility that others may feel quite different. ... An important corollary of developing this appreciation is that one comes to grasp that mental states may be variable from one time to the next and from one context to the next. Further, mental states may also be fallible, and they may differ from one person to the next. (pp. 120–21)

Fonagy and colleagues have shown that the development of the reflective self function is a demonstrable correlate of secure attachment in children (Fonagy et al., 1991). Children who are securely attached to at least one parent develop a theory of mind earlier and are better able to use it in situations that are emotionally charged.

By allowing reflection on attachment experiences (a fortiori disturbing ones), *the reflective self function is the opposite of defensive exclusion.* The capacity for affectively informed reflection permits the self to tackle caregiving limitations without resorting to constricting and distorting defenses. It advances the individual's optimal adaptation by supplying yet another set of tools for managing fear, buttressing safety-engendering closeness and promoting exploration, even in the face of adversity.

By being able to exercise the reflective self function, the individual is able to transcend trauma. Being able to understand not only cognitively but also affectively and empathically the responses of others as reflecting their own experience gives the self more leeway and more options—for instance, whether to seek greater emotional closeness or greater distance. It introduces a crucial extra step before the internalization of the caregiver's reality, including her sense of the child. If the caregiver's behavior suggests, for example, that she believes the child to be worthless or bad, the child can process that view as being only *her* view, and need not automatically internalize (i.e., own) such a destructive, pain-engendering, and maladaptive view of himself. In the case of affectively aversive situations, a high reflective self function raises the threshold at which the need for defensive exclusion kicks in; it helps the individual transcend trauma and sows the seeds for resilience rather than pathology.

AFFECTS ASSOCIATED WITH ATTACHMENT PHENOMENA

Affect is fundamental to the working of the attachment process. The entire attachment endeavor is guided by affective experience, namely, the self's experience of the safety feeling. The functional goal of achieving one experiential state (felt security), and avoiding and counteracting another (fear/alarm/anxiety) is essentially what regulates attachment (van den Boom, 1990). Affective experience—the relative balance of fear and felt security—is what is used by the individual to navigate the three attachment behavioral systems.

What makes all attachment experiences psychologically challenging is that the affects they generate are so intense: feared and actual loss, separations, abandonments, alone states, and reunions all evoke powerful emotions. The feeling of closeness with the responsive attachment figure is associated with states of calm, well-being, and self-confidence, and with the safety feeling (Sandler & Joffe, 1965). Separation and loss—either actual or feared—elicit fear, anger, sadness, distress, and grief, as well as the affective experiences associated with painful alone states, such as feeling forlorn, helpless, and abandoned. Reunions with the attachment figure elicit relief and joy, as well as restoration of well-being; exuberance, zest, and emotions associated with mastery experiences accompany the explorations undertaken against a background feeling of safety. Finally, closeness with a responsive other itself leads to deep loving feelings toward that other.

The Experiential Component
of Attachment Experiences

The phenomenology of affective experiences associated with attachment—their actual experiential quality—has not been sufficiently attended to, either theoretically or empirically (Eagle 1996, p. 111). We need to become familiar with the phenomenology of loss, grief, fear, and joy, as well as that of states of well-being, calm, and confidence. In addition to core emotions (e.g., grief, anger, joy) and core affective states, however, there is a panoply of *receptive affective experiences* (Fosha & Slowiaczek, 1997; McCullough Vaillant, 1997) that need to be recognized and elaborated; for instance, many deep feelings arise in response to being taken care of well, particularly in more mature individuals. As Bowlby states, "[A]n urge to keep proximity or accessibility to someone seen as stronger or wiser, and *who if responsive is deeply loved*, comes to be recognized as an integral part of human nature and as having a vital role to play in life" (Bowlby, 1991, p. 293, italics added).

Our conceptual models need to be stretched to include ways of describing and talking about receptive experiences, as well as about love, gratitude, connection, appreciation, and all the other emotional states that occur as a result of feeling deeply cared for and understood. To make the most of the affective experiences associated with attachment phenomena, both conceptually and clinically, it is crucial to explore them as accessible phenomena with experiential correlates and characteristics, not simply as abstract constructs. Eagle, for instance

(1996), characterizes the adult manifestations of secure attachment as including "the capacity to experience one's attachment needs openly" (p. 133). To that should be added the capacity to experience and express openly—that is, without anxiety or shame—the affects associated with attachment experiences, both negative and positive. Chapter 7 is devoted exclusively to the phenomenological exploration of core affects, including affects associated with attachment phenomena. Facilitation of experiencing these affects requires knowing their phenomenological foundation. Their viscerally based working through not only enhances the solidity of therapeutic change but is essential to the transformational process.

SUMMARY

Thus far we have reviewed several aspects of the construct of attachment: the three behavioral systems that comprise it; its representational aspects (i.e., the internal working model of relationships and the reflective self function); and the affects associated with attachment phenomena, which play a fundamental role in the regulation and internalization of attachment experiences.

The feeling of safety, fostered by the bond with a trusted companion counteracts fear (alarm/anxiety), promotes exploration and risk-taking, and fosters a full affective experience. If there is no feeling of safety, anxiety, the mother of all psychopathology, takes hold. Anxiety is a reaction to the nonavailability or nonresponsiveness of the caregiver and is rooted in the feeling of being alone in the face of psychic danger. Defenses arise to reestablish safety where the attachment relationship has failed to do so, and to optimize the caregiving available from the attachment figure, given her limitations. Their function is to exclude both intrapsychic and interpersonal affective experiences that threaten the integrity of self and the viability of the attachment relationship.

Internal working models capture these patterns, which then become represented in psychic structure. The reflective self function, an adaptive alternative to the development of defense, promotes security of attachment and resilience. Indeed, the capacity for reflective self functioning is the inverse of defensive exclusion, as it encompasses a sure-footed, full knowledge of the state of the other. The operation of the reflective self function raises the threshold for the development of pathology in the face of environmental failures.

Secure attachment and a high reflective self function are also correlated with maximal affective access. Insecure and disorganized attachment, as well as functioning based on a low reflective self function, are correlated with reduced access to affective experience, which in turn reflects a compromised adaptive capacity. Without full access to affective experience, the compass used by the individual to navigate the relational world is compromised, and the personality is robbed of vitality and richness.

The therapeutic implications of the attachment model are clear. The patient's feeling safe in the relationship with the therapist is essential: it reduces anxiety, precludes the need for relying on defenses, and supports the deep exploration of affective experience, which is the key to the profound transformation AEDP seeks to facilitate and work through.

In the next chapter, we move to consider how secure attachment is promoted: what makes the good-enough caregiver good enough. A major theme throughout is the issue of affect management and the application of the findings to therapeutic endeavor.

CHAPTER 3

THE GOOD-ENOUGH CAREGIVER AND THE OPTIMAL DYADIC PROCESS

Having established the power of secure attachment to promote optimal development, we now turn our attention to the caregiving system to explore what qualities and responses lead a caregiver to be able to function as a secure base for the child, and how the therapist in the affective model of change can incorporate essential aspects of caregiving into the therapeutic role. Our quest is informed by asking the following:

▼ How does caregiving transform the developing self?

▼ What use can therapy make of the lessons of good-enough caregiving?

▼ What promotes secure and less defended interaction, in both attachment and the affective model of change?

▼ How are the AEDP therapist's stance and techniques—uncannily—suited to the task of promoting secure and less defended interaction?

Affective competence—how affect is handled relationally—will emerge as the foundation of what makes the good-enough caregiver good enough. The extent of her own sensitive responsiveness, security of attachment, and capacity for a high reflective self function can be reframed as manifestations of affective competence. Moreover, tracking the theme of affect management will shed light on the therapeutic endeavor and its potential for evoking and supporting change.

If affective competence in the child involves managing intense affects associated with attachment events—separations, reunions, losses—while maintaining the caregiving relationship and continuing to discover the world, the ante is upped when the affective competence of the good-enough caregiver is examined. Affective competence in the caregiver encompasses the capacity to help the child with his feelings, in addition to managing her own: she has to be able to move fluidly between self and other, feeling and action, empathy and authenticity, sensitivity and effectiveness. It is when these dichotomous terms are experienced as clashing or incompatible that trouble starts. Optimal affective competence in the caregiver reflects the delicate balance of dialectical engagement, without needing to sacrifice attunement to the affective state of either member of the pair.

SENSITIVE RESPONSIVENESS AND HELPFULNESS IN THE CAREGIVER

Many studies (e.g., Ainsworth et al., 1978; Bates, Maslin, & Frankel, 1985; van den Boom, 1990) document the correlation between attachment status and the caregiver's sensitive responsiveness and helpfulness. It is important that sensitivity and attunement can be learned and enhanced (van den Boom, 1990), that is, attachment status is flexible and responsive to environmental changes.

Maternal Sensitive Responsiveness and Helpfulness

Mary Ainsworth's consistent yoking of two sets of terms characterizing the mothers of securely attached children—their tender *and* careful holding, and how sensitive *and* responsive they are to infant signals and communications—refer implicitly to different aspects of affective processing. One term in each yoked set is concerned with the feeling aspect of the mother-child interaction (tender, sensitive), while the other term is concerned with how the mother's feelings for and attunement to the baby inform her interaction (careful, responsive). The use of all four terms indicates that, optimally, the mother needs to simultaneously access the affective state of the baby as well as her own emotional response, processing moment-to-moment shifts in the interaction.

Such processing is one aspect of affective competence. Another depends on the caregiver's capacity, when appreciating the infant's emotional state, to "go beyond mirroring" to mastery of it, to "deal with distress" rather than be overwhelmed by it (Fonagy et al., 1995, p. 243). This is the dimension of active helpfulness (Bates, Maslin, & Frankel, 1985). In the words of Fonagy and Target (1998), the mirroring by mothers who effectively soothe their babies following an injection "is 'contaminated' by displays of affect that are incompatible with the child's current feeling (humor, skepticism, irony, and the like), which reflect coping, metabolization, or containment" (p. 94). Such noncontingent responsiveness, whereby the caregiver reveals herself as distinctly other, at once reflects the child's distress and uses the mother's (or therapist's) own affect-coping skills. Accordingly, the recipient of the caregiving (child or patient) will more readily be able to internalize that capacity, eventually becoming able to autoregulate his distress.

THE SECURE INTERNAL WORKING MODEL OF ATTACHMENT AND REFLECTIVE SELF FUNCTION

To assess which parent characteristics promote secure attachment in children, Fonagy and his colleagues and Main and her colleagues studied the impact of the quality of the caregivers' *representational processes*— their internal working model and reflective self function—on the child. The notions of secure internal working models of attachment and the high reflective self function constitute a remarkably powerful typology of affective competence. Both involve positive experiences for the child that can be internalized and provide him with the means for engendering his own safety and relatedness, and for exploring the world—and both are highly transposable to thetherapeutic endeavor.

Good-enough caregiving based on the caregiver's own secure internal working model of attachment facilitates the kind of affective–relational experience that produces affective competence and does not require defensive maneuvers. Good-enough caregiving based on the caregiver's high reflective self function engenders in the child the powerful sense that he is deeply and lovingly understood. The child develops his own ability to reflect on experience, which enhances his resilience and capacity for transcending adversity.

Affective Competence and
Caregivers' Attachment Patterns

Studies of adult caregivers' representational processes all are based on the Adult Attachment Interview (AAI), an instrument that taps the adult state of mind in relation to attachment (Main & Goldwyn, 1990). The semistructured interview, using a technique that has been described as "surprising the unconscious" (George et al., 1985, quoted by Main, 1995), probes memories of attachment-related experiences during childhood, such as feeling loved or unloved, memories of being upset or ill, and memories of separations and losses. Subjects are classified into four attachment patterns: secure—autonomous, insecure—preoccupied, insecure—dismissing, and unresolved—disorganized.

SECURE ATTACHMENT:
AFFECTIVE COMPETENCE

Feeling and dealing while relating. The *secure—autonomous* caregivers who have the ability to process painful affects without resorting to defensive strategies can hold a child on the roller coaster of attachment-related emotionality, feeling neither overwhelmed nor in need of distance themselves. The child internalizes the emotional confidence and poise that eventually develops into his own affective competence.

INSECURE ATTACHMENT:
COMPROMISED AFFECTIVE COMPETENCE

Feeling but not dealing. The *insecure—preoccupied* caregivers are unable to modulate their affect; the anxiety generated by its intensity overpowers them and interferes with functioning. They have difficulty reliably handling the child's distress, and the child who is not being helped might even be called on to take care of his caregiver. The insecure resistant children of such caregivers have to contend with inconsistent parenting. Their coping style—watching mother like a hawk and clinging to her to reassure themselves that she won't disappear again—is their way of managing the fear and pain associated with inconsistency.

Dealing but not feeling. The *insecure—dismissing* caregivers maintain their composure by defensively minimizing the importance of relationships, remembering little of their past, and being affectively flat. These caregivers do not emotionally engage with either themselves or the other. The child's emotional arousal would only exacerbate emotional distance, with the result that the child feels abandoned, experiencing his emotions as worthless and shameful. Overwhelmed by his initial emotional arousal and further isolated by feeling devalued, the now avoidant child internalizes the caregiver's internal working model as a way of coping with the pain of rejection associated with emotionally unresponsive parenting. The pain is beyond the child's emotional capacity to handle alone.

UNRESOLVED DISORGANIZED ATTACHMENT:
FAILED AFFECTIVE COMPETENCE

Not feeling and not dealing. The unresolved–disorganized caregivers lose both contact and coherence; momentarily paralyzed on one side or the other of a dissociative state, they become unable to parent, and in that moment the child undergoes the trauma of loss. Fear, a major disruptive affect if not relationally contained, is transmitted to the child, who is left completely unprotected in the face of helpless parental abdication (Lyons-Ruth & Jacobvitz, 1999).

As the foregoing demonstrates, caregivers transmit their internal working models to their children, documentably so in terms of the child's attachment *to them*. Secure parents have babies who are securely attached to them; insecure parents have babies who are insecurely attached to them—usually similar types of insecurity that characterize both parental and child attachment status (Fonagy et al., 1991; Levine, Tuber, Slade, & Ward, 1991; Main & Goldwyn, 1990; Steele, Steele, & Fonagy, 1996). Attachment studies also document the responsiveness of experience to environmental factors, particularly the *relationship-specific* nature of attachment patterns during infancy (Fonagy et al., 1991); Steele, Steele, & Fonagy, 1996; Main, 1995): "on the basis of manifestations of the parent's working model in relationship, *the child develops and maintains distinguishable sets of expectations in relation to each of his or her primary caregivers*" (Fonagy et al., 1995, p. 240, italics added). At this age, security of attachment is not a characteristic of the child that describes his relational patterns across the board. Instead we find different internal working models for different parent–child relationships. (Little or no research has explored the attachment status of different siblings to the same parent; most likely it too would be specific to the relationship, reflecting also the *caregiver's* different internal working models informing relational patterns with each of her children.) Attachment status also is responsive to change in the other: in a short time, children's attachment status becomes increasingly secure in response to increases in their mothers' sensitive responsiveness, which changed in response to interventions designed specifically to enhance it (van den Boom, 1990).

In the affective model of change, the continuity of patterns over time, side by side with responsivity and flexibility to specific conditions, allows both for the shaping power of the past (what the patient comes in with) and the power of the moment (what happens between patient and therapist). Both there and then (formative past) and here and now (current dynamic) contribute to and shape the construction of the moment-to-moment experience of the two partners and their interaction.

Traditional psychoanalysis has privileged the power of the past to shape the present. The affective model of change maintains that both are powerful influences, a contention that echoes the position expressed by Beebe, Jaffe, & Lachmann (1992), Beebe & Lachmann (1988, 1994), Beebe, Lachmann, & Jaffe (1997), and Lachmann & Beebe (1996):

> Our view of transference acknowledges its interactive organization and developmental transformations. The contributions of analyst and patient are neither similar nor equal but, through their interaction, the patient's rigidly retained structures can be engaged, responded to analytically, and transformed. Analysis therefore provides opportunities for new experience and new expectations can organize new themes. (Lachmann & Beebe, 1992, p. 145)

These opportunities for new experiences, with the new expectations that new experiences can organize, are at the heart of the affective model of change. The interactive structures generated by experiences with the therapist become part of the patient's repertoire and shape his expectations of and contributions to future interactions (they also restructure his representation of past interactions).

Caregivers' Reflective Self Function and Attachment

Reliance on the reflective self function can be understood as the opposite of reliance on defensive exclusion in the face of psychic adversity. High reflective functioning in parents is highly protective for the next generation (Coates, 1998; Fonagy, Leigh, Kennedy et al., 1995; Fonagy et al., 1995; Main & Hesse, 1990). Indeed, this research has shown that a caregiver's capacity to process the emotional events of her life is a much more powerful predictor of the security of her child's attachment to her than her actual history of trauma and early loss.

The reflective self function is a major intervening variable between trauma and the quality of one's internal working model. The ability to reflect promotes resilience, robs traumatic stressors of their pathogenic force, and has the power to interrupt the intergenerational transmission of predisposition to pathology (Fonagy et al., 1995, p. 255). Thus, the reflective self function provides a *second chance*—and it appears that "even a single secure/understanding relationship may be sufficient for the development of reflective processes" (Fonagy et al., 1995, p. 258). Here further evidence is adduced for the tenacity of the self-righting tendency: *through only one relationship with an understanding other* (who by no means need be the dominant attachment figure), *the impact of trauma can be transformed*. These studies illuminate the power of the reflective self function to contribute to resilience and self-healing even under highly adverse circumstances. This is very much in keeping with two central AEDP themes: the emphasis on the patient's resources and capacities, and the potential for transformation that the relationship with the therapist holds.

These data now provide empirical support for a core assumption of AEDP: the ability to process experience, together with an understanding other, is mutative: it transforms the experience, the self, and most likely the other (cf. Beebe & Lachmann, 1994; Beebe, Lachmann, & Jaffe, 1997; Seligman, 1998; Tronick, 1989). Now we also have powerful evidence that it transforms that which is interactionally communicated and intergenerationally transmitted.

In therapy, as in life, a developed reflective self function has the potential to put a stop to the intergenerational transmission of pathology. Those who do not have it can nurture and develop it in the context of being in *one relationship* with an other whose capacity for it is high (e.g., the therapist). What therapists must do to bring this potential to fulfillment is a central concern of this book. What follows examines specifically how the therapist's stance and interventions—the embodiment of a therapist's high reflective self function—can activate and enhance the operation of patients' reflective self functioning.

The proof that relational experiences with caregivers become immortalized in psychic structure supports the premise that early experience has the power to affect lifelong patterns, and implies, if not intransigence to change, the limited impact of new experiences on the structure of the personality shaped by the old ones. Yet the evidence for responsiveness to current conditions, especially those favoring self-righting tendencies, suggests that new experiences can and do have a rapid, significant impact on internal experience and therefore psychic structure. How then to reconcile these seemingly contradictory conclusions and their implications for therapy?

Emde (1981, 1988) makes the point, echoed by Eagle (1995), that the apparent stability of psychic structure over time is predicated on the stability of environmental conditions. That is, although a child internalizes his parents' attachment status by the time the child is twelve months old, his own attachment status will change when that relationship changes (van den Boom, 1990; Lamb, 1987) or when the child is engaged in other relationships, to reflect patterns consistent with the new experiences.

Such responsiveness to current conditions, particularly those favoring reparative or self-righting tendencies (Emde, 1981, 1988), is very good news for a psychotherapy based on the affective model of change. And yet, if psychic structure is plastic, then how can it remain responsive to good affect-facilitating conditions yet develop immunity to pathology-engendering environments? Our concern is the process whereby experiences with the therapist can become generalized across situations, particularly those in which the other is not always good enough (i.e., is not affect facilitating). How then can a highly adaptive internal working model come to dominate other, less healthy internal working models, particularly in nonfacilitating conditions?

The answer is in the capacity to reflect on experience. Here we find the strongest vote of confidence for the therapeutic process and its transformational powers from the get-go. Fonagy demonstrated that just one relationship with a secure other can enhance resilience and protect against trauma (Braithwaite & Gordon, 1991; Fonagy, Leigh, Kennedy et al., 1995). There is also evidence that parents with traumatic histories but high reflective self function triumph over their histories and break the intergenerational cycle of transmission (Fonagy, Leigh, Kennedy et al., 1995; Fonagy et al., 1995; Main, 1995). Applied to psychotherapy, these findings indicate that one secure relationship holds the potential for engendering in the individual the resilience to triumph over, or at least not be undone by, adversity.

Awareness can generate change. More specifically, the affective model of change advocates an awareness solidly rooted in and growing out of deep emotional experience. In AEDP, waves of experiential work alternate with waves of reflective work. The aim is to foster new security-engendering experiences that can be internalized in new adaptive internal working models, and then reflect on those experiences. The capacity for affectively informed reflection provides the *second chance* to transcend current aversive experiences; it also creates the opportunity to generalize from positive new experiences and make the most of them beyond current conditions. Reflection empowers the patient to generate environments conducive to well-being, and to immunize against vitality-draining experiences by understanding them to be emotionally inimical to well-being. A model that recognizes both the continuity of patterns over time and their plasticity in response to environmental conditions—particularly those favoring self-righting tendencies (Emde, 1981, 1988)—allows us to consider both the power of the past to shape the present and the power of the here and now to transform the individual.

Existing in the Mind and Heart of the Other

Seligman (1998) noted, "Understanding is not *about* experience. It is itself an experience, and this experience involves the crucial presence of another person with whom one feels secure, in part by virtue of feeling understood by that person" (p. 84). Why should it be that having a high reflective self function "is a critical factor in experiencing security" (Eagle, 1996, p. 135)? Fonagy (1996) proposes that the child of a caregiver with a high reflective self function has the experience of *existing in the mind of another*; in other words, he has the *experience of being understood*: "The biological need to feel understood ... takes precedence over almost all other goals" (Fonagy et al., 1995, pp. 268–69).

The need for being understood has been elevated to the level of a biological need. Through the reflective self function, Fonagy joins the moment-to-moment attunement of sensitive and responsive caregiving with the complex, survival-dictated functioning of the attachment system. In one bold move, empathy becomes a central tool for serving the most basic adaptational aims of the human being.

> Placing our emphasis upon the parent's confident anticipation of the child's mental state as one of the essential processes underlying secure attachment may force us to reconsider the nature of security in the child's mind. ... [A] child may be said to be secure in relation to a caregiver to the extent that, on the basis of his or her experience, he or she can make an assumption that his or her mental state will be appropriately reflected on and responded to accurately. (Fonagy et al., 1991, pp. 214–15)

In therapy, as in child rearing, the caregiver's empathy and the individual's experience of it provide the foundations on which the entire enterprise of change rests. As Seligman (1998) states, "[P]rogressive developmental and psychoanalytic processes are all, at their core, constituted by special types of transformative two-person interactions that are simultaneously reliant on reflective understanding and social interaction as inextricable parts of dynamic, integrative relationship systems" (p. 83). The capacity to metabolize affective experience—that is, affective competence—is fundamental to the reflective self function. As Fonagy et al. (1991) declare, "The development of the capacity for mental representation of the psychological functioning of self and other is closely related to affect and its regulation" (p. 206).

Though Fonagy emphasizes "existing in the *mind* of the other," for the reflective self function to lead to security of attachment, the child must have the sense that he also *exists in the heart of the other.* Even more deeply than cognitive holding, the reflective self function offers affective holding: not cool, detached reflection but reflection informed by empathy and caring. The mother's capacity not only to reflect the child's distress but to go "beyond mirroring" (Fonagy et al., 1995) and be effective in reducing that distress means that she knows him, that he exists in her mind as himself, and that she cares.

Intrinsic to the reflective self function is the capacity to reflect on and be mindful (Epstein, 1995; Goleman, 1995) of emotional experience (see *meta-experiential processing*—i.e., the experience of experiencing—in chapter 8). The operation of the reflective self function results in "making space" to feel and be, both for the other and oneself. Mindfulness allows the individual to be fully in touch with his experience, at the same time understanding how different the other's experience might be. Two realms of emotional experience—separate and touching, interacting, constantly shifting and modified by one another—can coexist and inform action. Intimacy is enhanced.

Ordinary, good-enough caregiving involves keeping the other in mind and expressing that mindfulness through sensitivity, attunement, and genuine helpfulness. The result is that the child feels safe in existing in the mind and heart of the other. He also develops a notion of the existence of different minds, that is, his own reflective self function, which will stand him in good stead.

THE ABILITY TO HOLD ONESELF
IN ONE'S OWN MIND AND HEART

Like maternal sensitivity and secure attachment, a high reflective self function involves being able to shift back and forth between self and other, and being able to experience and regulate affects. In addition, in the operation of the reflective self function, there is the back and forth between empathy for the other and empathy for the self. It is crucial that the caregiver be mindful not only of the child's emotional experience but also her own: she also must exist in her own mind as herself. If she focuses exclusively on the child and loses herself, she will pay the price of being disconnected from viscera, authenticity, and the intricate system of checks and balances that keeps the bio–psycho–social system of attachment humming. The caregiver who devotes herself to care of the other at the expense of her own self actually loses track of the other and ends up unconsciously taking care of her own self, treating the other as she herself yearns to be treated (Winnicott, 1949). The development of the false self has its roots in being the recipient of such caretaking.

THE ABILITY TO REFLECT ON CAREGIVING LAPSES

Another aspect of the reflective self function that has important clinical reverberations and partakes of affective competence is that it allows for caregiving lapses and their reparation (cf. Safran & Muran, 1996; Safran, Muran, & Samstag, 1994). Here the overlap is with Winnicott's notion of *good enough*. Mindful of self and other, it is possible to reflect on and acknowledge caregiving lapses. With acknowledgment comes ample opportunity for reparation.

The key to affect facilitation in the face of relational disruption is keeping things in the psychic space between child and caregiver. The caregiver's acknowledgment, honesty, and acceptance of lapses and failures, as well as her readiness for reparation, brings painful matters back into the realm of what can be talked about, felt, experienced, and processed together with a trusted other—particularly when the negative feelings are about that very other. In a truly affect-facilitating environment, losses, disappointments, offenses, lapses, and emotional pain that accompanies them do not require defensive exclusion (Bowlby, 1980): they need not be put away and disconnected or borne alone. The complete processing of intense affect culminates in communication with an open, receptive other, whose own affective experience is not distorted by defensive exclusion.

The caregiver's openness to communication about emotionally

painful matters allows difficult emotional experiences to be incorporated into the *child's omnipotence* (Winnicott, 1963a). Initially overwhelming experiences become manageable in that psychic space where the child feels a sense of control, mastery, and autonomy; thus they can be used to enrich and deepen relational experience and give the individual access to an increasingly supple self. The caregiver's openness to communication fosters the child's emotional access to her. This open emotional dialogue becomes internalized and reflected in intrapsychic fluidity, where the individual can freely think to himself (Bowlby, 1991). Once again, what is required in good-enough affect facilitation is not the perfection of seamless empathy or flawless selflessness, but rather something more akin to the willingness to engage authentically, compassionately, and responsibly: "One gets the impression that children get over even severe shocks without amnesia or neurotic consequences, if the mother is at hand with understanding and tenderness and (what is most rare) with complete sincerity" (Ferenczi, 1931, p. 138).

AFFECTIVE COMPETENCE AS MIRRORED
IN THE REFLECTIVE SELF FUNCTION

Affective competence is reflected in the mother who is in touch with her experience and can attune and focus on her child. She can respond to him in his own terms, yet do so with tenderness and sincerity (Ferenczi, 1931) and pleasure (Ainsworth et al., 1978; Winnicott, 1963b). The mother "has a special function, which is to continue to be herself, to be empathic toward her infant, to be there to receive the spontaneous gesture, and to be pleased" (Winnicott, 1963b, p. 76). It is this quality, whether we call it the reflective self function, meta-cognitive monitoring (Main, 1995), or affective competence, that is key in promoting the child's secure attachment.

The roots of resilience and the capacity to withstand emotionally aversive situations without resorting to defensive exclusion are to be found in the sense of being understood by and existing in the mind and heart of a loving, attuned, and self-possessed other. The reflective self function thus precludes the need for defensive exclusion. In this way, the reflective self function is related (but not identical) to Winnicott's (1949) understanding of mind as arising in response to inevitable environmental failure. Winnicott's notion of mind focuses on its defensive, *disembodied* aspects (i.e., its resulting from the split of psyche–soma); reframed through the lens of affect, the essence of the reflective self function is in its *embodied* (affectively full) bridging of the gap created by the inevitable lapses of caregiving and blows of fate.

OPTIMAL DEVELOPMENT: MOMENT–TO–MOMENT MOTHER–CHILD AFFECTIVE INTERACTION

Having examined the contributions of the caregiver, we now turn to explore the contributions of the dyadic interaction itself. What characteristics of the optimal interactive dyadic processes bring secure attachment about, and thus optimal development? In terms of therapy, what is the nature of the optimal patient-therapist interaction that can foster a process of deep affective exploration and resolution? The developmental literature examined here documents how experience *co-constructed* through the interaction of dyadic partners promotes optimal development (Beebe & Lachmann, 1988, 1994; Beebe, Jaffe, & Lachmann, 1992; Gianino & Tronick, 1988; Lachmann & Beebe, 1992, 1996; Stern, 1985, 1998; Tronick, 1989, 1998).

Tronick (1989) maintains that in the first year of life, the optimal dyadic interaction is essentially an affective communicative exchange; in resonance with the affective model of change, Tronick sees affective experience in an interactive context as the central agent of change. The specific constituent elements of affective competence are being identified with increasing precision. It has been shown that secure attachment has its roots in feeling understood. Tronick (1989, 1998; Gianino & Tronick, 1988) demonstrates further that feeling understood has its roots in early experiences of moment–to–moment mutual emotional attunement of caregiver and child.

The Affective Communication System

A critical feature of affectively resonant interactions is that each partner is transformed by and transforms the other. The affective interaction of each actually changing "the emotional experience and behavior of the other" (Tronick, 1989, p. 112) brings about corresponding changes in the self. This process description articulates the essence of the affective model of change; it also is borne out by empirical research: for instance, imitating another's emotional expression by facially reproducing it evokes a psychophysiological state in oneself that corresponds to that of the other (e.g., Ekman, 1983; Zajonc, 1985). Through the act of matching, each person's psychophysiology changes.

The mother's regulation of her own emotional experience is crucial in the regulation of the infant's experience. Regulation that results in modulated, attuned, and responsive affective processing sustains optimal development in general and security of attachment in particular. The mother uses the infant's affect to read his state and to guide her responses accordingly. In turn, the infant uses the mother's affect to obtain valuable information not only about her and their interactions, but also about the safety of new experiences in the world (Emde et al., 1978; Klinnert et al., 1983). For Tronick, as for Fonagy, affective mutuality goes "beyond mirroring."

> Clearly, the emotional state of others is of fundamental importance to the infant's emotional state. And carefully note that this importance is not the result of passive processes such as mirroring. Rather it results from the infant's active use of another's emotional expression in forming his or her appreciation of an event and using it to guide action. (Tronick, 1989, pp. 114–15)

Such an account clearly assumes that the other *can* be read, and accurately enough. As Stern (1985) notes, "[m]ental states between people can … be 'read,' matched, aligned with, or attuned to (or misread, mismatched, misaligned, or misattuned)" (p. 27). Mutually good readers generate states of resonance and positive affect. Partners who are functionally illiterate with one another cannot construct the desirable state of mutuality.

Emotions are part and parcel of ordinary, ongoing interactions. Here construction of the affective holding environment takes place. The goal is to keep affect integrated in everyday life, encouraging its experience, expression, and flexible management in ways that are "predictable, expectable, coherent and coordinated" (Beebe & Lachmann, 1994, p. 133). As we shall see, *coordinated* is the operative concept. This is the realm in which the tone of emotional life is set and in which affective expectations are structured: the level of arousal that promotes optimal interactions (what's too little to elicit a response or too much, which ends up being disruptive); the range of affects and affective intensities that can be regulated reliably within the flow of interaction (what is responded to and what isn't, what is approved of and what isn't, what is expressed and what isn't, etc.). These dyadically constructed patterns are based in a give and take that reflects the temperamental requirements of both members of the dyad. The dyadic pattern reflects the nature of the coordination they are able to achieve, given who they are and how they respond to one another. Yet here as throughout, by virtue of having a greater range of options, the caregiver plays a greater role in constructing the parameters of each affective holding environment.

Coordinated States and Their Affective Markers

Tronick operationalizes optimal affective interactions as the "reciprocal positive exchanges" that result in a "coordinated state" in which mother and child are attuned to one another. In this coordinated state, mother and child match each other's expressive displays (e.g., mother and infant sobering) and the direction of the change of expressive display (e.g., mother brightening as infant smiles). Such matching can involve facial expressions, vocalization patterns and rhythms, eye contact, or any other index of engagement. Lachmann and Beebe (1992) proposed that "such matching experiences are crucial ingredients of later symbolized experiences of feeling known, understood, and involved" (p. 146). The striving for the state of mutual coordination is powerful and essentially guides the dyad's interactions; Gianino & Tronick (1988) use the label *interactive errors* to refer to the often-occurring departures from it: failure to get in sync reflects "interactive error" and leads to a "miscoordinated state."

These constructs have affective markers that are linked to powerful motivational vectors:

▼ Pleasurable positive affect accompanies the coordinated state. Given both partners' vigorous striving to achieve it strongly suggests that we are designed to seek states of mutual coordination.

▼ Negative affect is the marker of the "miscoordinated state" (Tronick, 1989, p. 116); its occurrence occasions the desire to alleviate the highly unpleasurable state that it is, and seeks its rapid transformation into positive affect. Negative affect thus becomes a motivational spur to reparation.

▽ Positive Affects That Accompany Matching Experiences

Positive affects that accompany matching experiences in mother-infant interactions have three counterparts in the core affective experiences of adults in psychotherapy:

▼ Receptive affective experiences, associated with feeling understood and empathized with, that register the self's experience of the dyadic partner's responsiveness.

▼ The healing affects (see chapter 8) that arise in response to other positive core affective experiences.

▼ The affects of resonance and mutuality (see chapter 8), e.g., "peak experiences of resonance, exhilaration, awe and being on the same wavelength with the partner" (Beebe & Lachmann, 1994, p. 157) that arise in response to reaching a coordinated state. ▽

Tronick uses affective markers to evaluate the status of the interaction. Similarly, in a therapy informed by the affective model of change, if affect is accessible and the patient is communicating openly (including *freely expressing negative affect*), then the patient-therapist relationship is on solid ground created by affectively coordinated states. While increases in resistance occur for many reasons, often a lack of in-syncness—that is, a miscoordinated state between patient and therapist—and the patient's corresponding experience of not feeling understood might be responsible for interrupting the flow of the therapeutic process.

What Constitutes Good Enough

Although the "affectively positive mutually coordinated interactive state" is striven for, departures from it are frequent. In normal, optimally interactive dyads, only about 30 percent of their time together is actually spent in the affectively positive, mutually coordinated interactive state (Gianino & Tronick, 1988). The rest of the time is spent in miscoordinated interactive states, accompanied by negative affect, attempts to get back to coordinated states, and positive affect. There is a constant oscillation between matched and mismatched interactions, and back again: "Tales of ecstasy are endless tales of failure. For always comes separation. And the journey towards the essential, fleeting unity begins again" (Hart, 1991, p. 75).

As good as it gets is not some uninterrupted state of mutual bliss with perfect attunement; instead what obtains is some paradise, lost and regained as a result of focused efforts on the part of both partners. Optimal is 30 percent of the time spent in a good psychic place; though a long way from perfect, 30 percent turns out to be, much as Winnicott said, good enough. Furthermore, what matters as much as (if not more than) the natural capacity to be in sync is the capacity to repair out-of-syncness so as to reestablish optimal connection. The importance of successful reparation over states of in-sync bliss is echoed by Malan (1976): speaking of a difficult case where therapist and patient managed to repair a therapeutic rupture, triumphantly getting back on track, Malan, the supervisor in the case, commented, "I think we want it to go wrong and then be made right again several times" (p. 333).

The Moment-to-Moment Operation of the Reparative Function

Gianino and Tronick (1988) named the process of moving from miscoordinated states to coordinated ones *interactive repair*. Repeated experiences of interactive error followed by successful interactive repair establish "the expectancy that repair is possible" (Beebe & Lachmann, 1994, p. 143).

Both the urge toward and capacity for reparation are already present—and strong—in infants. The baby works hard to repair interactive errors and regain the coordinated state with the mother (Beebe & Lachmann, 1994, p. 144). Moreover, the baby is wired to make the most of the mother's reparative efforts, and in the absence of major pathology, she is deeply responsive to the baby's reparative efforts. Here we see the moment-to-moment operation of the reparative force. "[There is a] biological predisposition ... such that there are built-in self-righting tendencies after any deflection from the pathway due to adverse environmental circumstances" (Emde, 1981, p. 213).

> The experience of interactive reparation and the transformation of negative affect into positive affect allow the infant ... to be able to maintain engagement with the external environment in the face of stress. With the accumulation and reiteration of success and reparation, the infant establishes a positive affective core. (Tronick, 1989, p. 116)

A history of successful reparations is linked with infants' resilience and adaptive stick-to-it-iveness (Gianino & Tronick, 1988); maintaining engagement in the face of stress is a key factor in resilience:

[I]nfants who experience more repairs during normal interactions are more likely to attempt to solicit their mothers' normal behavior when their mothers are acting in a disturbing, stressful manner (i.e., still-faced). These infants, on the basis of their experience of normal interactions, have *a representation of the interactions as reparable and of themselves as effective in making that repair.* (Tronick, 1989, pp. 116–17, italics added)

With that kind of confidence, hope is not so easily disrupted; possessing a positive affective core (Emde, 1983)—the heart of affective competence—these children can keep going for a while, feeling and dealing, without either falling apart or needing to develop defensive strategies. Here is a parallel with the reflective self function—the good news and second-chance scenarios. Coordinated states are wonderful. Even better, however, in the long run is what accrues after something has gone wrong and one has been able to fix it (Kohut, 1984, pp. 66–67; Safran & Muran, 1996; Safran, Muran, & Samstag, 1994). In addition to feelings of effectiveness and self-confidence in adversity, such success fosters a sense of the reliability and responsiveness of others, particularly their openness to reparation.

Associated with an internal working model of the self as effective, the other as responsive, and the interaction as reparable is both the positive affect of mutually attuned, effectively coordinated interacting and the bearable negative affect marking miscoordinated states. What makes negative affect in the securely attached bearable is the individual's confidence that, with some effort, it can be transformed into positive affect (i.e., it is not accompanied by undue anxiety). When efforts to restore coordination fail, despite repeated attempts at repair, anxiety then renders negative affect unendurable and triggers defensive strategies.

For therapists who seek to facilitate deep affect, Tronick's conclusions illuminate how to understand the relational implications of different affect states, and what to aim for therapeutically when they occur. It is not a stretch to suggest that optimally interactive patient-therapist dyads are effective in restoring mutual coordination and positive affects *between* them. The patient does not experience long periods of negative relational affect, because both partners work hard to restore in-syncness (i.e., a good therapeutic alliance). The therapist in such dyads has the capacity to respond in an attuned manner, correct her responses, and be sensitive and responsive to the patient's reparative initiatives. Between them, interactive errors—and the accompanying negative affect—spur reparative efforts that succeed. In such circumstances, the patient is effective in righting a wrong. Focusing on the healing affects, the positive affects attendant on reparation, (see chapter 8), further solidifies the bond and deepens therapeutic work.

The State of Mutual Coordination and the Determined Striving for Interactive Repair: Implications for AEDP

It is important to note that the foregoing refers to *positive relational affects, that is, affects arising in response to the patient's and therapist's experience of their interaction.* Positive relational affects, the hum of the dyad working effectively, produce the safety feeling that allows in-depth therapeutic work to take place: the positive relational affects will only enhance the patient's ability, with the therapist's help, to do the difficult exploratory work of the therapy, which requires processing intense, negative, painful affects. The patient's capacity to experience and work through negative affects associated with the core of his pathology also reflects on the therapeutic relationship: inasmuch as the patient is able to experience, *without anxiety or defense,* core affects previously feared to be unbearable suggests that the patient feels safe, and that the background of good relational affect is allowing this difficult work to proceed. Negative relational affects, however, suggest that something is amiss in the therapeutic interaction. If this is the case, the core intrapsychic experiences of the patient—negative or positive—will remain off limits until the interactional error is repaired. Thus, there are two indices of the health of the therapeutic relationship, one explicit, one implicit: the presence of the positive relational affects associated specifically with the patient-therapist interaction; and the flow of the deep therapeutic work, which can only take place against a background of relationally constructed safety.

A PLEA FOR MORE THAN JUST A MEASURE

OF THERAPEUTIC RESPONSIVENESS

The reparative drive in psychotherapeutic endeavors is evidence of a basic motivation, a powerful drive active from infancy that seeks to restore optimal conditions—specifically, to restore responsiveness and attunement in the other; it is a moment-to-moment drive for health and healing. AEDP profoundly recognizes this primary source of motivation we wish to harness. Rather than being focused on pathology, reading the clinical material primarily for evidence of self-destructiveness, and so forth, we are primed to be on the lookout for evidence of the patient's profound adaptive strivings, reflected in his reparative drive and self-righting capacities: we ferret these out, deal with them in glimmer form, and seek to use them from the get-go; we privilege them over the more conservative, self-protective tendencies that result in stasis and stagnation—and we respond to them.

The importance of providing the patient with the opportunity for succeeding in reparative efforts cannot be overstated. If only from this perspective, the notion of neutrality and nonresponsiveness seems untenable (Tronick et al., 1978). The therapist's responsiveness to and facilitation of the patient's success in repairing emotional miscoordination is a key factor in healing.

THE AFFECTIVE COMPETENCE OF THE GOOD-ENOUGH CAREGIVER

The good-enough caregiver—here defined as one who fosters secure attachment—functions as a secure base for the child, evoking a sense of felt security and promoting ever-widening explorations. Her affective competence (management of emotions) in all these processes generates an affect-facilitating relational environment. She has the capacity to engage in attuned mirroring, in "positive, reciprocal exchanges" (Tronick, 1989), and also to go "beyond mirroring" and actually help the child cope with stress and distress until he can regulate his own experience.

The underpinnings of self and relational connection are to be found in the capacity to adaptively process strong emotions in oneself and others without being affectively, cognitively, or functionally overwhelmed. The goal in affect facilitation is to tolerate intense affects—positive and negative—while keeping the interaction going, without forsaking the relationship, the self, or in-the-world functioning; if this is achieved, adaptation is enhanced as the self is able to fully rely on affects as regulators.

Through "analogy and metaphor" (Lachmann & Beebe, 1996), we as therapists need to look to the defining features of the good-enough caregiver to understand which aspects of our own functioning to highlight, downplay, or refine, so as to promote optimal functioning in our patients. The AEDP therapist needs to be emotionally engaged and willing to share in affective experiences that are being worked through. Like the mother who fosters secure attachment in her child, the AEDP therapist has two modes of relating: sensitive responsiveness (attunement), and going beyond mirroring, using one's own affect management skills to help the patient process what previously had been too overwhelming or outside his sphere of mastery. Both relational modes, reflected in the little-step-by-little-step process and in the affect-releasing process, contribute to the achievement of a coordinated state and to the repair of miscoordinations.

The therapist's stance and techniques aim to create an environment in which affects can be experienced, dealt with, and reflected on. Through holding, support, empathy, and affective sharing, AEDP makes affects more tolerable so that patients can process and use them without resorting to defensive measures. Moreover, the focus on the *therapist's* experience of the patient and how to actively use that experience (see chapter 10) promotes, accelerates, and deepens the patient's experience of existing in the heart and mind of the other.

Like the good-enough mother, the AEDP therapist must have access to but not be overcome by the intensity of her feelings; she must be able to attend to her own experience while focusing on the patient; and must be able to fluidly move between the two. Furthermore, the therapist can model how to manage feelings, instead of denying them altogether or ceasing to function, as the patient needed to do in the past; also, she seeks to support the patient in her role as a way station to his competence to manage his own affective life. Finally, the therapist must have the courage to acknowledge and process her lapses and tolerate the intense affects that come in the wake of processing therapeutic ruptures.

In addition to being able to deal with negative affects evoked by disruption and taking responsibility for her part in the creation of the crisis, the good-enough, affect-facilitating therapist must be on the lookout for repair opportunities. Both partners participate in the process of repairing a disruption. The therapist need not invariably be the initiator of the reparative process, but she needs to be responsive to the patient's reparative efforts. The urge to repair, right a wrong, and restore coordination and well-being are powerful, operative adaptive forces. When fostered and facilitated, we find in these forces "expectancies of coping, ... re-righting and hope" (Beebe & Lachmann, 1994, p. 140), which are powerful contributors of long-term mental health. Failing to recognize reparative efforts not only cancels an opportunity for restoring security and coordination, but also does damage by undermining a powerful adaptive force that resides within us.

One of the obstacles that must be overcome in making the most of reparative initiatives is how difficult it is to process relational affects generated by experiences of intimacy, closeness, and appreciation. Much more than is generally recognized, intense positive affects are quite difficult to tolerate for many people. (How well do you accept compliments? How do you feel when a patient expresses deep gratitude or love to you?) Intense positive affects make people feel embarrassed, self-conscious, out of control, and vulnerable. Being able to tolerate the positive affects of repair is sometimes as hard as tolerating the negative affects of disruption. These positive experiences are singularly disarming, and vulnerability can be a frightening experience (Fosha, in press). Fear of these affects can interfere profoundly with the natural course of relational reparation—or at least interfere with its maximal healing potency.

The high-wire balancing act of affective competence, essential in good-enough parenting, is also essential—and demanding and difficult—in therapy. AEDP seeks to balance

▼ attuned empathy with genuineness and authenticity (Osiason, personal communication, 1998; Slavin & Kriegman, 1998);

▼ fully accepting where the patient is with striving to excavate deeper layers of experience (Greenberg, Rice, & Elliott, 1993);

▼ allowing the patient to discover his own resourcefulness with being willing to help when he is feeling overwhelmed (Fosha & Slowiaczek, 1997).

The attachment literature provides validation for some of the AEDP departures from a traditional psychodynamic stances, which revolve around the therapist's *active* use of her own emotional experience in the context of the metaphor of caregiving or parenting (Bowlby, 1988; Costello, 2000; George & Solomon, 1999) rather than in the context of a metaphor of a blank screen. While many therapists use their emotional experience to inform their understanding of the patient, most process this privately for fear of unduly influencing the patient. By making active use of it, the AEDP therapist, however, seeks to harness the transformational potential of personal experience rather than sacrifice half of the dynamic residing within the dyadic affective communication system. It would be self-defeating to do deep affect work with a poker face.

CHAPTER 4

THE DEVELOPMENT OF PSYCHOPATHOLOGY

Things fall apart; the centre cannot hold;
Mere anarchy is loosed upon the world.

W. B. YEATS, "THE SECOND COMING"

Psychopathology is rooted in the failure of the individual's emotional environment—either through *errors of omission* (neglect, inadequacy) or *errors of commission* (outright abuse, humiliation, rejection)—to facilitate the regulation of his affective experience when he is unable to do so alone. When the individual's affective needs exceed the affective competence of his others, the self must compensate for the environmental failure. The self divides, of necessity becoming its own caregiver, and much effort becomes invested in security operations (Sullivan, 1953, 1956). The individual needs to develop defenses, the adaptive goal of which is to restrict the impact of affects, feared to be unendurable and overwhelming to the psyche. The consequences of internalizing these defenses and building affective restriction into psychic structure is what pathology is—and what therapy seeks to undo. By being what the environment was not (i.e., affect-facilitating and willing to be there to bear, share, understand, and empathize with the patient), the therapist seeks to undo pathogenic conditions and set up an environment where self-righting tendencies can kick in.

The ability to experience and process intense affective experiences is fundamental to psychic health. Interference with this capacity is a major factor in the genesis of psychopathology. Optimally, affects develop in the transitional space between self and other, where they can unfold, evolve, and resonate, acquiring meaning and enrichment as they are reflected by the other. By seeing one's affects outside oneself, so to speak, in the countenance of the other, they become more real. The experience of affects becomes more alive, textured, and differentiated with layers of associations; affects thus shared are integrated into the individual's repertoire to contribute to inner resourcefulness. As long as affective experiences, both good and bad, can be experienced and processed in this way, the child's personality develops, acquiring its unique shape and flavor; there is character, but no character psychopathology, even if things do not go smoothly.

It is in the absence of an affect-facilitating environment that trouble begins—that is, when affects generated by self and relational experience cannot be processed. The goal of optimal development is for the individual to have self and relational needs met against a background of safety, such that he doesn't have to sacrifice his feelings. Here the emotional environment, or the affective competence of the caregiver, plays a major role. A facilitating emotional environment can help a child make the most of his internal resources (Kohut, 1977, 1984; Winnicott, 1965); it does so by being responsive to the child's needs.

Good-enough parents are aware of and responsive to the child's self and relational needs for care, safety, love, understanding, and respect. Good-enough caregiving promotes growth and doesn't require perfection; in fact, some discrepancy between the child's needs and his emotional environment often catalyzes psychic growth. Self-other boundaries, the separation-individuation process, healthy aggression, symbolic and creative capacities, and intersubjectivity can blossom in a context of frustration and lack of harmony (Mahler, Pine, & Bergman, 1975; Stern, 1985; Winnicott, 1963c). This level of discrepancy and failure is almost inevitable and very much covered by the notion of good enough.

Good-enough caregiving cannot protect a child from the blows of fate, but it can, however, "hold" a child through difficulties by protecting the child's emotional resources from being overwhelmed by demands and circumstances that are beyond his developmental capacity. Providing structure, help, guidance, support, physical contact, affection, and understanding are ways in which caregivers share their psychic resources with a child whose resources need buttressing or supplementing. Such responses go a long way in helping a child process extremely painful events, thereby reducing the likelihood of traumatization and long-term psychic distortion. Whatever painful emotions are generated in time can be psychically processed, and need not be warded off in fear of their wreaking psychic havoc.

Core affects are an expression of the wisdom of the human organism. The seeds of healing are contained within them. If supported and not interfered with, basic emotions, like all natural processes, are self-regulating and will function in the interest of optimal adaptation. A perfect example is the social and religious rituals following death: the emotional environment they create at once facilitates the process of normal mourning and decreases the likelihood that frozen or pathological mourning will develop (Volkan, 1981). Yet what happens when core affects are not supported, when the emotional environment fails the individual?

Parental failure "challenges the child's very basic and essential capacity to trust and, therefore, to depend" (Davies, 1996, p. 199). When the child's affective needs stretch beyond the limits of the caregiver's affective competence, the caregiver most often leads with defensive reactions, spurred by feeling inadequate, helpless, and panicked. The child's emotional experience arouses intense emotions in the caregiver, taxing her regulatory capacities. Rather than facilitating the child's experience, emotions—both hers and the child's—are denied, avoided, minimized, or dealt with through a variety of more primitive mechanisms; thus the caregiver's characterologic defenses against affective experience sow the seeds for the intergenerational transmission of pathology.

When emotional experiences are met by environmental failure, the attitude toward affects changes: rather than being a source of information and liveliness, affects become a source of anxiety, helplessness, guilt, shame, and fear (of loss, loss of self, love, rejection, etc.). These highly aversive experiences must be avoided at all costs; the push toward solutions that eventually lead to pathology intensifies.

THREE PRINCIPLES
OF AFFECTIVE HANDLING

Beebe and Lachmann (1994; Lachmann & Beebe, 1996) articulate three principles that account for ways in which interactions can have a mutative impact—that is, ways in which they become salient to transformational processes. *The principle of ongoing regulations* deals with how the regular, ordinary, day-to-day, moment-to-moment is handled and what expectations get thus generated; this type of change process is slow, gradual, cumulative, and powered by repetition. *The principle of heightened affective moments* addresses the process of change ushered in by intense emotional experiences: here the crucial factor responsible for transformation is intensity, not duration. Finally, *the principle of disruption and repair of ongoing regulations* organizes deviations from a relational norm: change occurs through how relational disruptions are dealt with.

Recast as principles of affective salience, these interactions may be used to explore how affect shapes development and how failures to relationally handle affective experience result in pathology. How a particular child–caregiver dyad handles affect becomes encoded in the child's internal working model of attachment (Cassidy, 1994, p. 230). The dyad's affective methodology gets internalized and shapes how the individual approaches affects—major and minor, ordinary and extraordinary, negative and positive, mild and intense. Thus, how affects are handled in a relationship influences the overall quality of attachment, which in turn affects the nature of affective experience in a constant feedback loop. Ultimately, the attachment bond is the context in which the child learns to regulate emotion (Fonagy, 1997). Under conditions of safety, where defensive operations are not necessary, affective experience is not constricted; with no aspects of self experience requiring defensive exclusion, the attentional, motivational, and communicative properties of affect have the opportunity to fully inform relational functioning. States of mutual coordination can be established on the basis of whole self functioning. As mentioned earlier, compromised affective competence is the price of restoring safety with caregivers whose own affect-handling capacities leave something to be desired. With access to affect blocked by defenses, the individual's adaptive capacity is compromised. States of mutual coordination can only be achieved by excluding vital aspects of self experience.

1. Failure in Handling the Affects of Everyday Life

Failures in regulating affects of everyday life occur when emotions are denied, ignored, and avoided as a matter of course, or when they are greeted with emotional misattunement, which invariably leads to negative affect (Gianino & Tronick, 1988). In the following examples, affects do not have the opportunity to develop through the back-and-forth resonance between members of the dyad; they either have to be borne alone (Stern, 1985) or excluded (Bowlby, 1973, 1988). Note that these affects are not particularly intense or problematic in and of themselves; they become so by virtue of the response (or lack thereof):

▼ A little girl looks sad and fearful at the prospect of an upcoming doctor's visit; her mother starts crying and ends up canceling the appointment.

▼ A birthday party generates much excitement, and the exhilarated children laugh and run wild. Without warning the parents come in and chastise the birthday boy, declaring the party over.

▼ Every time a ten-month-old "evidenced some affect and looked at her with a bright face and some excited arm flapping," his mother consistently undermatched him, falling "just short" of his level of activation and thus deflating his excitment. When asked about her strategy, she said she worried that her son would "lose his intiative if she joined in fully and equally with him"; further inquiry revealed that "she thought he was too much like his father, who was too passive and low-keyed" (Stern, 1985, pp. 211–12).

▼ An adolescent boy comes home proud of his third-place finish in the science fair. His father accuses him of immodesty though later brags to all his friends about his son's achievement.

If these everyday affective experiences are responded to, acknowledged, shared, and dealt with, they neither escalate to disruptive intensity nor are they forced to go underground. The flow of interactive life is not interrupted. This applies to positive as well as negative experiences. In these situations, however, emotional signals are not responded to (Cassidy, 1994) laying the groundwork for pathology.

2. Failure in Handling
Intense Affective Experiences

Affect-facilitating failures in the face of heightened affective experiences imprint the psyche in proportion to the more profound impact they generate, in keeping with the affective valence of such experiences. Events—impersonal or relational, intentional or accidental—occur that profoundly affect the individual, generating intense emotions that often leave him feeling overwhelmed and helpless. While affective intensity provides unequaled opportunities for mutative growth, it also can be overwhelming. The individual's capacity to deal with intense affects—both negative and positive—in a modulated and appropriate way is challenged by the high arousal associated with such experiences.

▼ A man watches helplessly as his son's hand gets caught in an escalator.

▼ A child's favorite teacher—the only person who has taken an interest in her—dies of cancer.

▼ Two-year-old Edgar Allan Poe (Terr, 1990) is found alone with the corpse of his beautiful young mother, who had been dead for two days.

▼ After several miscarriages, a woman's full-term baby dies within hours of delivery.

▼ In combat, a man sees his best friend die a sudden and violent death.

▼ A child witnesses a neighbor beat a dog to death.

HARD-TO-HANDLE

POSITIVE AFFECTIVE EXPERIENCES

▼ A teacher, overwhelmed when her students publicly present her with the year-end teaching award, is nowhere to be found the following final day of school, when they come to say good-bye and thank her again.

▼ A young professional, brimming with excitement at being elected president of his national association, becomes increasingly disorganized and ends up in disgrace.

▼ A dancer performs for an eminent person in his field, who tells him he has real talent and a promising career ahead of him. Soon thereafter, he gives up dancing.

When the environment fails to hold the individual through that which is unbearable, whether positive or negative, the overwhelmed self must attend to itself, for its very survival is at stake.

3. Failure in Handling Affect-Laden Interactions

Caregiving interactions often are very emotional, and herein lies the third challenge of good-enough affect-facilitation and management. Affect-facilitating failures in the face of relational disruptions and repairs on the part of caregivers are what Tronick (1989) calls *interactive errors.* When the caregiver's affective competence cannot handle the affective task at hand, the fate of the relational connection and affects become entwined. The individual must deal simultaneously with relational disruption and affective intensity, and must do so alone. In these instances, the caregivers' own difficulties with affective regulation make them unable to optimally deal with their children's affective experience.

The emotional environment may fail the individual by failing to help despite good intentions, resulting in *interactive errors of omission*—or by not only failing to help but actively hindering the individual's adaptive reparative efforts, resulting in *interactive errors of commission.* In both instances, the caregiving other cannot tolerate the individual's actual or feared emotional reaction, and this intolerance of affect creates the intrapsychic crisis that starts the sequence that so often culminates in pathology and its attendant suffering.

Each example that follows links an interactive error on the part of a caregiver with a patient's later presenting problem.

THE BAD NEWS:
INTERACTIVE ERRORS OF OMISSION

▼ A baby's cooing and smiling elicits no response from her depressed mother, who rocks the baby in the cradle next to her and stares at the floor. The patient presents with pervasive feelings of being "no good," and tremendous difficulty making eye contact with the therapist.

▼ The children of a couple who seldom argue witness a violent fight between their parents, during which they see their mother raise a knife, then drop it, run out of the house, and drive off. No one says anything. The next morning, the mother returns and the family resumes its routine as though nothing happened; the myth of the happy family is restored without comment. The patient presents with a perfect facade and a charming manner—which masks a long history of eating disorder, severe depression, and paralyzing procrastination.

▼ A boy's father dies while the boy is at camp; the boy is not told about it until he comes home two weeks later, when his mother matter-of-factly gives him the news. She tells him she did not want to interfere with his having fun, and urges him not to let this "event" interfere with the new school year. Twenty years later, the patient is admitted to a hospital in a fugue state, having walked more than twenty miles to his father's grave, and lacking all awareness of where he had been.

▼ Day after day, a preadolescent girl runs into her room and cries uncontrollably. Haltingly opining that she probably wants to be by herself and without ever asking what's wrong, her father closes the door to her room and takes the rest of the family out to dinner "to give her some space." When the patient presents to treatment, she is depressed and paranoid, convinced that any kindness toward her is evidence of ulterior motives and hidden agendas.

With *errors of omission*, denial rules and the caregiver's emotional inadequacy is reflected in avoidance, anxiety, paralysis, and neglect. The child, sorely in need of "holding," implicitly is given the choice of imitating the parent's defenses or dealing with his feelings on his own. Ignored or neglected, urged to deny his feelings and needs, the child is left to cope with mind-boggling emotional situations unsupported and pretend that there is no affective elephant in the room. He is not attacked, however, for being in emotional need: the attachment bond is maintained through affective denial and disowning of affect, and through the individual's managing to somehow absorb the additional pain associated with the environmental failure to respond and help. In the resulting self–other–emotion schema, AEDP's internal working model *cum* affect (see chapter 6), the self is too needy and demanding; the other is idealized as being in control, or else protected and treated gingerly as fragile and unable to deal, or else hated as cold and indifferent; and affects are experienced as shameful or overwhelming or explosive or annihilating—in short, as trouble and "too much."

THE EVEN WORSE NEWS:
INTERACTIVE ERRORS OF COMMISSION

▼ On the rare occasions when a six-year-old boy resists his mother's attempts to control his every move, she has a fit and runs out of the house agitated and hysterical, threatening to kill herself. The boy runs after her in a panic, repeating, "I'm sorry, I'm sorry, I'll never do that again" until he convinces her to return to the house. As an adult, he presents to treatment highly constricted, afraid to risk displeasing his wife lest she leave him, and driven by an extraordinary need for control.

▼ A psychotic mother who cannot tolerate her adolescent daughter's independence and budding sexuality grabs an eyelash curler from the girl's hand as she experiments with makeup at the mirror, attacks her with it, and calls her a whore. The patient presents with paralyzing depression, deeply dissatisfied with yet unable to leave a demeaning husband whose sexual demands border on abusive.

▼ A young girl screws up her courage and tells her mother how much she's missed her. With a sweeping gesture of dismissal, the mother replies, "Don't be tedious, darling. Feelings are *pour les oiseaux.*" As an adult, the patient presents to treatment with depression and physical symptoms mimicking multiple sclerosis for which there is no neurological basis. In the initial evaluation, she has a deep emotional response to her therapist's empathic responses, though she has difficulty finding words to match her emotional reactions. In the second session, sarcastic and contemptuous of the therapist, she is dismissive of her own responses.

Errors of commission tend to occur with caregivers who are more disturbed and more fragile. In this scenario, not only is the child not helped to bear the feared-to-be-unbearable feelings but also is shamed, blamed, rejected or punished, and forbidden from (or taunted for) experiencing or expressing them. The feared-to-be-unbearable feelings become even more unbearable when compounded by fear of abandonment, shame and guilt, and the great psychic pain of disappointment, rejection, and humiliation. Finding the child's affects profoundly disturbing, the parents feel out of control, helpless, and shamed, and they resent the child responsible for exposing them as such. Since the child's sense of self and relationship are at stake, his emotional experience becomes hostage to the parents' self-regulatory needs. Emotions become not only frightening and painful but also bad, deserving of shame, guilt, or punishment. In addition to a failure to process intense emotions, here is a further attack on the self or on the security of the attachment tie, which generates its own toxic and intense emotions. The greatest damage is done when those who are supposed to be protectors turn out to be the sources of danger, and when the things that make life worth living become the object of a powerful person's wrath and disdain. Positive emotions (e.g., pleasure, joy, tenderness), particular traits, qualities, ways of being that are either highly positive or at least benign (e.g., gentleness, independence, emotional sensitivity, intelligence, generosity) can become sources of great emotional pain when, for historical-dynamic reasons, the caregiver finds them intolerable, usually because they evoke intolerable vulnerability.

Unlike one-shot events that can reverberate on psychic development, the preceding *model scenes* (Lachmann & Lichtenberg, 1992) condense endlessly repeated interactions indicative of misregulation, misattunement, and affect-nonfacilitation, which in turn come to characterize the ongoing regulation of everyday affective life. When the infant develops expectancies of misregulation, he also develops an associated self-regulatory style (Beebe & Lachmann, 1994; Gianino & Tronick, 1988; Tronick, 1998) that already bears the hallmarks of the need for defensive exclusion and distortion. How the individual handles trauma much compounded by environmental failure will be examined after the notion of unbearable affective experience is explored.

UNBEARABLE AFFECTIVE EXPERIENCE

> I've sometimes thought that the body, our very physical existence, puts a limit on how much pain a mind can bear.
>
> PETER HØEG, *Smilla's Sense of Snow*

There is a profoundly physical aspect to the experience of emotion, particularly psychic pain of unbearable proportions. Mind and body can endure only so much before other mechanisms—shock, numbing, dissociation—take over. The painful feared-to-be-unbearable quality applies to

▼ affective experiences that are intrinsically painful and too much to bear, such as grief and loneliness;

▼ affective experiences, positive or negative, feared because their intensity threatens to overwhelm integrity of self (loss of control, disintegration);

▼ affective experiences, positive or negative, that elicit negative responses from the individual's emotional environment, such as sexual feelings met with shaming, angry feelings met with abandonment, expressions of need and vulnerability met with sadistic ridicule, expressions of joy met with criticism disguised as morality, and so forth.

Any of these characteristics—*intrinsic painfulness, intensity,* and *aversive consequences*—in any combination can lead to the quality of experience that is feared to be unbearable.

A defining quality of the unbearable experience involves a temporal dimension as well:

▼ Fear, anxiety, or terror arises in *anticipation* of a threat or a danger that has not yet materialized.

▼ Helplessness is experienced when the overwhelming situation is *in progress*: the individual feels helpless to stop what is happening to him as well as helpless to control his own reactions to it.

▼ What Joffe and Sandler (1965) call the *primary depressive reaction* (a neuropsychological response of defeat when the environment is unresponsive to efforts to change it) includes hopelessness and apathy, and it surfaces *after* the conclusion has been reached that the painful or overwhelming situation is immutable. The inability to exert any control over the forces impacting us is unbearable. This reaction arises as a consequence of past experiences that are generalized to the present and projected on the future.

Fear, helplessness, and the primary depressive reaction are also the hallmarks of anxiety disorders, traumatic disorders, and depressive disorders, respectively.

THE QUALITY OF
UNBEARABLE MENTAL PAIN

Freud, ever the great analogist, goes to the notion of physical pain to understand psychic pain: something impinges on us and we have no sense of control over it (Freud, 1926, addendum C). Similarly with mental or emotional pain, something external impinges and intrudes on us, breaks through protective devices, and is unresponsive to the individual's efforts to stop it. We feel helpless to avoid or stop it and powerless to get away from it.

THE SENSE OF BEING TAKEN OVER

Powerful emotions take us over, temporarily subordinating our sense of self. At their most intense, visceral phenomena such as grief, exuberance, passion, anger, and even love push to the limit our ability to contain them; intense emotions, particularly if we are not accustomed to them, can feel like an invasion. Often there is an accompanying fear that unless we step on the emotional brakes, loss of control will result. Cognition, in contrast, has a much more in-control quality that permits us to retain more of a sense of ourselves as initiators or executors.

The sense of being taken over applies not only to negative or painful emotions, but to any affective experience that challenges our control (see Kissen, 1995). A patient who persistently avoided positive emotions wasn't confident that he could contain them; his well-honed affective competence lay in managing disappointment and adversity. To feel deeply happy or tender, he said, would mean "I would no longer be 'me.'" Only through experiential processing, expression, and communication do intense emotional experiences come to be our own.

Emotions experienced as unbearable are at the extreme end of the control continuum, personal to each of us. In an individual with healthy boundaries, emotional surrender is not inconsistent with control: having a history of positive experiences with emotion, he *allows* himself to be taken over. The closer to optimal an individual's functioning, the higher his threshold for what is tolerable. Among more vulnerable individuals with tenuous affective organization and regulation, affects even at lower levels of intensity can seem overwhelming, threatening to undermine boundaries, identity, and sense of control. In these cases the self will try to curtail such emotion at any cost, in an effort to preserve some sense of identity and cohesion.

The specter of being overwhelmed by emotion creates the need for intervention. If others are willing and able to lend their psychic resources until the individual again can regulate his own affective experience, hope remains that the self can survive emotionally without long-lasting damage; if they are not, a major opportunity for healing vanishes.

THINGS FALL APART:
ALONENESS IN THE FACE
OF UNBEARABLE EXPERIENCES

> [W]hen a child finds himself abandoned, he loses, as it were, all desire for life. ... Sometimes this process goes so far that the patient begins to have the sensations of sinking and dying. ... What we here see taking place is the reproduction of the mental and physical agony which follows upon incomprehensible and intolerable woe. (Ferenczi, 1931, p. 138)

"Solitude, psychological solitude, is the mother of anxiety" (Wolf, 1980, p. 128, quoted in Stern, 1985, p. 109). If the caregiver is unavailable or unresponsive, the child finds himself alone with his overwhelmingly terrifying and painful emotional experience. Aloneness and loneliness, terrifying and painful in themselves, potentiate any other painful experience we are going through. When faced with the failure of the emotional environment to help him process his affects (i.e., when affective experience disrupts the individual's basic feeling of safety), what can the child do to preserve the integrity of his attachment ties, his self, and his affective life?

Occasionally, with resilient individuals, we encounter either unusual creativity or awe-inspiring resourcefulness arising out of profound crisis.

> The sudden, surprising rise of new faculties after a trauma [is] like a miracle that occurs upon the wave of a magic wand. ... Great need, and especially mortal anxiety, seem to posses the power to waken up suddenly and put into operation latent dispositions, which ... waited in the deepest quietude for their development. (Ferenczi, 1933, p. 165)

In more common scenarios, however, the individual must choose between preserving the integrity of his attachment ties and that of his affective self experience. Almost invariably, affective experience is sacrificed; access to affects—and with them, all the adaptive resources and richness inherent in experiencing them—becomes deeply compromised. This Faustian bargain (giving away the affective soul in exchange for a measure of security) is effected through defense mechanisms employed against affective experience.

THE CENTER CANNOT HOLD:
THE INSTITUTION OF DEFENSES

The institution of defenses is the emotional equivalent of shock, the body's adaptive response to physical trauma. The aim of defenses always is to restore the feeling of safety and to eliminate aversive emotional experiences. "Defenses consist of cognitive, emotional and interpersonal strategies employed by patients to keep anxiety-provoking thoughts and feelings out of awareness" (Coughlin Della Selva, 1996, p. 8). More specifically, defensive strategies seek to:

▼ protect against affects that threaten to disrupt the individual's functioning in the world as well as in self and relational experiences;

▼ avoid unbearable experiences (anxiety, shame, helplessness, hopelessness) linked with those affects;

▼ manage relational reality to minimize further arousal of disturbing, disrupting affects.

Bowlby (1973, 1988, 1991) wrote about the defensive exclusion of all that threatens the bond with the attachment figure; yet defensive exclusion also applies to all that would threaten the integrity of the organization of the self. Defenses against affect, anxiety, and relational reality therefore share the adaptive goal of restoring the background of safety associated with a sturdy attachment bond and cohesive sense of self—adaptive in the short term, that is, but maladaptive over time. This is the secondary felt security (Main, 1995) associated with the self-distortions necessary to maintain attachment ties and body and soul together in far less than optimal circumstances.

A Taxonomy of Defenses

Defensive strategies (A. Freud, 1937; Vaillant, 1993) include

▼ formal defenses that operate intrapsychically (e.g., repression, denial, minimization, isolation of affect, reaction formation);

▼ more primitive defenses that aim to manipulate reality (e.g., externalization, projection, somatization, introjection, projective identification);

▼ defenses that affect the organization of the self (e.g., dissociation);

▼ defenses that operate on relational contact (e.g., the barrier, the wall).

Davanloo extended the realm of defenses to include the nonverbal aspects of communication. Thus, avoidance of eye contact, mumbling, postural shifts, hardening of face and voice, body armoring, and so forth all can serve defensive purposes. Davanloo also called attention to the *tactical defenses*: habits of speech (e.g., vagueness, equivocation, use of passive voice, changing the subject, speaking in the third or second person) that also function in the service of avoiding affect and connection. As Coughlin Della Selva (1996) describes them,

Tactical defenses include all verbal and nonverbal maneuvers patients use interpersonally to deflect or prevent meaningful contact. Verbal tactical defenses include vagueness and a tendency toward generalities, the use of contradictory statements, sarcasm, a high level of verbal activity making dialogue impossible, or diversification (jumping from topic to topic). Some examples of nonverbal tactical defenses include avoidance of eye contact, smiling and giggling, weepiness, or an air of detachment. Posture is also included here, with either great stiffness and immobility or limpness indicating the presence of a defensive barrier against meaningful interpersonal contact. (P. 9)

Affects (though not core affects) also can function as defenses. The *defensive affects* can be deployed to run interference and preempt the experience of other, even more frightening affects. As McCullough (1991) points out, "borderline rage ... hides enormous sorrow over unmet, and natural, longings for validation of experience" (p. 42).

HOW DEFENSES FUNCTION

The nature of the failed emotional environment and, more specifically, the nature of the self-other interaction is uncannily reflected in the operation of defenses. In essence, the child internalizes the caregiver's compromised affective competence: the child deals with himself, with his own affective experience, and eventually with others, as his caregiver dealt with him.

Dreaded aloneness spurs on defensive processes, which not only deal with the problem of affective experience, but also solve the pain of isolation. Internalizing the defenses of a significant other in some way satisfies the need for psychic proximity. Just as the toddler runs to the attachment figure for a hug, even when that figure is responsible for the very stress and distress the child is laboring under, adults too seek psychic proximity, though in more symbolic ways, through adopting the safety measures of caregiving with which we are most familiar. Benjamin (1997) calls these mechanisms of internalization *copy processes,* the equivalent of the "interpersonal DNA." She identifies three copy processes in relation to an emotionally significant, designated caregiver (Benjamin, 1997):

▼ *identification*: be like her in how you deal with emotions and particularly how you deal with others, treating them as she treated you (this is similar to A. Freud's (1937) identification with the aggressor);

▼ *recapitulation:* act as though she is always there and in charge (be in a state of anxiety about punishment, humiliation, or neglect; carry her mental presence with you at all times and treat others as though they are her);

▼ *introjection:* treat yourself as she did (react with shame, guilt, self-contempt, and other forms of self-punitiveness for being emotional).

Thus the defensive patterns, and the personality that emerges, reflect some version of the "rules" governing interaction with the significant other. The aim of managing experiences guided by these ancient rules (and putting up with the attendant suffering) is the die-hard hope for affirmation by the principals in the emotional environment.

THE CONSEQUENCES OF DEFENSES

With regard to the development of psychopathology through identification with distorted functioning, Fonagy points out that developing the psychopathology is a way of resonating with the other. The magnitude of our need to be understood and affirmed is vast; it constitutes the motive for reliance on defenses. As Sandler (1960) made clear, defensive operations go beyond getting rid of aversive feelings: an actual positive affective state, a feeling of well-being, ensues. Decreasing the anxiety associated with threatening affective experience by reengaging the positive feelings associated with familiar ways of relating is construed as a gain, albeit a short-lived one.

People rely on defensive strategies, as with drugs, because they work; they achieve what they were instituted to achieve. Psychic equilibrium is restored, the self regains coherence, and the relationship with the primary caregiver regains its stability. The immediate experience of safety and affective well-being associated with reliance on (what will become) maladaptive mechanisms is one of the most powerful factors in what maintains them. Defenses buy the individual a respite from terror, guilt, shame, humiliation, and helplessness; the price tag of the respite, however, is exorbitant.

Chronic reliance on defenses constricts and distorts both relational and affective experience, for what gets defensively excluded and buried are not only emotions such as grief and rage that are too painful and intense, but also adaptive functions intrinsic to these emotions, such as a sense of perspective, self-worth, and strength. Tragically, the very experiences that the security measures were instituted to safeguard— self-integrity and relatedness to others—suffer and become distorted without the fuel of natural, spontaneous affective flow.

THE ADAPTATION MODEL
OF PSYCHOPATHOLOGY

The individual, guided by adaptive strivings to maintain connection and self-regulation and minimize aversive experiences, develops defense mechanisms. To ensure emotional survival and restore a feeling of safety, the individual internalizes environmental intolerance of affective experience, in the process sacrificing the transformational properties of affect and accepting the resulting damage to his core sense of aliveness and authenticity. Defenses are adaptive, but only in the idiosyncratic environment in which they arise; in the emotional world at large, they are maladaptive. Psychopathology—the long-term reliance on defenses against genuine affective experience—is the maladaptive consequence.

The view that adaptation is the driving force behind the development of psychopathology has clinical implications, and informs the technique that distinguishes accelerated experiential-dynamic psychotherapy.

PSYCHOPATHOLOGY AND
THE NONPATHOLOGICAL SELF

It's just that the mind won't quit. As long as you're alive, it will never stop looking for ways to survive. As if there were someone else inside you, someone more naive but also more tenacious.

PETER HØEG, *Smilla's Sense of Snow*

Despite the strength of defensive tendencies in those who adapt to destructive emotional environments, the potential for healthy emotional responses remains alive within even the most disturbed individuals, awaiting the right environmental conditions to become activated (Emde, 1981; Winnicott, 1960). Repetition is not inevitable: it dominates only when dread is pervasive. When hope-fueled motivation prevails, new responses leading to the generation of new patterns become possible. The self is always on the alert for an environment in which natural affective processes are allowed to flourish, and where there is opportunity to correct, repair, or create anew. When the individual has reason to hope that a given situation has such potential, defenses can be momentarily withdrawn and the individual can lead with his genuine, spontaneous emotional responses. This is what AEDP seeks to facilitate.

Particular internal working models are rooted in particular relationships. When the dominant one leads to pathological functioning, it is important to remember that others arising from other relationships are somewhere in the repertoire, although they may be repressed, dissociated, or less prominent. The fact that they can more readily come to the fore in affect-facilitating environments is a crucial point for understanding how accelerated therapy can work.

CHAPTER 5

A NURTURING UNDERSTANDING

A Case Illustrating the Reflective Self Function in Clinical Action

The following clinical vignette is a bridge between the theoretical building blocks (core affect, attachment through the lens of affect, and the reflective self function) and technical tools and materials to be introduced and elucidated hereafter.[1]

The four segments of the clinical vignette highlight the importance and operation of the reflective self function in therapeutic work, where the empathic supportive relationship with the therapist constitutes a secure base. The more the patient feels safe in that relationship—that is, the stronger the bond of attachment between patient and therapist—the more intensive and accelerated the therapeutic work. The question is, What can we do to facilitate the development of such a bond?

The lesson of the reflective self function is that the patient will feel securely attached to the therapist in proportion to the strength of the evidence that he exists in the therapist's mind and heart. Accordingly, any intervention or remark that reveals the patient's presence in the therapist's psychic reality and resonates with the patient's reality manifests the therapist's reflective self function applied toward the patient. Yet an insecurely attached patient, whose defenses derive from an internal working model drenched in pain, anxiety, and disappointment, will be unable to experience the therapist's connection to him. In addition to relying on optimal responsiveness, empathy, support, and effectiveness to establish the requisite safety and security in their relationship, the therapist therefore must help the patient overcome his defenses against emotional and

---

[1] While some terms in the annotation of clinical material will not be defined explicitly until later chapters, their meanings are implicit in the context of the illustration, and their pivotal role in the idiom of the affective model of change will become apparent.

relational experience; otherwise the patient will not be able to be aware of and fully benefit from the positive therapeutic connection.

Personal reflections can affirm the patient's existence in the therapist's consciousness, independent of his presence in the session, informally ("You know, after you left last week, it occurred to me that ..." or "I thought of you when I saw that movie/read that article ..."). On the formal level, therapeutic self-disclosure—specifically, self-disclosure of the patient's impact on the therapist—can be radical and dramatic; so can focusing the patient on the emotional reality of the therapeutic relationship.

A goal of AEDP is to make the implicit explicit, as expressed in the transcribed and annotated therapy session that follows. The aim of the work with this patient is to help her focus on her relational experience, her experience of the therapist, and *her experience of the therapist's experience of her*. The further development of her reflective self function is facilitated in part by discovering that she has an impact on the therapist. The sense of having an impact on the other is an equally important existential experience for both members of the dyad.

THE CLINICAL WORK

The patient is a thirty-one-year-old woman who sought treatment for severe depression. A central source of despair was that she had never been in a relationship and was afraid that she would spend the rest of her life alone.

Barbara's life was the embodiment of a painful attachment history whereby emotional connection meant emotional pain, hence her avoidant relational style. As is typical of patients with an avoidant pattern of attachment, there is no "other" in the internal working model: integrity of self and avoidance of emotional pain is maintained by avoiding relational contact; the other is altogether defensively excluded and the patient is alone. The unbargained-for consequence of the safety afforded by an isolated, exaggeratedly self-reliant way of being in the world is the development of psychopathology—specifically, a loneliness and emptiness of suicidal proportions (poignantly, the patient's relationship to Gòd has operated as a protective factor against total despair).

By the last of the segments—the first from her eighth psychotherapy session, the other three from her ninth—the patient is functioning from within an internal working model where there are two people, and her experience of emotional connection is not painful but safe and helpful. The groundwork for further exploratory therapeutic work is set.

Segment 1

DEFENSES AGAINST RELATEDNESS

AND PROTECTION OF THE SELF

In her own words, the patient describes her psychic structure: defenses she has needed to protect herself from unbearable pain and rejection, all against relational closeness ("clam up ... nonchalant ... don't want people to see it ... a wall"); anxiety she feels at the prospect of not relying on those defenses ("scary ... uncomfortable ... exposed ... vulnerable," the fear of getting hurt as she has been in the past); and finally, the core affective experience—in this case, her true self—these defenses are designed to protect (the "soft," "tender," hidden part of the self, "sensitive to everything").

In the following segments, comments in parentheses describe nonverbal and paraverbal aspects of the clinical material, and annotations appear in brackets, along with the chapters in which terms are defined and elaborated.

PATIENT: **I guess I know I need to and I want to do this** [i.e., therapy], **and it feels good. ... This is my time to focus on me and stuff. ... But it also feels ... uncomfortable ... like ... it's scary.** [anxiety]

THERAPIST: **Yes.**

PATIENT: **I don't like to open myself up ... I feel exposed, I feel vulnerable, and I do not want to get hurt. And so I clam up and just go on like if nothing bothers me ...** [defense: ch. 6]. **So ... all that soft part of me** (very soft, tender tone), **it's like really inside, it's really inside** (cups her hands together) [core affective experience] **and I don't let people get to it. ... Because I have been hurt already in the past ...** [roots of defenses in past hurts]. **Maybe I don't want people to get that. ... Because that's me. ... I do not want to open myself that much, I will open myself up to a certain point, and it's really tender, too ... really tender.** [quality of core affective experience: ch. 7]

THERAPIST: **Uh huh.**

PATIENT: (very soft, tender, hurt voice) **So ... it's not something that I expose to people or anything ... I ... put a wall around it, ...** (because) **in there it's all soft and sensitive to, to everything ... really ...** [relational defenses against vulnerability]

THERAPIST: (very soft) **It's tender.** [affective resonance: ch. 12]

PATIENT: **Yes, it's very, very soft.**

THERAPIST: **Yes, and it feels private.** [empathic elaboration: ch. 10]

PATIENT: **So it's inside here** (cups her hands again) **and I don't want peo-**

ple to get to it, I'd be crazy to, I think, in this world. ... You got to have ... logically, you got to have a self-defense. ... When I get to heaven *(voice cracking)*, I can allow that to come out ... because it can never happen, I don't think, in this world *(her eyes swimming in tears)*.

In this segment, the patient clearly outlines her avoidant style and spells out her defensive structure: afraid of getting hurt, she defends her core sense of self through relational distancing; she puts up a wall between herself and others. Note that the patient's idea of an affect-facilitating environment where defenses can be relaxed is heaven; experience on earth is too tainted for her to hope that she might be able to be herself here. Her utterance conveys simultaneously utter (and bitter) hopelessness and (albeit idealized) hope.

Note that while the patient speaks about her mistrust of people, she relates openly to the therapist, and reveals ever-deeper aspects of her innermost experience. This is a quintessential example of the little-step-by-little-step process (discussed in chapter 10).

Segment 2
THE CONSEQUENCES OF DEFENSES, EXPERIENTIALLY EXPLORED

In the following segment, the patient articulates the emotional conse-quences of her defense style: depression, loneliness, isolation, and despair of an intensity bordering on suicidal proportions. The quality of her experience that results from her reliance on defenses against relational closeness is "empty" and "black." Directly and explicitly, the focus is on bypassing defenses against her own internal experience. The therapist, by accessing a deep affective state within herself (note the slow, feelingful tone of voice) hopes to engage the patient, through the operation of res-onance and the drive toward coordinated states (Tronick, 1989) in a more affective mode of being, which in fact happens as the patient slows down and experiencing deepens. Note how the therapist's mirroring of the patient's experience easily bypasses defenses (her pressured, matter-of-fact speech), and leads to a deepening of experience, allowing the patient to contact the depth of her despair. Painful feelings, borne alone, can be unendurable; together with a trusted companion, they can be borne, which is the first and crucial step in their eventual transforma-tion. The bulk of work is aimed at facilitating the patient's experience of painful feelings (loneliness and despair) through experiential focusing and empathic experiential mirroring by the therapist.

PATIENT: Life is just empty for me. ... Is there more than this? And if there is no God, and if there is no happiness at the end, that's my light at the end of the tunnel. ... If you take this light away, it's pretty dark. [despair and hopelessness: ch. 6]

THERAPIST: *(soft, deep, somber tone, speaking very slowly)* It's dark ... [affective resonance]

PATIENT: Yeah.

THERAPIST: It's dark.

PATIENT: So what, you go through life proving, you go through life working, I mean this is ... *(speaks pretty fast here, dismissive tone of voice)* [nonverbal defense: pressure of speech, cynical attitude: ch. 6]

THERAPIST: OK, OK, OK. ... If *(slowing down)* for a moment, ... or two *(mild joking tone)*

PATIENT: Or two *(laughs)*

THERAPIST: If, instead of doing the "so what" with a joke or "that's life." [defense identification; urging patient to relinquish defense: ch. 11]

PATIENT: Uh huh.

THERAPIST: If you let yourself stay with this feeling *(slow, deep, somber tone)*, the sense of emptiness, this inner sense of ... uh *(deep sigh, grave tone of voice)* ... having to work so hard to keep something away. [affective resonance with the dark quality of her isolation, a vitality affect: ch. 7]

PATIENT: Yeah ... *(also slowing down and sombering)* it's tiring. [visceral experience of consequences of defenses: ch. 6]

THERAPIST: It's very exhausting *(amplified exhausted intonation)* ... mmm ... [amplifying affective experience: ch. 12] I mean right now it seems to me like we're sort of approaching this from the outside [defense] because it's such a scary place to be [anxiety].

PATIENT: Yeah, it is ... mmm ... I don't know. ... Sometimes I wonder is this it? Is that what life is about? ... It feels empty ... *(pained tone)*

THERAPIST: Which means what? When you say that you feel empty ...

PATIENT: So, so is that what life is about? That's it?

THERAPIST: In this dark moment, what is that emptiness like? [invitation to experiential elaboration]

PATIENT: It's black ... *(long pause)*

THERAPIST: Black ... *(long pause)* [affective resonance]

PATIENT: It's like ... *(fighting tears)* I don't have to be here ... if I thought of it that way. [deep despair; further elaboration of consequences of relational distancing defenses: ch. 6]

THERAPIST: Mmm huh.

Segment 3

AFFECTIVE SHARING OF EXPERIENCES

AND THE RECEPTIVE AFFECTIVE EXPERIENCE:

FEELING UNDERSTOOD

The patient's capacity to deeply experience such painful core affects without anxiety or defense is evidence that, this time, she does not feel alone. Her relational defenses, however, must be overcome if she is to have awareness and fully experience the intimacy and closeness of her evolving relationship with the therapist—a relationship being elaborated along lines quite different from her dominant internal working model. Thus, a few minutes later in the same session, the therapist urges the patient to focus on and articulate her experience of the therapist, and more specifically, her experience of the therapist's reactions to her. The metaphor of the cave, another representation of her defensive structure, sets the scene of the relational breakthrough: the patient spontaneously urges the therapist to join her in exploring her inner world. Note that the patient is the guide: she has a sense of mastery and control, and, rather than anxiety, experiences the associated positive affects ("it's *nice* to show someone that this is how I feel"). Despite being on unfamiliar relational territory, with the surefootedness characteristic of core affective experiencing, the patient takes the lead.

THERAPIST: **To me ...** *(deep sigh)* **about this profound dread-filled place ... this blackness ... this isolation ...** [more affective resonance and amplification] **mmmmm ... I was going to say this private hell** [upping the ante—statement of psychic reality: ch. 12], **what is, mmm how can I say this, what is it like to talk about it with me? What's it like for** *you?* [inviting patient to elaborate her experience of sharing her private pain with therapist: chs. 10, 12]

PATIENT: **Well, it's sort of like ... it's like we are walking through or hiking** *(starts to brighten up).* **... And we are walking through this cave that gets darker and darker, and gets really really dark.** [accepts invitation; spontaneous portrayal: ch. 12]

THERAPIST: **Mmm huh.**

PATIENT: **And ... there is this little hole in the wall maybe** *(makes small circle shape with her hands)* **and I kind of like go like this to you** *(makes beckoning motion).*

THERAPIST: **Uh huh.**

PATIENT: *(animated now)* **And I open this door and it already feels like we are crowded in like this, and there is this tunnel with this wide** opening that's getting narrower and narrower, and there is a door to that hole and I am opening this door and I am telling you like "Dr. Fosha, look inside, open the door." [breakthrough defenses against relational closeness: patient spontaneously invites therapist to share her inner experience]

THERAPIST: So you have been in there ...

PATIENT: Yeah, that's how I feel ... I guess it's nice to show someone that this is how I feel ... [more relational breakthroughs: patient owns her desire for sharing her emotional reality with another]. I guess since you sort of made me think more about who I am, I feel you are a part of it too because you sort of sparked it in me unknowingly, or whatever but ... [connection through being on the receiving end of therapist's reflective self function]. So I feel like you are part of it, part of the process of me showing you me putting the mirror in front of my face, and me even looking at myself and examining ... examining myself and ... [spontaneous experiential elaboration of relational closeness and affective sharing; patient's own reflective self function is kicking into gear]

THERAPIST: (deep, slow tone) Where am I? Or how am I, maybe even more than where am I, how am I? [aiming to elaborate patient's experience of therapist within the portrayal; this is no time for the therapist to be retiring or shy: ch. 12]

PATIENT: In this whole scenario?

THERAPIST: Uh huh.

PATIENT: You're sort of right behind me ... [patient feels she is in charge of process; she is leading the therapist, guiding a tour of her inner world]

THERAPIST: So what's that feel like? At this time when we're in this cave, going to this place that's darker and darker and darker ...

PATIENT: Right.

THERAPIST: And I am right there behind you, and you are telling me about it, and I ...

PATIENT: Sort of like ...

THERAPIST: ... see it with you.

PATIENT: Yes, it's the first time, you're the first. ... And it feels like you don't mind seeing it, I feel you are not offended, you are not taken aback by it, you're not like "yeah, right Barbara, I don't want to see that." ... You want to see it, like you always prod me ... [patient's experience of therapist's active desire to be there with her]. And I am showing it to you, so there is an understanding I get from you that this is where I am coming from ... [sense of self developing through seeing herself in the eyes of the other]. I guess there is a nurturing understanding about my situation. ... So it's like ... I see where you're coming from. ... And you are trying to get a better understanding of who I am so I am allowing you to look at it ... [spontaneous articulation of her experience of being with an affirming other; contrasted implicitly with experience of rejecting, dismissive others in the past; being with an affirming other makes her want to be open and share her experience]

THERAPIST: ... yeah

PATIENT: And you're a very safe person to show it to because ... naturally we kind of talk about all this stuff these last weeks. ... Because you try to understand and you don't make light of it, or so it's okay for me to show you. ... Because it makes me feel that I can show it to somebody, so it makes me feel like there is someone with me [current experience of not being alone with unbearably painful feelings implicitly contrasted with previous experiences]. Maybe you don't quite understand what's happening when I open the door, but ... I am sharing with someone "this is what I have to live with, this is how I *really* feel." [experience of being with an affect-facilitating other who does not get frightened by her feelings allows patient to share the depth of her negative feelings, revealing her yearnings for relational resonance, until now disavowed] ... And I never show people that side of me so ... I don't know, it just feels mm ... *(moved, tears in her voice)* comforting. ... It feels like a little bit of a relief too. ... Like maybe there is somebody else in this world *(fighting back tears now)* that might have an understanding of who I am *(patient cries).* [articulates deep yearnings for feeling understood; having the experience of being understood, first is relief, then a breakthrough of the emotional pain associated with previouly thwarted yearnings for feeling understood]

By getting the patient to focus on her experience of the therapist, the therapist gains a *felt reality* in the patient's world and her connection with the therapist becomes real. By focusing on the therapist, the patient viscerally realizes that the other is right there, beside her and inside her (see Mann & Goldman, 1982), and that she is no longer alone. The sense of connection has prevailed throughout the work. At no point in this instance of the little-step-by-little-step process (described in detail in chapter 10) was there any sign of resistance or entrenched defensiveness. The patient did not see that in *speaking to the therapist* about not letting anybody into her private world, paradoxically she was letting the therapist into that very world. By getting her to focus explicitly on her experience of the therapist, she not only is emotionally connected with another person but becomes aware that she is connected, and that experience, with full awareness, becomes experientially elaborated.

When the patient says, "I guess since you sort of made me think more about who I am, I feel you are a part of it too because you sort of sparked it in me unknowingly, or whatever but ... *So I feel like you are part of it, part of the process of me showing you me* putting the mirror in front of my face, and me even looking at myself and examining … examining myself," she is articulating the development of her reflective self function through one relationship with an understanding, accepting other, of whose reflective self functioning she has been the recipient.

Also significant here is that her experience of the therapist's attitude toward her intense, negative painful affects is openness and acceptance ("you want to know") and a desire to know more. Without specifying detail at this point, this new experience is contrasted with caregivers of the past, presumably significant contributors to the patient's avoidant style of attachment. Apparently they were offended and disgusted by the patient's emotionality; scared of the depth of her negative feelings, they urged her to deal and not feel—and she obliged them. Unlike them,

> you don't mind seeing it, I feel you are not offended, you are not taken aback by it, you're not like "yeah, right Barbara, I don't want to see that." … You want to see it, like you always prod me. … And you're a very safe person to show it to because … Because you try to understand and you don't make light of it, or so it's okay for me to show you.

A lifetime of pain is condensed in these few utterances. The patient does not require perfection: she knows all about the sufficiency of good enough: "Maybe you don't quite understand what's happening when I open the door, but …" it's OK. Through being accepted and feeling understood, the patient feels deeply taken care of:

> And I am showing it to you, so there is an understanding I get from you that this is where I am coming from. …I guess there is a *nurturing understanding* about my situation. … So it's like … I see where you're coming from. … And you are trying to get a better understanding of who I am so I am allowing you to look at it …

What better articulation of the recipient's experience of existing in the heart and mind of the other as herself can there possibly be?

Segment 4
UNDOING PATHOGENIC ALONENESS:
EMERGENCE OF THE GENUINE SELF

The therapist asks the patient specifically to focus on her experience of the therapist's emotional response to her: what she sees in the therapist's eyes and how that makes her feel.

THERAPIST: Barbara, you are telling me ...

PATIENT: Uh huh.

THERAPIST: ... that what is developing is the sense that though, in a way, this is your journey, but in a way it's our journey and I am there with you in some way. [promoting intimacy and closeness through explicit acknowledgment]

PATIENT: *(nods through tears)* [tears of recognition: experience of "having" puts the patient in touch with "not having had"]

THERAPIST: ... Ah huh.

PATIENT: Yeah, definitely ... I couldn't put it into words but what you just said, yeah ... that's it, I can't put it into words but it's like you just said, that we're going through this thing together. Yes ... that's pretty much what it feels like. *(long pause)* [though patient has been speaking about the feeling of being in it together with the therapist, hearing the therapist reflect togetherness makes it seem new]

THERAPIST: Oh, that's a lot, that's a lot *(pause)* [acknowledgment of work done thus far, before moving to do another round of work: ch. 10]. ... Because I wonder also, *I* have *told* you how I feel at different times *(referring to previous interactions not included here)*. ... But I wonder what you see? ... What you see in my face, what you see in my eyes in response to what you are telling me? [encouraging patient to engage in her part of the reciprocal monitoring of nonverbal responses of therapist, and put into words her experiential observations: ch.10; encouraging elaboration of patient's receptive experiences]

PATIENT: *(looking very carefully at therapist's face, much like a baby surveying the mother's face)* Oh, like you understand where I am coming from, and you're sort of there, like we are in this trip together so ... I feel like there is a connection, you know. ... That's how I feel, like there is a connection, and there is an understanding ... mmm ... compassion. ... You *really feel* where I am coming from, and ... mmm, you know, ... I feel like a certain amount of ... the feeling of trust. ... Because honestly, your face, you know, like every time I talk to you, like you're *really feeling* it *(laughing, scrunches up her face in imitation of therapist's expression)*. ... Like, when I am telling you things, you *really* get a good feeling for where I am coming from, it's like you almost got a *pained* feeling on your face ...

THERAPIST: Well, yeah ...

PATIENT: *(interrupting, laughing)* I don't know if that's just how you are, but you definitely, you're looking very pained ...

THERAPIST: At times, the things you are talking about are very painful *(pained tone of voice)*, and ... I was wondering about that. ... You know, what that feels like for you. ... I mean, you are very much in touch with *(your)* pain. It is a very, very difficult, very painful, almost unbearable way to feel. ... And then you see my reaction, of also feeling very pained by it. [exploring patient's experience of therapist's empathic mirroring of her painful affect: ch. 10]

PATIENT: It's funny though, but it makes me feel like someone out there understands *(light tone, open smiling)* so I don't have to dwell on it ... [sharing emotional pain, and acknowledging the sharing, transforms it: ch. 7]

THERAPIST: Mmmm *(matches patient's mood, smile in voice)*.

PATIENT: It's like a relief, thinking that there is another someone in this world that understands where I am coming from. ... It feels good *(energetic voice, increasingly brightening mood)* so I can put it [i.e., the pain] in a box for a while. I don't feel all alone in that world, someone's looked at it, so that I am not by myself. When I discovered that this is how it made me feel, I told my friend. It's weird, but I was all happy after last session ... [sharing emotional pain with another deepens the experience then transforms it; relief and happiness become associated with the experience of connection, even when connection involves sharing dark, painful affects: ch. 8]. Because it's like, "oh, someone knows, I don't have to hide it all the time, someone else knows out there" *(exhale of relief)*. ... And I can move on. ... It's nice that I can be real with you, I don't have to be anything I don't want to be. I can be me. I can be myself. That's nice ... I can be myself. At work I am not myself, I mean, I am myself but I am not, you know what I mean?

THERAPIST: I know what you mean.

PATIENT: I can be myself and it makes me feel. ... It feels a little like when you show people this side of you, this private part of yourself, it makes you feel a little bit lighter *(takes a deep breath)*, you know, I can breathe a little bit better too ... [affective markers of state transformation; relief and feeling "light": ch. 8]. I guess it's the whole process that's cathargic *(sic)* or whatever. It just feels better too, because someone else has seen it too. You don't feel all alone. ... And, in a way, that's a good feeling too.

When the patient says that now that someone else has witnessed her pain she can at least temporarily put it away ("It feels good ... so I can put it in a box for a while. I don't feel all alone in that world, someone's looked at it, so that I am not by myself"), the implication is that she has needed to hold on to her pain because it is such a large part of her experience of who she is. To let pain go before it is witnessed and gains reality through existing in the emotional reality of another would be to lose touch with a part of herself. Once her pain is witnessed and apprehended by an other, however, it acquires reality and becomes validated; she no longer has to talismanically hold on to it.

SUMMARY

The foregoing clinical vignettes are an example of alternating waves of experiential and reflective work. The initial experiential work of mirroring a patient's affective experience to bypass defenses deepens the patient's experience of extremely painful affects. The therapist's resonance deepens the patient's experience of her pain: in so doing, she is able to *show* someone what she truly goes through, not just talk about it. The depth of the experience allows her to reach the pit where painful affects—rendered close to unbearable by her aloneness with them—turn to suicidal considerations. The patient is deeply connected with the therapist, yet her mood is driven by the content of actual experience, and relational closeness is revealed in the patient's openness—but it is not something she is directly in touch with. Unless it is focused on, she could well walk away from the session immersed in the black and empty isolation she's describing without experiential access to the relational experience she has just been through.

The reflective work shifts the focus of her experience from "what do you experience?" and "how do you experience your pain, your aloneness?" to "what is it like for you to share your pain and your aloneness with me?" Background and foreground shift. The patient is asked to reflect on an aspect of experience that was implicit until the beam of reflection shone on it: once in focus, therapist and patient shift back and forth between experiential and reflective work with the relational connection.

Fewer than twenty minutes elapsed since the beginning of segment 2. Breathing better, feeling lighter, and thriving on showing the private self to someone else is a long way from blackness, emptiness, and the specter of suicide.

PART II

Tools and Materials

CHAPTER 6

STRUCTURING TOOLS

Three Representational Schemas

To facilitate affective experience, the therapist must be quick to recognize defenses, anxiety, and repeating relational patterns. She also must be able to recognize genuine emotions, however fleeting, as well as budding attempts, however tentative, at genuine relating. AEDP techniques rely on precise moment-to-moment assessment of the clinical material. Defense-driven material requires different interventions than material spurred by the desire to make contact. Tools are needed to perform this assessment easily and rapidly, so that appropriate techniques can be applied. The schematic representation of basic psychodynamic constructs is essential to this work. When the conceptual framework is schematized—stripped to its barest essentials—it becomes more readily able to be used, taught, and learned.

Two schematic representations have helped experiential short-term dynamic therapists perform a moment-to-moment, psychodynamically informed, functional analysis: the constructs of the *triangle of conflict* and the *triangle of person,* here renamed the *triangle of comparisons.* Initially introduced by Ezriel (1952) and Menninger (1958) respectively, then developed and elaborated in the work of Malan (1976, 1979), these schemas have been at the foundation of many STDPs (see Crits-Cristoph & Barber, 1991; Messer & Warren, 1995) and are all but indispensable to the therapist attempting deep dynamic work in a short period of time. In the affective model of change, a third schema, the *self—other—emotion triangle* is introduced: it represents the relational-affective context within which any emotional experience takes place.

The triangle of conflict, the self—other—emotion triangle and *the triangle of comparisons* help the therapist functionally categorize clinical material, structure listening, assess the impact of interventions, and select the next intervention. In organizing the wealth of material at any given moment, these constructs facilitate precise tracking of affective and relational experience and allow the therapist to forge a path of intervention through the thicket of clinical possibilities. The back-and-forth resonance among these structures leads to a deep understanding of the patient's dynamics and way of being in the world, intrapsychically (triangle of conflict), relationally (self–other–emotion triangle), and historically, over time (triangle of comparisons).

THE TRIANGLE OF CONFLICT

The triangle of conflict remains the main tool for the experiential/psychodynamic therapist. With it we are able to zoom in and explore the moment-to-moment structure of the patient's affective experience, which occurs within a relational matrix (represented by the self–other–emotion triangle, to be discussed).

Suppose an affect-laden situation triggers intense emotional responses. Further suppose that these responses were followed repeatedly by negative reactions from important people in the person's life, reactions that in turn evoked negative affects, such as anxiety and shame, in the person. Over time, a visceral conclusion is drawn whereby any stirring of emotion (i.e., core affective experience) comes to automatically elicit anxiety or shame (i.e., signal affects), which became a spur to institute protective strategies (i.e., defenses, whose function is to ensure that what happened in the past doesn't happen again). The triangle of conflict depicts the intrapsychic structuring of emotional experience in terms of a feedback loop that arises among *core affective experiences*, the *signal affects* they generate, and the *defense mechanisms* used to avoid what is anxiety-provoking (see Figure 6.1).

It is unfortunate that despite the best adaptive intentions (Pao, 1979), chronic reliance on defenses leads to trouble. Warded-off affective experiences invariably are reactivated by interpersonal situations reminiscent of the situation in which they arose. The individual is unable to process them as they continue to grow in force and intensity. Their threat to erupt generates further anxiety, which in turn intensifies defensive efforts aimed at maintaining the status quo. The increasingly greater reliance on defense mechanisms and avoidance of spontaneous emotional responses eventually interfere with the individual's psychic growth and development; moreover, patterns of defense and avoidance create distressing emotional consequences of their own. The symptoms associated with some Axis I disorders (e.g., depression, anxiety disorders, dissociative disorders) and the problems in living that result from character disorders are the clinical manifestations of adaptive efforts gone awry (see Figure 6.2).

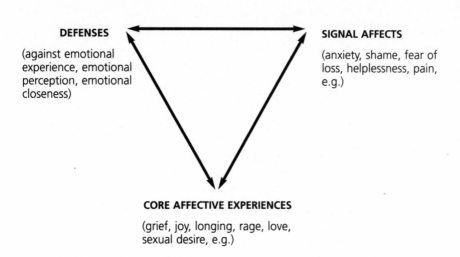

FIGURE 6.1
THE TRIANGLE OF CONFLICT

DEFENSES

(against emotional
experience, emotional
perception, emotional
closeness)

SIGNAL AFFECTS

(anxiety, shame, fear of
loss, helplessness, pain,
e.g.)

CORE AFFECTIVE EXPERIENCES

(grief, joy, longing, rage, love,
sexual desire, e.g.)

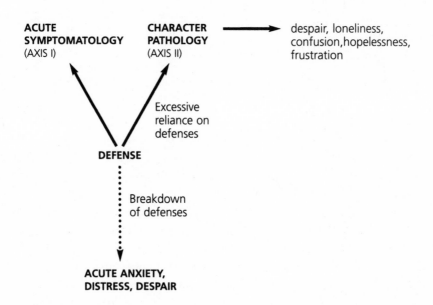

FIGURE 6.2
THE GENESIS OF PSYCHOPATHOLOGY

**ACUTE
SYMPTOMATOLOGY**
(AXIS I)

**CHARACTER
PATHOLOGY**
(AXIS II)

despair, loneliness,
confusion,hopelessness,
frustration

Excessive
reliance on
defenses

DEFENSE

Breakdown
of defenses

**ACUTE ANXIETY,
DISTRESS, DESPAIR**

For Barbara (the patient discussed in chapter 5), the reactions of her emotionally dismissive caregivers caused her enormous pain. As a result, the *fear of getting hurt again* (signal affect) led her to put up a *wall* (defense) in her interactions with others, thus keeping her *vulnerable sense of self* (core affective experience) to herself. Yet the wall between herself and others led to an emotional isolation marked by excruciating despair, loneliness, and chronic depression (consequences of defenses).

The triangle of conflict can be used to understand the dynamic structuring of inner experience. The clinical phenomena best assigned to the categories at the top of the triangle of conflict reflect solutions that are maladaptive despite the best adaptive intentions. At the same time, the core affective experiences represented at the bottom of the triangle of conflict contain within them the potential for optimal emotional functioning, awaiting "right conditions" to be activated. With most people, this potential at times is realized, even if partially or fleetingly.

It is important that our schemas can capture the dynamic structuring of healthy as well as pathological responses. Two versions of the triangle of conflict are discussed in the following: the *triangle of defensive response* and the *triangle of expressive response*, which depict the structuring of an individual's worst and best functioning, respectively.

Two Ways of Being: The Triangle of Defensive Response and the Triangle of Expressive Response

> It's a phenomenon that I've often observed without understanding it. Inside someone, another person may exist, a fully formed, generous, and trustworthy individual who never comes to light except in glimpses, because he is surrounded by a corrupt, dyed-in-the-wool, repeat offender.
>
> PETER HØEG, *Smilla's Sense of Snow*

Psychological functioning is radically different in different relational environments: conditions of optimal safety and conditions experienced as threatening tend to evoke different ways of being (see also Mitchell, 1993). One mode of functioning, conservative and dread-driven, is manifested in what Freud (1923) labeled *repetition compulsion*. The other mode, risk-taking and hope-driven, is powered by the drive for *reparation* or *corrective emotional experiences* (Alexander & French, 1946; Beebe

& Lachmann, 1994; Emde, 1981; Fosha, 1995; Tronick, 1989; Winnicott, 1960). We all function in each of these modes at different times. As a rule, psychopathology makes the individual more likely to perceive danger and the inevitable repetition of harmful past patterns, and less likely to experience safety and the possibility of new scenarios. Resilience has the opposite effect: it raises the threshold at which environments are experienced as threatening. One of the hallmarks of the vibrant resilient self is the capacity to create environments conducive to growth and make the best of environments that appear immune to enlivening attempts.

Since different emotional environments can activate different experiential patterns, the individual's dominant experience of a given relational environment activates one of two possible triangle-of-conflict configurations: the triangle of defensive response and the triangle of expressive response.

In situations perceived as potentially dangerous, patients lead with their defenses. The *triangle of defensive response* captures the dread-driven configuration characteristic of pathology-perpetuating patterns (see Figure 6.3a). This schema represents functioning that results from experiences with caregivers whose affective competence is compromised, leaving the individual psychically alone in face of overwhelming affects. Feeling and dealing while relating is not possible in these circumstances.

When a patient perceives a situation as potentially affect-facilitating, his emotional responses emerge more directly. The *triangle of expressive response* represents the hope-driven configuration in which the patient's

---

FIGURE 6.3a
THE TRIANGLE OF DEFENSIVE RESPONSE
DEFENSE-DRIVEN FUNCTIONING

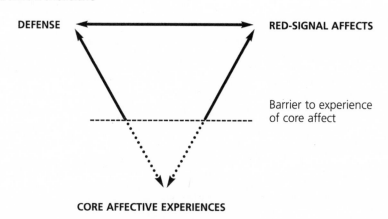

FIGURE 6.3b
THE TRIANGLE OF EXPRESSIVE RESPONSE
AFFECTIVE MODE OF FUNCTIONING

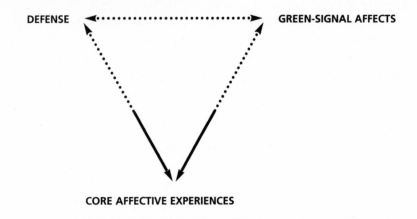

DEFENSE ◀┄┄┄┄┄┄┄┄┄┄┄┄┄▶ GREEN-SIGNAL AFFECTS

CORE AFFECTIVE EXPERIENCES

cautious trust is engaged and his emotional responses are more available (see Figure 6.3b). This schema is more fluid: although anxiety and defense still are present, they are less pronounced and less entrenched. The functioning depicted by the triangle of expressive response reflects affective competence in action: it schematizes the microdynamics of feeling and dealing while relating, which has its origins in relationships with affectively competent caregivers, who both initiate and are responsive to reparative efforts in the face of miscoordination.

The therapeutic relationship plays a major role in determining the nature of the affective processes that prevail in the therapy. Affect and attachment are joined synergistically: a principal function of attachment is anxiety abatement, and anxiety abatement (and the consequent decrease in the need for defense) is exactly what is required to release the transforming power of affect. By promoting a therapeutic relationship that enables the patient to feel safe, core affect can be pressed into immediate therapeutic service for the patient. At the fulcrum of mental life, we are poised between expression and protection: Does a relational environment (let's say the therapeutic environment) tip the balance toward anxiety, where defense mechanisms must be introduced if we are to simultaneously maintain psychic integrity, sustain attachments, and function in the world (triangle of defensive response)? Or does the environment tip the balance toward the predominance of the safety feeling that underlies self-at-best functioning (triangle of expressive response)?

From the first moments of initial contact, the AEDP therapist aims to facilitate functioning best represented by the triangle of expressive response. The desire to grow, connect, and feel authentic begins to then drive experience, engaging psychic healing capacities. This in turn facilitates the eventual unearthing of relationships with affect-facilitating, competent others—past relationships in which the individual felt held, accepted, and understood.

The two versions of the triangle of conflict suggest different experiences within the therapeutic relationship and call for very different therapeutic responses and interventions (explored at length in chapters on technique). If the material is best understood in terms of the triangle of defensive response, it is a signal that the patient is not feeling safe: interventions to address lack of safety, to lower resistance, and decrease anxiety are called for; the possibility of "interactive error" requiring "interactive repair" must be considered (Tronick, 1989; Gianino & Tronick, 1988). If the material is best understood in terms of the triangle of expressive response, it is an indication that the patient feels safe, understood, and supported within the therapeutic relationship and good, strong, capable, and clear within himself; this is a green light for proceeding with deep affect work.

The structural relationship among core affects, signal affects, and defenses applies to both versions of the triangle of conflict. What differs is whether the overall thrust is toward maximal self-protection or toward self-expression and communication. This is where the qualitative impact of the emotional environment is felt.

▼ In the triangle of defensive response (Figure 6.3a), the patient operates from a position of needing to protect himself, and there is resistance both to intimacy and closeness with the therapist and to self-expression; there is not a great deal of confidence in the possibility of interactive repair or in the other's responsiveness to his reparative efforts. As the figure illustrates, a barrier is blocking access to the individual's core affect; functioning (marked by the dark line) is defense-driven.

▼ In the triangle of expressive response (Figure 6.3b), there is much less resistance to intimacy and closeness with the therapist and to exploration of personal experience; here the motivating factor is a desire for self-expression and optimal contact. Underlying this is the individual's sense of "interactions as reparable and of [himself] as effective in making that repair" (Tronick, 1989, p. 117). Note that in the figure there is no barrier between the top and bottom of the triangle: functioning is driven by expressive and communicative strivings (indicated by a dark line at the bottom of the triangle).

EXAMPLE Upon entering treatment, Clark offered a highly idealized view of his parents, declaring that he had had an idyllic childhood and that his current difficulties—the paralysis he felt in his relationship with his wife—surely must have their roots elsewhere. Midway though his treatment, Clark dreamed that a Hell's Angels gang was wrecking his childhood home. In discussing the dream, he spoke of how the therapy was shattering his illusions and how angry he was at the therapist. In this case, *the triangle of expressive response is reflected in the directness with which negative feelings can openly be expressed. This defines the positive therapeutic experience.* Feeling safe, the patient is free to explore negative feelings openly, something he never felt he could do in his family.

Categories of the Triangle of Conflict

What experiences are represented in the different categories of the triangle of conflict? How did they evolve, and what is the relationship among them? What are qualitative differences in those categories, depending on which version of the triangle is in operation? These differences are represented in dynamic sequence in Figures 6.4 and 6.5, illustrated throughout with examples from Barbara, the patient presented in chapter 5.

CORE AFFECTIVE EXPERIENCES

Core affective experiences, represented at the bottom of the triangle of conflict, are identical in both versions: these are the natural, adaptive emotional responses directly experienced when anxiety and defenses are absent. (What is and isn't core affect will be further discussed in the next chapter.) Grief or joy or anger, or a state of relaxation and openness (i.e., the *core state*; see chapter 7), are adaptive by nature; they reflect an intrinsic motivation for expression and communication. A resilient sense of self and the presence of affect-facilitating others maximize the likelihood that the adaptive potential of core affects can be realized.

BETWEEN CORE AFFECTS AND SIGNAL AFFECTS:
SECONDARY AFFECTIVE REACTIONS

The expression of the individual's core emotions elicits a response from the other, which in turn produces a second wave of affects, the *secondary affective reactions*. Aversive secondary affective reactions (the *aversive affects*)

FIGURE 6.4

THE DYNAMIC SEQUENCE OF CATEGORIES OF EXPERIENCE LEADING TO THE TRIANGLE OF DEFENSIVE RESPONSE

**CORE AFFECTIVE EXPERIENCES
(PRIMARY AFFECTIVE REACTIONS)**

(grief, joy, longing, rage, love, sexual desire, experiences of intimacy and closeness, attachment strivings, "true self" states, vulnerability, "in sync" states of affective resonance, core state of relaxation, openness, and clarity about one's own subjective truth)

↓

NEGATIVE RECEPTIVE EXPERIENCES

(feeling hated, dismissed, criticized, or abandoned; experiencing oneself and one's affects as objects of contempt, discomfort, revulsion, pain)

↓

**AVERSIVE AFFECTS
(SECONDARY AFFECTIVE REACTIONS)**
(fear, shame, emotional pain, feeling alone, primary depressive reaction: helplessness, hopelessness, and despair)

↓

RED-SIGNAL AFFECTS

(anxiety, shame, fears (of loss, helplessness, loss of love), affect phobia, pain phobia)

↓

DEFENSES

(formal defenses, tactical defenses, nonverbal defenses, defensive affects)

↓

**CONSEQUENCES OF
TRIANGLE OF DEFENSIVE RESPONSE FUNCTIONING**

(symptom formation: e.g., phobias, depression, panic attacks; character pathology: feeling and not dealing, dealing and not feeling; isolation, dependency, feelings of inadequacy, depression, despair)

FIGURE 6.5

THE DYNAMIC SEQUENCE OF CATEGORIES OF EXPERIENCE LEADING TO THE TRIANGLE OF EXPRESSIVE RESPONSE

CORE AFFECTIVE EXPERIENCES
(PRIMARY AFFECTIVE REACTIONS)

(grief, joy, longing, rage, love, sexual desire, experiences of intimacy and closeness, attachment strivings, "true self" states, vulnerability, "in sync" states of affective resonance, core state of relaxation, openness, and clarity about one's own subjective truth)

$\downarrow$

POSITIVE RECEPTIVE EXPERIENCES

(feeling held, understood, appreciated, supported, loved, encouraged, helped; experiencing oneself and one's affects as acceptable, welcomed, and responded to)

$\downarrow$

FACILITATING AFFECTS
(SECONDARY AFFECTIVE REACTIONS)

(feeling of safety trust "in sync" states, intimacy and closeness, curiosity, excitement)

$\downarrow$

GREEN-SIGNAL AFFECTS

(hope, anticipation of pleasurable consequences, curiosity, excitement, trust, self-confidence)

$\downarrow$

SOFT DEFENSES

(coping stategies; social manner; defenses that can be bypassed)

$\downarrow$

CONSEQUENCES OF
TRIANGLE OF EXPRESSIVE RESPONSE FUNCTIONING

(affective competence, resilience, capacity to feel and deal, capacity to postpone)

arise in response to negative reactions to core affect; facilitating secondary affective reactions (the *facilitating affects*) arise in response to positive reactions to core affect. These experiences are crucial in shaping the relative predominance of pathology or psychic health, determining whether functioning is driven primarily by defensive or expressive aims.

Aversive affects and the triangle of defensive response. Responses to the individual's emotional expression that are either inadequate (cf. interactive errors of omission) or else derisive, punitive, or demeaning (cf. interactive errors of commission), give rise to aversive affects that are painful and overwhelming (see Figure 6.4). Emotional expression comes to be associated with emotional distress. Aversive affects include fear, shame, emotional pain, loneliness, and Joffe and Sandler's (1965) primary depressive reaction: helplessness, hopelessness, and despair. Shame, for example, is a quintessential aversive affect and plays a major role in the development of pathology. For Barbara, the expression of her true self (core affective experience) led to dismissiveness and rejection from her parents (negative receptive experience) that in turn elicited emotional pain (aversive affect).

The release of adaptive action tendencies is a defining characteristic of core affective experiences; aversive affects (e.g., bone-crushing loneliness, mortifying shame, primary depressive reaction, etc.), in contrast, are marked by the individual's inability to do anything to restore his essential self. What makes these affects unendurable is that their end is not in sight: the individual becomes motivated to do anything that will stop the pain. The aversive affects and red-signal affects they evoke (to be discussed further) are at the center of the development of psychopathology, and thus constitute the ground on which essential clinical work needs to be done. While the experience of core affect is transforming, the presence of aversive affects signals the need for transformation.

Facilitating affects and the triangle of expressive response. If the other is essentially accepting and supportive of the individual's emotions, however, then emotional expression evokes facilitating affects, positive secondary affective reactions that encourage emotional responsiveness (see Figure 6.5). Positive receptive experiences (i.e., feeling held, loved, understood, supported) elicit facilitating affects. These include joy, relief, hope and trust, feelings of closeness, strength, and authenticity; they motivate further experience, expression, and communication. Facilitating affects evoke the green-signal affects that communicate essential safety and the go-ahead to feel: Barbara's experience of the therapist's deep wish to share in all her feelings, good and bad, led to her feeling "relief" and "trust," an integral requirement for optimal development.

Signal affects reflect a reading of the emotional environment, in which the likely outcome of self-expression is anticipated. What begin as full secondary affective reactions (shame, pain, helplessness, fear—or alternately, hope, excitement, gratitude, trust, etc.), eventually become experienced only partially or minimally, enough to signal psychic threat (red-signal affects) or safety (green-signal affects). Intrinsic to signal affects such as anxiety or hope is the process of appraisal, what Lazarus (1991) calls "cognitive emotion-focused coping processes" (p. 285).

Red-signal affects. When living in not-good-enough emotional environments establishes an association between core affective experiences and disastrous consequences (i.e., the aversive affects), the threshold for experiencing the environment as unsafe drops and emotionally loaded situations more readily trigger red-signal affects. Red-signal affects communicate the same information as aversive affects, without full-blown psychic pain: experienced in small doses, they function as signals.

Anxiety, signaling anticipation of danger (Freud, 1926), is a major red-signal affect. Anxiety can be evoked by any of the aversive affects. Fear of experiencing these affects (fear of feeling shame, helplessness, loneliness, pain, or fear) as well as an overall fear of feeling—an *affect phobia* (Perls, 1969)—motivates the defensive exclusion of experiences that threaten to trigger them (Brenner, 1974; Jacobson, 1994, p. 20; Sandler & Joffe, 1965). The power of anxiety to motivate behavior is central to all psychodynamic understandings of psychopathology (Wachtel, 1993).

Shame is another major red-signal affect. Tomkins (1963) and later, Nathanson (1992, 1996), argue that while shame is a powerful feeling in its own right, it functions as "an auxiliary to the affect system. Shame affect *interrupts* the interest or enjoyment amplifying whatever good scene has been going on only a moment ago by producing a loss of tonus in the neck, downcast and averted gaze, and the blush" (Nathanson, 1996, p. 11, italics added). Pleasurable experiences leave the individual open and undefended. A negative response from the other in this state of unsuspecting vulnerability can be all the more shocking and humiliating. Over time, the individual learns to stay away from whatever evokes the other's wrath and condemnation—which in turn evokes shame; the result is restriction of aliveness. Ferenczi (1933), Suttie (1935), and Guntrip (1961, 1969) have written about the psychic devastation that ensues when the individual feels that what is best about him—his love, for example—elicits the other's rejection and destructiveness.

Emotional pain, and the primary depressive reaction all have red-signal aspects as well. Joffe and Sandler (1965) postulated that emotional pain in general and the primary depressive reaction in particular have unusual motivational power to evoke a variety of defenses, lest the individual be flooded with the agony of feeling despair. Pain, like anxiety, can be restricted to a signal or a warning function (Sandler & Joffe, 1965; Jacobson, 1994).

Green-signal affects. Having one's needs met with responsiveness and the success in feeling and dealing that follows leads to facilitating affects, which in turn produce green-signal affects that encourage more open and less defended experiencing.

Hope is one of the most important green-signal affects: it signals an openness to experience, a willingness to take chances, and an internal aliveness that does not have to be controlled. Feelings of safety and well-being, trust in the other, and confidence in oneself all have signal aspects, as does curiosity, the marker of the urge to explore when conditions of safety prevail. Successful explorations contribute to feelings of zest, efficacy, and pride (Emde, 1983, 1988; Kissen, 1995; White, 1959, 1960) that inform the individual's future risk taking.

DEFENSES

Defense mechanisms are designed to prevent psychic disruption and restore the experience of safety. Defenses function by blocking emotional experience so that the individual feels neither the feared core affects nor the aversive affects that become full-fledged if their signal function fails. Included here are *formal defenses*, such as isolation of affect, projection, and denial; *tactical defenses*, such as vagueness and verbal mannerisms; *nonverbal defenses*, such as avoidance of eye contact; and *defensive affects*, where the individual leads with one affect so as not to feel another, feared to be more painful.

Defenses represent the choice to protect one area of psychic life at the cost of another, as in the case of environmental failure, when self and relational needs are in conflict. For example, one patient's defenses manifested in constant focusing on inadequacies and disowning her considerable strengths; to acknowledge her independence and competence meant risking losing the other, relinquishing the hope that one day she would be cared for. For another patient, whose superficial relationships (the defense) did nothing to alleviate a crushing sense of aloneness, to relate honestly with an important other meant to risk loss of self-esteem and self (i.e., the other would feel contempt, reject him, think him not a man; he would lose track of who he is).

To minimize the impact of the other's negative response to the self (Bowlby, 1973, 1988; A. Freud, 1937), defenses can fulfill this mandate by acting

▼ intrapsychically, blocking emotional experiences;

▼ perceptually, blocking full awareness of the reality that provoked the emotional reaction;

▼ relationally, transforming interpersonal reality to defend against intimacy and closeness.

In an anger-provoking situation, for example, formal defenses such as reaction formation can be invoked to transform the anger; but the individual also can defend through emotional distancing, withdrawing to minimize the likelihood of anger even being triggered. As discussed earlier, these exclusionary strategies have their origins in the individual's attempts to preserve an attachment relationship and represent the internalization of strategies for maintaining closeness.

Adaptive in the short run, long-term reliance on defense mechanisms constricts the experience and functioning of the individual and eventually leads to the development of symptoms and "major problems in living" (Sullivan, 1953, 1956). By restricting experience through *defensive exclusion* (Bowlby, 1973, 1991) or *selective inattention* (Sullivan, 1953), defenses restrict learning and thus normal growth and development. Certain areas of experience are never enlarged and the individual loses the opportunity to define skills and responses in those areas. For instance, one of the many devastating consequences of childhood depression is that it isolates the child from his peers, severely interfering with the development of social skills.

Loneliness as the result of a high interpersonal barrier or feeling weak and frightened as a result of the defensive exclusion of anger are examples of emotional experiences that result from chronic defensive reliance. The depression, frustration, confusion, and desperation that brings so many to seek treatment are the emotional by-product of defense-dominated living, or else the "disintegration products" (Kohut, 1984) that result from the breaking down of defenses. Note that these are neither core affects nor secondary affective reactions; though such experiences are genuine for the patient, they are neither transformational nor adaptive.

When defensive efforts are overwhelmed, one is no longer dealing simply with signal experiences that operate largely outside of awareness:

instead, the individual is flooded with anxiety, fear, shame, helplessness, hopelessness, and despair. No longer just signals, they revert to being full-fledged aversive reactions, confirming the individual's worst fears about the consequences of feeling. The loss of control that many patients associate with being "emotional" is not an aspect of core affect experienced directly; unmodulated, out-of-control feeling results from the mixture of core emotion with shame or anxiety or guilt. Core affects rarely are unbearable if the individual has adequate support; the seeds of healing are contained within them. Core affects become unbearable and overwhelm the self only when they become inextricably linked with the experience of anxiety or shame; the combination, with its out-of-control quality, is disastrous.

Soft defenses. Soft defenses can be bypassed merely by heightening affect or relaxing anxiety; this is the realm of the triangle of expressive response. Affect-facilitating environments have a way of transforming what might appear as entrenched mechanisms into infinitely less formidable barriers. "A social manner, something which is adaptable" (Winnicott, 1960, p. 150) is a soft defense, as is the capacity to postpone affect and steel oneself when circumstances demand it, if one can then relax when safety is restored.

While the focus here is on the association between primary and secondary affective reactions, it isn't only core affects that elicit signal affects that lead to the institution of defenses: *any* aspect of an individual's psychic functioning can elicit a strong affective response from the other. Secondary affective reactions can (and do) become associated with any aspect of the self and self-experience (e.g., intellect, sexuality, talents, vulnerabilities, aspirations, physical or mental attributes, personality characteristics) and determine the fate of those aspects.

An Application of the Triangle of Defensive Response to Insecure Attachment

Let us consider the avoidant pattern. Suppose that a child responds with grief and anger (core affective experiences) to separation from the caregiver. Upon reunion, the caregiver ignores the child's emotion, which makes him feel rejected (Main, 1995). The rejection (negative receptive-affective experience) elicits fear, pain, and shame (aversive affects), as well as more grief and anger. Given sufficient iterations of this cycle of emotional pain and the failure to achieve greater closeness with the other, the child gives up any hope of expressing negative affect as a spur to reparation (Tronick, 1989). Instead he becomes absorbed trying to manage his negative affect on his own; he learns to defend. An inkling of emotional pain (red-signal affect) will suffice to trigger defenses. For avoidant children, attachment-related emotional reactions become linked with red-signal affects for initiating relational defenses; these children rely on defenses that dismiss the significance of the all-important attachment relationship. Thus, they come to deal and not feel. This is a perfect distillation of Barbara's dynamics prior to treatment.

The emotionality of the preoccupied individual, however, is often mistaken for core affect; the product of anxiety and regressive defenses, it is quite distant from core affect, which is other-attuned and releasing of adaptive action tendencies. The preoccupied attachment style developed in a setting in which emotionality and clinging (i.e., feeling and not dealing) maximized the likelihood of emotional contact with an unreliable attachment figure. The regressive defensive style (that in adults involves overemphasizing the inadequacy of the self and selectively glossing over the limitations of the other) is built on the defensive exclusion of relational information that would threaten the attachment bond: the other's unreliability is dreaded, and fuels emotionality and clinging—defenses that deny it. Without these defenses, with clear-eyed access to the reality of his emotional situation, the individual would have to contend with frightening feelings of aloneness and vulnerability, as well as with anger and grief. The preoccupied pattern is a powerful example of emotionality as defense against genuine emotion.

THE SELF—OTHER—EMOTION TRIANGLE

No emotional experience can be fully grasped or appreciated without understanding the relational matrix within which it occurs. The dynamically linked experiences schematized in the triangle of conflict occur in a relational context that is constructed through the affect-laden interaction of self with other.

The self—other—emotion triangle (see Figure 6.6) allows us to delineate how relational dynamics organize affective experience and generate emotional environments. This triangle captures how the individual's experience of an emotionally significant event (schematized by the triangle of conflict) is embedded within a matrix of self-other inter-

▽ The Triangle of Defensive Response vs. the Triangle of Expressive Response

When the clinical material doesn't flow (i.e., either gets stuck or goes around in circles), we're in the triangle of defensive response (see Figure 6.3a and 6.4). Defenses seem rigidly entrenched and core affective experiences largely inaccessible. There is resistance to relating openly and feeling deeply. High-risk emotional situations only intensify the patient's defensive efforts, which in turn derail dyadic processes of attunement and mutual state coordination.

In contrast, when the clinical material flows relatively easily and the patient needs only some acknowledgment of his fears before proceeding to new emotional depths, we're in the triangle of expressive response (see Figures 6.3b 6.5). Defenses are "soft" and anxiety is relatively manageable (Fosha, 1995). Expression is more suffused with affect, spontaneous, and more from the gut than from the head. It is important to note that while green-signal affects such as hope may win the day, anxiety, fear, shame, or pain may still be present; red-signal affects, however, are balanced by somewhat stronger green-signal affects, so the former do not automatically trigger rigid defenses. This is yet another illustration of affective competence in action: aversive affects do not automatically trigger defenses. The resilience-promoting impact of the reflective self function also is evident here. The individual, for example, can experience some shame connected with deep yearnings for being taken care of, yet this shame does not automatically shut him down. The urge to shut down is balanced by a sense that pushing through and expressing true feelings is likely to lead to the diminution, if not outright dissolution, of shameful feelings. This is the essence of confident expectations of reparation: positive experiences teach the patient that mindful emotional expression is the best way to overcome fears and shame; inhibiting expression only intensifies fears and shame.

Secure attachment (feeling and dealing while relating) leads to triangle-of-expressive-response functioning; yet both types of insecure attachment (feeling—and reeling—but not dealing, or dealing and not feeling) represent triangle-of-defensive-response functioning.

Functional and Qualitative Distinctions Among Core Affects, Signal Affects, and Defenses

At every moment, there is a tug-of-war between taking risks and seeking what we yearn for, or, alternately, listening to fears and playing it safe. The fate of this tug-of-war is reflected in the individual's moment-to-moment emotional experience, informed in its relative balance of expression and defense by either hope or dread. The moment-to-moment categorization of clinical material as core affect, signal affect, or defense is based on the *function* served by—and thus the motivation reflected in—a patient's communication.

Affects (though not core affects) can function at all three corners of the triangle of conflict, and thus can be deceptive.

▼ *Defensive affects* exist so that more troublesome and scary feelings need not be confronted, as in regressive disorders where emotionality functions as a defense (Davanloo, 1986–1988). One patient, for example, shamed by her arrogant father, used anger defensively so as not to feel the more humiliating experiences of need and loneliness.

▼ *Aversive affects,* such as anxiety, shame, fear, humiliation, and helplessness, function as warnings and conveyors of information about the nature of the emotional environment.

▼ *Core affects* serve a profound expressive function, with tremendous transformational potential.

For reasons having to do with how we evolved and therefore how we are wired, relief follows expression of core affective experiences, regardless of how painful they may be initially; also, they are finite in their experiential contour (cf. Stern, 1985). Aversive affects and defensive affects lack these two features: Whereas grief wanes, regressive crying can go on and on; similarly, shame and humiliation are not finite, nor is their experience in any way satisfying. Anger, for instance, can function either as a core affective experience or serve as a defense against grief and vulnerability. Whereas in the former the expression of anger represents a major and direct therapeutic opportunity, in the latter the experience and expression of anger is not likely to be mutative. The expression of defensive affects is therapeutically important primarily as a way station on the road to feelings that are being masked; defensive expression alone will not lead to therapeutic results of lasting value. However, having that affect understood and affirmed can paradoxically allow the patient to relinquish, at least temporarily, defensive reliance and risk bearing the deeper experiences.

Experiential Distinctions Among Defense, Signal, and Core Affects from the Patient's Point of View

The patient's experiential knowing of the difference between these states is of the essence and plays a major role in the healing process: becoming attuned to them is the first step in reclaiming mastery of his emotional experience.

▼ Defensive communications, with little or no access to core experience, have the sense of boredom and futility: they don't go anywhere.

▼ Communications from the top of the triangle of expressive response feel essentially meaningful, though there is static on the line. This static is anxiety and the catch of the defenses; however soft and manageable they may be, they still muffle the therapeutic impact that core affect can have.

▼ In communications from the bottom of either version of the triangle of conflict, the line is crystal clear.

For one patient, being in contact with core affect felt like "speaking from the place that breathing comes from." She spoke about how when she was in touch with her core feelings, not only did communication flow clearly and easily, but she had a physical experience of inner spaciousness. When speaking through static, she said there was no such sense. Spaciousness was accompanied by a clear sense of self: "I feel like a full person and I know exactly what I think. I am not ambivalent." Clarity and true self-being (Bollas, 1989) flow from this "place" of core affect. ▽

actions, and how representations of self and other are dynamically linked. Self-other interactions provide a set of dynamics that become internalized, shaping psychic structure, and also generate the affective background that strongly influences what state configurations come to the fore (a *state* being the experiential summation of a particular self–other–emotion triangle). Such configurations can accommodate data from attachment studies showing how the same child can have different internal working models in relation to different caretakers, with *emotion being differently processed in each configuration.*

The self–other–emotion triangle also captures patterns of relatedness and affect. Countless iterations of similarly structured moments become generalized into affective relational patterns that embody the individual's experience in a particular dyad. These patterns characterize what has been and shape interactive expectations, which in turn shape the individual's perceptions and actions. What connects such experiences into a single pattern is their affective fit: they are structured along similar motivational, relational, and experiential lines.

Although patients often lead with their experience of just one aspect of the self–other–emotion triangle, it is important to fill out the matrix, of which the particular experience is only one element. In the breakup of a relationship, for example, the individual must deal not only with the *loss of the other*, but also with the *loss of a way of being with another*, as well as with the *loss of a particular way of being oneself*, and all the emotions associated with that configuration. Where there is a specific version of the self, there is a specific version of the other and a

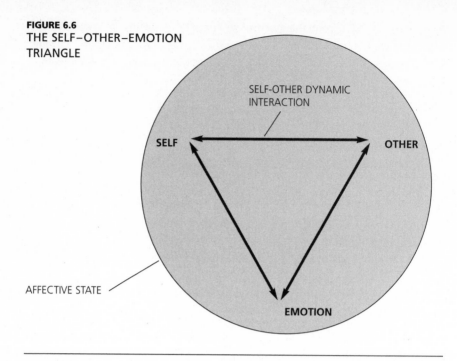

FIGURE 6.6
THE SELF–OTHER–EMOTION
TRIANGLE

SELF-OTHER DYNAMIC
INTERACTION

SELF

OTHER

AFFECTIVE STATE

EMOTION

characteristic dynamic interaction between them. Where there is an interaction, there is an associated emotion and a particular way of dealing with it. Everything—self, other, their connection, and the associated emotions—is state-dependent, contextualized, and dynamically linked.

EXAMPLE Oliver, a patient with substantive evidence of competence and achievement, had what he eventually came to call a "two-headed conception" of himself. At times he experienced himself as strong, resourceful, and as someone "useful and good." At other times he experienced himself as weak and inadequately equipped to deal with life's challenges. Elaborating the self–other–emotion triangles associated with each of those self experiences, it became increasingly clear to him that he was prone to experience the inadequate, "afraid-of-not-being-enough" version of himself either in the presence of a critical, judgmental other who "represented virtue" or as a result of his suppression of angry feelings. This version of the other could be traced to his formidably dysphoric mother, with whom he surely was "not enough" to ever be able to cure her depression. With others, appreciative of his considerable intellectual gifts and personal warmth, Oliver could relax and be himself. The self in the "not enough" self–other–emotion triangle was the result of defensiveness (i.e., tense and without great emotional access to his resources). In the "useful and good" self–other–emotion triangle, he was more in touch with true feelings, more relaxed, and as a result, more resourceful and supple.

Categories of the Self–Other–Emotion Triangle

The categories of the self–other–emotion triangle are conceptualized "from the assumed subjective point of view" (Stern, 1994, p. 11) of the individual engaged in the interaction (see Figure 6.6).

SELF

At the left corner is a representation of the *self,* with its specific perceptual, cognitive, and experiential aspects. This can include the self-concept and the representation of self in action (self as agent), self as experiencer, or self in relationship with the other.

OTHER

At the right corner is a representation of the *other,* as perceived and experienced by the individual in the context of their specific interaction. The representation of the other also has perceptual, cognitive, and experiential aspects. A crucial aspect of the representation of the other includes her feelings toward the individual. The self's registering and responding to the other's feelings and attitudes toward him constitutes the domain of receptive affective experiences.

SELF-OTHER DYNAMIC INTERACTION

The line connecting the self and other represents the *self-other dynamic interaction,* a "schema of being with another person [that] is a memory of a dynamic series of events" (Beebe, Jaffe, & Lachmann, 1992, p. 73). The self-other dynamic interaction allows us to explore the rules that govern the dyadic dynamics of moment-to-moment interplay involved in reciprocal coordination, miscoordination, and repair. Is the dynamic one of mutuality or dominance? Under what condition does one partner take the lead? How does one partner respond to the other's withdrawal or exuberance?

At the bottom of the triangle are *emotions* that accompany the interaction. Note that the category of emotion occupies the same plane as the entities of self, other, and the self–other dynamic interaction: though emotions are an aspect of self experience, experientially often they feel separate and independent of the self; they have the quality of otherness or separateness that makes them unique affective experiences. Spezzano (1993) addressed this phenomenon when he wrote, "affective truth is not something we find; it finds us" (p. 214).

AFFECTIVE STATE

The *affective state* is represented by the circle that has within it the triangle of self, other, and emotion. In addition to specific emotions associated with their interaction, the ongoing dialogue between self

▽ Emergent Dyadic Phenomena and the Transformational Model of Mutual Influence

The dynamic interactive process itself has the power to shape individual experience. Beebe, Jaffe, and Lachmann (1992) propose that the sense of self, the sense of the other, as well as the sense of the dynamic interaction of self and other are all "emergent dyadic phenomena"; they cannot be explained by referring to just one person alone.

> [W]hat is initially represented is not an object per se, but an object relation: actions of self in relation to actions of partner and their pattern of dyadic regulation. Thus, what is represented by the infant is an emergent dyadic phenomenon not residing in either partner alone. (Beebe, Jaffe, & Lachmann, 1992, pp. 73–74).

To understand the individual's personality as reflecting the contributions of the individual, his emotionally important others, and their interaction requires a "transformational model of mutual influence" (Beebe, Lachmann, & Jaffe, 1997). This concept addresses the bidirectionality of change and the active role of both partners in constructing the individual's psychic structure. While the influence is mutual and transformational, and while both partners contribute, their contributions are neither equal nor equivalent: the caregiver, having a wider and more flexible repertoire, has more opportunities to shape the process (Tronick, 1989). Such a model describes the affective model of change. The focus is not only on the attributes of the patient but also the contribution of the therapist (her person, stance, technique) and the patient-therapist interaction in shaping the process and determining the outcome of the treatment. ▽

and other generates an emotional climate—of safety or threat, affect-facilitation or affective intolerance—that profoundly influences and is influenced by the individual's experience of any emotionally significant event. As Kihlstrom (1987, p. 1451) notes, "some representation of the environments in which these events take place" must get linked with the mental representation of the experience and the self. The affective state is that environment, the affective hum that characterizes the self's subjective experience of a particular self–other–emotion triangle. Affective states that promote optimal interactions generate an emotional microclimate of essential safety, experienced by the individual as the sense of well-being.

The Experiential Quality of the Categories of the Self–Other–Emotion Triangle

Any dyadic emotional interaction has the potential to produce five types of affective phenomena, all of which are emergent dyadic phenomena and all dyadically constructed: self experiences, relational experiences, categorical emotions, feelings toward and about the other, and affective states. These affective phenomena are the self's affective *experience* of the basic categories of the self–other–emotion triangle. In any relational–affective event, these affective phenomena coexist, and are there to explore, express, and reflect on. The therapist's choice of which to focus on depends on what the patient is dealing with, and in turn what emerges on its own or is dynamically related to the patient's issues. A change in any one of the experiential categories is sufficient to catapult us into a different self–other–emotion triangle.

We all have felt at ease and confident with one person one minute, only to feel shy and uncomfortable with someone else the next. Depending on the interaction and emotional background it generates, our sense of who we are in the moment, our sense of the other, and the emotions we experience at the time can and do shift.

Just as there are two basic configurations of the triangle of conflict, there are two basic self–other–emotion triangles to capture self-at-worst and self-at-best functioning: the *compromised self–distorted other–blocked emotion triangle* (Figure 6.7a) and the *effective self–realistic other–core emotion triangle* (Figure 6.7b). Over the course of a successful therapy, states in which functioning is best characterized by the effective self–other–core emotion triangle come to predominate, and states in which functioning is best captured by the compromised self–other–blocked emotion triangle recede in frequency and emotional salience.

THE RELATIONSHIP BETWEEN THE TRIANGLE OF CONFLICT AND THE SELF–OTHER–EMOTION TRIANGLE

The experience of self and other is related intimately to how emotional experience is structured. How emotional experience is structured in turn is related intimately to how self and other are perceived and experienced. To understand how emotion is processed differently in different self–other–emotion triangles, imagine a triangle of conflict at the bottom of each, where emotion is represented.

The Self-at-Worst

THE COMPROMISED SELF–DISTORTED
OTHER–BLOCKED EMOTION TRIANGLE AND
THE TRIANGLE OF DEFENSIVE RESPONSE

In the case of emotional functioning best captured by the triangle of defensive response, the compromised self–distorted other–blocked emotion triangle captures the functioning that often brings patients to seek treatment (see Figure 6.7a).

The individual's sense of self is in some way dysphoric, painful, or inadequate; the other is perceived in a distorted, two-dimensional fashion; the self-other interaction is at best fraught with frustration and dissatisfaction, at worst, overwhelming, painful, and in some way destructive to either self or other (or both); the possibility of its repair does not occur to the patient. This configuration is evoked by the patient's habitual reliance on defenses against experience; it also can be evoked by a critical, punitive, or humiliating other. Indeed, interactions with such figures is what led to this kind of functioning in the first place. The block against feelings feeds the sense of inadequacy, as the individual is cut off from many important resources, and inadequacy reinforces defensive reliance, as the individual feels ill-equipped to handle emotional events.

The Self-at-Best

THE EFFECTIVE SELF–REALISTIC OTHER–CORE
EMOTION TRIANGLE AND THE
TRIANGLE OF EXPRESSIVE RESPONSE

The effective self–realistic other–core emotion triangle is associated with a type of emotional functioning best captured by the triangle of expressive response (see Figure 6.7b).

With access to core affective phenomena and the psychic resources residing therein, the individual experiences himself as effective, the other realistically, and the interaction between them—positive or aversive—at least manageable or potentially reparable. The therapist's reparative initiatives (her responsiveness to the patient's reparative efforts) play a crucial role here.

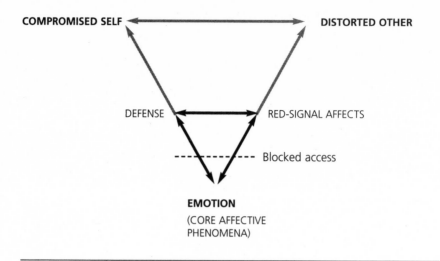

EXAMPLE Overwhelmed by what she experienced as a rejection by her therapist that occurred in the last minutes of a session, Aggie was in excruciating emotional pain in between sessions when her therapist could not be available to her. She described the pain and the vulnerability that went with it as "too much"—so much so that death, with its relief from pain, seemed appealing. She "steeled" herself against the pain by instituting her old defense mechanisms so that she could function. While her defenses cut her off from the pain that was increasingly intolerable, they also cut off her access to all sources of liveliness. The result was that while the patient was able to function, she felt "out of touch" with herself, numb, irritable, "depleted, and running on empty." She experienced herself as weak and needy and the therapist as self-preoccupied and indifferent. At the next session, despite feeling humiliated by her reactions, the patient decided to tell the therapist how she felt, which the therapist welcomed and encouraged. The therapist's response to her was, in Aggie's words, "totally embracing." The therapist reiterated her appreciation of the patient for letting her know exactly what had gone on with her, and reframed Aggie's experience from an empathic perspective; she also reaffirmed her wish that she could have been there for the patient. As they continued speaking together, Aggie

FIGURE 6.7b
THE SELF-AT-BEST
THE EFFECTIVE SELF–REALISTIC OTHER–CORE EMOTION TRIANGLE
AND THE TRIANGLE OF EXPRESSIVE RESPONSE

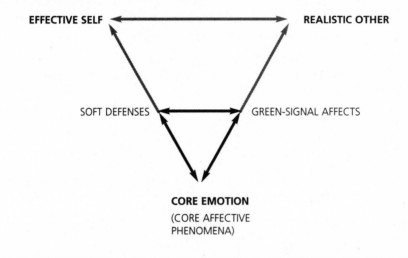

EFFECTIVE SELF   REALISTIC OTHER

SOFT DEFENSES   GREEN-SIGNAL AFFECTS

CORE EMOTION
(CORE AFFECTIVE
PHENOMENA)

---

felt herself "coming back to life," her subjective experience of the relaxation of her defenses. Her capacity for deep feeling restored through connection that saved her from aloneness and self-punishment, the patient said, "I have regained a sense of who I am." She spoke of feeling "the conduit restored": her connection to her core feelings and essential self was reestablished through the affect-facilitating, affirming, loving connection with the therapist.

A highly specific version of the self–other–emotion triangle—the true self–true other–transforming emotion triangle—figures prominently in AEDP work that goes well: it arises in the aftermath of deep genuine experiencing. Functioning best characterized by this configuration can be brought about by an experience of the other as deeply understanding and loving, of oneself as authentic, of the affective environment as safe, and by experiencing visceral, deep emotions. These are moments when enormous therapeutic changes can occur. These moments have been called "heightened therapeutic moments" by Lachmann and Beebe (1996) and "now moments" by Stern and colleagues (1998). In this state, the individual experiences himself at his best and the other as true. Their interaction is marked by openness and relaxation, as well as by generosity and empathy and at times even a ruthless honesty. These moments are tremendous therapeutic opportunities: through these experiences, the patient—and often the therapist— inhabits previously unavailable worlds. Once experienced viscerally, the phenomena can be processed, reflected on, and worked through until they are part of the patient's more standard repertoire. (See also Mahrer, 1999, on the "new person.")

The true self–true other–transforming emotion state has been described by one patient as follows:

> In this state, I am in touch with me at my most undefended, expansive, unconstrained, unblocked, affirmative, flowing, feeling, thriving, doing. I also feel like there is a shucking off of other ways of being. It's like those old ways of being are loosening and falling away. They're withering and they are much less easily invoked. More and more, I'm seeing those other ways of being as distortions, not reality, not the real me.

Many therapeutic strategies can be pursued for shifting the balance of power from the compromised self–distorted other–blocked emotion triangle to the effective self–realistic other–core emotion triangle. With increased awareness of these patterns, the patient learns which emotional environments foster positive self experiences and which are likely to evoke compromised self states. The most effective route, however, remains that of getting past defenses and accessing core affective experience. Once this is accomplished, natural core affective reactions release adaptive action tendencies that invariably release a good self experience.

Largely unexplored in the examples thus far is how the patterns revealed in the therapeutic relationship relate to other relational patterns in the patient's life. In what other relationship, if any, do these dynamics—healing or pathological—get played out? How is the therapeutic relationship similar to or different from those others? To find out, we must consider our final schema, the triangle of comparisons.

THE TRIANGLE
OF COMPARISONS

The triangle of comparisons examines the relationship among three sources of transformational influence: current relationships (C), the moment-to-moment therapeutic relationship (T), and past relationships (P) in which relational patterns were forged. It thereby links, across time boundaries, three self–other–emotion triangles, each with its own triangle of conflict embedded within it (see Figure 6.8). Any constituent element (e.g., type of defensive strategy) or pattern of elements of either the self–other–emotion or the triangle of conflict (e.g., the sense of self and a particular affective state) can be tracked temporally and across different relationships.

Mann and Goldman (1982), for instance, focus almost exclusively on emotional pain, "that privately felt, rarely verbalized, *present and chronically endured pain*" as a subjectively experienced constant across time. They believe emotional pain to be "*an important statement about how one feels and has always felt about the self*" (p. 21). By considering patterns of affective congruence, it is possible to link "past, present and future; that is the patient's private time line and the affects that accompany memories. … One recognizes what the patient has been struggling with all his life, how he has tried to master it, and the unrelenting pain he has suffered nevertheless" (Mann & Goldman, 1982, pp. 23–24).

This schema traditionally has been used to explore how the patient's current patterns of relating, with current others and with the therapist, repeat earlier pathogenic patterns. T-C-P linking is a staple and identifying feature of psychodynamic work (Malan, 1976, 1979). AEDP's use of the triangle of comparisons is more comprehensive; it is used to explore affective similarities, but also affective differences. The focus is on both repetition and exception to repetition. Once a pattern has been identified—especially one that has played a major role in the patient's difficulties—finding what relationships (if any) are characterized by some diametrically opposed pattern becomes just as important as finding those (if any) described by similar patterns. Moreover, the AEDP focus is not only on pathogenic, affect-aversive relational patterns; the exploration of affirming, affect-facilitating relational patterns is equally crucial. The therapeutic relationship, rich in opportunities, can be used as a living example of a relationship based on trust (Wachtel, 1993). The patient's good experience with the therapist facilitates recovery of memories of other good relational experiences, either long-forgotten or believed to be insignificant.

As in the other two representational schemas, here too are in essence two triangles of comparisons to capture the two ways of being: the triangle of affect-inhibiting relationships and the triangle of affect-facilitating relationships. Even when the work is very much focused on repetition of affect-inhibiting patterns (the realm in which the compromised self operates), the potential for things being good enough remains a powerful force in the patient's mind: a positive triangle of

FIGURE 6.8

THE TRIANGLE OF COMPARISONS
ITS INTERRELATEDNESS WITH THE TRIANGLE OF CONFLICT
AND THE SELF–OTHER–EMOTION TRIANGLE

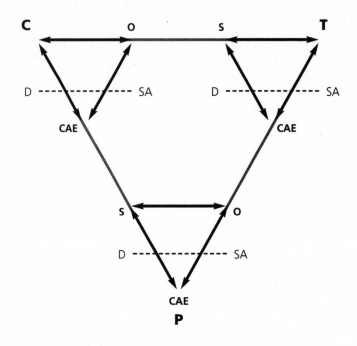

TRIANGLE OF COMPARISONS

C   Current relationships
T   Therapeutic relationships
P   Past relationships

SELF–OTHER–EMOTION TRIANGLE

S   Self
O   Other
SA   Signal affects
CAE Core affective experience

TRIANGLE OF CONFLICT

D   Defense
SA   Signal affects
CAE Core affective experience

comparisons is there either to be "discovered" or as a potential to be realized.

The power of the AEDP therapist's opening gambit is to act at once in a way that disconfirms the patient's pathogenic beliefs (Weiss, Sampson et al., 1986): instead of joining the not-good-enough others in the patient's current life (C) and in the past (P), thereby completing the T-C-P linking of not-good-enough others, blocked affect, and compromised self, we immediately seek to kick into gear the T corner of the triangle of comparisons (i.e., the triangle of expressive response, linking patterns involving interaction between a good-enough other and an efficient self, with potential access to core emotion). Having one self–other–emotion triangle, with its specific triangle of conflict, experientially elaborated acts as a magnet: once that schema is primed, it "attracts" other similarly structured schemas.

Very often the patient's affirming experiences with the therapist are experienced and described as happening "for the first time." It appears as if only the T corner of the affect-facilitating triangle of comparisons is in operation. The therapy is successful when the patient is able to generalize his wonderful new T experiences to the C realm, where he lives his life (Mahrer, 1999). The work at first appears to be about encouraging the patient to fill in the C corner of the new triangle of comparisons by developing new current relationships based on his positive experiences with the therapist. The positive therapeutic experience then is usually accompanied by discovering what was believed not to exist: in the process of elaborating the new triangle of comparisons, often some long-forgotten, deeply affirming past relationships (P) become unearthed, to fully complete the new triangle of comparisons. In this category, we often find grandparents, teachers, next-door neighbors, and pets. In the following example, we find a sister.

EXAMPLE A patient was sobbing as she described stark life experiences with both parents that left her feeling "bad," "unlovable," and forever compliant. The therapist asked her for an example. She related an incident when she had been cruelly and unfairly punished by her mother. In passing, she mentioned that afterwards, Maggie, her older sister, had come to her room to comfort her. The patient's affect shifted from hard despair to a softer feeling. The therapist gently urged her to focus on her experience of her older sister. The patient remembered Maggie telling her she could borrow a new skirt the patient much coveted. The patient cried as she realized that Maggie had always been there for her, no matter what. She felt moved, grateful, and uplifted. Having discovered a relationship where she had been nourished and treasured, she felt more able to deal with the starkness of her early painful experiences with her parents.

The repetition–exception mode can be quite powerful when a patient becomes aware of the repetition of pathological patterns and their prevalence in his life, *and becomes resolved to do things differently*. It is a profound moment when the patient realizes he has options. Shane, Shane, and Gales (1997) formulate the patient's options in terms of three possible relational configurations involving the new self (note that the "new self" is integrated within a self–other–emotion triangle where there is good access to core affect and the adaptive action tendencies intrinsic to it):

▼ *new self with old other* (i.e., patient comes to terms with the limitations of a particular person in a particular emotional setting); or

▼ *new self with old other on the way to becoming a new other* (i.e., the other changes in response to patient's changes—a more frequent phenomenon than one might expect); or

▼ *new self with new other* (i.e., patient goes on to be different in an environment conducive to a healthy configuration).

In the next example, the patient, hoping to bring about the *new self with old other on the way to becoming a new other* configuration, bangs her head against the other's defensive wall. Accepting the intransigence of the *new self with old other* configuration, she says good-bye to him, mourning the limitations of a current but genetically reverberating relationship; she is very clear that she will foster and nurture *new self with new other* configurations elsewhere in her life.

EXAMPLE During painful working-through of her relationship with her affect-intolerant father, Susan was increasingly struck by the extent to which her current relationship with her boss replicated her past relationship with her father. Knowing how damaging the relationship with her father had been, she went out of her way not to repeat that pattern with her boss; her boss proved unable to rise to the challenge of relating more openly and honestly, clinging to defensive and destructive patterns; he could not join her in making a new configuration. Distressed but not devastated, the patient said of her new-found ability to be assertive and intimate, "I'm learning that there are other people I can do this with." Then she was able to do with her boss what she had not been able to do with her father in real life: say good-bye, mourn and move on. The corrective emotional experience (Alexander and French, 1946) undid the pathological mourning that was at the core of the pathology that had made treatment necessary.

When the patient experientially compares two relationships of opposing emotional valence that leads to realizations about both and his differential experience within each, a powerful piece of therapeutic work has been accomplished.

SUMMARY

While many versions of each of these three configurations are in play at any given time, for the sake of clarity, the focus throughout has been on the two versions characteristic of functioning under conditions of safety and unsafety. Such a focus also captures a clinical truth: there does tend to be a main version of the compromised self and a main version of the efficient self that dominate our most pathological and our best functioning.

In moving from the triangle of conflict to the self–other–emotion triangle and then to the triangle of comparisons, we have moved from the microscopic, moment-to-moment examination of the structuring of affective experience to a naked-eye view of affective–relational states to a telescopic perspective that captures relational–affective essence across time. What we discover, though, is that when dynamically understood, the structure of the sweeping patterns of a lifetime resembles the moment-to-moment dynamic shifts of the current relationship with the therapist. It is what poets have always understood:

> To see a World in a Grain of Sand
> And a Heaven in a Wild Flower
> Hold Infinity in the palm of your hand
> And Eternity in an hour
>
> WILLIAM BLAKE, *Auguries of Innocence*

CHAPTER 7

VARIETIES OF CORE AFFECTIVE EXPERIENCE

One can never fathom an emotion or divine its dictates by standing outside of it. ... Each emotion obeys a logic of its own, and makes deductions which no other logic can draw.

WILLIAM JAMES, *Varieties of Religious Experience*

Core affective phenomena, when accessed, activate deep transformational processes. The visceral experience of core affect involves a state transformation (Beebe & Lachmann, 1994). In this altered state, deep therapeutic work can be accomplished as the patient gains access to

▼ deeper layers of unconscious material that can now be worked through (Davanloo, 1986–1988, 1990);

▼ vital sources of liveliness and energy that were lost when affect was warded off (Herman, 1982; Winnicott, 1960);

▼ adaptive action tendencies intrinsic to the experience of core affects (Darwin, 1872; Frijda, 1986; Goleman, 1995; Greenberg & Safran, 1987; Lazarus, 1991; Safran & Greenberg, 1991) and reflecting the individual's freedom to pursue exploratory strivings (Ainsworth et al., 1978; Bowlby, 1982);

▼ adaptive relational action tendencies, manifested in a capacity for greater openness and deeper and more satisfying relating;

▼ adaptive self action tendencies, based on clarity about basic needs and wants (Greenberg, Rice, & Elliott, 1993; McCullough Vaillant, 1997) and commitment to staying true to the fulfillment of those basic needs and wants;

▼ a sense of being in touch with the essential or true self (Bollas, 1987, 1989; Hart, 1991; Perls, 1969; Winnicott, 1949, 1960).

Experiencing deep emotion viscerally within the therapeutic relationship helps the patient master a vital psychological process with profound implications. Visceral experiencing is crucial: it is not sufficient for the patient to say that he is sad or fearful, or for the therapist to presume that he is from a dynamic processing of the clinical material; the patient must feel the sadness or the fear in his gut or his heart or his face or his sinew.

Accessing core emotions and achieving a core state are both pathways to genuine transformation. The term *core* is not to be confused with the terms *primary* or *basic* in emotion theory. *Core* qualifies clinical phenomena and has two referents: functionally, it refers to a state wherein profound opportunities for deep, rapid, and mutative therapeutic work exist; qualitatively, it refers to affective expressions that are free of defense or red-signal affects.

The *categorical emotions*, or core emotions, include sadness, anger, joy, fear, and disgust. In pure form (i.e., free of defense and red-signal affects), their experience and expression lead to an automatic state transformation. The *core state* refers to an altered condition, one of openness and contact. Within it, the individual is deeply in touch with essential aspects of his own self and relational experience, which themselves are considered varieties of core affective experience and become potentially mutative. These affective experiences include feelings toward and about the other (e.g., compassion, delight, hatred); authentic self states or self experiences (e.g., feeling powerful, sexy, aggressive, vulnerable); and relational experiences (e.g., feeling close, distant, or in sync). Finally, *vitality affects* refer to those "dynamic, kinetic qualities of feeling" (Stern, 1985, p. 156) such as "surging," "fading," or "explosive" that distinguish the ongoing, continuous aspects of affective experience.

Within the realm of core affective experiences, one distinction is between categorical emotions and the core state. Another distinction is based on what realm of experience (e.g., events, the self, or the relationship) the individual inhabits. For example, *categorical emotions* (and feelings) are the individual's reactions to events, usually interpersonal events involving others, based on an experiential reading of his environment. *Self-affective experiences* involve the individual's experiential reading and appraisal of the self and its state. *Relational–affective experiences* are the individual's experiential reading of the relationship and relational states, based on what Emde (1988) calls "the active experiencing of shared reality with another."

In what follows, each of the varieties of core affective experience is described to identify the possible forms of potentially transforming experiences and expose their attendant clinical and technical implications.

THE CATEGORICAL EMOTIONS

Categorical (or core) emotions, such as grief, anger, fear, sadness, joy, or disgust, for example, are core affective phenomena characterized by "distinctive biological signatures" (Goleman, 1995, p. 6). The categorical emotions

> are said to express universal biological rules handed down genetically through evolution because they have proved adaptationally useful. They arise from an inherited neural structure, involve a characteristic neuromuscular response pattern, and are correlated with distinctive subjective qualities for each emotion. ... The face, through a complex and interconnected set of muscles, gives innate expression to the primary emotions that humans inherited in the evolution of the species, and ... the pattern of expression for each emotion is universal for that species. In humans, there is, in effect, an anger face, a fear face, a happiness face, and so on, although to some extent sociocultural variables can affect the pattern and timing of expression, and an emotional face can be inhibited, disguised or produced for effect. (Lazarus, 1991, pp. 70–71)

The categorical emotions are the phenomena represented at the bottom of the triangle of conflict (both versions) and the self–other–emotion triangle: distinct feelings that arise in response to an emotionally meaningful interpersonal event involving a self, an other, and an action. Like the infant Winnicott (1960, p. 141) spoke of whose impulses seem as external to him as "a clap of thunder or a hit," we often experience categorical emotions as phenomena that have a life of their own. Phenomenologically described, the categorical emotions

> often are experienced as either *a surge of energy* or *a gentle flowing sensation that moves from the area of the torso toward the extremities, out from the body.* ... This *surge* or *flow* generates an *action tendency*, which if applied adaptively is an appropriate *reaction* to an event, leading to a sense of *relief* or *satisfaction.* In some circumstances, such as with grief or assertion, such reactions can lead to the resolution of an issue. (McCullough Vaillant, 1997, p. 232)

Categorical emotions differ from other varieties of core affective experiences (Darwin, 1872; Ekman, 1983; Goleman, 1995; Izard, 1977; Lazarus, 1991; Nathanson, 1992; Tomkins, 1962). The experience and expression itself of the categorical emotions involves a state transformation. (In the case of other affective experiences, as we will see, their experience and expression becomes mutative when it occurs in conjunction with the core state, that is, the altered state of openness, relaxation, and deep relational connection.)

Some of the core emotions—for example, anger, grief, joy, and being in love—have primarily activating or expressive functions. Others, such as fear and shame, can operate both at the bottom of the triangle of conflict and as red-signal affects; as red-signal affects, their main function is to inhibit the experience and expression of other affects. Shame most often functions as an inhibitor of other usually pleasurable affective states (Nathanson, 1992, 1996).

Categorical emotions are deep-rooted bodily responses with their own specific physiology and arousal pattern (Ekman, 1983; Zajonc, 1985) as well as their own set of characteristic dynamics (Darwin, 1872; Nathanson, 1992; Tomkins, 1962, 1963). Anger or rage, for instance, goes with the physiological profile preparing one for fight or flight; and from Darwin's extensive discussion of the phenomenology of rage (1872, pp. 238–41): "The face reddens or becomes purple, with the veins on the forehead and neck distended. ... The chest heaves and the dilated nostrils quiver. ... The excited brain gives strength to the muscles, and at the same time energy to the will." Furthermore, "[b]lood flows to the hands, making it easier to grasp a weapon or strike at a foe; heart rate increases, and a rush of hormones such as adrenaline generates a pulse of energy strong enough for vigorous action" (Goleman, 1995, p. 6). Shakespeare's Henry V, inspiring his men moments before battle "when the blast of war blows in our ears" thus tells them:

> Then imitate the action of the tiger;
> Stiffen the sinews, summon up the blood,
> Disguise fair nature with hard-favour'd rage:
> Then lend the eye a terrible aspect;
> ... Now set the teeth, and stretch the nostril wide,
> Hold hard the breath, and bend up every spirit
> To his full height!
>
> *Henry V*, 3.1.6–17

Typical anxieties associated with the experience and expression of anger involve fears of loss of control or fears of retaliation, and guilt about fantasies of destroying the object of one's anger. The adaptive action tendencies released by fully experienced anger often include a sense of empowerment and an assertiveness rooted in the rediscovery of psychic strength, self-worth, and affective competence.

Grief and emotional pain. Within the safety of the therapeutic relationship, the patient becomes able to face what he has had to bear and what he missed out on. These losses, deprivations, and missed opportunities—often further compounded by the patient's subsequent withdrawal from full engagement—evoke deep *emotional pain*, which is a grief whose object is the self. The phenomenology of grief or emotional pain—or distress, in Tomkins's (1963) schema—includes tears, rhythmic sobbing, downcast eyes, arched eyebrows, downturned mouth, and sometimes actual physical pain, which patients localize in the chest, around the heart, and around the eyes.

The experience and expression of many affects is inhibited by the intense fear of emotional pain associated with them. The connection with the therapist gives the patient strength to face what he found unbearable to confront alone. "Emotional pain represents the sting that makes an experience unbearable. Generally, emotional isolation has made the pain unbearable, so that the connection with the therapist is paramount in healing" (McCullough Vaillant, 1997, p. 275). Together with an other who can share his pain, the patient can begin to mourn. The adaptive action tendencies released by the full experience of grief and emotional pain renew compassion for self and others and very often reaffirm the will to live fully, inspired by the desire to make up for lost time.

Feeling moved, emotional, and grateful. This affect complex arises in the wake of a healing experience, such as feeling understood or helped to master previously frightening situations. It is not present in infancy, as it requires mature cognition and life experience; its essence is the attainment of something yearned for emotionally—but never having experienced—in the past. Feeling moved and grateful is deep and mutative, and shares with the other categorical emotions distinctness and discreteness; its prominent physical and physiological aspects are tears that express both joy and pain, an uplifted gaze, and internal surges of energy. The associated adaptive self and relational action tendencies include greater capacity for empathy and self-empathy as well as for deeper and more confident loving and understanding of oneself and others.

THE CORE STATE

The *core state* is the self's internal affective holding environment, reflecting the self's affective competence vis-à-vis its own experience. The core state can either precede and shape interaction or evolve from it: the safety feeling, the experiential correlate of secure attachment, is a key element.

The core state is marked by effortless focus and concentration, ease and relaxation, a subjective sense of clarity, purity, even truth, and often, remarkable eloquence. Affective experience is heightened, unequivocal, and declarative: sensation is enhanced, imagery is vivid, pressure of speech is absent, and the material flows. Relating is characterized by clear and effortless contact. The core state is one of deep openness, self-attunement, and other-receptivity in which deep therapeutic work can take place.

THE CORE STATE AND VITALITY AFFECTS

Experiences that are continuous (e.g., the state of well-being), unless focused on, function as the background hum produced by the individual engaged in being in his emotional environment. "A background feeling corresponds instead to the body state prevailing between emotions. ... The background feeling is our image of the body landscape when it is not shaken by emotion" (Damasio, 1994, pp. 150–51). What Damasio here refers to as background feelings Stern (1985) calls *vitality affects*, conceiving them as that which happens between distinct categorical emotions; vitality affects are crucial to the process of attunement, also referred to as the *little-step-by-little step process* (see chapter 10):

> During an average mother-infant interaction, discrete affect displays occur only occasionally—perhaps every thirty to ninety seconds. Since this is so, affective tracking or attuning with another could not occur as a continuous process if it were limited to categorical affects. One cannot wait around for a discrete categorical affect display, such as a surprise expression, to occur in order to re-establish attunement. Attunement feels more like an unbroken process. ... Tracking and attuning with vitality affects permits one human to "be with" another in the sense of sharing likely inner experiences on an almost continuous basis. ... [O]ur experience of feeling-connectedness ... seeks out the activation contour that is momentarily going on in any and every behavior and uses that contour to keep the thread of communion unbroken. (Stern, 1985, pp. 156–57)

When attention is paid to these continuous experiences, however, background and foreground shift, and background feelings ease into the experiential forefront; they too acquire distinct experiential characteristics.

Physiologically, the core state partakes of the body landscape of happiness, love, tender feelings, and sexual satisfaction:

> Among the main biological changes in *happiness* is an increased activity in a brain center that inhibits negative feelings and fosters an increase in available energy, and a quieting of those that generate worrisome thought. But there is no particular shift in physiology save a quiescence, which makes the body recover more quickly from the biological arousal of upsetting emotions. This configuration offers the body a general rest, as well as readiness and enthusiasm for whatever task is at hand and for striving toward a great variety of goals. *Love*, tender feelings, and sexual satisfaction entail parasympathetic arousal—the physiological opposite of the "fight-or-flight" mobilization shared by fear and anger. The parasympathetic response, dubbed "the relaxation response," is a bodywide set of reactions that generates a general state of calm and contentment, facilitating cooperation. (Goleman, 1995, pp. 6–7)

In the context of a core state, (a) *feelings toward and about the other*, (b) *self experiences*, and (c) *relational experiences* deepen and become mutative. Adaptive action tendencies, adaptive self action tendencies, and adaptive relational action tendencies are released. These affective experiences correspond to the *self*, *other*, and *self-other dynamic interaction* categories of the self–other–emotion triangle.

Feelings

Feelings toward and about the other are core affective phenomena that

> are subtle variations of the five [categorical emotions] mentioned ... euphoria and ecstasy are variations of happiness; melancholy and wistfulness are variations of sadness; panic and shyness are variations of fear. This second variety of feelings is fine tuned by experience, when subtler shades of cognitive state are connected to subtler variations of emotional body state. It is the connection between an intricate cognitive content and a variation of pre-organized body-state profile that allows us to experience shades of remorse, embarrassment, *Schadenfreude*, vindication and so on. (Damasio, 1994, pp. 149–50)

Along with feelings such as remorse, embarrassment, and glee, we include in this category love, compassion, pride, hatred, and tenderness.

Categorical emotions are primal, universal, and visceral; feelings, broadly defined, are idiosyncratic and laced with personal meaning, a cognitive–affective mix. For feelings to have a transformational impact, they need to occur in conjunction with the core state.

FEELINGS OF PARTICULAR INTEREST TO AEDP

The patient's compassion and love. Of particular interest to AEDP are the patient's feelings of compassion, generosity, and caring toward the other (for our purposes, the therapist). In focusing on the patient's capacity to love, empathize, and give, we recognize profound relational capacities and resources (adaptive relational action tendencies) that often have gone unrecognized and at times may have even been the target of attack. The recognition of the patient's love and generosity, with the concomitant acknowledgment of his capacity to have a positive impact and be effective in a generative fashion, is empowering and validating.

These basic feelings are the best the patient has to offer. Nothing is more emotionally devastating than having one's loving feelings treated as toxic (Guntrip, 1961). When loving is met with derision, rejection, or humiliation, it becomes equated with loss, abuse, or self-annihilation (at which point love itself, and with it, intimacy, turn terrifying). Other patients, overwhelmed after the loss of a loved one, come to associate loving with death and elect a stance of global emotional distance that results in impoverishment of the personality. When the emotional environment can help the patient feel safe enough to take risks and lift defenses, however, he can gain access to these core emotions. Along with joy and relief at being able to own his capacity to be loving and being validated, the patient often feels grief over having had to choose between the destruction of a deep part of himself or loss of the bond with an attachment figure.

While the entire AEDP enterprise rests on the therapist's capacity to enter the patient's experience and the patient's being able to register her empathic response, the patient's capacity for empathy with others and for himself also is crucial. Loss of the capacity for empathy often is a casualty of defending indiscriminately against relational experiencing, and must be addressed.

EXAMPLE Clark was extremely close to his psychotically depressed mother. Her inconsolable sobbing and freely expressed suicidal yearnings had been utterly terrifying to the four-year-old boy, who felt himself "shattering to a million pieces inside." Over time, he developed the habit of going to his room, shutting the door, and creating a perfectly orderly environment in which nothing was ever out of place. His room became the objective correlative of his inner state, where he succeeded in shutting out anything and everything— almost—that had to do with messy emotions. In his adult life, he regarded emotions and needs as weaknesses, and was filled with self-contempt whenever he reacted emotionally rather than logically. A marital crisis triggered by his failure to react emotionally to his wife's miscarriage brought him to treatment. Though he felt guilty about his lack of response, he evidenced neither compassion for his wife nor any grief or sadness of his own. In treatment, however, the therapist's compassion pleased him deeply even as it filled him with discomfort. He urged her to be more "Freudian": "I thought you were supposed to be objective. Isn't it against the rules to have feelings for your patients?" The first breakthrough of empathic experiencing on his part occurred when she told him she needed surgery and would be out for a few weeks. His eyes immediately filled with tears: "I couldn't bear to have anything happen to you … I just do not want you to be in any pain. It hurts me to think of you suffering." She thanked him, moved by his response, and urged him to stay with his feelings and maintain eye contact. His eyes and facial expression continued to soften. He became aware of feeling scared. "I just feel too vulnerable right now. I just don't know where this is going to go." This mutative spontaneous moment was the first step in the slow restoration of his capacity to experience compassion, first for others, and eventually for himself.

Empathy for others often is more readily available than empathy for the self, even in those whose empathic responsiveness is not blocked, as Darwin recognized (1872, p. 216). In some patients, access to empathic responsiveness is intact, even though self-empathy might be problematic. When that empathy is directed toward the therapist, it is extremely important that she acknowledge it. Validating and appreciating the patient's empathy as evidence of generosity of spirit and capacity for relational engagement play a major role in strengthening the patient's self-esteem and confidence, empowering him to eventually extend his empathy to himself and his own predicament. The capacity for self-empathy is crucial to psychic healing and must be nurtured as a powerful antidote to corrosive self-blame and self-loathing.

Self Experiences, Self States, and Vitality Affects

"The basis of the self forms on the fact of the body. ... The self finds itself naturally placed in the body. ... It is the self and the life of the self alone that makes sense of action and of living from the point of view of the individual ..." (Winnicott, 1972, pp. 15–16). Self states and self experiences—for example, feeling powerful, worthless, active, old, weak, competent, lost, aggressive—involve exploration of the subjectively *felt sense* (Gendlin, 1991; McGuire, 1991). These are affective phenomena that refer to some prominent aspect of the self evoked by a particular self–other–emotion dynamic. Self states and experiences are the products of elaborating bodily based affective experience with personal meaning, thereby making it a feature of identity (Bollas, 1989).

In this context, vitality affects (Stern, 1985) refer to the qualitative aspect of an experience, how it is registered by the self. If, for example, the categorical emotion is grief, the self's experience of it may be feeling enlivened, or empowered, or drained. Vitality affects qualify self experience and convey what an experience means to the self.

Self experiences can be transitory, situation-specific phenomena, but when they become characteristic and take root in identity, they become the experiential correlates of personality traits. For instance, while feeling inferior or inadequate is an ordinary response to certain kinds of interaction, a pervasive feeling of inferiority is of profound consequence to the organization of the personality. A patient for whom inferiority was an essential aspect of his sense of self and identity described it as unrelieved: "My sense of my own inferiority was always there, it wasn't a momentary experience. It wasn't triggered by this or that. It was always with me. It always set me apart from everyone else. I thought that I was the only one who felt that way. It was only when I met Tom that I realized that there were others who also felt it and that it was possible to have it worse than me."

Openly exposing a self state to someone who meets and welcomes it with understanding can indeed transform it (see also Rice & Greenberg, 1991): the patient who can speak of his sense of inferiority to an empathic other ends up feeling less inferior.

EXAMPLE One man, whose considerable intellect had become a source of pain as his parents humiliated him, accusing him of showing off, was so reluctant to let himself shine that in fact he was functioning at a rather dull level. In the course of therapy, as he grew able to experience himself as smart and work through the shame and panic he associated with displays of sparkling intellect, a lusty creativity burst forth, empowering him to pursue his many interests and integrate them in new ways; and as he developed his reflective self function, his residual embarrassment at moments of recognition became increasingly manageable.

So much of self affective experience remains in the experiential background. When self states are not experienced affectively, the therapist can attend to their bodily rooted elements and thereby ground therapeutic work in visceral sensation. Change of focus has a salutary influence on the therapeutic process by relieving it of the aridity of disembodied insight and releasing the mutative power of affective processes. When the individual's attention is focused on these experiences through empathic understanding and resonance, he is presented with opportunities for coping, mastery, and growth. Informed by growing self-empathy and self-acceptance, *adaptive self action tendencies* are released: the individual realizes the nature of his basic needs and becomes committed to their realistic fulfillment.

SELF EXPERIENCES
OF PARTICULAR INTEREST TO AEDP

Vulnerability is an affective self state that often accompanies risk-taking and undefended experience. It also arises when the patient feels that he is alone and that his resources are about to be overwhelmed. If the patient can be helped to feel that this time he is not alone, that his therapist is with him, vulnerability can be exhilarating rather than frightening. Vulnerability is a particularly hopeful clinical indicator in those patients for whom an exaggerated self-reliance has been the means of psychic survival; it signals melting defenses, emerging trust, and willingness to reveal need and longing. Sensitivity and tact are required to allow the patient to feel held without feeling humiliated by his longings.

True self experiences. True self states and the experience of the essential self are core affective phenomena that arise in the wake of other profound affective experiences. For instance, the intense experiencing of a categorical emotion, particularly one that was previously feared to be unendurable, often is followed by an equally intense true self state. A true self experience, an aspect of the core state, may be accompanied by feelings of happiness, well-being, and relaxation, and by a sense that everything is simple, easy, and beautiful. One patient likened it to the sound of "a flute in a brass band." The experience of joy, authenticity, and aliveness, what the novelist Josephine Hart refers to as "the dazzling explosion into self" (1991, p. 41), echoes Fritz Perls's "explosion into joy, laughter, joie de vivre ... [that] connect[s] the authentic personality with the true self" (1969, p. 60). The therapist's threshold for registering these experiences—during which the individual feels authentic, "real," and "alive"—should be very low, as they need to be attended to and fostered.

Relational Experiences

[T]here are three interactive pathways of self and shared meaning, not two. These include the sense of "I," of other and of "we." ... [A] sense of "we" involves a profound shift of self-perspective—a shift to an active experiencing of shared reality with another. (Emde, 1988, pp. 36–37)

Relational experiences are the core affective phenomena conceptualized as *emerging dyadic phenomena*—that is, they are affectively constructed by both members of the dyad (cf. Beebe, Jaffe, & Lachmann, 1992). They are the experiential correlates of the self's experience of the self-other dynamic interaction in the absence of defenses and anxiety. Relational experiences include being with, feeling apart from, feeling close or distant, and being in sync or out of sync. By definition, all experiences, including relational experiences, are felt within the confines of the self: "a very significant feature of intimacy [is] that although dependent on the presence of another person, it is centered within the self of each individual" (Kelly, 1996, p. 59). The paradoxical term *relational experience* has been chosen deliberately to suggest the joint affective experience of the dyad (though clearly it consists of each individual having his or her own experience). This intersubjectivity (e.g., Stern, 1985) is being widely explored: "the child's developing sense of 'we' and the interpersonal world of shared meaning is now becoming an increased focus of research attention" (Emde, 1988, p. 36).

Feelings of relatedness and intimacy are relationally constructed phenomena with roots in the sharing of affects between infants and parents (Emde, 1988; Stern, 1985, 1998; Tronick, 1998). Through this affective communication, the mother-child dyad achieves (and reachieves after miscoordination) mutual states of coordination (Tronick, 1989); the dyadically coordinated state is the basis for affective resonance, the feeling of being understood, and thus, ultimately, secure attachment.

In AEDP, patient and therapist focus in on and elaborate the experiential qualities of feelings of closeness and intimacy. Making the implicit explicit augments and amplifies such relational experiences: thus transformed, their full experience releases *adaptive relational tendencies*. With growing awareness and access, the individual becomes increasingly motivated to act in ways that will further his relational agenda. More and more, intimacy and close contact come to be associated with safety and pleasure, and less and less with dreaded loss of self and accommodation to the other. Empathy and self-empathy are also increasingly summoned in the process.

RELATIONAL EXPERIENCES

OF PARTICULAR INTEREST TO AEDP

Matching, affective sharing, and resonance. Relational experiences of particular interest to AEDP are those likely to produce receptive affective experiences, such as feeling understood, seen, and loved; states of openness and relaxation; and intimacy and closeness. Crucial to these experiences are states of matching and of shared affect, which are "key moments in the interaction" (Beebe & Lachmann, 1988, p. 329). Stern (1985) considers state sharing, such as vocal coaction, or affect contagion, to be the basis of subjective intimacy. Reproducing our partner's emotional display, we evoke in ourselves a psychophysiological state that corresponds to that of the other (Ekman, 1983; Zajonc, 1985).

As Beebe and Lachmann (1988) note, "The process of becoming related and better attuned to another involves in part, becoming more similar. ... The implication is that similarity or symmetry in behavior is associated with a similar congruence of feeling states" (p. 320). This amounts to a mechanism by which the physiological substrate of intersubjectivity (i.e., shared affective states) is created, and helps explain why the therapist's emotional participation is so crucial in an affect-oriented psychotherapy. Without the therapist's emotional participation, the transformational potential of experiences of intimacy and empathy cannot be fully realized.

The process of affective sharing, in which patient and therapist share intense emotions, elicits powerful feelings of closeness and intimacy. Relief, lightness, closeness, melting experiences, and other in-sync states are experiential correlates of affective sharing and are aspects of the core state of openness and relaxation. Noteworthy is how often affective sharing of intensely painful and negative emotions brings with it relief and lightness for the patient. Here is the essence of the achievement—and reachievement—of coordinated states through open, undefended, mutually attuned communication of affective experience.

Moreover, expression itself can change these experiences, intensifying them or transforming them into different experiences altogether. For example, speaking about feeling disconnected and out of sync to someone who is validating and listens empathically can turn the experience of disconnection into one of closeness and feeling understood. Mutually acknowledging resonance can "crescendo higher and higher," leading to *"peak experiences of resonance, exhilaration, awe and being on the same wavelength with the partner"* (Beebe & Lachmann, 1994, p. 157, italics added). These kinds of experiences—matching, affect sharing, and resonance—lead to the core state and to relational experiences of openness, closeness, and intimacy. When both partners feel in sync—the experiential correlate of the coordinated state—and engage around their respective experiences, profound therapeutic work can take place.

Deep self experience and intimate relational experience are interpenetrating:

> The outstanding quality of the intimate experience is the sense of *being in touch with* our real selves. It allows us a fresh awareness of who, what, and how we are. It differs from introspection or meditation, which are ways of *looking* at ourselves. ... [I]n the intimate experience, our seeing happens in the presence of the other. It requires no thinking or looking but occurs directly; it is experiential. (Malone & Malone, 1987, p. 19, quoted in Kelly, 1996)

Experiencing deep relatedness and intimacy—direct, back and forth sharing of truthful feelings—entails openness, bareness, and willed vulnerability to the other. It is the essence of the little-step-by-little-step process, whereby each partner maintains simultaneously attunement to the other and to one's own authenticity of self experience. The back and forth of the little-step-by-little-step process involves the capacity to express feelings directly to the person whom the feelings are about, to remain connected while taking in the other's reaction, and to sustain this emotional conversation through time. In the core state, the relational process deepens and intensifies the experiences of each participant.

The task of emotionally and relationally engaging is a difficult one, as anxieties, guilt, shame, emotional pain, and a myriad of other aversive affects are often the patient's (and may well be the therapist's) associations to emotional engagement. This demanding process is one with which many people have no prior experience; the terror of the unknown and the fear of being inadequate and helpless, or of being found out and exposed, can be significant obstacles to overcome.

For therapists—aside from our own personal issues, which can be formidable—this little-step-by-little-step process of fostering openness and intimacy is one for which few of us are trained; it involves not only authenticity and empathy, but active involvement of one's self and active use of one's emotional experience. This demands more emotional risk taking than most training prepares us for. For this kind of work, the therapist's openness, emotional engagement, and attention to personal reactions are critical (Alpert, 1992; Fosha, in press). Without it, therapeutic work—in which affective and relational processes are inextricably intertwined—cannot take place.

The therapist's openness facilitates the patient's experience and deepens his participation in the process. When this goes well, the atmosphere is highly charged, superficial interaction disappears, awareness is heightened, and the work shimmers with meaning and importance.

The capacity for such mutual experience underlies mature interpersonal relating and growth-promoting attachments. As the empirical work of Main, Fonagy, Tronick, and their colleagues has demonstrated, the achievement of coordinated states through affective communication promotes knowing that we exist in the mind of our significant others, which is at the foundation of secure attachments that underlie our capacity to thrive.

FIVE CLINICALLY RELEVANT DISTINCTIONS

1. The Receptive Affective Experiences: Affect-Laden, Crucial, but Not Core Affect

The impact of the therapist's empathy toward the patient is at the heart of the affective model of change. Here we consider the individual's experience of that empathy. McCullough Vaillant (1997) notes that "the receptive capacity is the substrate for vulnerability, openness, emotional connection, empathy, and intimacy" (p. 294). Receptive affective experiences thus are the individual's experience of the other's affective response to him. The underlying process is comprised of perceptual, cognitive, and affective elements. Though usually expressed through the language of feelings—for example, "I feel loved"—what we are referring to is an emotionally laden *appraisal*. This appraisal leads to feelings, often core affects: for instance, feeling tingly, alive, and expansive (vitality affects); calm, confident, and serene (self states); or moved and grateful (categorical emotions); it can also lead to feeling shaky and drained, agitated and out-of-sorts, or feeling afraid and wary.

In a therapeutic model that relies on empathy and attachment-based relational experiences, we need to be able to assess the patient's *experience* of empathy and attachment. Receptive experiences precede and underlie emotional responses. It is very important that they be precisely explored with the patient; only then do we have the true context for his emotional responses. Receptive experiences are the result of appraisal—the capacity to read the environment—that lies at the heart of adaptation. This adaptive capacity needs to be reengaged in those for whom receptive affective experiences are defensively excluded: these are patients who are threatened by recognizing the impact of others on them.

Registering the love, hate, anger, emotional indifference, or compassion of the other—that is, registering the other's strong feelings toward the self—is vital. Being the object of someone's anger, for example, might make one feel either angry or afraid (categorical emotions), small (self-experience), or gleeful (feeling). Clarifying that the individual *registered* the experience of being the object of the other's anger allows us to put in context the individual's feeling angry, afraid, small, or gleeful himself.

As therapists, we rely on our ability to read the other (our patients). Similarly, explicitly or implicitly we rely on our patients' readings of others whom they talk to us about. Therapists recognize that misreadings and distortions may be part of any perception–appraisal (owing to the patient's history and motivations), just as they may be part of any psychic process, our own included. Yet we must assume that the other's emotional state can be known, albeit imperfectly at times, through moment-by-moment changes (Kiersky & Beebe, 1994, p. 389). The change occurring in oneself as a result of closely relating with another, where each influences the other, "provides each a behavioral basis for knowing" the other, thus enabling one to enter "into the other's perception, temporal world and feeling state" (Beebe & Lachmann, 1988, p. 331).

Let us consider the patient's experience of registering the therapist's empathy. Although we talk of the therapist's being empathic, it is the patient who deems it so—or not—and then has feelings about it. As

Henry Heatwole writes with regard to whether campers need to worry about unprovoked attacks from bears, "I've never heard of an unprovoked attack. But it's the bear, not you, who decides when he's provoked" (1988, pp. 45–46). Barrett-Lennard (in Greenberg, Elliott, & Lietaer, 1994) identified three phases of empathy, proposing the term *received empathy* for the third phase:

> [F]irst, a therapist resonates with the client (therapist experienced empathy); second, the therapist communicates empathy (expressed empathy); and third, the client perceives the therapist's understanding (client received empathy). Client received empathy was shown to have the strongest correlations with outcome. (P. 522)

RECEPTIVE AFFECTIVE EXPERIENCES
OF PARTICULAR INTEREST TO AEDP

We are particularly interested in receptive experiences in which the patient feels understood, appreciated, helped, and in those that produce the safety feeling. Healing affects (discussed in the next chapter) often arise in response to registering such matching experiences. When asked to pay extra attention to the sensations that arose in response to feeling loved, safe, or understood, several patients reported that the experience that follows in the wake of positive receptive experiences is one of relaxation, an almost physical sense of letting go of yet another layer of defense. One patient spoke of her experience of being cared about: "I tried to notice where I feel it. The sensation feels along the surface of my body, my skin and the muscles or tissues right beneath. I feel that safety of contact on my skin and my skin relaxes." Another patient experienced it more internally: "it's like my internal state is being caressed." In Josephine Hart's *Damage*, the protagonist describes the experiential consequences of being seen and feeling recognized: "A stillness descended upon me. I sighed a deep sigh, as if I had slipped suddenly out of a skin. I felt old, content. The shock of recognition had passed though my body like a powerful current. ... I had been home" (1991, pp. 26–27).

Here's how the narrator of Paul Auster's *Moon Palace* experiences being loved, illuminating how it can reverse the free fall of pathology:

> I had jumped off the edge of a cliff, and then, just as I was about to hit bottom, an extraordinary event took place: I learned that there were people who loved me. To be loved like that makes all the difference. It does not lessen the terror of the fall, but it gives a new perspective on what that terror means. I had jumped off the edge, and then, at the very last moment, something reached out and caught me in midair. That

something is what I define as love. It is the one thing that can stop a man from falling, the one thing powerful enough to negate the laws of gravity. (P. 50)

Auster's words recall one of Winnicott's unthinkable anxieties, *falling for ever* (1962). Yet he also evokes its antidote, *being held,* which can quell, quiet, soothe, and transform even unthinkable anxiety not only into thinkable anxiety (cf. the reflective self function) but even into a feeling of safety. This is the healing essence of positive receptive experiences.

2. Transforming Affects
vs. Affects That Need Transforming

The practice of AEDP, as of all experiential STDPs, is founded on a distinction between affective experiences that are transforming and experiences that we seek to therapeutically transform. In terms of the triangle of conflict, the essential difference is between bottom-of-the-triangle phenomena (core affects) that are transforming, and top-of-the-triangle phenomena (aversive and defensive affects) that need to be transformed.

TRANSFORMING AFFECTS: CORE AFFECTS

Core affective experiences (i.e., core emotions and core states) are conduits to contact with the essential self and to optimal relational, in-the-world functioning. All experiences of transforming emotions are integrated within a self–other–emotion triangle in which the self is authentic and effective, the other is accurately perceived, and the self-other interaction is optimally manageable.

AFFECTS THAT NEED TO BE TRANSFORMED:

A. AVERSIVE AFFECTS

In contradistinction to the core affects, another group of intense emotional experiences is comprised of affects in need of therapeutic transformation. These are aversive affects (e.g., anxiety, shame, pain, helplessness, loneliness, despair), responses rooted in the failure of the caregiving environment to be good enough. Whereas the release of adaptive action tendencies is a defining aspect of core affective experiences, paralysis marks aversive affects. "Instead of the freely flowing, inner-to-outer direction of adaptive affect, self-attacking or inhibitory affective responses are generally represented by a pulling in, a cowering, a shrinking, a withdrawing, a gaze aversion" (McCullough Vaillant, 1997, p. 143). When aversive affects are prominent, defenses truly represent the best the individual can do under the circumstances to psychically survive and function; otherwise, the psychic pain would be too great to endure. These responses—the aversive affects and red-signal affects into which they evolve—are at the heart of the development of psychopathology, and thus are the ground for clinical work. The aimed-for therapeutic transformation is that they no longer severely inhibit adaptive responding.

EXAMPLE A patient tearfully and painfully spoke of how "diminished" she felt by her father's unsolicited and critical appraisal of a piece of creative writing she had done. She spoke about how excruciating it was for her to always feel that she was just "not good enough." In itself, the breakthrough of these feelings (i.e., pain about not being good enough), through her cheery, bubbly facade, represented a major step toward increased authenticity in her therapy. An act of trust and opening up, it was elicited by the therapist's supportive, empathic response to her account of her interaction with her father.

Though representing a therapeutic opportunity, the breakthrough and direct visceral experiencing of pathology-engendering aversive affects is not sufficient for the kind of transformations AEDP seeks to foster. That the patient has courageously exposed her most vulnerable sense of inadequacy—something she has struggled with alone, in anguish, all her life—creates an opening where aloneness *can be* transformed by support and empathy; but it *must be* transformed if true healing is to take place.

The therapist can respond by appreciating the patient's courage, resonating with the pain she feels, speaking about how painful it must have been to endure all this alone, saying how moved she is by the patient's opening up to her, or sighing empathically. For any of these therapeutic interventions to stick, the patient needs to take in the therapist's emotional responsiveness. It is important to note whether the patient's affective opening up is followed by deepened contact after the therapist's emotional embrace, or whether, in the initial moments, emotional closeness evokes more anxiety or distancing from the patient. The transformational opportunity is to meet the patient's pain and shame about "never feeling good enough" with empathy, affirmation, and support. The next step is to help the patient take it all in.

If the patient in this example can accept the therapist's "holding," then she can relinquish her reliance on defensive strategies, and the self–other–emotion schema can change to one where the self is valued, the other is affirming, and the emotion not only bearable but enlivening. Feeling strengthened, the patient then can confront the feared-to-be-unbearable categorical emotions—whether grief about not having had good parents, or anger at her father—and benefit from their associated adaptive action tendencies. This in turn increases the effectiveness of her functioning in the world, strengthens and bolsters her sense of self, and eventually translates into affective competence. If, however, she cannot accept the therapist's holding, that becomes the focus of the work; the unconscious knows, so to speak, that empathy exposes us to grief about past deprivation.

B. DEFENSIVE AFFECTS

The other group of emotional experiences that need to be transformed are defensive affects. These often function to mask unmet longings for attachment and connection, and to protect vulnerable areas of self experience. Defensive aggression or defensive sexuality, for example, might cover up unexpressed grief or anger concerning unmet and valid longings for love, recognition, or understanding (McCullough Vaillant, 1997). In the preceding example, say, for instance, the patient responded with contempt to the therapist's empathy, accusing the therapist of being "too touchy-feely." Her contempt would be an example of a defensive affect: it protects the patient from feeling the grief associated with a lifetime of missed opportunities for closeness, and also protects the patient from the vulnerability associated with owning the depth of her yearnings for appreciation. Regressive affects (e.g., temper tantrums, weepiness, self-pity) are defensive affects par excellence: because they so closely mimic authentic emotion, they are particularly effective in camouflaging much more frightening experiences that the patient seeks to avoid at all costs.

3. *Adaptive vs. Maladaptive Aspects of Emotional Experiences*

Darwin's assertion that emotion is adaptive has clear clinical implications that further allows us to determine what is and is not core experience. Core affect is an integral aspect of a self–other–emotion schema in which the self is authentic, the other is perceived accurately, and the interaction is as manageable as the situation permits. A sense of calm, a quality of being and feeling real, or a genuinely self-accepting perspective goes with the self–other–emotion triangle. Here core affect and adaptive action tendencies lead to psychic health.

IMPLICATIONS OF MALADAPTIVE EXPERIENCES

If the self is perceived as bad, the other as larger than life or insignificant, and the interaction as simultaneously unsatisfying and unavoidable, then we are not dealing with core affective experience. When the experience of self is in some way under attack (i.e., is bad, worthless, or weak), we infer a self–other–emotion triangle in which access to core affective experience is blocked by defenses. Distorted, two-dimensional, or inaccurate views of the other or the self similarly suggest the presence of experiences rendered inaccessible by defenses. If the other is declared to be "nice" but the self "unworthy," for instance, this should alert us to core affects being held off-limits. When those affects are accessed, either self-representation or representation of the other will change, or both. If anger, for example, is the defended-against affect, when anger becomes viscerally accessible, the self can be reconfigured as effective (powerful, assertive, etc.) and the other as insincere, critical, fragile, self-involved, or any number of qualities other than nice. If, however, the individual is primarily avoiding feeling the other's love, then the sense of self as unworthy can be a defense against vulnerability associated with the yearned for but terrifying experience of being loved; with access to fear, such reconfiguration would result in a sense of self as open and vulnerable and the other as loving.

Maladaptive expressions of emotion are accompanied by a subjective experience of being out of control: anxiety is present, and the expression of affect is not for self-expression or communication; rather, it is the result of defenses overwhelmed by intense feelings and anxiety linking their expression with feared consequences (i.e., aversive affects). The subjective feeling of being out of control almost invariably is a marker for the maladaptive expression of emotion, which has undesirable consequences for the individual.

IMPLICATIONS OF ADAPTIVE EXPERIENCES

There is a key distinction between on one hand the *experience* of the emotion (e.g., rage experienced as murderous, as in the foregoing example) and its expression in fantasy, and, on the other hand, the *expression* of the emotion in reality. In fantasy, rage and attack facilitate contact with the essential self through intensity. However, actual expression (as opposed to expression within the therapeutic environment) must be appropriate and modulated, or else it is not in the self's best interests. In actuality, rage is adaptive when used in self-defense, in discriminating confrontations, and to inform assertiveness.

The adaptive expression of core affect is accompanied by a particular subjective experience: the self is in control, and the affect is an expression of the self's basic agenda.

The adaptive aspects of core emotions are revealed in their activation of action tendencies that enhance the patient's effectiveness (Coughlin Della Selva, 1996; Laikin, 1999). Consider anger. Losing impulse control is not adaptive: impulsive expressions of anger are not expressions of core affect; they are either defensive affects or reflections of primitive, unmodulated pathology. What is adaptive is to *fully experience* (though not enact) one's murderous rage; knowing the full extent of our feelings empowers us to take effective action on our own behalf. An adaptive sense of self assumes responsibility; attacks on the self and attacks on the other are not adaptive. Adaptive self experience leads to the release of adaptive self action tendencies, including empathy for the self. Just as the therapist must view the patient from an empathic perspective if she is to be useful to him, so the patient must come to care deeply about himself; ultimately, true responsibility is not possible without self-empathy.

4. All That Glitters Is Not Gold: Distinguishing Emotion from Emotionality

Mutative core affective experiences must be differentiated from emotionally charged experiences and states that serve a defensive or avoidant function. Genuine affective experiences have the following distinguishing features:

▼ sensation, visceral experience, and imagery are prominent;

▼ there is either an "outward *surging, flowing,* or *resonating* of some form of energy" (McCullough Vaillant, 1997, p. 232), or they are accompanied by a sense of ease, calm, or relaxation;

▼ a sense of openness and coming forward;

▼ cognitions associated with them are textured and specific (Marke, 1995), rather than global and stereotyped;

▼ regardless of how painful they are, their expression provides eventual relief;

▼ they are finite—that is, their experiential activation contour (Stern, 1985) is wavelike.

Red-signal affects and defensive affects lack these features. They are marked by the following:

▼ "the inner direction of energy (constriction, withdrawal, inhibition)" (McCullough Vaillant, 1997, p. 233), or by tension or frustration;

▼ "the generation of excessively thwarting or self-attacking inhibition of action" (McCullough Vaillant, 1997, p. 233);

▼ a sense of being closed off, held in, or out of control;

▼ a sense of stasis or stagnation, of not getting anywhere; or a sense of deteriorating, sinking, falling, disintegrating, etc.;

▼ cognitions associated with defensive or anxious affect are global and tend to remain so.

Given the phenomena of empathy, affect contagion, and affective sharing, the therapist's response may be useful in distinguishing emotion from emotionality. For the attuned therapist, states of core affect are moving and intense, and elicit strong emotional and empathic responses: the therapist feels something akin to what the patient is feeling, or feels pain, joy, or compassion for what the patient is going through. When emotionality is not authentic, the attuned therapist cringes. Just as out-of-tune singing is grating to a musical ear, so inauthentic affect makes the attuned therapist viscerally ill at ease; yet genuine affect draws one in.

5. Still Waters Run Deep:
Distinguishing the Declaration of Emotional "Truth" from Instances of Intellectualization

When someone is calm and speaks in measured tones it does not mean that affect is absent and that we are in the realm of defenses; quiet and simple communication can be a statement of affective truth, a declaration of deeply felt personal meaning, which is an aspect of core state functioning.

Declaring the "truth" of one's personal experience, when before that truth either could not be borne or was forbidden knowledge, involves the patient daring to state painful "facts," relinquishing the pathogenic need to remain loyal and protect the other (Kissen, 1995) regardless of cost to the self. This sober confrontation and declaration can be profoundly liberating for the patient.

Concentrated, clear inner conviction in the absence of defense and anxiety marks the emotional–truth-telling narrative. The quality of certainty, "the state of assurance" (James, 1902), is one of the characteristics of the core state experience. The tone can be passionate and emphatic, colored by a particular affect such as pain, sadness, wistfulness, or anger; or alternately it can be declarative, calm, and quiet, with little other emotion than intense, concentrated conviction. In any event, it is unequivocal.

It is important that these highly meaningful declarations not be mistaken for defensive intellectualization. Also important is not to mistake the *declaration* of personal truth regarding defensiveness, anxiety, shame, and so on for actual instances of defensiveness, anxiety, or shame. Acknowledging and owning defensiveness is very different from being defensive: the motivation for declaring personal truths is expressive and communicative, rather than protective or avoidant. The unflinching expression of a painful truth, such as confronting the depths of one's shame or the extent and consequences of one's detachment, is a bottom-of-the-triangle-of-conflict core affective experience.

CHAPTER 8

THE HEALING AFFECTS

Joy & Woe are woven fine
A Clothing for the Soul divine
Under every grief & pine
Runs a joy with silken twine

WILLIAM BLAKE, *Auguries of Innocence*

META-THERAPEUTIC PROCESSES AND THE AFFECTS OF TRANSFORMATION

Bringing about change is our raison d'être. Through our interventions, we seek to activate mutative processes to alleviate suffering and help our patients lead fuller, richer lives. What happens, though, when patients experience our empathy and *do* feel understood? What happens when patients are able to overcome a phobia and (re)gain a sense of freedom in their lives? What happens when, through deep experiencing of previously unbearable affects, patients at last are able to achieve mastery and work through traumatic pasts? What happens when depressions lift, anxieties are mastered, personality restrictions are overthrown, and symptoms disappear?

When change finally has been brought about, it is a new beginning, where *meta-therapeutic processes* and their markers, the *affects of transformation*, come into operation, thereby providing an opportunity to deepen and broaden the treatment's effectiveness. Regardless of the therapist's orientation, in any therapy that is going well, both patient and therapist experience a sense of accomplishment. Meta-therapeutic processes—the patient's experience of therapeutic processes—are associated with characteristic affects called the *affects of transformation*, the markers for processes of therapeutic change. *Acknowledging mastery, mourning the self,* and *receiving affirmation* are the three major meta-therapeutic processes. Each has its own characteristic affective markers.

▼ In the process of *acknowledging mastery,* the patient processes his success in overcoming the obstacles that stood in the way of his being able to fully experience his emotional life. The affective markers most common to mastery are the categorical emotion of joy and the feeling of exuberance, pride, and happiness (Tomkins, 1962; White, 1959, 1960).

▼ In the process of *mourning the self,* the therapeutic experiences activate the patient's awareness of what he didn't have, what he lost, and what he missed. Similar to the work of mourning (Freud, 1917; Lindemann, 1944; Volkan, 1981), mourning the self involves facing and working through the impact of the painful reality that resulted in the patient's psychic suffering. The affective marker associated with the process of mourning the self involves the experience of emotional pain, a grief whose object is the self.

▼ The process of *receiving affirmation* is the flip side of mourning the self. Affirmation involves fully acknowledging, feeling, and working through therapeutic experiences (i.e., those that alleviated the patient's suffering and engendered his nascent and growing sense of well-being). Affective markers associated with affirmation are the healing affects, of which there are two main types: feeling moved, touched, or strongly emotional within oneself; and feeling gratitude, love, tenderness, and appreciation toward the affirming other.

ALTERNATING WAVES OF EXPERIENTIAL AND REFLECTIVE WORK

Meta-therapeutic processes evolve as patient and therapist together trace the affective contours of a successful therapeutic collaboration. This work calls upon and further elaborates the development of reflective self functioning in both patient and therapist. This mutual relational exploration involves alternating waves of experiential (Greenberg & Safran, 1987; Greenberg, Rice, & Elliott, 1993) and reflective (Fonagy et al., 1995) work. The meta-therapeutic process is akin to advice given to public speakers: tell the listeners what you're going to do, do it, then tell them what you've done. What's involved here is (a) facilitating a therapeutic experience, (b) naming and acknowledging that therapeutic experience, and (c) exploring the patient's experience of the therapeutic experience. In other words, feeling and talking, and talking and feeling, and so on. The patient not only has been successful and has been helped, he deeply *knows* it. He has access to how he experiences that success and help, and to what that means to him. The process of change is identified and marked for the patient as a coherent experience and thereby becomes an accessible part of his affective-cognitive-behavioral repertoire. Experience, reflection, and meaning construction—in a relational context—all are integral aspects of meta-therapeutic processing.

META-THERAPEUTIC PROCESSING

Why are meta-therapeutic processes and their associated affects of transformation clinically useful? There are several reasons. First, by focusing explicitly on meta-therapeutic experiences, rather than allowing therapeutic processes to operate silently, we give patients the opportunity to process, and thus learn about, the nature of helpful experiences in which they already have been successful. This furthers the transfer of therapeutic learning to experiences outside treatment (see also Mahrer, 1999); patients then can reflect on these processes. As the work of Fonagy and colleagues (1995) and Main (1995) has demonstrated, the capacity to reflect on one's own experience, as well as on that of others, is strongly related to resilience and psychic health.

Second, acknowledging and focusing on the receptive aspects of positive therapeutic experiences gives rise to specific clinical phenomena that have enormous therapeutic potential as they tap the psyche's healing forces. Focusing on these processes and facilitating the experience of the affects of transformation leads to yet another state transformation, where deeper resources are accessed. This dual process is reflected in the *healing affects,* which are both markers for healing processes and heal in and of themselves. The following aspects of state transformation follow in the wake of a full experience of the affects of transformation:

▼ general awakening of adaptive action tendencies;

▼ awakening of adaptive self action tendencies (e.g., increased confidence and self-esteem), as well as greater self-empathy;

▼ access to states of well-being, calm, ease, and relaxation;

▼ access to true self states and experiences of aliveness, liveliness, and authenticity;

▼ awakening of adaptive relational action tendencies (e.g., deepened capacity for intimacy and closeness), as well as empathy;

▼ true insight (i.e., deep knowing and clarity about the nature of one's difficulties, as well as a felt sense of one's resources in being able to overcome them).

Finally, in the context of being the recipient of such therapeutic experiences, memories of good relationships reemerge. Affective experiences with the therapist help patients recover memories of positive relationships that had been vital to their psychic survival, but that had been forgotten.

EXAMPLE Work with one patient, for example, had focused on her deep grief and anger about her father's failure to understand, nurture, and appreciate her (i.e., the process of mourning the self). In the course of therapy, the patient was deeply moved by what she experienced as the therapist's loving interest in her. Her experience with the therapist liberated long-forgotten memories of early days with her father when he had been both loving and proud of her. She recalled a nickname he had for her, which she had not thought of in years. She also remembered how proud she had been of his interest in her writing when, at age six, she had declared herself an "authoress." The recovery of these positive experiences led to a better understanding of the dynamics of her experience. She had had her father's love until she lost it irrevocably and inexplicably during the latency years (it seemed to be related to the birth of another child, as well as to the patient's having reached the exact age at which her father had lost *his* father). The recovery of her memories of her father's early love, through her experience of feeling loved by the therapist, had a profound impact on her. While the loss of love and subsequent starkness of her relationship with both parents shaped her adult personality and concerns, the recovery of her memory of her father's love solidified her core sense of herself as good and worthy of love and understanding. It also helped us understand the origins of her incapacitating fears of loss, which had inhibited her growth and development. These more positive and consolidating memories of a past relational experience might never have been recovered without the meta-therapeutic focus on present relational experience (with the therapist).

ACKNOWLEDGING AFFECTIVE MASTERY AND THE EXPERIENCE OF JOY AND PRIDE

Tomkins (1962) has written that "[a]ny sudden mastery of a source of hitherto incompletely mastered fear will also produce joy" (p. 292). Very often, what prevents the patient from experiencing the more primary emotions or being emotionally connected is the fear of pain: as Perls (1969) said, "the enemy of development is the pain phobia—the unwillingness to do a tiny bit of suffering" (p. 56). With the release of primary emotions comes the patient's new ability to face painful truths.

By offering support, empathy, and an environment conducive to and facilitating affective processes, the patient, no longer alone, is able to experience what previously had been too frightening or unbearable. While each of these experiences contains its own therapeutic aftermath, often affective mastery follows, particularly if patient and therapist focus together on how the patient feels having just done what he has done. By acknowledging his affective mastery the patient is able to feel joy and pride. Joy, pride, self-confidence, and a new appreciation of one's abilities are some of the affective experiences that follow the experiential process whereby the unbearable becomes bearable. Note, however, that affective mastery is not limited to being able to feel what could not hitherto have been felt; the term applies to the processing of all emotionally meaningful triumphs and achievements.

The recognition and acknowledgment of experiences of mastery, effectiveness, and competence plays a crucial role in consolidating a sense of self, self-esteem, and self-confidence (White, 1959, 1960). It should be emphasized that the categorical emotion of joy is a marker of the psychic process associated with overcoming obstacles.

In the following quote from an article written during the last phases of a terminal illness, Harold Brodkey movingly describes the consequences of, *together with his wife*, having *fully faced* that he is dying.

> I feel very well, and for a week now, as part of some mysterious cycle, I have felt very happy. The world still seems far away. And I hear each moment whisper as it slides along. And yet I am happy—even overexcited, quite foolish. But *happy*. It seems very strange to think one could enjoy one's death. Ellen has begun to laugh at this phenomenon. We know we are absurd, but what can we do? We are happy. (Brodkey, 1996, p. 54)

As this example illustrates, joy can be the other side of fully faced and overcome fear.

MOURNING THE SELF AND THE EXPERIENCE OF EMOTIONAL PAIN

> Thus piteously they wailed in sore unrest,
> And on their weepings had gone down the day
> But that at last Telemachus found words to say.
> (HOMER, *The Odyssey*, quoted in Darwin, 1872, p. 215)

As patients gain access to previously warded-off affective and relational experiences, the process of mourning is activated. The realization of losses, deprivations, and missed opportunities triggers deep emotional pain, the experience of which sets in motion the healing process. Therapeutic work involves focusing on this experience and staying with it over time, as these losses have to be mourned.

Emotional pain. Emotional pain is the feeling of grief about one's own disappointments, deprivations, lost childhood, lost opportunities, the loss of the myth of wonderful parents, the experience of which assumes a reflective self. While emotional pain (a categorical emotion) is deep, pure, and potentially profoundly therapeutic, it is not an emotion of very young children: it is based on the belief that things ought not to be as they are, that as they are is not in the order of things, and that the reality that prevails is tragic. As Joffe and Sandler note: "[mental pain involves] a discrepancy between the actual state of the self on the one hand and a ... state of well-being on the other" (p. 396).

Another anxiety invariably is that the pain will be unbearable. Patients often say they are afraid that if they start crying they will never stop, or that they will fall apart. Helping the patient bear the pain, and with support, helping them go through the process of experiencing the pain and emerging intact goes a long way toward removing that fear.

Denial of painful reality is also used to preserve the myth of good parenting: parents are idealized, regardless of the cost to the self. Fully facing reality involves relinquishing this fantasy, and grieving. Prior to a visit home, a patient said, "I go with no expectations. I'm letting go of the hope that she [her mother] will provide the mothering she never has," and with that, she burst into deep sobs.

DYNAMIC ISSUES FOR THE THERAPIST

Therapists often have the same fears as their patients, namely, that they are putting their patients through an ordeal, and furthermore, that they themselves will be inadequate to the task: "I won't know what to do." Here too emotional pain, triggered by the patient's growing awareness of painful truths of his life, has to be fully borne. With therapists, as with patients, there is nothing like going through the full experience—and thereby benefiting from the activation of adaptive action tendencies— to help one overcome such fears. Watching other clinicians' videotapes is enormously helpful. Davanloo (1986–1988) referred to the process that takes place in the course of being exposed to affectively intense work—one's own and that of colleagues'—as "desensitizing the therapist's unconscious."

The healing that comes in the wake of mourning is profound. New capacities come to the fore, which often include a renewed thirst for life, wisdom, clarity, and new acceptance. The energy formerly drained by denial and avoidance of painful reality now can be harnessed into living, thereby increasing the patient's capacity for growth and experiencing emotions. As patients let go of hope founded on denial, they create emotional room for the experience of true hope and the possibility of genuine, fulfilling relationships. Post-grief healing includes acceptance, coming to terms with, letting go, and transcending.

In the following clinical vignette, the patient is living through a painful breakup with Charlie, a lover of several years, which he initiated. The patient had a long history of difficulty around separations, and he had been terrified to make this move; yet he did so. Prior to the following session, the patient had gone through a powerful mourning process, not shirking from any feeling, no matter how painful. The vignette is from a session right after the patient moved out.

PATIENT: I woke up on Monday and I was comforted by this thought ... "I have to find this out and we might be together again someday but this has to happen first. ... So let's go."

THERAPIST: Hmmm.

PATIENT: And I woke up on Monday and I said "Let's go" *(big full smile)*. And I've been checking with this feeling and asking, "Is it a defense?" And it isn't. It's just "Let's go."

THERAPIST: Let's go. ... That's wonderful.

(Later in the session)

THERAPIST: I am so taken with this "Let's go." It's very deep.

PATIENT: It feels very good.

THERAPIST: It comes from a very deep place. Deep happy place. *(happy voice)* It's really amazing.

PATIENT: I was walking down the street and I was thinking about all that I have gone through and leaving Charlie and I was thinking "I did it," I did it I did it. I separated from someone and I survived it, and it felt good *(pause)* ...

By being fully in touch with his grief about the loss and what it meant to him, by being able to tolerate his lover's distress without either pulling away or backing down from his position, the patient gained strength. The "Let's go" is a powerful phenomenon when it happens, and a clear instance of adaptive action tendencies coming to the fore. There is also a sense in "Let's go" that he's not alone, and that's also very important.

Facilitating the Mourning Process

As patients immerse themselves in understanding their history, defenses, and ways of coping, they inevitably must confront the many losses they have suffered. While losses due to uncontrollable events (e.g., the death of a parent) or inadequate caretaking experiences are very damaging, pathology resulting from adaptive efforts to cope with the primary losses leads to a second wave of losses: the patient's capacity to live a full, rich emotional life is compromised by chronic reliance on defenses. The therapist helps the patient acknowledge and experience the grief over both sets of losses. The therapist's use of her own grief and sadness for what the patient has had to endure facilitates and deepens the process: not alone this time, the patient now can bear these extremely painful experiences. The therapist's emotional involvement provides the supportive, holding environment that all cultures and religions recognize as crucial in assisting the mourner with the painful work of mourning, within which the seeds of healing reside.

As the end of treatment grows near, facing the constraints of the therapeutic relationship and the inevitable loss that's ahead can be a catalyst to grief. Patient and therapist must bear and share the pain, in the context of their relationship, of what can and cannot be. As together they struggle with the experience of the loss, the patient becomes more able to express it and bear it in other areas of his life. With this newfound ability comes a realistic appreciation for what they have been able to share.

RECEIVING AFFIRMATION AND THE HEALING AFFECTS

In this section, the concept of the *true other* as a counterpart to the true self will be introduced. Then the process of receiving affirmation will be explored in detail, and the phenomenology of the healing affects will be described.

The True Other

Winnicott's (1960) "true self," aside from its extraordinary importance as a construct for both patients and therapists, captures an essential quality of experience rarely encountered in pure form; nevertheless, it does exist experientially at those times we call peak moments. It is an experience-near construct and a deeply meaningful one for the experiencing self. The *true other* is the relational counterpart of the true self, and similarly describes a subjective experience: when one person can respond to another in just the right way, that person is experienced in that moment as true. The sense of the true other has experiential validity, and it is important to identify and validate the individual's experience.

Optimal functioning is characterized for the most part by the true-enough self, a mixture of true self with some defenses, either conscious (socially necessary) or unconscious (psychically necessary). There are moments of experience and self-realization, however, when we have pure true self experiences; these have been described variously as peak experiences, being in the zone, being in a state of flow, and so on. Similarly, in optimal case scenarios of the other's responsiveness, we have Winnicott's good-enough m/other. In the relational realm as well, there are peak moments in life when a particular other responds to one in such a way as to provide exactly what is needed, even when we were not aware of the need prior to its fulfillment; these are *peak relational moments*. The phenomenon refers to an essential responsiveness, a deep way of being known and understood, seen or helped, which is meaningful, attuned, appreciative, and enlivening.

Therapeutically, such moments are not something to strive for; they can only be genuinely spontaneous. Yet it is extremely important to be aware of the patient's experience of the other as true, for the therapeutic potential residing in such experiences is enormous: by being with a true other, the individual can more readily evoke and experientially connect with his true self.

It is important to localize the true other experience in the moment and not mistake it for a claim of perfection or any other thing that smacks of idealization. The true other has to do with responsiveness to need; it captures an experientially accurate assessment at a given moment in the particular emotional predicament. The true other is real, actual, deeply felt, unmistakable. Idealization would occur only if the patient went on to assume trueness as an invariant feature of the other—that is, assumed the other to be always-and-across-the-board true, rather than a human being with frailties and faults. Like its counterpart, true self experiencing, true other experiencing takes place in a state of deep affective contact; unlike idealization, it is contingent, not rigidly fixed.

A perfect example of how the sense of the true other captures an experientially accurate assessment that bears no relation to idealization occurs in the movie *Scent of a Woman*. Colonel Slade could not be a more frayed and contaminated individual. Narcissistic, arrogant, alcoholic, and abusive, his blindness, isolation, and alienation are the tragic consequences of a severe, lifelong character disorder. Charlie Simms, the other lead character, is a young prep school boy with an endearing mixture of innocence and integrity. A bond grows between the two, though Charlie has no illusions about Slade. There is a moment when Charlie faces a situation with a potentially disastrous outcome. At this precise moment Slade comes forward for Charlie, and does so very effectively. Deeply understanding what Charlie needs, he provides it: he is there, he is effective when it counts and completely counteracts Charlie's excruciating and poignant aloneness. In that moment, a lifetime of narcissistic pathology notwithstanding, Colonel Slade is a true other for Charlie Simms.

Receiving Affirmation

Less familiar than the mourning process, and certainly much less written about in the clinical literature, is the process of affirmation. In contradistinction to the process of mourning the self, being the recipient of affirmation involves processing the positive emotional consequences of *having* (as opposed to *not having*), and of having been (or being) in a relationship with a true other. The process of receiving affirmation is activated by and involves the experience of having an important aspect of one's self affirmed, recognized, understood, and appreciated. The affirmation can apply to recognition of one's achievements; it can underlie the other's actions toward the self; or it can involve a deep recognition of one's self-transformation. The source of the affirmation can be either one's self or the other.

Recognition of change for the much better is an essential aspect intrinsic to affirmation. A deep transformation occurs within the self as a consequence of being with another (a fortiori, with a true other); of being seen, loved, understood, empathized with, affirmed; of being able to do that which hitherto had been too frightening; of being in touch with the aspects of emotional experience that previously were feared to be beyond bearing; and so on. As a result of the transformation, one is closer to the true, essential self, the self one has always known oneself to be. As one patient put it: "thank you for giving me back the self I never had."

The response to receiving affirmation elicits a highly specific affective reaction that appears to have two aspects: feeling moved, touched, and strongly emotional, on one hand, and love, gratitude, and tenderness, on the other. There exists no word in the English language for this emotion, yet it appears to have all the features of a unified categorical emotion: a specific phenomenology (presumably with a distinct physiological profile), specific dynamics, occurrence of a state transformation, and adaptive action tendencies upon its being experienced. A marker for therapeutic experiences, the label *healing affects* seems apt; its elements are captured in the well-known hymn "Amazing Grace":

Amazing Grace
How sweet the sound
That saved a wretch like me
I once was lost, but now I'm found
Was blind, but now I see

Healing affects arise specifically in response to the realization that emotional suffering is being alleviated, to being seen or responded to as one has always wished, as well as to one's recognition of oneself in that moment as authentic and true. The healing affects register a welcome change: "I was blind, but now I see." This change is either witnessed and understood by the other, or reflects the impact of the other on the self.

The two types of healing affects differentiate two aspects of the affirmation process: what patients describe as feeling *moved, emotional,* or *touched* appear to be intimately involved with the process of self-transformation toward greater authenticity. The awareness of affirming receptive affective experiences gives rise to the second type of healing affects: love, gratitude, appreciation, and tenderness are feelings that arise specifically toward the affirming other.

The Phenomenology of Healing Affects

The physical, physiological manifestations of healing affects include a trembling, shaking voice associated with trying to contain emotion and hold back tears. The eyes are clear, light-filled, and usually moist. The gaze tends to be uplifted. There appear to be internal state changes related to gaze direction. It may be the case that gaze up and gaze down are linked to internal state transformations of an affective nature: gaze down seems to be a marker for grief and experiences of loss, while gaze up is a marker for healing affects and experiences of affirmation. The experiential correlate of the uplifted gaze often is a sense of something rising, a welling up, a surge, or feeling uplifted. Whichever words the individual uses, there is an upward direction to the sense experience.

The expression of feeling moved, touched, or emotional, as well as of love or gratitude, usually is accompanied by tears, though patients make it very clear that they are neither *primarily* sad nor *primarily* in pain; oftentimes they report feeling happy or joyful. When the reaction is mixed with sadness or emotional pain, the individual embraces and accepts the pain as one that is well worth feeling, without being frightened and trying to avoid it. Alerted to its existence by a Sesame Street episode, my daughter dubbed the phenomenon "happy crying" (Lubin-Fosha, 1991). Weiss (1952) has written about one aspect of this reaction, speaking of it as "crying at the happy ending" phenomenon. One patient came up with the phrase "truth tears." Eugene Gendlin (1991) captures the essence of these tears as a response to being touched at the core:

> Tears can be about life now, and not only when it is sad. A certain kind of tearfulness comes with the stirring of one's need for living *now*. There are also quiet, gentle tears. The deepest tears are not always uncontrollable sobbing. Very gentle tears can be deeper still. They can come when people are deeply touched, or when they touch a deep part of themselves. Tears can come when something new stirs, and comes alive for a moment. (P. 274)

The experience of change that emerges in the face of full self-expression and intense, validating relatedness has a particular quality. The healing affects possess simplicity, clarity, innocence, freshness, sweetness, and poignancy. The individual is in a state of openness and vulnerability, but a shimmering vulnerability without anxiety and without the need to be defended. There is also a sense of ease and relaxation. The mood (or primary affective state) surrounding healing affects can be either solemn, poignant, and tender, or else joyous and filled with wonder, often accompanied by a gentle, almost shy smile. William James referred to healing affects with characteristic eloquence and phenomenological precision as "the melting emotions and the tumultuous affections connected with the crisis of change" (James, 1902, p. 238). Overall, the quality of the healing affects is sweet, innocent, light, soft, melting. In "Amazing Grace" this quality is expressed in the musical phrase accompanying "how sweet the sound."

Contrast is an integral aspect of healing affects. Harold Brodkey (1996) wrote, "Perhaps you could say I did very little with my life, but the *douceur* ... was overwhelming. Painful and light-struck and wonderful" (p. 52). This is the joy experienced by someone who has known pain, the light experienced after years of darkness, the experience of feeling understood after having felt misunderstood. The following passages from Darwin (1872) and Homer, quoted by Darwin, speak of the tears of joy that gain their emotional charge by virtue of contrast with the emotional pain that preceded them.

> The feelings which are called tender are difficult to analyze; they seem to be compounded of affection, joy, and especially of sympathy. These feelings are in themselves of a pleasurable nature. ... They are remarkable under our present point of view from so readily exciting the secretion of

tears. Many a father and son have wept on meeting after a long separation, especially if the meeting has been unexpected. No doubt extreme
joy by itself tends to act on the lachrymal glands; but on such occasions
as the foregoing vague thoughts of grief which would have been felt had
the father and son never met, will probably have passed through their
minds; and grief naturally leads to the secretion of tears. Thus on return
of Ulysses, Telemachus:

"Rose, and clung weeping round his father's breast.
There the pent grief rained over them, yearning thus."

So again when Penelope at last recognized her husband:

"Then from her eyelids the quick tears did start
And she ran to him from her place, and threw
Her arms about his neck, and a warm dew
Of kisses poured upon him ..."
(Quoted in Darwin, 1872, pp. 214–17)

This is the essence of crying at the happy ending, of reunion triumph-
ing over the grim specter of loss and its attendant grief.

A similar sense is expressed in this next passage, where the contrast
is in terms of darkness and light. The metaphor of light is particularly
apt, given its connection to the uplifted gaze and the predominance of
photisms (light-seeing phenomena) James (1902) speaks about. Comparison and contrast also are to be found here, along with paradoxical
recognition with which new experiences are met: encountering for the
first time what one has always known.

> It seemed to him that he recognized the place in some way that he did
> not quite understand, as though it were a place he had been looking for
> without knowing it, like the perfect house one dwells in sometimes in
> dreams. *Standing in the dark at the border of light,* he felt an ache building
> inside him, a sweet, incomprehensible pain he yearned to hold to him, to
> probe, to understand, as if, grasping it, he might then become oblivious
> to pain, to loss, to death, to everything that might touch him save the
> occasional raindrop kiss. (Preston Girard, 1994, p. 240, italics added)

Heightened sensations and new perceptions define a sense of being
intensely alive. There is a "sense of clean and beautiful newness within
and without" (James, 1902, p. 248).

In the next two quotes, all the elements of the phenomenology of
the healing affects come together. Here is Casanova's description of
what he experienced after a narrow escape from the confinement of
prison and persecution:

> I then turned and looked at the entire length of the beautiful canal, and,
> not seeing a single boat, admired the most beautiful day one could hope

for, the first rays of a magnificent sun rising above the horizon, the two young boatmen rowing at full speed; and thinking at the same time of the cruel night I had spent, of the place where I had been the day before, and of all the coincidences favorable to me, I felt something take hold of my soul, which rose up to merciful God, exciting the wellsprings of gratitude, moving me with such extraordinary force that my tears rushed in an abundant stream to soothe my heart, choked with excessive joy; I sobbed and wept like a child. (Casanova, *Histoire de ma vie*, in Flem, 1997, pp. 66–67)

The elements we have been describing are all here: the contrast between narrowly avoided tragedy and currently joyful circumstances; the sense of a new state taking hold; the upward surge and heightened sensations and perceptions; the healing affects, first the experience of being moved, then "happy crying," weeping tears of "excessive joy"; and the feeling of gratitude toward the affirming, deeply holding other, in this case, "merciful God."

Now from a patient, a man in his thirties. Lately, he had mastered the fear and self-loathing associated with traumatic memories of being scapegoated, ganged-up on, and threatened by a bunch of his school-mates. Some weeks prior to his writing the note quoted in the follow-ing, as the patient remembered and relived the torment and terror of those times, he also recovered a memory of a place of safety: he recol-lected sitting under the shade of one particular tree and finding soul-soothing solace there. The feel of the tree trunk against his back, the cool air, and the welcome solitude all made him feel peaceful and grounded. On a recent visit home, he went to the school yard. To his surprise, there was no fear in his chest or nausea: the school yard, the site of childhood dreads, seemed so small. A couple of sessions later, he spoke about how anxiety-free and self-confident he had been feeling. He mentioned that the previous evening, as he was "just hangin' around" at home, he felt the impulse to write, and did so (an unusual occurrence). Moved and pleased by what had come out of him, he brought me what he had written and gave me his permission to include it here:

When I remember me as a little kid, a smile comes across my face, it starts down somewhere around that belly button space. It starts first as a thought, then there's a moment where it's caught in a white noise, silent place. Then, like it came, the silence breaks and it rushes up through my chest, my head and then falls into place. It is what's defined, as I said, you know, a smile. It comes to my face. The thought brings joy and feelings stir. A warmth crosses my skin, a feeling so large and present and yet, you could never see a thing. Love hits this way, peaceful and soft and *Right*. It

gives me a certain courage that strengthens a Dimming light. I sit and in
an instant, a tear is in my eye, the stinging kind, not the sad tears when
I really sit and cry. It's all a bit confusing, and I am left woundering *(sic)*
why a smile, a loving thought, then an emotion, should Bring a tear to
my eyes. Then I think, one step deeper, and just one second will pass.
I think of me as a little boy once again, and happiness at last.

Here too the phenomenology of healing affects is unmistakable: the
context of happiness at the site of past torment; the sense of the experience coming, unbeckoned, rather than sought or willed; the intense
sensations, including the upward surge ("the silence breaks and it rushes
up through my chest, my head") and the sensation of warmth; the tears
of being moved, differentiated from sad tears; the feeling of love; the
gentle yet certain quality of feeling "peaceful and soft and *Right*"; the
sense of an even deeper state transformation following the one in
which the healing affects occurred ("one step deeper"); and finally, the
next wave of positive experiences that follow the experience of healing
affects: along with "a certain courage that strengthens a Dimming light,"
the patient, going "one step deeper," experiences "happiness at last."

Reaping the Benefits
of Meta-Therapeutic Processing

It is important to describe the dynamics of the process of receiving
affirmation and the phenomenology of healing affects to alert the
therapist to what is happening in the therapeutic process—which is
that it is going well. It also tells the therapist that in this moment, in
this configuration, she is different from past figures who had starring
roles in the development of the patient's difficulties. This is especially
important for psychodynamic therapists who have a low threshold for
perceiving repetition of the bad-and-old and a high threshold for perceiving the good-and-new. It is essential, for instance, that "happy
crying" or "truth tears" not be confused with sad tears. Since the tinge
of the negative state is always there in contrast, the patient may go
easily to the negative state or emotional pain, if the therapist so guides
the process—but then a valuable opportunity is missed, for the full
exploration of meta-therapeutic processes provides additional therapeutic opportunities.

Meta-therapeutic processes ultimately involve tolerating and
acknowledging experiences of having (as opposed to deprivation) and
being in affect-facilitating rather than affect-hostile relationships. The

individual has to tolerate, acknowledge, process, and take in good stuff such as love, appreciation, understanding, and recognition. By virtue of feeling new and unfamiliar, good things can be scary, causing patients to feel helpless or inadequate; "What do I do now?" is a common refrain among patients who feel vulnerable and out of control in face of the unknown. Patients often feel an urge to retreat into painful, self-destructive but familiar modes of nonbeing and nonexperiencing. When this happens, another round of work is activated, fostering further working through.

Another difficulty is that positive experiences are often linked with painful ones; *having* only highlights the painful starkness of *not having*. To experience the positive is to risk being immersed in painful feelings. Patients rely on their defenses to prevent the experience of both. Other fears of experiencing and fully owning positive experiences include the fear of making oneself vulnerable to loss, which becomes even more unbearable in light of the realization of how good good can be. Issues of guilt and unworthiness also often require more rounds of working through before the affirming process can fully proceed.

By acknowledging and owning healthy functioning, resources, and emotional capacities, patients gain access to solidly based self-confidence in being able to handle emotional situations, and even score an occasional triumph in the face of emotional adversity, without fear of being overwhelmed. They grow confident that they can participate in creating positive relational experiences, and that they can readily identify such situations when they arise. Confidence in one's abilities and belief in the possibility of meaningful, mutually satisfying relating are important underpinnings of interpersonal relating. The healing affects themselves promote trust, hope, and confidence that goodness is possible. The dynamic task here is giving up defensive self-reliance and opening oneself up to experiencing the enormous positive impact that others can have. In giving up defensive self-reliance, the patient not only can reap the benefits of connection and relatedness, but paradoxically, by acknowledging the impact of the other on the self, emerge strengthened and energized.

By alternating experiencing and reflection (i.e., alternating feeling and talking), patients can take ownership of the process of transformation. As one patient said, by both experiencing it and speaking about it, "one begins to know the process of being healed, to believe in it, not just as a temporary aberration, or a fragile moment, but as an owned aspect of experience, as something one can do."

Resistance to Receiving Affirmation

A major factor for the relative dearth of clinical attention given to meta-therapeutic processes is most likely the discomfort this work evokes in therapists. Better trained in processing negative reactions toward us, we squirm when recognized, appreciated, and loved. Here the patient's defenses are not the main culprit, for healing affects occur when patients' defenses are in abeyance; rather, the problem lies with our discomfort. Therapists seem to be at a loss as to how to deal with positive patient responses, such as love and gratitude for being good at helping them change and feel better; often we use modesty—even false modesty—to cover up personal difficulties with being thanked for doing exactly what we most value. Psychodynamic practitioners, well-versed in investigating the depths of the patient-therapist relationship, are more comfortable focusing on and working through negative experiences, frustrations, and disappointments.

> Development in psychoanalytic theory is always described as a process in which, at each stage, the child is encouraged to relinquish something with no guarantee that what he or she is going to get instead will be better. *This is a hard school and we might wonder what it is in us that is drawn to stories of renunciation, to ideologies of deprivation,* whether they are called the symbolic, the depressive position, or Freud's description of the resolution of the Oedipus complex. (Phillips, 1997, p. 744, italics added)

Patients' difficulties too in receiving love and experiencing empathy are not as well understood by clinicians as difficulties resulting from being deprived of love and recognition. This is in part an artifact of the neutral stance of traditional therapists. Difficulties accepting and receiving love—much as it is craved when it is not available—more readily come into view with a therapist who can initiate a loving exchange than with a withholding therapist (Coen, 1996). Similarly, difficulties in owning emotional competence, resourcefulness, and resulting pride become evident more rapidly and pointedly when the focus is more on the patient's strengths than on his pathology.

Gratitude, for instance, often arises in the course of a successful therapy; its importance lies in its being the patient's emotional acknowledgment of being helped by treatment. Taking in such deep appreciation can make the therapist feel vulnerable: insecurities about personal worth or competence, fears of loss or humiliation, feelings of being overwhelmed or at a loss as to how to deal with something yearned for are some of the more common disturbing responses stirred in us. Faced with earnest acknowledgment, our defenses kick up. False modesty, minimizing the magnitude of our contribution, a low threshold for inferring negative motives and a high threshold for positive ones interfere with meta-therapeutic processing. Aside from being a lost opportunity for growth for the therapist, it is an even greater loss for the patient.

In working through the meta-therapeutic processes and the affects of transformation, it is necessary to focus on and explore positive therapeutic experiences as thoroughly and systematically as in the case of negative experiences. It is equally important for therapists to develop competence in this area: we need to learn to tolerate being the focus of the patient's positive feeling and avoid modesty as a defense.

AFFIRMATION AND THE HEALING AFFECTS AT WORK

The clinical vignette that follows zooms in on a therapeutic moment when the process of receiving affirmation and the healing affects are in full view. Once these core affects emerge, they are privileged, focused on, enlarged, and explored with the same thoroughness and intensity as any other core affective experience.

The patient is a thirty-year-old single woman who, despite a history of severe depressions, had never before sought treatment. She felt "stuck and stagnant" in her work and in her personal life. The crisis that led her to enter therapy, despite major reservations, culminated in her bursting into sobs at work and not being able to stop crying. The patient entered therapy feeling somewhat hopeless and extremely helpless. She felt humiliated by having "fallen apart," by needing help, and by not being able to resolve her problems on her own.

The following clinical vignette comes from the last fifteen minutes of a two-hour initial evaluation. Much of the work preceding the vignette focused on the patient's self-reliant defenses and exposing their consequences, that is, their having led to her emotional isolation and loneliness. Throughout, the understanding of the patient's defenses, as well as all other clinical material, was framed within an adaptive–empathic perspective, emphasizing how they reflected the patient's best efforts to take care of herself. Both in her account of her current and past life, and in exploring the phenomena of the evolving patient–therapist relationship, the patient's strengths were noted and affirmed, as were her therapeutic efforts on her own behalf. The therapist was empathic, expressive, and supportive of the patient, emotionally self-disclosing, and highly encouraging of the patient's affective and relational experiencing. As a result, resistance was relatively low; despite the patient's characterological tendencies toward mistrust and self-reliance, much emotional work was accomplished in a warm, mutual atmosphere. (See Mann & Goldman, 1982, on how in-depth explorations from a stance of empathic attunement to the patient's pain do not elicit resistance but rather foster patient openness, trust, and the welcome experience that the therapist is "beside and inside" the patient.)

PATIENT: **And I also always thought like "alright I could do it by myself. I don't need anybody. I don't need anybody's help." That's always been my thing "Don't help me, I can do it." And that's why in the past even though I thought "OK, maybe I should talk to somebody, a therapist or somebody," another thought would come "No, I don't need to, I don't have to."** [patient is openly describing self-reliant defenses; high therapeutic alliance in operation]

THERAPIST: **See, I was realizing that I focused a lot on how hard it is for you to stay close to your feelings. But** *(speech slows down here)* **I am also so struck how open you've been with me. And so direct.** [affirmation of patient's therapeutic efforts on her own behalf]

PATIENT: *(nods head, swallowing hard)* [beginning of experience of feeling moved]

THERAPIST: **And I appreciate it all the more because I'm learning more and more what it takes for you to do that. That it's not just your reflex.** *(snaps fingers)* **to do that** [more recognition]

PATIENT: *(voice shaking a bit, some tears)* **Right. ... Yeah. Definitely I wouldn't say that it's in my nature, to just, like, tell people things ...** [more affect]

THERAPIST: **You have a feeling about my recognizing this about you?** [in response to incipient healing affects, meta-therapeutic inquiry: making affirmation explicit and inquiring about patient's experience of it]

PATIENT: **Do I have a feeling about it?** *(swallows hard)* **Ummm ... I feel that ... well, I'm glad, I mean** *(smiling broadly and shyly)*

THERAPIST: *(very sympathetic tone)* **Uh huh.**

PATIENT: **I'm definitely glad you can see it** *(rueful, soft laughing).*

THERAPIST: *(empathic, nonverbal affective resonance)* **Mmmmmm.**

PATIENT: I don't know what else I feel ... I kind of feel like, uh, ... relieved *(moved, voice starting to shake, talking through tears)* in a way, you know like, wow, maybe, like I'm glad that you can understand what I'm trying to tell you. [healing affects in response to feeling understood]

THERAPIST: Tell me what that sense of relief feels like. ... Once again, you start to talk and it touched something deep. [eliciting deeper experiencing of healing affect, through inquiry and empathic mirroring and labeling]

PATIENT: Hmmm, let's see.

THERAPIST: *(empathic, nonverbal affective resonance)* **Mmmmm.**

PATIENT: I'm trying to like ...

THERAPIST: Don't try, just tell me. [bypassing tactical defense]

PATIENT: OK, I don't know if I can ... I don't know

THERAPIST: It's alright.

PATIENT: Ummmm. ... It does feel good to like be able to you know get it off my chest, like ...

THERAPIST: *(deeply empathic tone)* You've been carrying so much, so much ...

PATIENT: But like you know, I think that I have ... I think. ... When I called you last week I think that's what I was feeling too, like *(emphatic, determined, feelingful tone, crackling with withheld tears)* "yeah, you know what? Like, *it's time,*" you know. *(her voice breaking, starts to cry)* [takes in and owns empathic acknowledgment of her psychic suffering; deepening of healing affects: affirms validity of her own needs]

THERAPIST: *(feelingful, emphatic, and tender)* It's time *for you.*

PATIENT: *(shakes her head in affirmation, cries; gaze down, voice breaking, sobs for a while)* ... I do feel like. ... Yeah, like I do really like push down a lot. And I feel like "No, OK *(vigorous arm motions with hands in fists of pushing down)*, I'm just gonna go, I can deal with that, I can just move on," but maybe I don't allow myself to kind of, I don't know, "indulge" myself. ... I don't know if that's the right word, but. ... Maybe like ... feeling like ... not so much that I come last, but maybe that I'm the last one I want to deal with or something. [emotional pain, mourning the self; detailed, specific description of her defenses and felt sense of their negative consequences; starts to make emotional space for basic needs and yearnings, the very experiences she customarily defends against]

THERAPIST: Like you feel that you can take it.

PATIENT: Yeah, like I feel that I can take it.

THERAPIST: What about this sense that you're the last one that you want to deal with?

PATIENT: Yeah, like I think maybe that's it. I think I was kind of like afraid to really see ... you know ... like what is behind ... my persona, that people see me as, like at work. People see me as a certain way. And like ...

THERAPIST: What else is there?

PATIENT: Yeah. Like, I don't know, I was afraid to deal with what was inside. Like it's unknown, like "Oh, oh, it could be too scary, I don't know if I want to do it, so let's just pretend like I don't have a problem or that I can deal with it or that it will go away, or it'll get better somehow" or whatever, even though I don't know how it will, but somehow it will, you know. Or maybe "OK, really, I don't want to deal with it now, I'll deal with it some other time." *(voice very moved)* But I think like now, it *is* the other time. *(shakes head affirmatively)* [deeper description of defenses leads to a deepening of the material and patient articulates her fears; with deepening affect, she spontaneously affirms and validates the "rightness" of seeking help]

THERAPIST: Yes.

PATIENT: Because I feel like I can't really move on, like I feel really stuck and stagnant. And even though I've felt stuck for a really long time, now this whole thing [crisis that brought her to treatment], like this is the thing that's like pushed me to do it. Because of this situation, it is forcing me to do it, which is a really good thing. ... Like it took this to do it. [patient clearly and without ambivalence declares her motivation for treatment]

THERAPIST: To shake things up.

PATIENT: Yeah. Like I just felt that I know something's gonna happen, I don't know what, it's going to be scary, it ...

THERAPIST: It has to do with *you* and *growth* ... [affirmation]

PATIENT: *(moved)* Yeah. Yeah. [receptive experience; healing affect]

THERAPIST: And taking care of something.

PATIENT: Yeah. *(Light giggle).* That's what's been happening. [end of one wave of work]

THERAPIST: What's it been like to talk together, for you to talk to me? You have sense of me? [Therapist-initiated transition: the end of one wave of work having come to a satisfying resting point, the therapist makes the decision to elicit patient's relational experience of the therapist and of the patient–therapist connection; this work is particularly important for a patient who uses defensive self-reliance; she has just allowed herself to get help from someone, it has worked, and it is important for her to register and experientially process that this is so; regardless of whether this line of inquiry evokes defenses or core affects, this is a significant opportunity; thus, the beginning of relational meta-therapeutic processing]

PATIENT: I guess it's felt like I've wanted to let you know where I'm coming from and maybe in talking to you like ... Do you feel like it's something that I can ... maybe because of your experience, do you think that we can work together? Is there a way ... to help? Or something? [bare, vulnerable, undefended expression of her yearning to be helped, despite her fears; a long way from defensive self-reliance]

THERAPIST: Ohh *(very tender, somewhat surprised tone, touched)*, I feel I can say a lot more than that, you know. That I really have a lot of feeling for you, and what you're telling me and for what you're going through. And that you've been able to be so open with me, it's ... very touching to me, actually. [patient's vulnerability elicits tenderness in therapist, who starts to respond directly to patient's bare statement of need through more affirmation of the patient and affective self-disclosure of her own healing affects evoked by patient]

PATIENT: *(feeling touched; mouth quivering)* [receptive experience; healing affects]

THERAPIST: There's something about that, about how you've been with me ... that I appreciate. [more self-disclosure of therapist's experience of patient and her own healing affects in response to patient]

PATIENT: *(feeling moved)* Uh huh. ... I feel like it's been easy to talk to you.

THERAPIST: *(appreciative)* Mmmmmm.

PATIENT: Like, you really, you've listened to me. You've really ... Like ... like ... OK ... like I was going to say, like even when I talked to you on the phone.

THERAPIST: Uh huh.

PATIENT: Uh, there's something about like ... your tone *(moved, holding back tears)* in your voice that like, it feels good, you know ... it feels like warm ... and kind of like, I don't know, embracing or something. ... So like I feel that I can kind of like talk to you and I can kind of just ... *(soft crying, gentle smile)* like cry ... if I want to ... you know. [patient articulates her experience of being affirmed and accompanying healing affects; breakthrough of experience and expression of yearnings for relational contact]

THERAPIST: *(tender tone)* Mmmmmm.

PATIENT: So that's kind of like the feeling that I get, you know ... like uh, *(crying softly)* you know, concern, something like that. [acknowledging concern; healing affects]

THERAPIST: *(warm voice)* Where are these tears coming from?

PATIENT: mmmm I don't know *(holding back bigger crying)*.

THERAPIST: *(very tender)* Mmmm.

PATIENT: I just feel that ... *(very definite gaze up, eyes uplifted)* like I feel that I wanna be ... uh, able to just like relax and, you know that feeling ... of just being able to, kind of if you wanted to ... to be embraced and feel like ... warm and feel safe, you know, and I guess maybe that's maybe some of the feelings that I feel like that makes me wanna ... cry, you know ... 'cause I feel like I want to be not so strong all the time, that I just wanna be able to let it all out, *(vulnerable)* to ... [further breakthrough of experience and expression of yearnings for relational contact and of healing affects (note the gaze up)]

THERAPIST: ... to let go.

PATIENT: Yeah, like let go and just kinda like feel comfortable enough to do that. ... Kinda like falling back and havin' somebody to catch ya, you know, being able to do that. I feel like ... I keep having this image in my mind of like ... you know that experiment where, you know, where two people stand up and you have to let yourself fall back ...

THERAPIST: ... without putting your hands down to

PATIENT: ... yeah, and having somebody catch you, I've always wanted to do that and I don't think that ... I don't think I can or I haven't been able to. ... [continued elaboration of core affect: experience and expression of yearnings for relational contact, accompanied by healing affects]

THERAPIST: Mmmmm.

PATIENT: So when I talk to you I kinda feel like maybe I am on the way to being able to do that ... or something *(blows nose; calm now, peaceful)*. [end of another wave of affective work; state transformation and experience of new phenomena in the wake of taking in affirmation and the experience of healing affects: trust, hope, relaxation]

THERAPIST: *(moved)* That's such a deep thing to say to me ... I really, I mean ...

PATIENT: *(laughs softly and girlishly, a little shy, with evident pleasure)*

THERAPIST: Uh, thank you. Thank you. [acknowledgment of patient's impact on therapist through declaration of therapist's gratitude toward patient]

PATIENT: *(a bit shy, pleased, open)* So that's kind of like the best way I can describe the feeling.

THERAPIST: Oh, it's very eloquent. It's very eloquent. You know, and I think that's what makes me feel hopeful, very hopeful about our working together. I think it's a sense of connection, you know, I mean you've just expressed it to me in a very deep way, and I have felt it as well with you. And I think that there's something about your trust, and again, trust, particularly when trust doesn't come easy. ... [using evidence of the meta-therapeutic experiences and accompanying affects they just shared, as well as her growing understanding of patient resulting from the patient's increasing openness and expressiveness, therapist addresses the patient's question and expresses her own hope and confidence in their capacity to do good therapeutic work together]

PATIENT: **Yeah.**

THERAPIST: **... that's very meaningful.**

SUMMARY

Through meta-therapeutic processing, that is, through acknowledging and owning the resources and emotional capacities involved in their therapeutic successes, patients gain access to solidly based self-confidence in handling emotional situations, and even in scoring occasional triumphs in the face of emotional adversity, without fear of being overwhelmed. There also accrues a growing confidence in being able to make use of, as well as actively participate in the creating of, positive relational experiences. Here are laid the foundations underlying the sense of confidence in one's effectiveness (the opposite of helplessness) and the belief in the possibility of meaningful, mutually satisfying relating, a very important underpinning of the capacity for trust, intimacy, and closeness (the opposite of hopelessness). Furthermore, the very experience of healing affects brings in its wake trust, hope, ease, clarity, empathy, and self-empathy, as well as the ability to risk believing that goodness is possible and that the self can be resilient when optimal conditions do not obtain.

CHAPTER 9

YOU DON'T LOVE ME ANYMORE

A Case Illustrating the Collaborative Construction of the Psychodynamic Formulation

USING THE THREE TRIANGLES TO TRANSLATE PSYCHODYNAMIC UNDERSTANDING INTO CLINICAL ACTION

From the first moment of the patient's telling his story—or not telling it, for that matter—the therapist has access to two potent sources of dynamic information: the content of the story, manifest and latent, and the interactive process between herself and the patient. Taking whatever the patient offers, the therapist uses it as the starting point of a dynamic interaction. The schema of the three triangles helps the clinician remain oriented in the thicket of clinical material. She can categorize emerging clinical material as defense, signal affect, or genuine emotional experience and then aim specific interventions at that phenomenon. The therapist also can see the different defense, signal affect and core affect constellations that underlie particular self states and self-other patterns. Finally, she can explore "the genetic and adaptive relevance" of these patterns (Mann & Goldman, 1982): where they arose, other situations in which they operate, and—a particular emphasis in AEDP—those in which they do not. The moment-to-moment translation of patient material into the categories of the triangle of conflict is equally useful for rapid assessment of the impact of a given intervention (e.g., Did it make the patient more or less defensive? Did it lead to greater or lesser emotional openness and spontaneity?) and in using that assessment to guide the choice of the next intervention. Each response is the patient's on-the-spot supervision of the therapist as well: if she can accept this immediate feedback, the therapist will be able to alter course when necessary, increasing effectiveness.

Any specific emotional experience (one whose intrapsychic structuring is represented by a particular triangle of conflict) leads to a specific version of self, other, and self-other interaction. Any of these elements can trigger a particular configuration of the triangle of comparisons, linking it with others like it across time. Thus we arrive at a deep understanding of the patient's dynamics, his way of being in the world intrapsychically (triangle of conflict), relationally (self–other–emotion schema) and historically (triangle of comparisons).

In a thorough review of short-term dynamic psychotherapies, Barber and Crits-Cristoph (1991) state, "one of the important tasks for any dynamic therapist, but especially important for therapists involved in brief treatment, is to infer the link between the patient's presenting symptoms and the core conflicts" (p. 338). Translating rich and complex clinical material into the categories of the three representational schemas helps systematize the linking of symptoms, core conflicts, and transference phenomena. Moreover, clinical use of this set of constructs is eminently teachable and can provide the "articulated heuristics" advocated by Barber and Crits-Cristoph (1991, p. 338).

THE PSYCHODYNAMIC FORMULATION: FROM SYMPTOMS AND MOMENT–TO–MOMENT SHIFTS TO CORE ISSUES

A psychodynamic formulation is the affect-based organization to be found in the stories our patients tell us (McCullough Vaillant, 1997). Right off the bat, in the initial complaint and the dynamics of the example the patient chooses to illustrate it, as well as in the dynamics of the patient-therapist interaction, there is abundant psychodynamic information, already organized to some degree as the therapist's listening is guided by the three schematic representations.

We always begin with the present situation. "The precipitating event is, in truth, the final blow that simply cannot be tolerated" (Mann & Goldman, 1982, p. 24). By following the patient's pain, it is possible to see how it links present and past, and how it becomes manifest in the evolving patient-therapist relationship. The relationship with the therapist evokes intense feelings: from the first minutes of the first session, the therapist declares that she wishes to relate to the patient. By focusing on the patient's feelings, asking for specifics, and responding empathically and emotionally to the patient, the therapist activates the patient's complex feelings about intimacy and closeness.

In the presenting complaint and the specific example are the patient's response to the therapist's first and second questions, "What brings you here now?" followed by "Can you give me a specific example?" The presenting complaint represents a "final common pathway" (Mann & Goldman, 1982, p. 20) of core conflicts, anxieties they elicit, defenses deployed, and consequences of those defenses. The request for a specific example announces the departure from vagueness: the work of therapy has begun. The emotionally charged atmosphere of the first minutes of the first session offers tremendous opportunities as the first set of dynamics that underlie the suffering the patient is seeking to remedy is exposed.

That the first session presents a unique opportunity is recognized by many STDP therapists (e.g., Coughlin Della Selva, 1996; Davanloo, 1990; Magnavita, 1997; Malan, 1976, 1979; Mann & Goldman, 1982; McCullough Vaillant, 1997). Gustafson (1986) goes so far as to speak about the "sacred nature of the first session" and how important it is to focus on what brought the patient to treatment. If the precipitating event is a "common pathway," hope and dread inspired by the encounter with the therapist shape the dyadic interaction, making their encounter the second common pathway.

The greater the crisis, the greater the opportunity. Affective charge creates an intrapsychic crisis and therefore fluidity (Lindemann, 1944); the result is an unmatched opportunity to get past the patient's customary defenses. During such a crisis, the patient's customary ways of handling intense feelings becomes evident, as does his ability to respond differently as the therapist engages him in new ways of relating.

In this first session, patient and therapist, as members of a brand-new dyad, are creating their own unique patterns. As both bring best and worst configurations, much is possible and nothing is yet determined. Such a fortuitous chance for creation might never arise again in the course of their relationship. Another source of dynamic information present in this first session, as throughout the therapy, is the moment-to-moment therapeutic process. Making interventions and observing their impact is a form of hypothesis testing.

The following are some questions for the therapist to ask herself during the initial interview.

▼ Has contact been made? If the therapist thinks so, does the patient? If the patient thinks so, does the therapist?

▼ What are areas of defensiveness, and areas of ease? What are areas of difficulty in the patient's life, and areas of pleasure?

▼ What defenses does the patient use, and what resources are available?

▼ What makes the session flow? What makes the session get stuck?

▼ How does the patient respond to empathy, validation and support, and confrontation?

▼ How does the patient respond to his own emotionality, or to his lack thereof?

▼ What are the patterns of relational repetition, and what kinds of environments trigger them? What are the exceptions?

▼ What feelings are difficult for the patient, and what feelings not so hard? Can the patient experience, for example, sadness but not anger, or anger but not vulnerability? Are positive feelings more difficult than negative feelings (or vice versa)? Are all feelings difficult?

▼ How does the patient handle negative feelings such as anger, pain, and disgust?

▼ How does the patient handle positive feelings such as joy, love, pleasure, and tenderness?

▼ Can the patient tolerate negative aspects of the session, that is, areas of stuckness, disagreement, confrontation, or disappointment?

▼ Can the patient tolerate positive aspects of the therapeutic interaction, that is, empathy, collaboration, and hope?

▼ What brings out the best in the patient? What is he like at his best?

▼ What brings out the worst in the patient? What is he like at his worst?

The AEDP process tracks affect and relatedness: we track the pain associated with the patient's suffering; but we also follow the patient's joy and relief when pathogenic expectations are disconfirmed and hope for creative solutions in living seems warranted. Each response to an intervention results in opening or closing, in flattening or deepening of rapport, or in fostering or blocking unconscious communication, *and does so for a dynamically coherent, meaningful reason.* The weaving of those reasons together produces the psychodynamic formulation, our affect-based account of what makes the patient tick, and why. More specifically, what we aim for is to get to the core affect at the bottom of the main triangle of conflict—the assumption being that its defensive suppression accounts for the presenting symptoms and difficulties—and that by getting to the genetic past (the P corner of the triangle of comparisons), we will understand why that core affect was so troublesome for the patient that it necessitated defensive reliance. We might even be able to understand the patient's reliance on specific defenses by seeing in action his identification with pathogenic agents of the past and his internalization of them, reflected in his way of dealing with himself (Malan, 1976).

The first interview has several purposes: to establish contact with the patient; to learn the story of what brings the patient to treatment; and to uncover the way in which the patient's seemingly excessive or incomprehensible reactions make complete sense. The most important goal for the first session, however, is that whatever else may happen, the patient should have a therapeutic experience.

While the focus of this chapter is on the infrastructure of the treatment, the clinical process has one overarching aim: to relieve the patient's suffering and free up emotional resources. The emotional pain and the patient's wish to be rid of it are the therapy's greatest allies.

CASE ILLUSTRATION:
THE AMATEUR BOXER

The interview that follows is far from perfect; to the contrary, it is full of errors. Yet errors present opportunities for correction, and patients are forgiving: ultimately eager to get to what matters, they give us many chances. Despite wrong turns, by the end of the first two-hour evaluation, patient and therapist get to where they need to be. What follows illustrates one way to get from presenting symptoms to core conflicts and back through the dynamic formulation.

Presenting Symptoms, Precipitating Event:
The First Question

The patient came to treatment with a relatively common precipitant: "the blues" following the breakup of a relationship. It becomes apparent within the first fifteen minutes of the interview, however, that the current blues sit atop a more long-standing despair, of suicidal proportions.

THERAPIST: **Can you tell me what led to your coming to see me now?**

PATIENT: **Gosh. ... Hmm ... I've been having a hard time lately** *(breathing heavily, exhaling forcefully).* **... I'm trying to calm down a little bit. ... I'm at the end of a three-year relationship and it really hurts** *(starts crying, trying to control it, can't talk, trying to talk through tears).*

THERAPIST: **Let yourself be, let your feelings come, don't fight them, hmm?** [focus on experience, encouragement]

PATIENT: **Yeah.** *(takes deep breaths)*

THERAPIST: **You're struggling with something very painful.** [mirroring, validating]

PATIENT: **Yep. ... The same thing happened when I went to see Dr. X** [whom he saw for a consultation]. **As soon as I started talking, I started crying. I think it's 'cause I usually put it away, so when I take it out it hurts.** [patient declares himself to be a psychological person, aware of his defenses and able to be conversant with his emotional patterns. Therapist appreciates efforts, and encourages him to stay with his feelings]

THERAPIST: **Uh huh.**

PATIENT: **OK. ... So a three-year relationship just ended only a couple of weeks ago. Very difficult but I'm kind of getting used to it** *(starting to tear again).*

THERAPIST: **Tell me just what's inside.** [focus on experience, rather than events]

PATIENT: **Hmm. ... Well, I feel really tight. Right here** *(taps his chest).* **... It's very strange.**

THERAPIST: **Uh huh. ... In your chest?** [mirroring physical concomitants of experience]

PATIENT: **Yeah! ... A lot of tension.**

THERAPIST: **You're holding a lot of stuff in?**

PATIENT: **I think so, but I don't quite know what it is. ... That's one of the reasons why I am here. ... To work through it and talk it over ... I don't really get a chance to talk with people.** [here is an early unconscious communication that there is more there than he is aware of. Patient declares himself to have high ego adaptive capacity: his coming to treatment is evidence of his hope and belief that he can get to the other side of this. There are a lot of green lights to proceed even in face of the enormous pain and massive anxiety and tension he is struggling to contain. Yet he also is communicating that he is quite emotionally isolated: "I don't really get a chance to talk with people."]

THERAPIST: **Yeah ... So you're dealing with a lot of this totally on your own.** [mirroring, amplifying theme of aloneness in face of intense feelings]

PATIENT: *(nods head)*

THERAPIST: **It's hard.** *(very compassionate tone)*

PATIENT: **Yeah** *(sobs for the first time for a few seconds* [mini breakthrough], *then swallows tears* [mini defense] *and catches breath).* **... So, I guess, let me give you a little bit of history. I've been living with this woman Wanda for three years. About four months ago, we started having problems. These problems, I don't really understand them. About two months ago, uh, it kind of came to a head and she moved out. ... Then two weeks ago, she told me she wanted to totally break it off. ... It didn't work out** *(trying to choke back tears)* **and it hurts. 'Cuz I thought that she was the one** *(grimacing in pain).* **...** *(deep breath)* **So basically for the last two months, I've really had the blues. And I don't know if this is a reasonable response to everything that's going on but ...**

Note that the first affective mini breakthrough of emotional pain follows an instance of compassion; after the mini breakthrough, for the first time in the interview he is able to talk. It's important to him, he needs to catch his breath, literally and figuratively, and the therapist appreciates having the information. The momentary defense against affect is quite functional here; less than five minutes have elapsed since the beginning of the interview and the affect is not going to vanish. Last but not least, we find evidence of strengths: he is as open and communicative as he can be, and he is trying hard. It is likely that the crisis has made his defenses more fluid (Lindemann, 1944), and so he probably has somewhat more affective access than usual. That only works in our favor.

Within the first few minutes of the initial interview, two basic issues arise, which the psychodynamic formulation should be able to address:

1. Why is the loss the patient has experienced so resonant (and with what does it resonate) that it is beyond his capacity to absorb?

2. Why has he needed the defenses that are having such disastrous consequences?

Dynamics Revealed by Specific Example: The Second Question

PATIENT: *(Deep sighing)* ... I have a hard time dealing with uh ... There's like a conflict between emotion and intellect. And I have been wrestling with that for the last couple of months. [patient very aware of his dynamics; defenses are ego-dystonic]

THERAPIST: What do your emotions say? [attempt to privilege emotion]

PATIENT: I don't understand them well enough to know. [more defense]

THERAPIST: Yeah. ... But there is pain and loss and ... [second attempt to bypass defenses]

PATIENT: Yeah, pain and loss *(starts crying again)* and loneliness and ... anger. *(deep sigh, wipes his eyes)* ... I came today hoping to know what's going on. ... Well, I don't *(shakes his head)*. [deepening of communication; puts on the table issue of anger and emotional isolation; declares how important is his need to understand: very important not to dismiss this as intellectual defense only]

THERAPIST: Well, what I would like us to do is to make some room for these feelings that you are struggling with so mightily and let them come out and share them with me and don't fight so hard to keep them in *(patient is nodding head vigorously as I am speaking)* and let's see what sense we can make of what you're going through and where this deep-seated struggle is really coming from beyond what you know about it already ... [setting up for collaborative work with patient by making explicit some therapeutic agendas, such as focus on emotion and affective sharing; communication to patient that he is not alone; mirroring patient's awareness of deep-seated issues affecting current experience]

PATIENT: Okay.

THERAPIST: We'll get to the intellect too *(long pause, patient nodding his head and looking expectantly, with a clear gaze and momentary calm)*. ... Now you said there is this terrible feeling of tightness in your chest. [expressing understanding of patient's need to make sense of his experience; check on anxiety before proceeding]

PATIENT: *(fighting back tears again)* It comes and goes. ... That's something that is really confusing. The fact is that most of the time I am really positive

THERAPIST: Uh huh.

PATIENT: ... and outgoing and relaxed and confident and with it, and other times I'm just sulky and depressed, it's very strange. [patient's communication about two modes of functioning noted]

THERAPIST: And the last couple of months, you've been ...

PATIENT: **Yeah, much more. ... I take things too seriously, kind of obsessing on them, think about them all the time, kind of bother myself with them again and again, kind of like rolling a videotape around.** [whatever this reference is about, I decide to leave it alone]

THERAPIST: **Uh huh.**

PATIENT: **... less so lately. I was definitely in an emotional limbo in the two months I was sort of going out with Wanda. That was a really hard time. Honestly, the time after we've broken up is better. I kind of know where I am standing at least.**

THERAPIST: **Uh huh. So that was a painful and confusing two months.**

PATIENT: **Very confusing ... very painful. ...**

THERAPIST: **What happened?** [whether or not patient needed a break, the therapist seemed to have needed one, so we now go to content for a little while]

PATIENT: **What happened? Well ...**

THERAPIST: **Give me an example of the problems that started to come up.** [therapist recovers and asks for a specific example; this is the second question]

Through working on the example the patient gave of difficulties with his girlfriend, it emerges that he had denied his angry feelings at his girlfriend (defensive exclusion) and had tried to bend over backward to be sweet and accommodating (defense of reaction formation), which only made him more distant, creating more relational difficulties (triangle of defensive response in relation to girlfriend, filling out self–other–emotion schema). The other side of his defensive exclusion of anger, however, is his occasional "loss of control," as the patient sees it: in the second example, the patient got mad at his girlfriend; he felt she acted in a "silly and foolish manner" and her behavior revealed her as "careless, inconsiderate, and stupid" in her handling of other people's monies (precious resources). The bottom line for him was that he thought she was acting in a "childish manner." The patient became very angry, verbally lashing out at her in a way that "hurt her. 'Cause she started crying," about which he feels terrible remorse.

The self-other dynamic interaction is between an angry, critical self and an other accused of being "silly, foolish, and childish," or differently formulated, a big, strong self, critical of and angry at an other, who is small and hurt and crying. Here the patient is big and angry and the other is small. It will be interesting to see if past reverberations of this dynamic emerge. In terms of the triangle of conflict, with his girlfriend we see the triangle of defensive response in operation. Defenses against anger include exclusion and reaction formation. When defenses are pressured, angry feelings burst forth, unmodulated, out of control. The out-of-control quality always suggests anxiety. With the adaptive expression of core affect, anxiety is not prominent; the self is in control and the expression of the affect is the expression of the self's basic agenda. When the affect is not adaptive, the self is not in executive control; anxiety pervades (or other red-signal affects) and the expression of the affect is not the result of desire for deep self-expression but rather the result of defenses overwhelmed by the pressure of intense feelings and anxiety. Feeling out of control is the subjective aspect of nonadaptive outbursts of affect; almost invariably, they have disastrous consequences (unless expressed to an other perceived as "stronger or wiser," whose affective competence is able to contain the patient's outburst and can prevent the disastrous consequences).

Deepening

A little later in the session:

PATIENT: **I have a very strange way of looking at the world that I'm going to explain to you.** [patient announces introduction of a new topic]

THERAPIST: **Uh huh.**

PATIENT: **... I try to do things in my life based on reasons, I try to make everything sort of interlock, I do. ... I ... and I have a deep metaphysical problem ... I do not see the underpinnings of all of our existence ...** [more evidence of pervasive use of intellectualization and its disastrous consequences]

THERAPIST: **Uh huh.**

PATIENT: **... and it's a bother** *(through tears)*. **I do not see a reason for people to go out and work** *(deep sigh)*, **and it causes me despair** *(more dry sobs, no relief; deep sigh)*. [deep affect: secondary affective reaction; we have to learn what despair is a reaction to]

THERAPIST: **Now if you were to remove just one set of barriers and let yourself feel what you're feeling ... and not fight it so much ...** [seeking to bypass intellectualizing defenses; pressing for affective expression; failure to acknowledge patient's risk taking and deepening of communication that preceded this intervention; therapist not sufficiently attuned to how hard he is fighting for control; no wonder this lapse of empathy leads to heightened defenses and a mini resistance]

PATIENT: *(deep sigh, long nonproductive pause)* [missed intervention triggers more anxiety, tension, and defense; communicative flow gets blocked]

THERAPIST: 'Cause you're telling me about very profound feelings, very scary and very profound feelings. [correction of oversight: therapist acknowledges and validates deepening of communication; by adding the word *scary,* she conveys that she understands the gravity of what the patient is struggling to communicate and expresses empathy with patient's experience of meaninglessness and despair]

PATIENT: *(more dry sobs and deep sighs)* ... really very frightening feelings *(hyperventilating)* ... I'm trying ... [back in contact; with lowering of defensive barrier, anxiety very high again]

THERAPIST: I know. ... These are feelings you've been struggling with for a long, long time, not just three, four months. [empathic; planting seeds of triangle of comparisons by introducing idea that these symptoms must predate current crisis]

PATIENT: *(sobbing now and nodding head in agreement; deep sighs)* ... Yeah. *(shakes head)*

A Bit More Working Through

THERAPIST: I have a sense that you are struggling with such deep deep pain, but that there is also a lot of anxiety, that you are really frightened about opening up. [articulating content of the anxiety; making sense of it]

PATIENT: *(really crying now, but also breathing hard)* No one is acknowledging that, my fear of the metaphysics of the world. [stark statement of aloneness]

THERAPIST: ... You're talking about the meaning of your life.

PATIENT: I worry that life has less meaning for me than somehow it should, that the things I do also have less meaning for me and that hurts. [deep communication linked with deep pain]

THERAPIST: Tell me what it's like to just articulate that and to start talking about it with me? [I want him to be aware that he is not alone; refocus momentarily on patient-therapist relationship]

PATIENT: The more I sit here and say it, actually the more it feels better 'cause I start to understand why it hurts, it's a real struggle. There is something about talking about it with you which is helpful. [putting it out helps; making sense of things and communicating with another helps]

THERAPIST: Uh huh.

PATIENT: I don't do this with other people, which is maybe why it is so hard for me to talk.

THERAPIST: But at the same time, you're being so courageous and very honest, which I really appreciate. I mean you're not shirking from any of it. [affirmation]

Moment-to-Moment in the Here and Now
Gets Linked with There and Then

Staying close to the alternating waves of affect, anxiety, and defense, and intervening accordingly, depending on which was most prominent, the patient's anxiety about his angry feelings becomes increasingly apparent (red-signal affect of anxiety: first triangle of defensive response completed). Anxiety also appears linked to the patient's yearning for closeness: this emerges in the context of the relationship with the therapist, as he reveals that, much as he yearns to, he is terrified of letting his guard down (beginning of elaboration of second triangle of conflict: anxiety linked with fears of closeness; need to understand where these fears of closeness come from). As the session continues, exploration of bodily correlates of anxiety reveals a numbing of the face, in addition to other common anxiety manifestations. Regarding inquiry about the patient's anxiety, the guide for the therapist is to keep going until the patient's anxiety decreases and until the therapist has a clear and comprehensive sense of the patient's physical experience.

THERAPIST: **How's that tingling in your face?** [checking to see if more contact reduces anxiety]

PATIENT: **It's weird, I've never had that numbness before.** [hint from patient that patient-therapist relationship needs to be explored, inasmuch as a symptom is being generated in the here and now]

THERAPIST: **Just let yourself focus on it and describe it to me, the sensations.** [therapist misses the hint; another round of anxiety work, which is not a bad next best thing]

PATIENT: **It's kind of like my face is falling asleep, it's not painful, I don't exactly know how to describe sensations, it's strange.**

THERAPIST: **As if what? What image comes to mind?** [having explored physical sensations, introducing a different realm of experience]

PATIENT: **Like when your arm falls asleep.** [remember this simile: its layers of meaning will become comprehensible later on]

THERAPIST: **Let's just keep track of that. … If you let yourself look at me, what do you see in my face?** [therapist is floundering; been there, done that]

PATIENT: *(sigh)* [when therapeutic alliance is good, patients are very kind and tolerant]

THERAPIST: **It's hard?**

PATIENT: **Yeah. I don't have a hard time looking at people. That's**

actually one of the things I'm pretty good at. [patient tactfully lets therapist know this ain't where it's at]

This is a very interesting moment. While the work is proceeding and deepening, at the same time the patient's anxiety is not decreasing sufficiently. Something important is not being addressed. The therapist repeats a type of intervention already used only minutes earlier and the patient tactfully declines another go-round. However, at this point, given that the therapeutic alliance is very strong despite the momentary floundering, the patient's unconscious weighs in and offers the therapist some on-the-spot supervision about where patient and therapist need to go. The therapist finally gets it, takes the hint, and accepts the help. We continue:

PATIENT: **... I guess I'm uncomfortable because I don't know where we're going and it's hard. ...** [patient reflects on the floundering and then goes about repairing it] **One thing stuck with me from my consultation with Dr. X. He thought I had a hard time with feelings of anger, that I didn't feel safe enough to express, and that maybe that came from my father, the way my father dealt with his anger.** [major reorientation: patient introduces core affect of anger in context of a primary relationship, i.e., between him and his father]

THERAPIST: **In what way did that stick in your mind?** [therapist gratefully accepts patient's reparative efforts]

PATIENT: **It rang a bell; I remember these episodes with my father when he got very very angry when I was a child, I remember cringing.**

THERAPIST: **Can you give me a specific example?**

PATIENT: **Pretty silly, I was playing in a field outside a McDonald's. For some reason, my father got angry at me and chased me down,** *slapped me across the face* **and wrestled me to the ground, yelling at me. It was so scary.** [therapist should have gotten more details about exactly what he was doing; self–other–emotion configuration, a P corner of triangle of comparisons: self is small and terrified; the other is big and out of control; the self-other dynamic interaction is of big other attacking small self, and the emotion that is accesible is anxiety and fear connected with the attack. Note especially that now we know why his somatic experience of anxiety was tingling and numbing in his face]

THERAPIST: **How old were you?**

PATIENT: **Gosh, I guess I was eight or nine. I mean it wasn't anything that traumatized me, or anything.** [denial of impact; protecting father; defending against full realization of his vulnerability]

THERAPIST: **What did he look like in that moment?**

PATIENT: **When people get that angry, you know they look kind of possessed. I don't get angry that much ... I don't know if it's because of this or because of that.** [spontaneous link between defenses against anger and experiences being the victim of his father's anger]

THERAPIST: **When you think about that time and your father being in a rage, an irrational rage, from what you're saying, it's not something that makes any sense to you from what you're saying. ... That stirs up another wave of feelings in you.**

PATIENT: **Confusion.**

THERAPIST: **Confusion. ... Put it into words.**

PATIENT: **Well it didn't make sense. Maybe that's why I have trouble getting angry myself because it doesn't seem to make sense.**

THERAPIST: **I think that makes it ten times more scary. Dealing with anger that big is really scary no matter what. But dealing with anger that big when you don't know what triggers it, or what it's about, or what you've done to elicit it, is really like a nightmare. ...** *(pause)* **I mean, I put myself in that situation, it seems infinitely more terrifying.** [validation and making sense of patient's experience; amplifying it through labeling it a "nightmare"; empathic elaboration]

PATIENT: *(listening intently)*

THERAPIST: **Now if we approach that scene now, from your vantage point as an adult. If you're the boy's advocate, what would you say to your dad?** [attempt to use a portrayal here to heighten patient's empathy toward himself, rather than have efforts focused on protecting his father]

PATIENT: **I would say, "He, meaning me, he wasn't doing anything bad, that's what boys of that age do. They play. There was a McDonald's and everything was calm and there was some play time." It doesn't seem like that kind of response was appropriate. For that situation.** [Note shift: patient gains access to his own perspective of its not being fair. No more confusion] **Things might have been going on for my father that made him more angry than was appropriate for that situation. So ...** *(wipes eye)* **it doesn't seem fair.** [patient introduces here the theme of children being children, boys being boys. Accusation of childishness will come up again]

This has been a key portion of the interview. A number of associative links have suggestively emerged. The slap across the face from his father has begotten the numbing and tingling in his face. The accusation of being "childish" that he threw out at his girlfriend has a historic resonance: it was his childishness that triggered his father's rageful attack.

Positive Experience with Therapist: Derepressing Early Instances of Emotional Deprivation

An hour has passed. The patient says he's thirsty and asks if there's any water. I offer him a bottle of peach ice tea, which I happen to have in the office. Thinking it's apple juice, in a Proustian moment, the taste of the drink—and most likely, the experience of feeling cared for—catapult him to relive an early experience. The memory is accompanied by a breakthrough of deep pain (affective breakthrough: visceral experiencing of core affect). The material revolves around the patient's loneliness, sense of being emotionally abandoned by his father by whom he used to feel loved, and feeling that no one understood him. Here is a potential triangle of comparisons around the theme of loss and fears of loss, linking girlfriend (C), therapist (T), and father (P), but these connections are not made as the material is flowing and we are following affect.

PATIENT: **Is it apple juice?**

THERAPIST: **Ice tea ... peach ice tea.**

PATIENT: **Ice tea, it's funny ... I thought it was apple juice** *(drinks some more)*. **I don't drink apple juice very much ... so**

THERAPIST: **Is it something about apple juice?** [follow the detail: gifts from the unconscious come in unexpected guises]

PATIENT: **It just struck me as funny ... OK. I thought it was apple juice and I don't drink apple juice and all the associations about apple juice are from childhood.**

THERAPIST: **Uh huh.**

PATIENT: **So it's just kind of funny that I thought it was apple juice.**

THERAPIST: **Uh huh.**

PATIENT: **Hmmmm ... strange.**

THERAPIST: **What memories does it bring ... ?**

PATIENT: **Kindergarten.**

THERAPIST: **Kindergarten ... uh huh.**

PATIENT: **Even before kindergarten.**

THERAPIST: **Three, four, like that?**

PATIENT: **I guess. ... The Lilly Pad Kindergarten ... I remember drinking apple juice there. ...**

THERAPIST: **What's the feeling of the memory?**

PATIENT: *(nods)* **Happy mostly. But some very strange things hap-**

pened to me during that period. I was superactive as a child. Really, really active. I don't know whether they were thinking of me as ... I think the term was at that time, uh ... hyperactive. ... But I managed to break all kinds of limbs. I broke both arms and my foot ... [crucial diagnostic and historical information emerging in an affectively resonant dynamic context; very important communication about environment's failure to hold him; he may have been hard to hold, but three broken limbs before age of five doesn't bespeak safety]

THERAPIST: **You did?**

PATIENT: **Different episodes.**

THERAPIST: **That young ... ?**

PATIENT: **Yeah, pretty young. ... Yeah. ... Let me get my chronology straight ... yeah that was certainly before kindergarten.**

THERAPIST: **So by kindergarten you had already broken two arms and a leg?**

PATIENT: **I was really really outgoing, active, very much a leader of my peers ... I just managed to break arms and legs.**

THERAPIST: **Uh huh.**

PATIENT: **Strange. ... Let's see if I can remember how I did it.** *(relating this with matter-of-fact, boyish earnestness)* **One time I fell off a jungle gym, another time I broke my foot when somebody else jumped off a table and it rolled over my foot. ... A big, heavy marble table** *(very expressive now)*. **Another time I ... another time** *(now shaking his head, something meaningful is coming)*. **... There was this tall tree and ... it was maybe twenty feet up in the air ... it couldn't be that tall 'cause I was real small, let's say ten feet, ten feet up in the air.** [patient is absorbed in what he is saying, language highly detailed and specific, there's no anxiety now, he is reliving a moment; this is a core state in the absence of specific core emotion; it is about presence, authenticity, and engagement]

THERAPIST: **Uh huh.**

PATIENT: **... and I got a ladder, I kind of made a ladder with the assistance of some people in this wood class ... and the ladder was not made the way that normal ladders are. ... It had one very long leg and one very much shorter leg ... and one leg made it to the tree and the other leg didn't ... so I climbed up the ladder and I was able to reach the tree branch, grab it** *(motions with his hands, very animated now)* **and the ladder fell out. ... And I was hanging there for a while and then** *(dropping motion with his arms)* **and I broke my arm. ... Very strange** *(laughs a bit uncomfortably)* **... rambunctious child ...** [patient very unself-conscious, but also not aware of emotional significance of lack of environmental support he is describing; overly self-reliant style much in evidence: he expects little from others, much of himself; this is an ego-syntonic pattern]

THERAPIST: Mmmmmm.

PATIENT: ... who did not understand the laws of physics

THERAPIST: Uh huh ... [therapist is horrified but at the moment keeps horror to herself] *(pause)*

PATIENT: None of those things ... huh. ... Thinking about them now, none of them really scared me, yeah

THERAPIST: Mn hmm.

PATIENT: ... and I don't remember if that was because of where I was, of who I was at the time

THERAPIST: Uh huh.

PATIENT: ... or that I was putting the fear away somewhere ... [insight]

THERAPIST: Already. ... [marker: by age three-four-five, these patterns were already in place] Who was there with you?

PATIENT: When? *(totally surprised)*

THERAPIST: When you fell out of the tree.

PATIENT: *(shakes head vehemently)* I was alone. ...

THERAPIST: You were alone? ... So what happened? You fell out of the tree, you broke your arm, and?

PATIENT: My arm was at a very strange angle. I was crying because it hurt. So I picked it up *(refers to the arm)*, walked over to the class, showed them my arm, and we went over to the hospital. It got fixed.

THERAPIST: Oh, my. ... That's so ... upsetting to hear. ...

PATIENT: Well ...

THERAPIST: That's a lot of very scary stuff to tolerate. ... For anybody ... [addressing defense against experience of fear, implication being that it was all the more scary for a little boy]

PATIENT: It didn't scare me ... *(starts to cry softly)* I didn't feel afraid. It just hurt.

THERAPIST: But you tell me about it and you start to cry

PATIENT: Well, I don't know whether or not. ... It doesn't feel scary now.

THERAPIST: Uh huh.

PATIENT: But I don't really know whether or not it felt scary then.

THERAPIST: Right, right. ... But there's also something about the aloneness.

PATIENT: *(nods head emphatically)* Well, the aloneness was worse ...

THERAPIST: **It hurts.** [empathic reflection]

PATIENT: **Well, ... That was. ... That was really bad. I was hanging ... I was probably hanging for a minute or so. ... That was! ... I was yelling, I was really yelling for help. ... No one came. ... That was. ... That was scary ... because I was hoping for somebody to come and help me** [memory and experience of fear are derepressed in context of empathic connection with therapist]

THERAPIST: **Yes ...**

PATIENT: **Nobody did. That was pretty scary. Towards the end ... I knew no one would come ... it just seemed to me all along like, like someone would be there** *(makes holding gesture with hands)* **to take me. ... But ...** *(even more tearful)* **I guess towards the end I realized that it wasn't going to happen** [very poignant: the painful realization that yearning for help would not be met]

THERAPIST: **... that it wasn't going to happen.** *(pause)*

PATIENT: **Hummm. ...** *(sad)* **Do you think that the things that stand out from our childhood are the things that don't ... that aren't resolved?** [a beautiful example of openness, of patient's leading to open up new areas; anxiety addressed, deep exploration no longer seems a Pandora's box]

THERAPIST: **Yes. ... A profound yes.**

PATIENT: *(he nods as well)* **... I just find it really strange that I am remembering flashes from childhood.** [we are in realm of core experience and deep unconscious communication]

THERAPIST: **It just seems to me that ... the experiences that are coming up, the memories triggered by the ice tea that tasted like apple juice, but it's in a particular context ... you were having very very deep deep poignant feelings that had to do with not being cared about** [integrative comment, puts us on solid ground, integrates cognition with affect, names and labels core theme of not being cared about; solidifying ground before going further]

PATIENT: **Yeah. ... Definitely.** *(crying, but bearable now)* [core affect of pain]

THERAPIST: **Awful feelings, awful feelings.** [mirroring, empathy, verbalizing deep feelings]

PATIENT: **Yeah, I remember that was the worst feeling in childhood was ... the phrase was "you don't love me anymore." I remember it distinctly.**

THERAPIST: **... in your mind saying it.**

PATIENT: **No, saying it like when I was crying. That was one of my worst fears. ...** *(crying)* **It just hurt.** [further derepression, further deepening; no anxiety now]

THERAPIST: **"You don't love me anymore"?**

PATIENT: *(nods)*

THERAPIST: **And who was that to?** [let's link core feeling with specific other]

PATIENT: **It was mostly to my parents. I mean, they seemed like really loving people. They've always seemed like really loving people ...** *(shakes head)* [now that we have triangle of conflict, let's fill in self–other–emotion schema and triangle of comparisons]

THERAPIST: **What?**

PATIENT: **I'm just thinking about it. ... I'm looking through my mind for instances, trying to think of when they were not loving. The only times my father was not loving was when he was really angry.** [working through: patient is spontaneously asking questions, fine-tuning, making key distinctions, elaborating key dynamics]

THERAPIST: **In that rage?**

PATIENT: *(nods)*

THERAPIST: **It's a big exception.**

Spontaneous Links: C–P Link and Triangle of Defensive Response

We pick up from where we left off. Again the patient takes the lead.

PATIENT: *(nods)* **They're at opposite ends of the spectrum.** *(drinks some tea)* **There's something that I noticed in myself now that we are putting it in those terms. Normally, I'm pretty passionate and caring and loving and nice. But when I get angry, I really fly off the handle.** [he brings core affect of anger under aegis of self; crucial link: we have explored his being the victim of father's anger. Now he spontaneously brings up his own anger]

THERAPIST: **Uh huh.**

PATIENT: **At least emotionally. Even if I am not expressing it, I feel it.** [nice spontaneous differentiation between experience and expression; augurs well for work ahead]

THERAPIST: **Inside you feel that flying off the handle.**

PATIENT: **Yeah.**

THERAPIST: **In a rage.**

PATIENT: **Yeah.**

THERAPIST: **Give me an example.**

PATIENT: *(sigh)* **An example. ... An example with Wanda. She was running an event. She was in charge of the money and she mismanaged it. She was inexperienced and had some misunderstanding of** her task. I feel I treated her harshly. More harshly than I should have. I really insulted her

THERAPIST: I am interested in hearing two things from you. One is that I'd like to have a sense of what was inside you, what you experienced in reaction to what happened, the other is what you said and did. [reinforcing distinction between experience and expression patient made spontaneously a minute earlier]

PATIENT: *(nods)* I was really angry with her because it seems like it was very badly managed. ... But ... let's see. ... I'm working on the inside part. ... *(mumbles)* [we are now exploring core affect of anger at the C corner of triangle of comparisons]

THERAPIST: Yeah.

PATIENT: I kind of worked myself up, I got more and more angry. What she did just seemed so silly and foolish. It was careless. ... And ... what I said to her was "I guess in the future we need to keep it out of the hands of children." And that's what I really felt, that she was being really childish with how she was handling the finances. ... But I really hurt her. 'Cause she started crying. [his father's attack on him was because he was being childish or boyish, in that case; here, another self–other–emotion schema is being elaborated: self is big and angry and out of control, the other is small and "childish," the interaction is still about attack, but this time it is self attacking other]

THERAPIST: Hmmmm.

PATIENT: *(very sad)* I regret that. ... *(sigh)* See. [appropriate remorse over causing pain shows he is deeply in touch with anger and its consequences]

THERAPIST: Uh huh.

PATIENT: *(teary)* I feel like the anger alienates people. I think that's one of the reasons why I don't feel safe expressing anger. That I feel like in the same way, when my father when he was being angry with me, that whenever I am expressing anger I am alienating people the same way my father alienated me *(very painful feeling, then slowly becomes peaceful)*. ... Ahhhhh *(big deep slow exhale)*. [spontaneous declaration of identification between him and his father around experience of out-of-control rage and its consequences, explaining reason for his defending against it]

THERAPIST: You said Ahhhhh *(mirroring exhale)*. What was that?

PATIENT: I liked that insight.

THERAPIST: Yeah *(long drawn out, matching contour of the exhale of relief)*.

PATIENT: It felt good.

THERAPIST: To make that connection and to realize it.

PATIENT: *(nods)*

Deepening Trust Leads to Deepening of Material:
Traveling the Royal Road to the Unconscious

We go on, continuing to explore the patient's reactions to the consequence of emotions—and then go much further. Throughout, I try to stay very close to him, so that he feels safe and not alone, which allows him to explore. In so many places, he leads, I follow.

PATIENT: *(drinks)* **It's very frustrating. Because it seems like the emotions are definitely what causes trouble. And I think in terms of problems you can solve, yet with emotions, with bad emotion, I haven't had a lot of luck.** [specific statement of cognition maintaining defenses against emotion]

THERAPIST: **That's where I hope our work can do something about that. Because I don't think there's ever such a thing as a bad emotion. And I do not think they are problems to be solved. Emotions are ways of dealing, ways of expressing.** [education, restructuring]

PATIENT: **When I say bad emotions, I think of emotions that cause hurt.**

THERAPIST: **And I want to make a distinction with you between the emotion that we feel inside and the way in which it becomes expressed.**

PATIENT: *(nods)*

THERAPIST: **For instance, with anger. Your father's anger was almost traumatic at that moment that you described to me. What was traumatic was not that your father got angry, but that he lost control.** [another round of distinction between experience and expression]

PATIENT: **I am worried about it. I am definitely worried about letting my anger get out of control. ...** [patient finally explicitly reveals red-signal affect of triangle of conflict: his fear of loss of control of his anger]

THERAPIST: **Did that ever happen?** [key inquiry in deep work with intense anger]

PATIENT: *(looks equivocal, grimaces)*

THERAPIST: **Any instance when you ...**

PATIENT: **... I need to think about that ...** *(pause)* **Hmmm. ...** *(looks down, sad; sigh)* **Hmmm, actually it did once ... I was training a parrot and ... he bit me and I killed it. I just hit it. ...** *(breaks down sobbing; deep sighs as he is sobbing, looks up at me, makes eye contact; unintelligible as he speaks through sobs)* **Letting up that guilt. ... I think that's where it comes from.** [deepening; note the specificity and graphic quality of his language. Major breakthrough]

THERAPIST: *(very soft tone of voice)* **What was the bird's name?** [though patient rapidly completes affect sequence, let's stay with incident a little longer, getting more specifics to make it even more immediate; ride the wave of core affect a little longer, allow his psyche to absorb and start to metabolize what has just happened]

PATIENT: **I forgot.**

THERAPIST: **What did you do with it afterwards?**

PATIENT: **I hid it. I didn't hide the bird. I hid that I killed it from my mother. I just said it died. And we buried it in the garden.** *(calmer now)*

THERAPIST: **This guilt is so painful. ... I feel so much pain from you** ...

PATIENT: **... It's just pretty amazing if I think about it that that might be where a lot of the fear that I have about expressing anger might come from. ...**

THERAPIST: **... yes**

PATIENT: **... of hurting something that I love ...** *(nods head, clear gaze).* **I think that's why I am scared about expressing my anger. It seems if it gets out of control, I can hurt who I love. I mean that's the sort of thing I've done with Wanda. Letting myself become unloving when I am angry. ... I am not worried about doing physical harm. 'Cause I don't really have those impulses anymore. I also have a good outlet for that. ...**

Psychodynamic Formulation Using the Representational Schemas and Relational Work

By the end of the session, it was not difficult to put together the central role that conflicts around anger and thwarted yearnings for closeness played in his presenting problem, the depression that had been plaguing him for many years, which became severely exacerbated by his girlfriend's breaking up the relationship. Afraid of loss and the destructive power of his anger, the patient defended against his anger in a way that made him more distant, false, and uncommunicative, and contributed to the difficulties in his relationship. When his girlfriend left him, he felt grief, which he could experience, despite its intensity, and anger, which he could not experience. Once again, he found himself alone. Grief and anger turned inward (he blamed only himself for the demise of the relationship) combined to produce the painful and acute state of anxiety and depression that brought him to therapy.

The sensations of anxiety—numbness in the face—is linked with the very spot of his father's attack, the slap across the face. Interestingly, when asked to elaborate the sensation, he says it feels like when one's arm falls asleep. This is purely speculative, but there is a possibility that the association of an arm falling asleep is suggested by the wish to inhibit the destructive rage: if the arm is asleep, then it cannot strike out in rage.

The time for the session is almost over. There has been a major breakthrough and connection between a determining early event (from identification with the father) with the precipitant for the current depression, which the patient is able to make. Before the end of the interview, it is absolutely necessary to return to the issue of suicide. The core affect breakthrough signals a very solid therapeutic alliance, and the patient shows excellent capacity to work with it and not be over-whelmed by it—an excellent sign. The assessment must be made directly, however, not just implicitly. We pick up the thread of the interview where we left off.

PATIENT: The ...

THERAPIST: ... the boxing.

PATIENT: ... The boxing practice. It's very aggressive. When you fight, you fight with all your being. Your opponent is wearing pro-tective gear. There is nothing that you can do to your opponent effectively to injure him. Or her. So ... it's a very safe place to express aggression. And anger. I let my feelings of aggression go when I fight and I do not hate the people I am fighting. And I best like fighting with my friends because I feel l can express anger at them without ... without danger. ... *(moved)*. That's something I really like. [this is a profound therapeutic communication about making a safe place for anger in the therapy with me. Notice communications about safety. Had I heard it I would have addressed it]

THERAPIST: Yes. ... I want to offer you a thought. This fear of loss of control has two sources: one of them is in your own loss of con-trol in what happened with your beloved parrot, the other in what happened at the hands of your father.

PATIENT: Yes. Seeing in my father and then seeing in myself defi-nitely makes me fearful of it. [note openness, directness, and clarity of the dialogue]

THERAPIST: But my sense is that your reaction to it has been to try to eradicate all angry feelings from your responses.

PATIENT: Eradicate the emotion?

THERAPIST: Yes ...

PATIENT: Could be.

THERAPIST: And the price that you have paid is that you get withdrawn. ... You called it unloving, I've just referred to it as withdrawn. Maybe unloving, maybe withdrawn, maybe it's the same thing.

PATIENT: (nods vigorously, very focused) I think I see what you're saying. ...

THERAPIST: ... and I have a sense that it is not your anger that got you into trouble. It's your fear of your anger.

PATIENT: Well, I believe that. What you say makes sense.

THERAPIST: The withdrawal, the detachment, and maybe the loss of feeling, what you call "becoming unloving" ...

PATIENT: That makes sense. (long pause) Hmmm (moved). [very important communication, given that what he wanted from this session was to make sense of what was happening to him, that that was a very important aim for him; core affect of being moved supports this assessment]

Before the session comes to a close, the therapist goes back to feelings of meaninglessness and directly asks about suicidal feelings and intent, to which patient responds.

THERAPIST: I want to do one more piece of work with you.

PATIENT: Okay.

THERAPIST: I want to go back to those very scary feelings of meaninglessness. In terms of your personal experience at these moments of despair ... Have you ever had thoughts of suicide at these moments?

PATIENT: (shakes head) I believe I have a good instinct of self-preservation. Good friends to talk with. Also there are good things in life. And in my experience, though I might feel despair at human existence, I feel there is stuff to live for though I do not always know what it is. I do not feel self-destructive. On a small scale, I know I contribute to the betterment of the world. ... It's hard to talk about these things. ...

THERAPIST: Just stay for a while with the experience.

PATIENT: (resonant, full silence)

THERAPIST: I find you very very lovely.

PATIENT: (tears up) Thank you. ... I know as a person, I'm really a good person. ... [now session can come to an end; the last piece of necessary work: the need to process experience of having done the work]

Wrapping Up the Initial Evaluation

THERAPIST: I was going to ask you to reflect with me, we're now approaching the end of the time we set aside.

PATIENT: I thought we were, it felt like it was the time.

THERAPIST: Yeah, yeah, I want to reflect together on these two hours that we spent together and then go to talk about what next.

PATIENT: Okay.

THERAPIST: I know it'll take you some time to think about and digest and process. ... But what's the feeling right now about what we've done, that you can share with me?

PATIENT: As a feeling, I feel quite relieved, because I didn't know what was going to happen.

THERAPIST: Tell me some about the feeling of relief.

PATIENT: Well, I feel like we have been talking about the kind of stuff I've put away. I have felt safe to feel these things and safe to think these things and it's becoming more safe to explore. ... It's a relief to talk about these things.

THERAPIST: You have a sense about what it is that we did together that's making it safer?

PATIENT: I'm not sure. ... *(silence)*

THERAPIST: What you did? ... What I did?

PATIENT: What we did. *We* did it ... I think it's two things. Me being honest with you and you being a professional and being honest, empathetic and ... caring. [aloneness undone]

Psychodynamics are the transformational rules or principles by which various mental contents are linked with one another so as to produce experience and behavior. So, for instance, the way in which the categories of each of the three representational schemas are linked represents a set of dynamics. Yet there are many possible interrelations, between different versions of each schema or between different elements of different schemas. Finally, the most parsimonious way of linking together the various explanations in a way that makes sense of the patient's symptoms, precipitating incident, functioning, way of being in the therapy, subjective experience, and past conflicts and how they all interrelate is the psychodynamic formulation. The psychodynamic formulation should be able to suggest the patient's core issues and dominant motivation.

Of interest in the foregoing interview is the dynamic suggested by two different self—other—emotion schemas: in one, the self (as a rambunctious nine-year-old) is small, the other (his father in a rage) is big, the self-other dynamic is one of big other attacking small self and the dominant emotion is fear, followed by sadness and withdrawal; in the other, the self (as a nine-year-old again) is big, the other (his rambunctious bird who bit him) is small, the self-other dynamic is big self (in response to small provocation) attacking small other, and the dominant emotion is rage, followed by enormous guilt. The linkage between these two triangles of self—other—emotion echoes the identification with the aggressor operative in abused children: the child overcomes his sense of utter helplessness and feels powerful by acting toward a weaker other, much as his parent acted toward him. Moreover, the rage that could not be expressed toward the original aggressor finds a displaced target in a powerless other.

The horror, guilt, and grief at the transgression are so powerful, however, that they become the focal point from where the psychopathology gets generated, the grain of sand producing the toxic pearl. In our psychodynamic narrative, the patient draws a moral: rage is dangerous, and it both kills and kills love; so it must be extirpated from the patient's psyche. The moral becomes generalized: feelings are trouble and need to be put away. So defenses are instituted. Very concretely in this case, the patient's reliance on defenses set him up for the relational loss that brings him to treatment. Abandoned and no longer loved, he ends up alone, despairing and bereft, much as he was as a child.

The last exchange of the transcript catches the essence of why his healing in the first session of psychotherapy could begin: through a relationship in which he felt both understood and helped to simultaneously connect with his feelings, stay in control, and make sense of his experience, he is able to face what previously felt too overwhelming. Aloneness undone, he has a visceral experience, counter to his previous ones, of the power of emotional experience to decrease rather than heighten anxiety, and to heal.

PART III

Strategies of Intervention

INTRODUCTION TO STRATEGIES OF INTERVENTION

I have had a kind of fanatical belief in the efficacy of depth-psychology, and this has led me to attribute occasional failures not so much to the patient's "incurability" as to our own lack of skill, a supposition which necessarily led me to try altering the usual technique ...

FERENCZI, 1931, P. 128

STANCE: PROMOTING PATIENT SAFETY
AND THERAPIST RISK TAKING

Establishing the trust needed for deep affect work requires that the therapist's sense of self be engaged (Casement, 1985), and that she be able to share her emotional experience in a genuine, nondefensive way, striving to be as authentic as she possibly can. AEDP's clinical stance demands at least as much from the therapist as from the patient: the patient cannot be expected to rapidly open up to a therapist who remains hidden and shielded.

The emotional atmosphere should be one in which the patient feels safe and the therapist brave. The patient's sense of safety within the therapeutic relationship is enhanced in part by the therapist's risk taking.

Her willingness to share feelings and take emotional risks also models affective engagement for the patient, and shows him that she practices what she preaches. Implicit in the therapist's affect-rich stance is a message that affects are valuable, tolerable, enriching, and that they need not be draining, overwhelming, or shameful. The therapist's emotional openness and expressiveness also serve to deepen the patient's affective experience, which is AEDP's principal technical goal. Emotional phenomena are contagious. Affective mirroring and affective sharing appear to be wired-in: emotion in one partner facilitates emotion in the other; similarly, one partner's emotional unavailability can inhibit the other's emotionality. The therapist's judicious affectivity enhances and deepens the patient's emotional access.

What is the therapist's stance when the patient is in the state where he allows himself to believe that it is possible to risk trusting and being open? If the therapist's internal state can meet the patient's, and the therapist's own hopefulness and openness can come to the fore, allowing her to feel free to be as therapeutic as she is capable of being, something profound can happen: in that moment, the therapist has the opportunity to go beyond being good enough, to actually be downright good.

THE UNIT OF INTERVENTION

The unit of intervention is not the therapist's comment, but the therapist's comment and the patient's response. What matters is the patient's experience of the intervention and his subsequent response. Thus, while a therapist's validating some aspect of the patient's experience is offered in empathy and with the aim of reducing defensiveness, the patient is the judge: he can experience that as empathic or not, and respond to it with a heightening or lowering of resistance. This gives the therapist enormous technical freedom. Regardless of whether the intervention leads to affective deepening or relational distancing or more anxiety, the dynamic question implicit in the therapist's intervention will be answered: as much can be learned about the patient's inner world from understanding the dynamics of what scares him and makes him withdraw as from what he reveals in the aftermath of an affective breakthrough. The therapist does not have to walk on eggshells, afraid that powerful interventions might arouse too much resistance; their doing so is as informative as their not doing so. The only thing that matters is that the shifts in the patient's moment-to-moment experience be dynamically processed and empathically used to inform the therapist's next response.

There are many ways to access core affective experience. For instance, aesthetic experiences (movies, songs, works of art, a beautiful landscape), intense moments of achievement, personally or vicariously experienced (e.g., Mark McGwire's breaking the home-run record), falling in love, socially shared experiences (e.g., the death of Martin Luther King, Jr.) all have the power to effect deep and moving transformations (Bollas, 1989; Gold, 1996; Winnicott, 1974). It is the goal of AEDP to take core affective experience out of the realm of serendipity and gain access to it with some degree of reliability.

The change from traditional analytic techniques to experiential and STDP techniques—integrated in AEDP under the aegis of the affective model of change—primarily has been a process of *turning passive into active*, as it applies to the therapist's activity. Much of these techniques brings out what formerly had been kept inside the heart and mind and guts of the therapist and offers it up for use in the interpersonal space between patient and therapist, where both members of the therapeutic dyad have access to it.

The notion of communication is expanded beyond the verbal and the notion of defense is expanded beyond the formal defenses (such as denial, intellectualization, and reaction formation). The domain is enlarged to include nonverbal behaviors: avoidance of eye contact, tone and volume of voice, and body movements or their absence become the focus of therapeutic attention. As the body is the locus of core emotion, AEDP requires overcoming therapeutic prudery and inviting the body and its language to take formal part in the therapeutic discourse.

Technique is how theory becomes translated into clinical practice: here the goal is to articulate transformational rules that inform the process of bringing about "affective change events" (Greenberg & Safran, 1987). AEDP's strategies of therapeutic action (Strupp & Binder, 1984) are the means by which the good-enough therapist puts into action her affective competence. These therapeutic strategies are organized into three groups: *relational, restructuring,* and *experiential-affective* (see table 1). The basic aim of all AEDP strategies is to allow therapeutic work to get done in a place of deep affect and subjective "truth" (Fosha & Osiason, 1996): the three intervention groups highlight alternative pathways to minimizing the impact of defenses and the red-signal affects and facilitating affective experience within a close relationship.

Relational interventions rely on the development of a two-way affective bond between patient and therapist to help the patient feel safe

TABLE 1
AEDP STRATEGIES OF INTERVENTION

Relational Strategies

Facilitating patient-therapist relational experiences
Tracking and focusing.

Expression of therapist's support and affirmation:
Making the nonspecific factors of treatment treatment-specific
Validating, affirming, and appreciating the patient and his experience: expressing care, compassion, and concern; offering encouragement and being helpful; acknowledging, validating, and amplifying healthy responses; recognizing, validating, and appreciating self-empathy and self-care; exploring the patient's reaction to support and affirmation.

Expression of therapist's empathic response
Explicit expression of empathy; empathic elaboration; exploring the patient's reactions to empathy.

Expression of therapist's affective experience
Affective self-disclosure; acknowledging errors, vulnerability, limitations; receptiveness to patient giving and acknowledgment of impact; self-disclosure to counteract therapeutic omnipotence; exploring reactions to therapist's self-disclosures.

Promoting intimacy and closeness through
little-step-by-little-step attunement
Sharing with the patient his moment-to-moment experiences; exploring reactions to therapeutic intimacy.

Collaborative work with patient
Reciprocal monitoring of nonverbal communication; comparing views; recognizing and making use of the patient's psychological expertise.

Meta-processing of affective–relational experience
End-of-session processing.

Restructuring Strategies

Tracking fluctuations in openness vs. defensiveness

Working with defensive responses
Identification, labeling, and clarification of defenses; experientially focused defense work and evocative shorthand; appreciative reframing; cost-benefit analysis; removing the pressure; the coach approach—i.e., encouraging the patient to persist and affirming the value of trying to do so.

Working with red-signal affects
Working with anxiety: Exploration of physical concomitants of anxiety; explo-

ration of cognitive, fantasied, and experiential aspects of anxiety; finding meaning and making sense; reassurance, reframing through accurate labeling, education; removing pressure and appreciating the patient's hard work and accomplishments.

Working with shame

Validating emotional experience.

Working with green-signal affects

Focusing and tracking green-signal affects.

Working with the self–other–emotion triangle: Tracking fluctuations in positive vs. negative aspects of self and relational experience

Coming to understand how self, other, and emotion are interdependent; juxtaposing good and bad states.

Working with the triangle of comparisons: Tracking fluctuations in repeating vs. emergent patterns of interaction

Comparing relationship patterns; sensitizing the patient to repetitions of interpersonal patterns, both painful and affirming; sensitizing the patient to "new" patterns, or departures from repetitions, both painful and affirming; exploring the role of self and other in the construction of interpersonal patterns, while exploring their consequences for self experience.

Integrative processing

Creating a new autobiographical narrative

Experiential-Affective Strategies

Facilitating genuine affective experience

Direct tracking of affect; translating ordinary language into a language of feelings and motivation (or desire); encouragement to stay with and tolerate deepening emotional experience.

Mirroring and going beyond mirroring

Mirroring the patient's affect; affective resonance; anticipatory mirroring; amplifying affect.

Naming and acknowledging affective experience

Aiming for specificity and detail

Focusing on bodily rooted correlates of experience

Portrayals: imagined interactions and their dynamic—experiential correlates

Portrayal; completion of portrayal; affective portrayal to complete interrupted affect sequences; internal dialogue portrayals (to help with issues of shame, guilt, ambivalence, and dissociation); impulse, affect, and interpersonal desensitization portrayals; reparative portrayals.

Affect restructuring

Experience and expression of affect, and feeling and dealing within the relationship, thereby rendering defenses functionally vestigial. Relational strategies are designed to get past defenses that result in interpersonal barriers, and to foster the development of an environment in which patients are able to intensely experience and explore, in depth, emotions, feelings of intimacy and closeness, as well as "we" experiences of resonance, mutuality, and in-syncness. *Restructuring* interventions address the patient's awareness and understanding of his own emotional and interpersonal experience through the lens of empathy toward oneself. A key aspect of the self-empathic understanding is that in the past, defenses were necessary for psychic survival, reflecting the self's "best efforts" at adaptation. The therapist uses restructuring strategies to rapidly process the moment-to-moment interaction and help the patient become attuned to patterns in his experience of himself and with others. *Experiential-affective* interventions aim to bypass defenses through direct enhancement of the core state and the experience of core affects.

AEDP strategies for therapeutic action, all ultimately aimed at facilitating affective experience within an emotional relationship, are based on a therapeutic stance characterized by empathy and the willingness to share in the bearing and processing of emotionally intense experience.

CHAPTER 10

RELATIONAL STRATEGIES

One of the tasks of therapy is to make a meaningful connection. ...
This frees [the patient] from the toxic association of closeness and
intimacy with pain, anxiety and humiliation; instead, intimacy comes to
be associated with the intense pleasure of the success of the relationship
with the therapist. (Marke, 1995)

When the therapeutic relationship activates the patient's potential for
more open, less defended relating, it is crucial to explore the patient's
response to the therapist's emotional involvement. Patients sometimes
will have a great deal of difficulty accepting and taking in care, compassion, and empathy. Frequently, these interventions stir deeply
repressed longings and can lead to an initial increase in anxiety and
defenses against those longings. Whether negative or positive, the
patient's experiential-dynamic reactions to what the therapist is
expressing then become the focus of the therapeutic work (Alpert,
1992; Foote, 1992; Fosha, 1995; Marke, 1995; McCullough Vaillant,
1997; Sklar, 1994).

Making the implicit explicit—not simply that the patient exists in
the mind and heart of the therapist, but exploring *how* he exists—gives
weight and staying power to the new experience to balance the perva-
siveness of defenses marshaled against the pain and disappointment
associated with intimacy. Moreover, such therapeutic work promotes
and intensifies, even accelerates, the process that primes the reflective
self function.

This work is not only affirming and empathic, but also intensely
interactive; it is not just about validation and support, but also about
intimacy. The patient needs to attend to and process both the repetitive
and nonrepetitive aspects of the relationship. The explicitly expressive
strategies that follow differentiate among affirming, empathic, and affective aspects of the therapist's experience. The latter two both involve the
expression of the therapist's more personal emotional reactions to the
patient; in the first of them, however, the emphasis is on her response
to the patient (his affect, his story, his experience) as it reveals *him,*

whereas in the second the emphasis is on the therapist's response as it reveals *her* as a separate person in the relationship with the patient (see also Bacal, 1995, on the delineating relationship).

Facilitating Patient-Therapist Relational Experiences

TRACKING AND FOCUSING

From the start, the therapist tunes in to how the patient feels talking to her, as well as to how she herself is feeling talking to the patient, and she encourages the patient to do the same. The message she conveys is that feelings that come up between them can and need be discussed openly, as the therapeutic relationship is a rich arena for exploring new experiences and interpersonal dynamics. We try to help the patient verbalize the experience of closeness and distance. Talking about what is happening—good and bad—intensifies the sense of closeness. Some of this work is similar to more recent analytic relational work (Coen, 1996; Ehrenberg, 1992; Ghent, 1995; Lindon, 1994), though in AEDP, the therapist closely attends to the moment-to-moment interaction and is free to redirect the patient's attention to current relational experience.

The psychoanalytic rule of thumb whereby positive transference remains unenunciated and negative transference primarily is addressed does not apply in AEDP: positive relational experiences also elicit real anxiety, as they are linked with the pain of frustrated past yearnings. The AEDP rule of thumb is to intensify patient-therapist relationship experiences, negative as well as positive, so as to process the material together. The generic questions here are, How do you feel here with me? and What's your sense of me? (or How do you experience me?).

Technically, the therapist tracks fluctuations in rapport, affect quality, and depth of unconscious communication (Malan, 1976, 1979). The therapist considers how each shift is related to the therapeutic relationship: with increased defensiveness, the patient is asked to tune in and see whether something in the interaction made him uncomfortable; similarly, when the material deepens, patient and therapist together seek to understand what allowed the expansion of trust and openness.

With greater closeness, just as important as understanding why it occurred is knowing that it did in fact occur. Defenses against this kind of emotional knowledge are profound. Even deep treatment experiences can be put out of awareness and "disappeared" if they are not identified and processed. Ill-placed modesty sometimes will prevent the therapist from drawing the patient's attention to their positive interactive experiences—but it is vital to remember that the same steadfast courage and thoroughness applies to working with positive relational experiences as with negative ones.

Could It Be That I'm Not Bad?

In the following vignette from an initial evaluation, the exploration of the patient-therapist relationship follows a powerful affective breakthrough (regarding the patient's incomplete mourning of the death of her mother in relation to whom the patient felt she was "bad"). Focus on the patient-therapist relationship was informed by the therapist's uneasy feeling that the patient was not experiencing sufficient relief after such a major breakthrough, and adaptive action tendencies had not kicked in. (Note that the therapist does not explicitly disclose her unease, although she might have; nevertheless, her feeling conditions her contributions to the affective dialogue.)

THERAPIST: **I really want to have a sense of how you're feeling talking with me.**

PATIENT: **I feel like I'm resisting you a little bit. Even though I'm telling you everything, I feel like I'm not letting myself really connect to you.** [triangle of expressive response: patient openly communicating about her difficulties communicating with therapist]

THERAPIST: **How come?**

PATIENT: **I don't know ... I'm scared. ... It's like—I'm protecting myself in some way, holding something back ...** [patient identifies anxiety and defense components]

THERAPIST: **In what way?**

PATIENT: **Something about vulnerability. ...** [self experience; completes triangle of defensive response]

THERAPIST: **Is a part of it** [i.e., resistance] **a reaction to me?** [now let's elaborate the self–other–emotion schema]

PATIENT: **Well, I don't know. ... I like that you've been able to follow this and figure things out and put it together and I feel that you're caring about me. ...** [the words are nice, but the subtext is damning with faint praise]

THERAPIST: **Wait a second. I was expecting a "but" in there.**

PATIENT: **Well ... the "but" has to do with your asking "well, what are you feeling?" with that question ... it's like "oh, no** *(young girl* *tone) ... you're asking a hard question."* One of those questions I can't answer. [demanding other–inadequate self–blocked emotional access]

THERAPIST: *(deep slow tone of voice; somewhat pained)* That makes me feel sad because I've tried to tell you that I think you have this amazing capacity for communicating and doing it in a way that has made *me* feel very connected to you. [therapist is using her own affective reaction to patient here to explore discrepancy between their takes, and to see if they can get to other side of resistant barrier; disconfirming pathogenic beliefs]

PATIENT: *(very open, in contact)* I don't know what I'm scared of ... [decrease in defense and anxiety]

THERAPIST: In a funny way, I don't think it's a resistance in what you're communicating *to me.* It's more like you're resisting taking something back from me, *resisting giving yourself something* ... [facilitating patient's self-empathy]

PATIENT: *(open, deeply receptive, seriously pondering)* Right. ... That's right.

THERAPIST: That, to my mind, there's zero missing from what you've done. ...The piece that's missing is that you should walk away from here today knowing that you've made a deep impact on another human being and with a sense of awe about what you can do. [acknowledging and affirming patient's achievements in the session; continuing to promote self-empathy]

PATIENT: *(open, soft, good eye contact)* Hmmm. ... [lowering of anxiety and defense; relational openness]

THERAPIST: To take something for yourself. [facilitating patient empathy through being her advocate]

PATIENT: *(moved, open, soft, clear-eyed, taking it in)* Yeah ... Thank you ... That's good. ... *(smiling, core state; long, long pause)* [defenses against positive experience undone; patient is able to take good stuff in and affectively experience it]

Expression of Therapist's Support and Affirmation: Making the Nonspecific Factors of Treatment Treatment-Specific

The patient's sense of the therapist's care, warmth, and understanding toward him has been shown to contribute strongly to good treatment outcome (Frank, 1982; McCullough et al., 1991; Orlinsky, Grawe, & Parks, 1994; Rogers, 1957). Rather than leave these matters to chance, the AEDP therapist systematically seeks to bring them about; *making the nonspecific factors of treatment treatment-specific* (Fosha, 1995) is what these interventions are all about.

Validating, affirming, and appreciating the patient and his experience: expressing care, compassion, and concern. The therapist validates the experience of the patient, and appreciates the meaning of that experience for the patient. She openly shows the patient that she feels compassion for him and expresses care and concern throughout. The therapist meets the patient with *empathic prizing* (Rice & Greenberg, 1991), affirming the patient's humanity and intrinsic worth. She also affirms the patient's positive qualities, such as courage, sensitivity, forthrightness, even when excessive reliance on them has led to trouble (i.e., character pathology, unfulfilling interpersonal patterns). (For how to deal with the negative aspects of the patient's personality, see *work with defenses* in the next chapter.) Such affirmation, when internalized, enhances the patient's trust in his own self-affirming beliefs and perceptions. It is particularly important for the therapist to see whether the patient is able to recognize these positive qualities, or whether he is drowning in harsh criticisms toward himself.

Offering encouragement and being helpful. The therapist is the patient's ally through and through, offering encouragement to keep going, pointing out accomplishments and helping to ease the road ahead. The therapist also can refer to previous moments, in the work or in the patient's life, when the patient's persistence paid off. The therapist can respond directly to the patient's requests for clarification, direction, and help, and initiate helpful responses. Speaking about what she has found helpful in similar circumstances has the potential to serve a dual purpose: offering a suggestion and decreasing the patient's sense of shame and isolation surrounding his difficulties.

EXAMPLE The therapist pointed out to the patient that he was most likely to be taciturn and avoid eye contact with her precisely whenever he seemed most in need of help and support (feeling particularly bad, stressed, and overwhelmed). The patient, confirming her observation, asked, "OK, so what can I do to change that?" Instead of seeing his response as evidence of passive aggressive or dependent tendencies, and rather than turn the question back on the patient, particularly in light of the therapist's awareness of his depleted resources, she replied: "Perhaps you can begin just by naming it to yourself when this happens, and also pay extra attention to what's going on inside you that's making you want to withdraw rather than want to come forward."

Acknowledging, validating, and amplifying healthy responses. The therapist zooms in on the actual achievements of the patient, no matter how small they may be. Metaphorically, as the blade of grass begins to grow through the cracks in the concrete landscape, without denying the formidable concrete, we focus in on the blade of grass. The therapist helps patients attend to their positive actual qualities and accomplishments, which patients—being filled with shame, guilt, and self-criticism—tend to be unaware of or minimize. Any patient, no matter what problems he brings to therapy, will also display a number of healthy, adaptive behaviors. The therapist can point these out, emphasizing that the patient is not starting from scratch, but rather has a repertoire of resources to draw on. Especially in areas where the patient has trouble, the therapist can highlight any achievement to show that there is a part of the patient who is already able to do what he is striving for.

EXAMPLE A patient who was despairing of ever being able to talk with his intimidating father suddenly felt a glimmer of hope when his therapist reminded him of just how effectively he had recently dealt with his daughter's irascible coach; the next session, the patient, more relaxed than he had been previously, came in remembering some moments of ease and playfulness with his father; later, he realized that all those memories were from a time before his mother's death. As his empathy toward his father kicked in, he felt less intimidated. He also increasingly came to feel that he had something to offer his father, with whom he then began to have more contact.

Recognizing, validating, and appreciating self-empathy and self-care. A particularly important area of therapeutic change is the patient's becoming increasingly able to be good to himself, have empathy for himself, and nurture himself; the therapist should be alert to ways in which the patient begins to be his own caretaker, as well as note lapses in self-care and self-empathy. She can help the patient identify the difficulties he has being his own self-advocate; until his self-empathy kicks in, she can be his advocate. One way of jump-starting self-empathic tendencies is to ask the patient how he would feel toward someone else who was describing a predicament identical to his; especially powerful is to ask the patient to imagine how he would feel toward his child (actual or imaginary) if that child had to deal with what he had to deal with.

As the patient's thoughts and feelings become more forgiving and compassionate toward himself, and as he learns to treat himself with love and understanding, the therapist recognizes these developments and expresses her own pleasure and delight in these changes. Here lie the seeds of the capacities that will enable the patient to end treatment but continue the lifelong process of healing and growing.

As the patient takes in a new awareness of himself in the treatment, he will begin to act on it. In treatment, the therapist observes that he is more aware of his emotions, more able to express himself openly, and more willing to look at his situation with an open mind. With others, outside of therapy, the patient learns to express himself more genuinely and live more genuinely himself. These achievements can be highlighted and celebrated with the therapist. They represent dramatic accomplishments, and acknowledging them will enhance the patient's self-esteem and help give him strength to go on. The pain of setbacks and difficulties can also be shared. The acknowledgment of his efforts will enhance the patient's self-esteem and help him open up even more.

Exploring the patient's reaction to support and affirmation. Affirmation often elicits anxiety, guilt, and defense.

EXAMPLE In response to an affirming comment, the patient said, "you're such a positive person," defensively switching focus from him to therapist. As she held him on it, clearly pointing out evidence in his behavior to justify the affirmation, he got more and more squirmy, finally bursting into a kind of helpless laughter, as though someone was tickling him. Eventually, after some little-step-by-little step dialogue, he said that while the recognition made him feel "wonderful," the feeling inside himself was so unfamiliar that he didn't "have a clue about what to do with it."

Affirmation can also elicit tremendous sadness, as the patient gets in touch with the consequences of years and years spent tolerating destructive environments that only further reinforced his self-dislike.

Expression of the Therapist's
Empathic Response

> Those who have suffered understand suffering and thereby extend
> their hand.
>
> PATTI SMITH, *"Rock 'n' Roll Nigger"*

Special to AEDP is the *explicit expression of empathy* (Alpert, 1992,
1996; B. Foote, 1992; J. Foote, 1992; Fosha, 1992; Osiason, 1995; Sklar,
1994). This strategy goes beyond letting the patient know that he is
heard by reflecting back his feelings: it makes active use of the therapist's empathic reactions. The therapist conveys her sense of the meaning a situation might have for the patient, in light of his experiences.

Through the therapist's *empathic elaboration* of his story, the patient
has the unusual opportunity of hearing a detailed, evocative narration of
his experience of events. This can be a stunning experience for one not
at all well-versed in self-empathy. Empathic elaboration is an amplified
version of the process whereby the patient knows that he exists in the
therapist's mind and in her heart; through seeing himself through her
eyes, his self-knowledge, and his self-empathy, expand unexpectedly.

The therapist is not only permitted to join in the feeling state of the
patient, but encouraged to do so, with one proviso: whatever she
expresses must be authentic; effectiveness depends on it. A facial expression, the look in one's eyes, just the right word that captures the quality
of the patient's experience are all vehicles for the communication of
empathic understanding, as are tears of sadness or feelings of anger on
the patient's behalf. When the patient experiences the therapist as
empathic, feelings glide back and forth between patient and therapist,
seemingly without effort (i.e., the little-step-by-little-step process). This
is a powerful intervention inasmuch as many patients rarely have felt the
impact of someone emotionally being with them (Osiason, 1995).

EXAMPLE A patient described a difficult telephone interaction with her
daughter; the therapist commented that she herself felt very tense listening to the interaction, as she could sense all of the feelings that were
being held back in the phone conversation. The patient acknowledged
her own tension and went on to talk about feeling trapped and having
difficulty breathing. Patient and therapist continued expressing the
tense feelings, with their words, clenched fists, and shallow, tight breath-

ing. Eventually, the patient became able to articulate all that she initially had been unable to say about the very disturbing feelings she experienced during the telephone conversation.

Exploring the patient's reactions to empathy. We express these reactions and focus on the patient's responses to see how he experiences the therapist, since defenses can lead to blocking, discounting the experience of empathy, or minimizing its significance:

> The therapist is concrete in her self-portrayal of her empathy for the patient ... to the degree that the patient is unable to recognize a safe, empathic other. The overt self-disclosure of warm, caring or sad feelings for the patient bypasses this aspect of the defensive wall. (Marke, 1995)

In addition to denial or other defenses, two other reactions are often encountered that present opportunities to deepen the work:

▼ Empathy—the sense of being understood—elicits healing affects (feelings of gratitude, love, appreciation, and feeling moved).

▼ Empathy often will elicit great pain and sadness. It evokes in the patient the visceral realization of the deprivation that was a fact of his emotional life. *Having* makes him poignantly aware of *not having* or *not having had; having,* however, with its strength-giving affirmation, also makes it possible to mourn that which he never had.

Making these dynamics explicit will help the solidity of the transformation. Beebe and Lachmann (1994) point out, "If these interactions are verbalized and labeled, this process may transform the original representation" (p. 132).

A word of advice to the therapist: all the while attending to the patient's experience, do not dismiss your own. It is to be hoped that the therapist has less defensive need to deny good mutual stuff than does the patient. Tronick's work (1989; Gianino & Tronick, 1988) has shown that good feelings in one partner are the result of an interactional process of mutuality and coordination. Chances are that if the therapist feels good about the work, the process has been good; the patient is likely feeling that as well. The therapist can gauge by her own reaction whether the patient's defenses against acknowledging the impact of the other's empathy can be bypassed, as in the following illustration from the end of an initial evaluation:

Getting by the Guard Outside the Tent

PATIENT: I am actually, I think that I am pretty good ... better than most people, at being open with my feelings.

THERAPIST: You deserve to say that you are *very very* good. You've done an amazing, amazing piece of work with me. And I ... *(therapist stops to make room for patient's deep reaction)* [affirmation]

PATIENT: *(closes eyes, breathes deeply, and seems very moved)* Thank you.

THERAPIST: *(speaking slowly, with a lot of feeling)* I am really moved ... by what you've been able to share with me, what we've been able to do together ... it's really tremendous ... and it's not easy to do ... it's very hard to do. [affirmation; therapist's tone of voice echoes patient's deep response]

PATIENT: I have to admit like, my first impulse, is to think "she is just saying that, you know" ... [relational defense]

THERAPIST: *(interrupting)* But this is not true. ... That's your second impulse. I will ... vouch for my intuition that that wasn't your first impulse. ... Your first impulse was to really take it in and be touched by what I said to you. [based on patient's initially very deep response to affirmation, therapist challenges his defense by relying on her own experience of the patient's reaction and her sense of the work done together]

PATIENT: *(pause, emergent sheepish smile)* Yes, I guess you're right

THERAPIST: Fair enough though that there was a second impulse but ... *(patient and therapist laughing)* Yes? [affirming patient's need for defense in order to feel safe]

PATIENT: Yes.

PATIENT: These defenses come up when you need to protect yourself.

PATIENT: It's like my self sort of sitting in a tent, and the second impulse is sort of ... is the guardian of the tent. And you have to talk to the second impulse before you can come inside to meet the real one in the tent. ... And I guess you sort of reached out to the one which is in the tent who is saying "yes, thank you" and the guardian is saying "wait a minute," like ... "Will I let you in so easily?" [beautiful experiential elaboration of experience of therapist's bypassing defenses to "reach in" to the true self inside the tent]

THERAPIST: Right. That is hard. And now we are also coming to the end of the session and that's a hard place to be in, so open and having gone so deep. Now I have told you how I feel and now you tell me just what your sense has been of these two hours we spent together. I think that it will take you some time and we will see how you will feel after you leave and we will see how, you know, it plays in the next few days. ... But for just now how are you feel-

ing? [over and over validating patient's experience of vulnerability and anxiety associated with being open and receptive]

PATIENT: It's, it's, it's a relief you know, it's a relief, and … I have been reading lately that the best way to get to security is by … you know, facing your fears, yes and you know, I don't like to look at my thoughts too closely because I don't know what to do with them, and I admit that it will be embarrassing or difficult for me to talk about some of them … but eventually I will, I will. [relief associated with recognition; increased motivation for risk taking and hard work ahead]

THERAPIST: Uh huh … so where do we go from here?

PATIENT: Well … I, I want, I want, I want to work with you and, and I feel very hopeful and I think that … I know that it's a moment of truth for me in some ways and I got to perform for myself. [empathy begets facilitating affects of trust and hope]

The therapist's affirmation of the patient initially elicited deep appreciation from him, which was rapidly followed by defensive mistrust. Challenging defensive mistrust, while simultaneously validating the patient's need to keep himself safe, reestablishes trust, engenders hope, and renews the patient's commitment to risk taking and the hard emotional work ahead.

When the patient's defenses cannot be bypassed, there is then an important opportunity to do another round of work to understand the reason the patient needs to defend. Careful inquiry and exploration will reveal the specifics of the dyadic experience for each patient.

EXAMPLE The therapist felt good about the work accomplished in an initial session. The patient had seemed to be deeply affected by the work; toward the end of the session, however, she avoided eye contact, commented little about the session's impact on her, and left in a way that left the therapist feeling unsettled. The following session, the therapist inquired about the patient's reactions. With tremendous trepidation, the patient revealed a sexual involvement with a previous therapist; somewhat relieved to have the issue out in the open, the patient was also saddened; she further volunteered her fear that, in acknowledging and exploring her positive feelings toward the current therapist—*and doing so with eye contact*—she was putting herself at risk for a repetition.

Expression of the Therapist's Affective Experience

Affective self-disclosure. By disclosing her emotional response to the patient, the therapist acknowledges the patient's impact on her (Ferenczi, 1931; B. Foote, 1992; Lachmann & Beebe, 1996; Mitchell, 1993; Winnicott, 1963b) in both positive and negative ways. The therapist uses her own affect to create an open and intimate interpersonal arena. She might speak of her fondness for the patient, or of her pain at how difficult getting close to him is, or about how meaningful and moving a session has been for her, or about how their work together has helped or a given aspect distressed her ("I would like to share my reactions to what you've just said. I found myself shaking ...").

Many patients rarely have felt that they have an impact on the significant others of their early life; if it were otherwise, they would not have felt neglected (Osiason, 1995). The experience with the therapist will precipitate feelings about the longed-for closeness that was unavailable when it was most needed.

Acknowledging errors, vulnerability, limitations: self-disclosure. In the face of a therapeutic rupture, the therapist explores and acknowledges her contribution to it, or her error, with feeling (see also Safran & Muran, 1996). Occasionally, in the service of the patient's treatment, she might go beyond the self-disclosure of affect to a disclosure that extends into the more private realm of personal experience (Alpert, 1992; Searles, 1958, 1979). This can be profoundly reassuring to the patient, demonstrating another level of the therapist's willingness to engage. Particularly if the patient appreciates and feels reassured by her risk taking, his own response to the struggling therapist is often empathic, supportive, and helpful. Insofar as the therapist's self-disclosure gives the patient the opportunity to experience himself as someone who has something to give (Winnicott, 1963b), and who can have a positive impact on the other, it can be a healing experience. As the patient apprehends viscerally that he is not the only person in the world who struggles and doesn't have it "all together," he can experience a reduction of aloneness, shame, and humiliation. Such self-disclosure also can be liberating for the therapist: it takes her lapses out of the realm of shame, self-blame, and guilt and puts them to work. The therapist herself actualizes the deepest ethos of the affective model of change: that each of us is a confounding combination of strengths and damage, gifts and wounds, and that what is essential is to communicate openly about it to the other and to oneself.

Receptiveness to patient giving and acknowledgment of impact. Helping others to deal with overwhelming feelings has been shown to have profound salutary consequences for one's own affective competence and resilience (e.g., Herman, 1982). As the more vulnerable member of the dyad empathizes with, supports, and gives comfort to the perceived-to-be "stronger or wiser" member, the therapist's capacity to acknowledge and accept what the patient has to offer is of enormous importance: it validates the patient's generative capacity, strengthens his confidence in his own goodness, and makes him proud.

Self-disclosure to counteract therapeutic omnipotence. On the other side of the clinical continuum are those patients who devalue themselves in order to maintain an idealized view of the other. For these patients, the experience of having to deal with a struggling, far-from-perfect therapist can kick into gear reliance on their own resources, a self-reliance otherwise defensively excluded. Self-disclosure to counter therapeutic omnipotence (Alpert, 1992) can promote separation, differentiation, and individuation (Bacal, 1995; Ferenczi, 1931), as well as awareness of the patient's own strengths. Patients want to hold on to the image of the omnipotent therapist, rather than face the disappointment of seeing her as all too fallible and themselves as capable. (Incidentally, therapists do too.) Undoing this denial through the therapist's disclosure of struggles and uncertainties contributes, for patient and therapist, to a visceral sense of everybody being more human than otherwise; it is also a remarkably reliable way of getting a stuck treatment unstuck.

For the patient with this dynamic, acknowledging and accepting his own competence is frightening: it often means letting go of the hope that his helplessness, confusion, and emotional inadequacy will someday elicit the always yearned-for nurturance and care. Such patients often had a critical and judgmental parent; the parent's self-righteousness suggested unshakable certainty and infallibility. Often, these parents are people who function effectively but are emotionally isolated (with dismissing attachment styles). The patient's bond with such a parent demands his uncertainty to his or her sureness, his inadequacy to his or her all-knowingness. The price of the patient's safety is low self-esteem, depression, dependency, and paralysis. Giving up inadequacy by owning his competence not only threatens the attachment bond, it means facing existential uncertainty and relinquishing the reassuring idea that order, fairness, and the "right answer" exist. In giving up this defensive dependence, the patient makes room not just for the rewards and pleasures of his own competence, he also makes room for the possibility of having relational needs and wants actually met.

Exploring reactions to therapist's self-disclosures. Because these are high-risk and intense interventions, the therapist must continually monitor herself; she must make sure that use of her own affective experience is in the service of the patient, and not primarily to fulfill her needs. The patient's reactions to the therapist's self-disclosures must be attended to all the more carefully. If the patient feels burdened, intruded upon, or disgusted by the therapist's disclosure, or if the patient reacts with numbing, blocking, or anxiety, those reactions become the focus of the therapeutic work. The same is true if the patient reacts by feeling strengthened, moved, or deeply valued and valuable. This sheds yet new light on the patient's experiences in interpersonal relationships.

Promoting Intimacy and Closeness Through Little-Step-by-Little-Step Attunement

All the interventions discussed thus far articulate how both partners affect one another and how the texture of experience, and therefore of relationships, is never static. Out of these conversations intimacy is forged: the therapist gets to know the patient as the patient gets to know himself; he also gets to know the therapist, and the therapist gets to know herself in a new way yet again. As Kelly (1996) says: intimacy between two people is based on "the dynamic interplay of the *inmost* parts of the self" (p. 60).

Sharing with the patient his moment-to-moment experiences. The little-step-by-little-step process encourages experiences of relational openness and closeness, and seeks to counteract pathogenic processes through attunement, authentic presence, contact, and "radical acceptance of the patient" (Osiason, 1997). Stern and his colleagues (1998) refer to this as a *moving* process. Yet attunement is not always exact; at times, it is off by a little bit—enough to leave room for the therapist's authenticity to weigh in (Slavin & Kriegman, 1998). Unlike the core affect–releasing process, where there is a particular goal (albeit with many ways to reach it), the little-step-by-little-step process is open-ended. The authentic, attuned therapist stays with the patient, little step by little step, with no sense of needing to get anywhere and no clear sense of where things are going. It is largely a patient-led process: all that is required is that the patient's reality be validated, the patient be affirmed, and the patient not be alone. Sometimes this is all that happens; sometimes, to the surprise of both participants, major transformation occurs.

Often the process begins with the patient deciding with trepidation to share with the therapist "shameful secrets," "weaknesses," and "ugly stuff." Such disclosures often are introduced with such phrases as "I've never talked about this with anybody, but ... ," or "I can't believe I'm actually telling you this." Unlike core affective experiences, the seeds of healing are not contained within their direct experience and expression. The transformative potential lies in sharing feelings drenched in anxiety, shame, guilt, or humiliation—feelings previously experienced alone—with an affirming, unflinching other. Through the other's receptiveness, empathy, and understanding, the aversiveness (or fear or shame) intrinsically associated with these feelings significantly diminishes. The intensity of relational connection and acceptance leads to openness and a lessening of resistance against relational intimacy and closeness; part of this is the patient's experience of sharing with the other what previously had been dealt with all alone; it often engenders core state experiencing in both partners.

When anxiety and shame dissipate and defenses no longer are necessary, what sometimes emerges is the core affect against which defenses were initially constructed—grief or anger, for example, or sexual desire. Just as often, however, the emerging core affect is not that which initially required the institution of defenses, but rather one that arises as a response to relational contact, such as love, gratitude, or relief. Here the aim is for the essential self to be revealed through intense contact with the other—through connection, closeness, and intimacy—side by side with the revelation of the essential other.

This also is a place to attune to nuances and shifts of mood and feeling between patient and therapist—of asymmetry in mutuality—since the therapist is skilled in navigating these waters. This is an opportunity for fine-tuned conversations about dynamics as well as feelings and experience: "I have the sense that you really enjoyed it when I was speaking about you needing some time alone, but that it was somehow difficult to own that"; "Yeah, you know there is something to that"; "You know it reminded me of the time a few sessions ago when ..." The tone of some of these exchanges can be conversational, but if maintained and not avoided, closeness and intimacy will deepen, and eventually the mood will deepen or intensify—either into a core affect or a core state.

Exploring reactions to therapeutic intimacy. The closeness that ensues can be very frightening to some patients. Boundary issues often are raised by the intensity of the process, particularly if the patient has not had a great deal of experience with intimate relationships.

Collaborative Work with the Patient

Although patients often come to therapy feeling helpless and hoping to find a savior, one goal of AEDP is to help the patient, from the first session on, to realize the depth of his own resources. While the therapist's role as expert in psychological processes is acknowledged, the patient is the expert of his own inner life (Gold, 1994, 1996; Greenberg, Rice, & Elliott, 1993; Rogers, 1961). Owning that sense of competence can help the patient feel more in control in his life, and encourages a feeling of mutuality and closeness rather than one of distance and hierarchy in the therapy. The therapist can enhance that sense of self-confidence by fostering the collaborative aspects of the relationship in many ways, three of which are detailed in the following:

Reciprocal monitoring of nonverbal communication. Patients and therapists communicate a tremendous amount through body posture, facial expressions, physical movements, eye contact, and tone of voice. Whether or not these aspects of communication are recognized consciously, they have an impact on what happens between therapist and patient and how they feel in the room together. The patient is not only invited, but also "trained" to participate in monitoring and commenting on nonverbal communication, with a focus on affect. Such *mutual affective attunement* or *mirroring* in the service of deepening contact often has to be taught. The therapist becomes the model, noting, for example, the patient's nonverbal affective fluctuations—discomfort with eye contact or nervous laughter—and her own reactions: "Your tone changed just then and I had an uneasy feeling you were moving away." The patient is strongly encouraged to articulate what he notices about the therapist's nonverbal communication, and how it makes him feel. To encourage the patient's engagement in this process, the therapist might ask, "What do you see when you look in my eyes? How does that make you feel?" In this way, patient and therapist collaborate in creating intimacy.

Comparing views about therapy experiences and interactions is also recommended. Rather than the therapist solely making interpretations, each participant shares his or her perspective. Areas of agreement and divergence are processed (Alpert, 1992). The therapist might follow a comment by saying, "This is how I see it. What's your take on this?" When the therapist is unsure of which way to go, it can be very useful to put the dilemma to the patient. Patients are wonderful supervisors. Comparing views enhances the patient's sense of control and feeling of the therapy being his; it also promotes intimacy and makes areas of therapeutic difficulty the stuff of progress rather than impasse, as the following vignette illustrates.

Avoiding the Washing Machine

In the following clinical vignette, the issue is whether the patient will acknowledge the deep emotional work accomplished in the session and the feeling of connection with the therapist, or whether she is going to revert to her usual M.O. for feeling safe and go back into "the washing machine," her phrase for defense-driven going-around-in-circles type of functioning. Earlier the session revealed how she closes herself off to avoid pain of separation, as well as the disastrous consequences of this strategy; much is at stake. This work differs from validating the patient's need for defense; instead, the therapist chose to pursue a divergent path. What follows is both an example of working with defenses (see next chapter) and of doing collaborative work while acknowledging differences.

PATIENT: So ... *(getting tearful)*

THERAPIST: **Go ahead. What's coming up? What are these tears about?**

PATIENT: *(looks at her watch)* **Yeah I have to get in control, I have to go, so ...**

THERAPIST: **Well, we still have a few minutes ...**

PATIENT: *(crying, covering eyes with a tissue)*

THERAPIST: **Let it out Brenda, don't keep it all in like that. ... Go ahead. ... What were you going to say?**

PATIENT: **I've got to get myself together.**

THERAPIST: **I just realized that I was just encouraging you to let go but that what you're doing is fighting for control.** [explicit statement of lack of attunement; different agendas]

PATIENT: *(nods)*

THERAPIST: **We were getting to a lot of painful feelings and your face was hidden in the tissue and I thought you were crying but I realize you're actually working very hard to keep it in.** [acknowledging patient's wish to defend against strong feelings; these are not soft defenses]

PATIENT: **Yeah, I'm trying to keep it in. I was on that verge but I can't right now 'cause I have to go and walk home so OK?**

THERAPIST: **Look, you could say to me "bug off, I need to do what I need to do," and I'll respect that. But you need to say that to me with words, you can't act it out.**

PATIENT: **Wait, wait, I don't know if we're on the same page.** [patient alerts therapist to their lack of interactive coordination]

THERAPIST: **Okay, then get us on the same page.** [urging patient to take the lead, responding to proto-reparative attempt]

PATIENT: I guess I have a hard time ... with ... oh man ... my more emotional side. I did feel I've got to zip up and I got to push off and I do have a difficult time with ... you trying to acknowledge this connection. [patient takes responsibility, precisely articulates she is trying to defend against emotion; resistance starting to be overcome; vector is toward communication and greater closeness; owning not wanting to acknowledge connection with therapist leads to greater closeness]

THERAPIST: Right. I'm trying to acknowledge that we got out of the washing machine. ... And even if you want to climb back into the washing machine so you could walk out the door more comfortably, that's OK with me. But at least let's acknowledge that we spent a large portion of our being together today doing something very different.

PATIENT: And I guess that's what I have a hard time. ...

THERAPIST: You took a big risk and you let yourself go to a very painful place and you stayed there and felt it and struggled with it. And you also let me in. I mean I feel that I was with you, I don't know if you felt that. [specifying nature of big emotional work that took place; therapist using her affective reactions]

PATIENT: I did, I did. I have a hard time with those type of emotions. ... I downplay that kind of stuff, ... it's uncomfortable for me 'cause it's too much feeling ... but like, it's not uncomfortable for you. [patient does her share of collaborative work, further articulating differences between herself and therapist; patient is speaking the language of the triangle of conflict; more emphasis now on red-signal affects than on defense]

THERAPIST: Fine. I'm comfortable and you're uncomfortable. I know that and respect it. [therapist begrudgingly acknowledges differences]

PATIENT: So with that type of thinking and emotional connection, I minimize it and you maximize it. [patient keeps pushing forward, being increasingly precise about the nature of the tug of war]

THERAPIST: I'll split the difference with you.

PATIENT: *(laughs)*

THERAPIST: Do you know what I mean?

PATIENT: Yeah. ... Not to go out of here and say it didn't happen. [echoing therapist's position]

THERAPIST: Right, I'll split the difference, I'm not going to push and ... [therapist allowing patient's desires to have an impact on her actions]

PATIENT: It's funny that you bring that up. ... I get afraid of your ... acknowledgment of this exchange, I'm afraid of your emotions ... I'm afraid of that closeness, you know what I mean? Like I feel you acknowledge it too much ... again I guess I minimize it. ... But like your emotional reaction to what I go through, maybe I don't know how to react to it, or to your caringness. ... **All that I'm sharing with you is scary for me.** [profound declaration of subjective truth in triangle of conflict language; patient deeply acknowledges her receptive experiencing of the therapist's "caringness" and how terrifying it is to her]

THERAPIST: **I appreciate your saying that to me.** [therapist expression of gratitude to patient; implicit acknowledgment of patient's generosity and courage]

PATIENT: **So I push it away and I close up ... does that make sense?** [open and direct communication]

THERAPIST: **Of course it makes sense.** [patient and therapist getting to be on same page]

PATIENT: **I mean I feel much different now than I felt before ... I feel softer now. ... Before I felt so hard. ... In a way this sort of guided me to acknowledge what happened and why it's important to acknowledge. ... And your reassurance that you're not going to push. ... You understand where I was coming from. ... But I do feel so much different now than I felt five to ten minutes ago ...** [patient affirms different visceral experiencing of being defended vs. being open; articulates importance of feeling heard by therapist and having her need not to be pushed understood; example of hard defenses becoming soft defenses]

With the patient's acknowledgment of our different tendencies ("with emotional connection, I minimize it and you maximize it") and with the therapist reassuring the patient that she respects her need to not be pushed, the patient is able to relax defenses, articulate their nature, name the fears that trigger them, and finally, experience some relief and ease. Comparing views turned what was threatening to become an impasse into highly productive work that ended up shifting the patient's functioning out of the washing machine (triangle of defensive response) and back into the triangle of expressive response.

Recognizing and making use of the patient's psychological expertise. We also rely on the patient's expertise and note that we are so doing to the patient, who often forgets his own strengths in the midst of the gloom of his problems. There can be many psychological areas in which the patient is knowledgeable and experienced. Growing up with mentally ill parents, for instance, or having to cope with a disability gives the patient the opportunity, however unwanted, to develop a specialized repertoire. Another area of often unutilized resources is that of the patient's responses to others who are vulnerable or in need of help (often his children, e.g.). When the patient is in trouble's spotlight, it is as if these extremely competent responses—ordinarily readily available on behalf of others' needs—become nonexistent. Recognizing and making use of the patient's psychological expertise, the therapist actively brings areas of strength and competence to the patient's attention. The goal is to be able to tap into, for himself, the resourcefulness usually reserved for others.

Furthermore, strengths from conflict-free areas also can be harnessed. For example, a therapist pointed out to a highly successful self-made businessman, who regarded himself as incompetent in his personal life, that the interpersonal skills honed in business relations are fine tools he already possesses that he can apply in the personal arena he finds so daunting.

Meta-Processing of Affective–Relational Experience

Throughout, the therapist actively promotes the patient's focus on meta-experiential processes: that is, the patient's experience of his experience (see also Damasio, 1999, p. 8, in which he distinguishes between "an emotion, the feeling of that emotion, and knowing that we have a feeling of that emotion"). The patient's experience of feeling understood and his reflective self function are actively stimulated by the very nature of AEDP's therapeutic processes.

End-of-session processing. An initial meeting with a patient ought not to end without spending some time processing the patient's reaction to being and talking with the therapist. The more powerful the session, the more crucial it is that meta-processing take place. If the session involved a major piece of affective work, it is important to explore the patient's experience of his experience in relation to the therapist: "So what has it been like for you to have us do such deep (or meaningful, scary, etc.) work together?" If the work has been primarily relational, it is important to see how the patient feels: "What is it like for you to feel so close (or vulnerable, exposed, comfortable, etc.) with me?" or alternately, "What is it like for you to experience me as being on your side (or challenging, understanding, vulnerable with you, etc.)?" In this kind of processing reside enormous opportunities to

▼ gain further understanding of the patient's experience and its dynamics;

▼ see if defenses and/or red-signal affects already have begun to creep in (in which case there is the chance to do another round of work before the session is over);

▼ give the patient the benefit of fully experiencing deep postaffective breakthrough affects.

These are extraordinarily powerful and intimate interventions. They place intimacy front and center and gently announce that this is no ordinary discourse, but rather one whose goal for both therapist and patient is risk taking against a background of safety.

Most experiential techniques focus on how to facilitate access to emotional experiences, so that therapy is not an intellectual exercise but rather comes from the gut (e.g., Gendlin, 1991; Greenberg, Rice, & Elliott, 1993; Mahrer, 1999; Perls, 1969). Less emphasized, however, is the importance of focusing the patient's awareness and attention on what he has just experienced. This aspect of the work addresses the defense of disavowal, which is the equivalent of a postsynaptic, after-the-fact defense. Awareness and subsequently, memory of what the patient just experienced, vanishes. This accounts for one of the most disheartening experiences for a therapist: after an unusually good session, which the therapist expects to be mutative, the patient comes in the next time as though nothing has happened and it's back to square one.

A related point is that it is very important to undo past associations. This is achieved not only through having powerful new experiences, but also by labeling and acknowledging these new experiences as new, and specifying why and how they are different. The tone of these discussions is not intellectualized and dry, but rather one of speaking subjective "truth": simply, with quiet conviction, clarity, and directness, or alternately, with passion and great feeling.

Faraway Eyes

In this last vignette, many if not most of the interventions described earlier come into play. The turning point, however, occurs around the therapist's self-disclosure and acceptance of help from the patient. Buoyed by the deep sense of having an impact on the other, the patient experiences new strengths and becomes motivated to pursue her independence. We join the exchange toward the end of the session; earlier, the therapeutic work focused on the pathogenic aspects of past and current relationships, with her mother and husband, respectively.

THERAPIST: **What you had to deal with was intolerable, just intolerable. Too much** [validation, explicit empathy]. **How are you feeling right now?**

PATIENT: **Sad. Then, I had no choice. No haven. No harbor in the storm.** [this kind of poetic eloquence often is a marker of core affect]. **But right now the saddest part is that I had some choice when I chose Dar-**

ryl [husband]. Owning my part, that's a very deep hurt. I don't know how to reconcile that.

THERAPIST: I think you *are*. I think you're really on your way. [affirmation; encouragement; recognition of therapeutic accomplishments]

PATIENT: *(deep sigh)*

THERAPIST: Just put into words what you're feeling. [linking affect with cognition]

PATIENT: I'm feeling comfortable. Being with you, I'm feeling very warm and comfortable and accepted. Not a concrete embrace, but I feel you very close to me. ... My mind is flipping back to scenes of my life at that time [when mother was emotionally absent due to major depression triggered by birth of younger brother]. My mother sitting in the playground. ... My grandmother across the way. ... My mother being depressed. ... I'm with Louis [baby brother] and another kid. I'm seeing how I lost my mother *(soft tears)*. When I began to look at her face and at her eyes and know she was thinking those thoughts. [having touched affective base with safe environment, patient goes right back and goes deeper into reliving conditions intimately related to her difficulties; this time, she's not alone]

THERAPIST: *(sigh)*

PATIENT: When I would come home from school and my heart would break. You know, I never mourned and grieved the loss of that vivacious, pretty, lively lady who I adored, who had hopes for life and who got wrecked on the rocks *(wave of pain)*. ... There were times when my grandmother would meet the bus and I knew my mother was depressed, upstairs in bed. I didn't want my grandmother. I wanted my mother.

THERAPIST: What do you see in my eyes? [abrupt refocusing]

The emotional intensity of this kind of material often elicits very strong emotional responses in the therapist. In this case, the therapist's taking the patient away from her absorption in the material to refocus her on the therapeutic relationship is the beginning of evidence of such a countertransferential response from the therapist. We resume:

PATIENT: I see you deeply touched by my pain and my sadness *(bites her lip anxiously)*. ... Now you're starting to have a faraway look. ... It scares me when that happens. [patient is completely in touch with her feelings and also attuned to therapist; no defenses. The ball is in therapist's corner]

THERAPIST: Stay with it.

PATIENT: It really makes me wonder if you go to a place in your life that hurts. If that cord rings too close. [patient's deep empathy for therapist]

THERAPIST: **Mmmm.**

PATIENT: **The look you get is so far away. Different than at other times.**

THERAPIST: **Let's keep staying with what's happening right now** [tracking and holding on relational interaction]

PATIENT: **It scares me. I can't reach you. You're not available. I feel that you're going away and I don't want you to go away. Or I feel you behind a wall. ...** *(with a lot of feeling, tears coming into her voice)* **And I want you closer, I want you with me because I really love you and I have a hunch about your pain too.** [having accessed core affect, adaptive action tendencies are released: patient is able to precisely articulate the nature of both her deepest yearnings and her perceptions, but she also accesses empathy toward therapist's pain]

By encouraging the patient to stay with her perception of what reaction the therapist is having, another opportunity for healing opens up. The emotional nature of the material has triggered an emotional response and corresponding defenses in the therapist. Encouraged to remain in the moment, the patient first describes her experience of the therapist, wonders about its origins in the therapist's own pain, then describes her experience of loss of the therapist, an uncanny repetition of the very process the therapy has just derepressed. Only this time, the patient doesn't dissociate or in any way defend against the experience. She stays right there, experiencing her feelings of loss, remains in contact with the therapist, then goes one step further: not remaining passive, full of emotional resources, she takes the risk and states her yearning for a meaningful emotional reconnection with the therapist. Her plea is responded to by the therapist with a continued deepening of the affective interaction.

THERAPIST: **I am so touched** *(voice trembling with tears).* **I have such a sense of love from you. There is something about how we know each other ... it is so deep. ... I'm learning something about the place I go to when I get that look, I'm learning something about it from you** *(with some tears).* **So I want to thank you.** [therapist self-disclosure: acknowledging patient's impact; receptive to patient's empathy and helpfulness; expressing gratitude]

PATIENT: *(very caring, calm manner and voice)* **What's the place you're hurting about?** [therapist's taking responsibility for her lapse and acceptance of patient's contribution eliminates patient's anxiety]

THERAPIST: **These moments have come when we're talking about your experiences with your mother. ... It touches something in me,** something about me too, in a way that I guess I'm trying to fight off. [self-disclosure]

PATIENT: I feel very good about being able to say it because I've felt nervous about it, not today, but in the past. But I felt cautious. I feel very good that I can say it when I said it. ... And that you can hear it. It's brought us closer. And that's a deepener and a helper rather than something that should not be there. ... And that's the delight and ... a pleasant surprise.

Inspired by the patient's courage, the therapist gets brave and, rather than hiding behind any of a plethora of technical interventions at this point, continues to remain open and vulnerable and trying to work with her emotional reaction. At the same time, she is owning her reaction, reaffirming the bond with the patient. What the patient gave was accepted, acknowledged, and received with gratitude. The patient is thriving. One issue remains to be checked out, that the patient is not thriving because she is in the role of caretaker—a role all too familiar.

THERAPIST: Part of what made me unable to respond to you in the first few moments is that I get worried. I get worried that you not get put in the caretaker role, in that split-off way.

PATIENT: I don't feel like that.

THERAPIST: It really doesn't feel like that. But I wanted to ask and to hear it from you. [therapist's use of her affective reactions]

PATIENT: (moved, speaking with conviction) I don't think I've ever been able to say it that way when it happens—"come back"—to anybody. "Come back (voice cracking with emotion), please come back, I want you here with me. Don't go away" ... and then have somebody respond. ... (pause; big smile; very tender voice) It makes me want to say "how can you say that I feel that all closeness is fraught with danger?" [referring to an intervention, made earlier in session] How can you say that? It's not being totally fair. [affective breakthrough; deep statement of core need, the need her mother could not tolerate]

THERAPIST: Well, you're not the only one with a talent for dissociation

PATIENT AND THERAPIST: (laughing together)

PATIENT: (with a very bright smile, full of affection and delight) Graduation is going to be a hell of an event around here. [patient with a history of passivity, paralysis, and dependency spontaneously mentions termination in tone of mastery]

This is the ultimate corrective emotional experience: in being confronted with a similar situation as the pathogenically traumatic one, the patient is able to respond with maximal emotional adaptiveness and receive a genuine emotional response in return. The importance of this last interaction cannot be overestimated. Through spontaneously occurring transference-countertransference responses, yet another piece of work gets done. At that moment, the patient is an adult who is able to retain her emotional vitality, sense of self, empathy and compassion for another while staying very much in touch with her needs, yearnings, and emotional responses, all while she's out on a limb with no guarantee of the therapist's response. The therapeutic benefit comes from the patient's perceptions being validated as accurate, and from enhancing her sense of self, self-esteem, and self-efficacy and resourcefulness by letting her experience herself as having an impact on the other, and having something valuable to give. When giving comes from the heart, it is evidence of great resources; acknowledging it, and even more important, receiving it and using it, only makes it blossom.

The patient is able to undo the core pathogenic experience of her life: threatened with loss of the caregiver, who recedes into a far-off world, the patient says, "come back." This time she is heard, responded to, and engaged until the alchemy of communication works its magic again: out of potential trauma and repetition comes reparation and renewal and a sense of effectiveness. Much as the original incident necessitated dissociation, the current incident fosters integration.

Once her capacity to give expresses itself and is not at the expense of herself but rather a deep expression of her true self and its resources, separation and future exploration can be contemplated. The patient spontaneously brings up the topic of termination, and does so with the zest and enthusiasm characteristic of the exploratory urge occuring against conditions of attachment satisfied by good-enough caregiving.

CHAPTER 11

RESTRUCTURING STRATEGIES

Restructuring work takes place through a psychodynamically informed, ongoing conversation between patient and therapist. The interventions, however, are filtered through content categories privileged by the affective model of change: adaptation as the principal motive force; the contribution of both self and other to the creation of any emotionally significant situation; and valuing—and thus having a lowered threshold for noting—the patient's potential for change, his healthy functioning, and his qualities (e.g., aliveness, courage, kindness, honesty, creativity, humor, etc.).

The interventions described here are most similar to interpretations used in more traditional psychodynamic psychotherapy. AEDP interventions, however, are made much earlier in the process and much more frequently. The interpretation of the patient's experience is approached collaboratively, presenting ideas as hypotheses for the patient to consider and inviting the patient to participate. When defenses don't melt as a result of the relational and experiential-affective techniques, the more frontal approach these interventions represent in fact may be more clinically indicated.

The specific example is the fertile soil in which such strategies of intervention do their work. AEDP interventions use the three triangles to process the moment-to-moment clinical interchange to facilitate affective access and relational openness. The restructuring work precedes and lays the groundwork for the affective–experiential work, and is used at all phases of the therapeutic process. These interventions use the three triangles to grasp both lifelong and moment-to-moment patterns of the patient's affective and relational responses and understand their roots and function. The patient's familiarity with and handle on his affective–relational patterns allow him to rely less on defensive constellations and more on responding spontaneously from an increasingly affect-laden place; they also promote his self-acceptance and self-empathy (Jordan, 1991; Kohut, 1984). By putting into words what he does and what he feels, by becoming aware of the determinants of his actions and their impact on others, the patient enlarges the scope of his reflective self functioning.

TRACKING FLUCTUATIONS
IN OPENNESS VS. DEFENSIVENESS

Moment-to-moment clinical material is classified as belonging to one of the categories of the triangle of conflict according to the function that the material serves. Is the patient moving toward deeper material and greater closeness, or is the patient moving away from deeper material and greater closeness? What does one's countertransferential experience indicate? Do the patient's verbal, nonverbal, and unconscious communications match? We assess whether an emotionally charged communication serves a primarily defensive or expressive function. This is important, particularly since affect (though not core affects) can be used in the service of all three functions. A simple question, such as "Where do these tears come from?" or "Do these tears come more from sadness or from fear?" can be very useful to distinguish between tears of fear (red-signal function), defensive–regressive tears, and tears of grief (core affect). This functional categorization is crucial, as we intervene differently when we are faced with core emotional material than when we are dealing with defense or anxiety manifestations.

EXAMPLE In the middle of an intense exploration of the experience of closeness with the therapist, the patient turned his eyes away and said, "My wife is right, I'm really a very cold person." Rather than regarding this as an expression of subjective "truth," the therapist processed it as a defense propelled by the patient's anxiety about closeness and said, "You get so scared of being close with me that you would rather regard yourself as incapable of it. Let's see what happens if you let yourself look at me again. ... What do you experience?" The patient responded by saying, "For one moment, I feel your warmth and it's so nice. But then, I don't know why, I feel like I must get away. I can't believe this, but I am literally shaking inside right now and my legs feel weak." Patient and therapist then went on to do yet another round of work on the terrifying experience of closeness.

Had the therapist regarded the patient's remark that he is a cold person as an expression of subjective "truth," reflecting his capacity to face the unsavory character consequences of his defense-based functioning, she would have responded very differently. In this case, the therapist's hunch that the patient's statement was largely a defensive maneuver was validated by the patient's response, which revealed the terror that his remark was intended to preclude.

Experiential processing, structured in terms of the triangle of conflict, tracks both the moment-to-moment material and the direction in which the therapeutic process is moving, that is, whether the material is deepening or becoming more superficial.

WORKING WITH DEFENSIVE RESPONSES

Active work with defenses is the hallmark of all STDPs. AEDP features an approach to defense work carried out from an engaged, empathic side-by-side stance with the patient rather than a confrontational one. The focus initially is on the adaptive motivation behind the patient's creative invention of these means of self-protection; we then address the negative consequences of entrenched defenses in his current life. The patient should feel validated and empowered to expand his repertoire rather than criticized, humiliated, or resigned to having to change his wayward ways.

Defenses prevent (and protect) people from experiencing their core emotions and interfere with close personal relationships. The vibrant life force on the inside is masked and often hidden, even from the individual himself, who lives life as a restricted and controlled or anxious and fearful person. Although defenses are a hindrance to the patient in his current life, they were developed to protect the self at an earlier time, when protection was necessary and adaptive. The AEDP therapist keeps this in mind when working with defenses. The defenses that appear in the adult patient who walks in for treatment often were created by an overwhelmed child who needed to simultaneously protect his vulnerable self and maintain ties of attachment with a highly problematic other.

Once the therapist has identified that a defense is in operation, several strategies of defense work are available. Restructuring work applies more to entrenched defenses (characteristic of the triangle of defensive response) than to soft defenses (characteristic of the triangle of expressive response).

Identification, labeling, and clarification of defenses. Using empathy, the therapist can simply begin to talk about defenses with the patient in a nonjudgmental way. She explores with him when defenses are most prominent and how they operate. She might say, for example, "Do you notice how you avoid my eyes when you feel sad?" Identification, labeling, and clarification of defenses can be very useful, as defenses often are ego-syntonic for the patient. Experiential–visceral correlates of his defenses are also explored (Coughlin Della Selva, 1996; Laikin, Winston, & McCullough, 1991; Magnavita, 1997). Nonjudgmental feedback to the patient of what it is like to be on the receiving end of his defenses can be powerful: the patient becomes aware how his defenses distance others and cut off his access to vital internal and relational experiences. Through empathic and nonjudgmental feedback, the patient also can learn what it is like for others to relate to him when he is so defended. By learning to become attuned to the moment-to-moment ebb and flow of these experiences, the patient becomes increasingly familiar with how and when he relies on defenses. McCullough Vaillant (1997) also discusses this process, labeling it *defense recognition*.

Experientially focused defense work and evocative shorthand. Another aspect of defense work is the experiential component (Davanloo, 1990), focusing the patient's awareness of the physical correlates of defense (e.g., "hard," "numb and light-headed," "cold"). The experience then is contrasted with how the patient feels when he is less defended (e.g., "supple," "tingly," "melting"). Evocative, graphic metaphoric labeling, particularly in the patient's own words, can be useful as a shorthand that patient and therapist use together. In one of the clinical vignettes in the preceding chapter, for example, the patient comes up with the phrase "in the washing machine" to denote her sense of defense-driven functioning (i.e., going around in circles, without getting any deeper). Another patient used the term "spinning," a similar metaphor. In addition to being evocative, such metaphors, by virtue of becoming a shared language between patient and therapist, promote intimacy and heighten the ego-dystonic aspects of the mechanisms themselves.

Appreciative reframing. Often, as the patient's awareness grows—that is, as defenses go from being ego-syntonic to ego-dystonic—so does his realization of how his defenses alienate and distance others, and severely restrict his life. As the patient becomes deeply in touch with what he has lost, defense mechanisms begin to be often viewed as personality flaws. When these aspects of personality become a target of self-blame, the therapist responds with *support and affirmation of the patient*, and *appreciative reframing* of the defenses (Alpert, 1992; Sklar, 1992). The therapist helps the patient see how necessary his defenses were in the past and how they reflect his strength and ingenuity in coping, while also acknowledging their current negative consequences. As defenses themselves, often a source of humiliation for the patient, are met with empathic understanding, self-blame decreases and self-acceptance increases. Recognizing the adaptive strivings reflected in defenses instead of seeing them as the enemy (Alpert, 1992; Kohut, 1977) provides an acceptance that makes it easier for the patient to become more empathic toward himself and the reality of his circumstances.

With defenses ego-dystonic, the patient goes through a period of grief and mourning about lost opportunities in the past. Particularly painful can be mourning the impact of one's pathology on others, especially one's children. Viscerally confronting one's contribution to the intergenerational transmission of pathological patterns can be excruciating. Going through this mourning leads to deepening empathy and self-acceptance, and motivates one to risk new, more open ways of interacting emotionally with others (Alpert, 1992; Coughlin Della Selva 1996; McCullough Vaillant, 1997; Sklar, 1992), and where necessary to attempt repair.

Cost–Benefit Analysis

Together patient and therapist can look at the defenses and discuss their purposes and usefulness, past and present, performing what McCullough Vaillant (1997) calls a *cost–benefit analysis of defenses*. What does the patient gain by responding in these ways? What is lost? Considering the costs and benefits of his defenses in the past and how his current life has changed enables the patient to see that his defenses no longer serve a needed function: they hinder his growth rather than protect him. Raising the patient's awareness of the pleasures and benefits of nondefended states is also tremendously useful in helping him to relinquish outmoded protective strategies.

The emphasis is on the patient being in the driver's seat. His knowledge of his defenses enlarges, rather than narrows, his field of options. The tone is not resigned, remorseful, tail-between-the-legs renunciation, but empowered; he now is in a position to make other choices as well.

Costs of defenses. The negative aspects of the patient's personality—those responses that tend to alienate and distance others—are empathically understood as the undesirable consequences of defenses in light of the patient's goals and desires. Patients' interpersonal patterns so often are ego-syntonic, and thus the negative responses of others mysterious;

to have these patterns and their consequences identified, without criticism, humiliation, or abandonment by the other, is a profound, eye-opening experience. Experiencing the costs of defenses can also be viewed as an aspect of defense work approached through relational interventions.

Benefits of defenses: resistance to relinquishing. For the patient, defenses, representing a lifetime of the means to safety (cf. secondary felt security; Main, 1995), are deeply connected with ties to the pathogenic object. Relinquishing a defense, however negative its consequence in the patient's current life, becomes equated with dreaded object loss, loss of identity, and terrible feelings of guilt for being disloyal (Searles, 1958). Making this explicit gives the patient the opportunity to examine other more adaptive means of maintaining connection. He ends up confronting the often illusory nature of the tie to the attachment figure: in the Wizard of Oz effect, confrontation of the emptiness of the bond can lead to further grief and mourning, as the patient increasingly becomes aware of having sacrificed the self to maintain a relationship that affords him little true caregiving; like Dorothy, he comes to realize that the strength is within him. A related source of resistance to relinquishing defenses is the sense that the patient is giving up and saying good-bye to a part of himself, a mainstay of his identity. Leaving those ways behind ends up feeling like abandoning a difficult and unpleasant but nonetheless reliable companion; mourning that loss often is the final step in relinquishing defenses. Confronting the debilitating effects of dual allegiances, a patient wept at renouncing a long-standing sense of herself as "a secret spy," a strategy to which she attributed her emotional survival.

Removing the pressure. As long-serving protective functions, defensive strategies may be difficult to relinquish; feeling frustrated, patients pressure themselves to do what they feel incapable of doing. It is important not to confuse this self-imposed pressure (that comes from self-punitiveness or lack of self-empathy) with positive motivation. Intensification of resistance often indicates a deeper level of anxiety-laden material closer to the surface, and we can help the patient be attuned to his need to proceed more cautiously.

The therapist's response to the patient's self-imposed pressure is twofold: removing pressure and helping the patient do so himself (Alpert, 1992). Focusing on the patient's therapeutic accomplishments to date, the therapist can empathize with how difficult it is to confront painful experiences and try to change lifelong patterns (Sklar, 1992). Not feeling pressured to proceed to any experience before he is ready, the patient feels more in control, less anxious, and has less need to defend. Paradoxically, removing the pressure often leads to therapeutic progress. When the patient feels that he does not *have to* proceed to an experience for which he is not yet ready, he will feel more control over it and therefore less anxious, and will have less of a need for defense. Saying that it is all right to stay right here often has the paradoxical effect of decreasing obstacles to progress, obstacles that in a prior moment seemed formidable. Furthermore, dealing with the patient's self-critical stance and rigid self-standards—that translate into impatience with one's needs for safety—the therapist can point out how far the patient has come, and recognize how difficult it is to confront painful experiences and attempt to change lifelong patterns. Since patients tend to be so self-punitive, the therapist's support and testimony that they are doing the best they can goes a long way. This kind of appreciation helps the patient feel less alone and less defeated by his pathology, and can lead to a renewed sense of strength and determination to continue. Removing pressure, and thus reducing anxiety and increasing self-acceptance, is an effective technique in the face of what often is a therapeutic impasse.

The coach approach. Finally, the counterpart of removing pressure is the coach approach, that is, *encouraging the patient to persist and affirming the value of trying to do so.* This refers to the therapist's expression of confidence in the patient's ability to sustain some discomfort and exert some effort, with support, toward a constructive end. Being cheered on, egged on, pushed some, and urged to persist in the attempt to get to a new place can be very therapeutic. Sometimes we need mirroring, sometimes nudging, and sometimes a major respectful challenge. There is no taboo against going beyond where the patient naturally goes. He can be encouraged to try, though it might be difficult, to maintain eye contact, or not run away from exploring the consequences of an imagined attack, or tolerate grief for more than a fleeting moment.

The patient ultimately determines whether the therapist's intervention is encouragement or pressure, just as his experience decides whether removing the pressure is affirming or disrespectful. To one person a simple comment or question can feel like a lot of pressure, while to another, a whole slew of questions and urgings to push the experiential envelope ends up feeling like deeply caring, empathic, and much appreciated help. The indicator that it is time to switch gears from *encouragement to persist* to *removing pressure* and *explicit empathy* is when the patient indicates he is being asked to do something he cannot do. The difference between AEDP and more confrontational stances comes in affirming the patient's no (instead of dealing with it as resistance) without in any way, either implicitly or explicitly, blaming or criticizing him for that which he cannot do. Rather, in the face of the patient's pressuring or blaming himself, the AEDP therapist works to foster self-empathy and use the therapeutic impasse in one area as an opportunity for therapeutic work in another.

WORKING WITH RED-SIGNAL AFFECTS

Anxiety, shame, guilt, helplessness, and despair are powerfully aversive states that arise in reaction to core affects and activate defense mechanisms. While the discussion of techniques that follows applies to all the red-signal affects, it will be centered around anxiety and shame, as these are prototypical red-signal affects.

Working with Anxiety

As the focus of an anxious patient is absorbed by the experience of anxiety, the therapist tries to stay as close as possible to what the patient is experiencing, both physically and emotionally, to help him feel less alone. Anxiety often signals that defenses have been broken through, but that the patient feels too vulnerable. Similar to defenses, anxious reactions are learned earlier in life, when real emotional danger existed and the patient felt alone without benefit of the reassuring presence of a trusted other. When the patient responds with anxiety, the therapist must be sensitive to his state, and help him feel less alone in his experience.

Exploring physical concomitants of anxiety. When a patient is feeling anxious with the therapist, his focus is on his immediate experience; he will be highly attuned to physical signs of anxiety and how they are changing. The therapist can stay right with the patient and be attuned as well. Asking a patient to describe in detail his physical experience of anxiety (i.e., where in the body it is located and what sensations accompany it) is an intervention that invariably lowers anxiety while providing dynamic information (Davanloo, 1990). As the patient shares his experience of anxiety in the moment, often he overcomes it; he also learns to identify the feeling of anxiety—when it is likely to arise and eventually, how to control it. In describing in detail what he experiences inside of himself to an interested other, the very conditions underlying the anxiety begin to change.

PATIENT: *(sobbing; deep sighs; shakes head)* **It's very strange, I have a physical sensation, a kind of tingling.**

THERAPIST: **Where? All over?** *(inquiry in gentle, sympathetic tone)*

PATIENT: **My face.**

THERAPIST: **Your face?**

PATIENT: **Uh huh.**

THERAPIST: **Uh huh. ... What's it like?**

PATIENT: **Strange. ... It's numbing.**

THERAPIST: **It's numbing. Where in your face?** [detailed exploration of physical correlates of anxiety reaction; also sets stage for understanding unconscious meaning of anxiety]

PATIENT: **... Here, above there** *(washes hand over cheeks)*. **... In my cheeks.**

THERAPIST: **In your cheeks. So not all over, but just here and here** *(mirrors movement)* **... uh huh.** [mirroring strengthens relational connection and reduces anxiety]

PATIENT: **Yeah, very strange. ... Okay. ... It's funny, saying that relaxes me. ... That's part of the problem I'm having. I'm so tense.** [note that, with relaxation, after naming and connecting, patient recovers his capacity to label his own state]

Another important reason for exploring the physiological correlates in detail is that they have unconscious significance: very often there is an unconscious one-to-one correspondence between how and where anxiety is experienced and the dynamics of the fantasy it represents. Later in the interview, it turns out that for this patient (the one described in chapter 9, who as a boy was slapped across the face by his father) anxiety is triggered by intense anger and fears of its consequences (i.e., loss of control). Having had the precise location of the tingling earlier in the interview activates the unconscious schemas and makes more likely the arousal of that memory and associated fantasies. Thus by getting specifics,

▼ anxiety lowers to a more tolerable level and a frightening state is shared with an other, both of which are reassuring to the anxious patient;

▼ anxiety can be more readily identified;

▼ detailed dynamic information is obtained, the specific meaning of which is likely to unfold subsequently;

▼ we prime the pump of the unconscious.

Exploring cognitive, fantasied, and experiential aspects of anxiety. The therapist can ask the patient to talk about what the anxiety is like, to relate it to other situations in which he has felt it, and imagine where the anxious feelings will go. The therapist also can ask the patient for fantasies and other cognitions associated with the experience of anxiety in the present ("What's the worst that can happen?") and in the past ("What's the worst that it has been?"; "What was happening then?"). To find the dynamic root of the anxiety, the therapist can try to pinpoint the exact moment when the anxiety began ("When was the first time you experienced this?"; "What was going on then?"). These kinds of questions can help the patient to see the extent of the anxiety and begin the process of reversing the helplessness or shame he feels by first acknowledging and facing, rather than denying and avoiding, what he fears.

Finding meaning and making sense. By linking the sensations of the anxiety with the content of the anxiety (what the patient is afraid of, why, how it links with past, etc.), therapist and patient together make sense of what he is feeling. An essential quality of overwhelming anxiety is that what is happening doesn't make any sense to the patient. The more meaningful the experience, the less out of control it seems.

Reassurance, reframing through accurate labeling, education. Therapists often assume that patients know that uncomfortable frightening experiences and sensations they contend with are manifestations of anxiety. In fact, that is often not the case. Reassurance, reframing through accurate labeling, and education from the therapist about these reactions and their prevalence can be very helpful. Other means for reducing anxiety are shifting to a less emotionally loaded topic, and exploring what the patient usually does to reduce or contain anxiety. This latter approach provides patient and therapist with more information about the patient's functioning, and can at times reconnect the patient with his momentarily discarded adaptive and self-healing capacities (Gold, 1994; Bohart & Tallman, 1999).

Removing pressure and appreciating the patient's hard work and accomplishments. In addition to entrenched defense work, this technique also applies to anxiety. When a patient responds with an increase in anxiety, it is important for the therapist to recognize what the patient is going through and not push him further. As with defenses, removing pressure and appreciation on the part of the therapist helps the patient feel less alone, and tends to dramatically decrease anxiety and other red-signal affects by reaffirming the patient's sense of being in control.

Exploring physical concomitants; exploring cognitive, fantasied, and experiential aspects; finding meaning and making sense; providing reassurance, reframing through accurate labeling, education; removing pressure and appreciating the patient's hard work and accomplishments are all strategies that can be applied not only to work with anxiety but all red-signal affects. Next we will briefly consider some issues specific to working with the red-signal affect of shame.

Working with Shame

Shame arises in response to the sudden condemning interruption of a pleasurable response. Very often, shame results in the inhibition of entire areas of human experience, which become not only painful, but also undeveloped. The aim of therapeutic work with shame is that the patient be able to recover and experience the positive nature of the responses that became distorted by shame. The therapist can respond to the patient's experience with admiration, appreciation, and encouragement rather than shock and condemnation.

The following vignette shows the careful exploration of a marker of the shame response, the averted gaze, in a relational context.

To Be or Not to Be Seen

THERAPIST: **I've been wondering throughout, from the beginning, about your eye contact.**

PATIENT: **Yeah.**

THERAPIST: **It's not that it's absent, but you look away from me a whole lot ...**

PATIENT: **Right. Right. ...**

THERAPIST: **Are you afraid that you'll see something terrible in my eyes?** [exploring relational anxiety; inviting patient to engage in reciprocal monitoring of nonverbal reactions]

PATIENT: **Where are my glasses?** *(reaches for them)* **... My glasses are like twenty years old. I really can't see even with them. Yeah. ...**

Yeah. I don't know, maybe I just ... want to stay stuck. I don't think that's the case, but ... [soft defense]

THERAPIST: Mn hmm. **Stay with just your feeling of avoiding my eyes.** [bypass soft defenses by refocusing on relational issue of gaze aversion]

PATIENT: I don't know it's like ... what would happen if I keep looking at your eyes? What could happen? I don't know. You're not going to hypnotize me. ... I think it's that you'll see something, but I've already shown you everything. What else could you see? It's shame. ... I think it's shame *(starts to cry)*. Like I can do it [i.e., "tell you everything"] but then I'm ashamed. ... My stupid glasses. *(takes them off again, ostensibly to wipe her eyes)* [visceral experience of aversive affect of shame]

THERAPIST: *(sympathetic noise)* **Hmmm.** [empathic holding]

PATIENT: *(patient cries quietly with head down)* [shame and pain]

THERAPIST: *(softly)* **What are you afraid you're going to see in my eyes?** [exploring cognitive, fantasied aspects of shame]

PATIENT: I don't know. ... What am I afraid I'm gonna see? ... I don't think it's that I am afraid of what *I'll* see, I'm afraid of what *you'll* see. *(good, clear direct eye contact now)*

THERAPIST: **It's what *I'll* see.** [echoing]

PATIENT: Or it's that I'll see you seeing it. *(lifting of oppressive affect)*

THERAPIST: **How do you mean that?**

PATIENT: *(clear, direct gaze, slight smile, open expression)* I can tell you anything, and that's okay, and you can look at me, and that's okay, as long as *I don't see you looking at me.* That's the really scary part. ... Wow! That's really something, isn't it?!!! [making sense of previously incomprehensible experience; relaxed; declaration of subjective truth; core state; openness and directness]

Naming the monster robs it of its power. By naming and making sense of her experience, the patient regains control of her experience and reclaims it within the sphere of her omnipotence.

Validating emotional experience. One of the keys in working with red-signal affects in general, and with shame in particular, is to disrupt the association between emotionality and weakness (or badness, or self-indulgence, e.g.). Similarly, it is important to disrupt the association between self-care (self-empathy, self-acceptance) and selfishness. Rather than being evidence of immodesty, weakness, narcissism, selfishness, badness, swelled-headedness, or any other of the many accusatory characterizations hurled at the patient, it is the therapist's task to help the patient realize that his responses reveal the extent to which he was merely trying to fulfill a developmental agenda (Ferenczi, 1931). Instead of criticism and humiliation, such reactions were in need of delicacy, admiration, acceptance, guidance, and tactful fostering. It is vitally important that the therapist support and validate the patient and reiterate his right to his own feelings, as well as his responsibility to himself. In addition, the therapist can take pleasure, and show it, in the patient's tentative forays in areas previously rendered off limits by shame.

EXAMPLE A patient whose mother had been sexually abused grew up in an atmosphere in which sexual responses were regarded as shameful and taken as evidence of being out of control. The child's age-appropriate exhibitionism had been squashed through heavy-handed and humiliating admonitions and prohibitions. As an adult, sexual inhibition was the patient's presenting complaint; painfully ashamed of her bodily responses, she spoke of feeling "betrayed" by her body whenever she became sexually aroused. Some of the therapeutic deshaming work included showing compassion for the patient's early experiences and reframing her childhood behavior as reflecting exuberance and the psyche's developmental mandate. The therapist also shared with the patient instances of her own young daughter's prideful exhibitionism; the patient was moved. The patient's forays into the exploration of her sexuality were affirmed and celebrated; fortunately, they were also supported by the patient's loving partner. Over time, the patient not only lost her shame, but started to revel in her capacity for sensual and sexual experience as a newfound expression of and vehicle for the further expansion of her new sense of self.

WORKING WITH GREEN–SIGNAL AFFECTS

Sometimes hope, trust, curiosity, openness, and the zest for exploration are experiences that are passed over in therapy, the focus being on negative and problematic responses. It is very important to track the green-signal affects, naming them and drawing the patient's attention to them.

Focusing and Tracking
Green-Signal Affects

When focused on, the patient's hold on green-signal affects can become rather tenuous. Like therapists, patients often are more practiced in dealing with negative experiences. Once attention is focused on these experiences, patients can retract and dismiss them as silly or foolish, becoming self-conscious and anticipating that the therapist will "interpret" them away.

Therapeutic work includes fostering the patient's attunement to what these reactions signal. It is important to sensitize patients to the information value contained within these reactions—that they represent a favorable reading of the emotional environment, including a positive assessment of the state of one's internal resources. Once acknowledged, it is important to explore with the patient the antecedents of green-signal affects so that these positive experiences can be incorporated into the patient's sphere of omnipotence and become the object of the patient's evolving reflective self functioning. The therapist also strives to facilitate their transformation from signal affects into a fuller affective experience. With experiential work, the patient not only comes to realize his incipient trust and hope, but also to experience them viscerally, and link them to environments conducive to such experiences.

In the following vignette, most of the work takes place under the aegis of the triangle of expressive response. This suggests some basic trust and willingness to take risks, as demonstrated in the clinical exchange. This is only the inference from the patient's behavior, however; when he directly and viscerally experiences those elements of his relationship with the therapist that truly allow him to be open, his anxiety shoots up. Trust as a green-signal affect and the full-fledged experience of the recognition and empathy that engender trust are different: the full, receptive experience of feeling understood and appreciated is very difficult for the patient to take in and stay with: though it is exactly what he craves, it is so unfamiliar as to be terrifying.

The Man Who Loved Sandpipers

PATIENT: **Let me try to do it without beating myself up. I'll just talk about how I feel** *(long pause).* ... [Patient goes on to talk about how his girlfriend does not join him in activities that make him feel "most alive"]

THERAPIST: **It's not about cross-country skiing or rock climbing. The issue is about how you feel. That this is something that is close to** your heart. ... There's something about your feelings that's very pure, that's not being recognized. [reframing issue affectively: translating from ordinary language to language of feelings and motivation]

PATIENT: I winced when you said the word *pure*. [declaration of anxiety linked with recognition of true self]

THERAPIST: Yes.

PATIENT: I felt it. I don't know why that made me uncomfortable ... but I ... the feeling is just of doing something that I really enjoy. ... [shifts topic: tactical defense]

THERAPIST: What was your reaction to my saying that there is something *pure* about your feelings? [refocusing: bypassing soft defense]

PATIENT: I don't know. It was so ...

THERAPIST: Try to focus here *(pointing to the heart)*, rather than here *(pointing to the head; laughing together)*. Do some internal focusing, closer to the heart. Because that wince didn't come from your head.

PATIENT: Mn hmm. I think I felt, somehow recognized, that my feeling is recognized in a way that caught me off guard and surprised me and made me uncomfortable. I think that's the closest I can come to it. It just felt very sort of positive. ... Just recognized and responded to, that my feeling was responded to. *(long pause)* I'm just not used to it. [links anxiety connected to recognition and responsiveness; a new triangle of comparisons is being elaborated, i.e., this experience is different and thus frightening from previous experiences]

THERAPIST: And the wincing? [refocusing]

PATIENT: I don't know ... just your use of that word *pure*—I thought of like sometimes when you cry in a movie, you just feel overwhelmed by the feeling in a way. [another restatement of linking anxiety—feeling overwhelmed—to intense feeling]

THERAPIST: Yes ... yes. ...

PATIENT: I'm always gasping.

THERAPIST: Gasping and I think, one is that you gasp and the second thing that I guess I'm getting a little familiar with in terms of your physical response is the "hmmm" ...

PATIENT: That sound that I make?

THERAPIST: Yeah. You know, hmmm, which I have a sense that that's also a way of disconnecting a little emotionally [identification of nonverbal defense]

PATIENT: It's true. It's like a shock absorber.

THERAPIST: Right.

PATIENT: It has that quality of putting up a little barrier. [patient and therapist working closely together; patient is open and discussing defenses rather than shutting down]

THERAPIST: That's right ... like you know, a little protection. [empathic reframing]

PATIENT: Yeah. ... And your saying, something about your saying *pure* kind of caught me off guard, like I didn't have time to think before it got under the barrier ...

THERAPIST: Mmmm. ... There's something about my recognizing and my seeing this very deep feeling in you and ... such a visceral reaction—I don't know if it's painful or scared. [implicit request for collaboration]

PATIENT: Scared. [request for collaboration met; very clear about aversive affect associated with positive experience of feeling understood]

THERAPIST: Wincing, uncomfortable ... you know, I want to note it. ... Something that on the face of it seems really very good ... is terrifying.

PATIENT: I don't know why it feels scary but it does. It feels sort of soft and melting [visceral experience of defenselessness in face of feeling understood]. That's scary. Mostly I'm aware of how much I just kind of want to block everything and cover it all over. It all feels dead in a way. [visceral experience of defense-dominated function; instant institution of defenses]

THERAPIST: Hmm?

PATIENT: It feels dead in a way. To just block everything and to see— to keep everything locked up. I really don't feel alive at all. But you're right. There's something uncomfortable about it. I don't know what it is. [consequence of defenses is deadness; patient refocuses on anxiety; back to area of aliveness]

THERAPIST: I feel a little torn, because there's a part of me that says, OK, if it's this scary, let's take it slowly because I'm sure you're scared for a reason. And there's a part of me that says, OK, let's see if we can take it a step further. ... [comparing views; putting therapeutic dilemma out to patient]

PATIENT: I would go for let's take it a step further. [patient chooses to go forward]. ... We'll be walking down the beach and I'll be noticing the sandpipers and I'll comment and she'll say "stop talking to me about the sandpipers. I'm not interested in sandpipers."

THERAPIST: *I* winced when you said that. [explicit empathy; anticipatory mirroring]

PATIENT: You know this doesn't happen a lot but it happens occasionally. [minimization]

THERAPIST: You seem uncomfortable with my having said that. [identify anxiety]

PATIENT: I'm waiting for you to say "you know, that's really fucking immature." [content of anxiety based on previous experiences, now deeply internalized in self-attacks, defensively projected]

THERAPIST: But it seems a little hard right now for you to take in my actual response. [empathic identification of defense]

PATIENT: I guess I just kind of brush it off, just go on. [owns defense]

THERAPIST: ... I just had the sense again that you were frightened. That it's scary for you to take in my being on your side. [back to anxiety, and its connection to closeness]

PATIENT: I guess it is. I don't know where it's going to lead if I just abandon myself to the feeling. ... But I'm not just scared of myself but I'm scared of something that you're doing. ... I wince when you are most accepting or most recognizing. ... That's really the thing ... it's true. It's physical, my whole body just jumps. [expression of visceral experience of anxiety about closeness]

THERAPIST: Right. We're coming towards the end. I'd love you to take a look at this tape. Because there is that part that reasonably enough if you feel frightened you're going to protect yourself. ... But let me also acknowledge the other side ... how much you are doing and how undefended you are being and how open with me. ... My sense is that we are going as far as we can in a very short time. [affirmation; summing up]

In the course of doing this work, we have elaborated very important patterns: that the acknowledgment and resonance he yearns for viscerally terrifies him; that aliveness and terror are linked, as are safety and deadness; and that a self-other connection based on his being supported and recognized goes counter to his previous experience, whereas connection based on dismissiveness, painful though it may be, represents relatedness as he knows it. In addition, the experiences of defense and anxiety were explored viscerally and the patient had a success experience in being able, as he put it at the beginning of the vignette, to avoid both beating himself up or shutting down, both defensive reactions against intimacy and closeness.

THE SELF—OTHER—EMOTION TRIANGLE: POSITIVE VS. NEGATIVE ASPECTS OF SELF AND RELATIONAL EXPERIENCE

Coming to understand how self, other, and emotion are interdependent. As the patient becomes aware of different states within himself, the work focuses on helping him decipher the constituent elements of the specific self—other—emotion triangle underlying each state. He can learn, for example, that a sense of himself as a "loser, a fat, stupid, ugly loser" is connected with an other who, like the mother of childhood, possesses the power to reject him. Furthermore, he can learn that the suppression of core affect is connected intrinsically with the dynamic of the subservience of an unworthy self to a perceived-to-be-powerful other: the defensive exclusion of what he really feels—anger, in this case—is driven by his fear of being cast out.

Juxtaposing good and bad states. By attending to experiences of feeling good, both in and out of therapy, the patient can also come to know—emotionally—that when he has access to core emotions, his experience of himself is radically different. Being emotionally in touch goes with a self experience of competence, ease, and the capacity to be direct and firm; it also goes with a sense of the other as not so big and overpowering: when he is in touch, the other doesn't hold his fate in her hand. Part and parcel of the experience of the good self state is a sense of options and choices, utterly absent from the more pathological self state, where a sense of being out of control and at the mercy of forces larger than oneself predominates.

By discovering the link between particular self states and others who tend to evoke them, then linking those with particular defense—signal affect—core affect constellations, the patient can get a hold of his differential dynamics in a manner that eventually will enhance his affective competence. The result of this kind of awareness has several therapeutic consequences:

▼ The patient learns that any bad state is just that, a bad state, and that other states of mind are available. A given state does not have to carry the weight of completely representing the individual's identity. In other words, the reflective self function kicks in. "*I* am no good" changes into "*For now, I'm in a state where I feel* I'm no good." The heightened awareness of multiple states often reduces the shame and self-contempt that accompany pathological, self-at-worst configurations.

▼ With experience, the patient comes to know the features of environments in which positive self states are more likely to be evoked, and those in which negative self states are more likely to come to the fore. This awareness not only will help him differentiate and selectively seek particular environments, but contributes to his evolving affective competence, so that he will be more able to construct environments in which he can thrive.

▼ Over time, the patient becomes able to give up negative self labels; he comes to understand his more compromised functioning in the context of particular emotional situations and habits of mind resulting from best efforts in difficult earlier situations. As awareness and self-empathy grow, the patient's self-esteem, rooted in substantive experiences of his own affective competence, rises. With it, the threshold at which external situations can trigger self-at-worst configurations gets increasingly higher. The patient's sense of control and mastery slowly transforms the prevalence patterns. What emerges out of this kind of reflective awareness is a restructuring of the sense of self and other (McCullough Vaillant, 1997).

▼ With increased self-empathy and access to core affect, the patient's capacity for empathy and attunement to others grows. As a result, the dynamics of the self-other interaction shift to include greater mutuality.

THE TRIANGLE OF COMPARISONS: REPEATING VS. EMERGENT PATTERNS OF INTERACTION

Comparing relationship patterns. The triangle of comparisons illustrates the key interpersonal relationships in every patient's life. Patterns of self–other–emotion can be linked, whether similar or contrasting. The link can be one of repetition, for instance: the patient treats the therapist with the same contempt with which she treated her father, experiencing herself as superior to and smarter than both. Or the link can be one of relatedness through opposition: having always craved understanding, the patient felt connected to his aunt, with whom he felt special, whereas he felt distant with his mother, in whose presence he felt invisible. Thus, we are attuned to repeating patterns and exceptions to repetition, and to similarities and distinctions. Whether the patient is moving toward or away from greater contact, processing relational fluctuations in terms of the triangle of comparisons tracks whether the patient's here-and-now therapy experience is part of a familiar pattern or represents something new. The therapist combines her observations of patterns and teaches the patient to make these observations and connections as well.

Sensitizing the patient to repetitions of interpersonal patterns, both painful and affirming. Important past relationships have been influential in setting the stage for interpersonal experience, and their consequences sometimes are seen repeated in both current relationships and the therapeutic relationship. Together, patient and therapist explore. This exploration focuses on self experience, the perception and experience of the other, and the pattern of interactions. The therapist helps the patient become sensitized to these repeating patterns, and the patient becomes engaged in trying to recognize them as they occur. Invariably, here the focal point is on how emotion is processed and what the nature of the patient's sense of self is during such interactions.

Once a particular pattern is identified—for example, fear of annihilation (anxiety) in response to anger (core affect), leading to "good girl" behavior (defense)—it is possible to further understand it by examining other situations in which the patient responded similarly. "Have you noticed this pattern in any other relationship?" and "From where does this fear of annihilation come?" are questions that elicit important information when defenses are relaxed.

Sensitizing the patient to "new" patterns, or departures from repetitions, both painful and affirming. We are just as interested in the exception to the pattern. "Can you think of anyone in your life with whom your getting angry wasn't such a big deal?" By examining congruent and discrepant experiences, the patient can have a handle on what makes him tick, what situations he is vulnerable to, and what conditions bring out his best. *New* is emphasized because when the first relational pattern that is a departure from a particularly painful pathogenic pattern is uncovered, it appears to be the only one, happening for the first time. As mentioned earlier, the identification of one such pattern often derepresses the memory of other such instances, even if not with the dominant attachment figures.

Attentive to the repetition of pathological patterns, the therapist also is on the lookout for the "exception to the rule," that is, those relational experiences, however short-lived, in which trust, giving, faith in the patient, and love prevailed. Such exceptional experiences are important indicators of the patient's capacity to make use of affect–facilitating environments. The therapist notes, affirms, and amplifies the patient's ability to respond nonpathologically in these situations.

Exploring the role of self and other in the construction of interpersonal patterns, while exploring their consequences for self experience. By connecting past patterns to current relationships, the patient will begin to realize the active (though usually unconscious) role that he plays in generating the scenarios of his adult life through his choices. It is important that the patient take responsibility for his contribution in constructing a given relationship. Equally important is for him to be able to acknowledge and come to terms with his helplessness in situations he was powerless to influence, such as traumatic experiences. (Fosha, 1990; Herman, 1982; Miller, 1981). As the patient becomes more aware of the specifics of the interpersonal patterns that cause him difficulty, it is important that he be able to recognize those aspects of the pattern that are due to his own limitations, fears, and perceptual preferences (i.e., distortions), and those that come from others. This can be done by pointing out circumstances to which the patient responds similarly; as the patient sees that he responds to many individuals with similar feelings of anger or defensiveness, for example, he will be able to look more closely at himself. He might also become interested in investigating whether the seemingly disparate others do not in fact share some subtle similarity to which he is particularly sensitive.

The adaptational slant of the affective model of change translates into fostering awareness of the emotional environment—in this case, the emotionally significant other—to which the patient is responding. Many defenses and anxious responses will be specific to particular interpersonal environments, and recognizing how they are linked is an important step toward mastering defense and anxiety and eliminating the underlying pathology. The patient also can become sensitized to his sense of self and how it is altered in different interpersonal environments. This is closely related to how anxious and defensive responses grow out of feelings of inadequacy and vulnerability. While the therapist can acknowledge that the patient has constructed reality in a certain way, she also can acknowledge that he has adapted and responded to some external reality. Just as it is important to correct the patient's distortions due to denial, externalization, and projection of personal responsibility, therapists also must correct the kind of distortions that lead patients to blame themselves and hold themselves responsible for mishaps that are by no means under their exclusive control.

EXAMPLE In the session that followed the therapist's return from vacation, the patient was closed and distant. He insisted that he was not angry. The therapist connected the patient's reactions to the way he felt about his mother, who often had abandoned the children to pursue her own good time. The patient admitted to feeling disappointed, and over several sessions recalled many incidents of loss and feelings of abandonment, but still denied feeling angry. The therapist continued to wonder about the anger, and in this context listened to the patient talk about how he could never let anyone know how he felt, even during the many years of his mother's chronic illness. The therapist commented, "You must have been angry, but how can you be angry with a mother when you are scared you will lose her?" The patient became more in touch with his feelings of needing the therapist and anger toward her, and then his feelings of anger toward his mother for negligence and inadequate parenting that had never been acknowledged.

A particularly useful application of the triangle of comparisons is to help the patient become aware of a specific kind of repetition that plays a potent role in the maintenance of psychopathology: this repetition involves the patient treating himself as he was treated by his pathogenic other. This is a key revelation in the psychodynamic undoing of the pathogenic past's hold on the patient, as shown in the following clinical example. Here the triangle of comparisons (which incorporates the other two triangles—see Figure 6.8) helps structure the material to give patient (and therapist) clarity, as is the case in the next clinical vignette.

MANAGING TIDAL WAVES

Emily grew up with an out-of-control mother, given to irrational outbursts of temper that occasionally would spill over into physically attacking her daughter. To the little girl these flareups were as frightening and overpowering as "tidal waves." She tiptoed around her mother, "managing" the relationship so as to reduce the likelihood of another blast.

Emily regarded her father as her real parent, a father–mother figure. She loved him very much and he adored her. Understandably, the patient resisted confronting her feelings about how her father abandoned her to the mother's irrationality and violence and never intervened, maintaining the importance of respect to one's elders. In early sessions, progress was followed by backsliding, as Emily questioned whether she was being disrespectful when being assertive (which she was not).

Emily came to realize the degree to which she herself had internalized her father's way of dealing with her: to maintain the tie with her father, her only sane and reliable parent, she had adopted his strategies toward herself. She invariably talked herself through tolerating situations highly counter to her best interests. Needless to say, she was a brilliant manager of impossible people. The realization that she had colluded with her own abuse rather than standing up and being an advocate for herself was deeply painful; but her understanding brought with it a new resolve. For the first time in over thirty years, the patient began to question her unwavering commitment to her husband, whose abusiveness, self-involvement, and only intermittent care and concern for her were disturbingly similar to her mother's.

The triangle of comparisons was complete. Emily's experiences with her father became internalized in her psychic structure: she squashed and ignored her assertiveness and her anger, protest, and self-protection so as not to rock the boat. The result of that internalization was evident in how the patient dealt with her husband and coworkers. Her experience with the therapist, and with her best friends, completed the triangle of comparisons by contrast: the therapist steadfastly being her advocate encouraged her self-advocacy. The process of change involved undoing the internalization of her father's ways and on her subsequent self-management, and substituting them by internalizing an affirming relationship that promoted self-assertion. In the relationship with the therapist, she also had access to her core affects, which could not be accessed if the compromised pattern was to be maintained.

In a further session, the specific incident involved the therapist: instead of being different, in the patient's eyes, the therapist's behavior was disturbingly congruent with her father's and her own "old" behavior toward herself. This time, however, she became angry and challenged the therapist. What happened was that with dire announcements of an upcoming hurricane, Emily called early in the day to cancel that evening's session. The therapist responded by saying, "I'm going to be here anyway, so you can let me know in the afternoon whether you want to come or not." In the next session, Emily reported that initially she had felt "intimidated" by the therapist's response, as it made her feel like a "wuss" for being so worried and making a mountain out of a molehill. On the surface, the therapist had seemed so accommodating; therefore it took her a while to admit that she was "pissed off." In discussing the incident, it became clear that in canceling the session, the patient was taking an active role in maintaining her own safety, protecting herself from the onslaught of the hurricane (as she should have been protected from the onslaught of the tidal wave of her mother's and husband's outbursts of rage). Instead of validating and celebrating her efforts on her own behalf, she experienced the therapist's comments as deeming her fear unwarranted and urging her to ignore it and manage the situation.

Having had a consistent corrective emotional experience in her work with the therapist, the patient had come to expect the therapist to be on her side, to advocate for her assertion and self-protection. When Emily experienced the therapist as similar to her old figures of attachment, she held on to her new self (see Shane, Shane, & Gales, 1997), openly declared her anger, and challenged the therapist. The therapist responded by validating the patient's perception. The discrepancy between her usual way of experiencing the therapist as distinct from her father, and this experience of the therapist as similar to the father, was the impetus for this round of crucial work: it proved to be the irritating grain of sand that led to the formation of the pearl. Emily's determination not to sell herself down the river was further fortified. The session ended with the patient determined—though somewhat scared—to rigorously examine her marriage; she needed to see whether her needs and aspirations could be fulfilled and supported within it if she started to advocate on her own behalf, instead of focusing her energies on managing an essentially untenable situation.

INTEGRATIVE PROCESSING: CREATING A NEW AUTOBIOGRAPHICAL NARRATIVE

A patient once said wisely, "It'll take me a while to catch up with my experience." He is right, of course, it does take a while. Such processing is about making sense of experience by integrating affect and cognition. Reflecting on experiences is an important tool of integration: it leads to the representation of experience that then can be translated into structure. The work of integrative linking is done postexperiencing: learning can be enhanced if one can put what happened into words, articulating the essence of the experience. This is where insight—what Greenberg and his colleagues (1993) call "the creation of meaning" and Marke (1995) calls "the creation of a new narrative"— plays a major role in an experiential–psychodynamic treatment. This kind of integrative work comes into play after affective breakthroughs, at the end of each session, and figures prominently in termination-phase work.

This aspect of therapy can be described as rewriting the narrative of one's own life. This new narrative is not a fixed construction: it can never be complete or definitive, as the person's subjective "truth" is not static. While patients develop many narrative voices, we focus on using a particular set of terms—the categories of the three triangles—to accomplish this task. Since these categories and their interrelationships are at the core of what informs the AEDP therapist's work, being the terms of the therapeutic language in which treatment is performed, their use only facilitates the patient's understanding of his experience, thereby increasing his sense of mastery and control. Being able to understand not only why his psychological difficulties developed, but also how they developed and how they work—what Davanloo (1986–1988) calls the "engine" of the patient's suffering—is empowering. The new narrative tells the psychodynamic fomulation in the patient's own voice. Thus, being able to know the connection between

▼ defense, anxiety, and core affect patterns;

▼ triangle-of-conflict patterning and resulting psychopathology (symptoms, maladaptive interpersonal patterns, character patterns, etc.); and

▼ one's responses and how one perceives and experiences the "other," given one's past experiences

helps the patient feel competent in dealing with his own psychological life, which stops being terrifyingly illogical, unknown and unknowable, and out of control. The patient also should have a sense of the relational context in which he feels good, strong, and in control (i.e., affective environments that bring out the best in him), and that in which he feels bad, weak, inadequate, and resourceless (i.e., affective environments that bring out the worst in him). Being able to rapidly identify such states in himself allows him the greatest leeway to shift states, and if that proves too difficult, at least be clearly aware that this is a state and not a permanent way of being. Optimally, he will acquire a facility and fluency regarding his own patterns, as well as those of others. Such integrative processing and creating new narratives by the patient allow treatment to come to end, even though therapeutic work is a lifelong endeavor. Most important, patients will have internalized a methodology for handling emotionally stressful situations and experiences:

> I asked myself what would you [i.e., the therapist] say to me in this situation. Then I *imagined* what I wanted to do to this guy [who had made him very angry]. Yeah. Yeah, I gave him a good beating, broken bones and all. ... And then I was able to calm down and I dealt with him very straightforwardly and told him what I didn't like about what he did. You know what the funny thing is? I think I might have made a new friend.

In this example, by concretely internalizing the therapeutic process in the form of the therapist's presence and words, this former patient is able to adaptively deal with intensely troubling feelings. Dealing with them directly in his own visceral experiencing, he is able to reap the benefits of clarity and the adaptive action tendencies they release—in this case, straightforward, direct assertion. (The example comes from a one-year follow-up session.)

This integrative work is rooted in the shared experience of patient and therapist. Up to this point, in all prior interventions (and a fortiori in those that follow), succinctness is of the essence in short-circuiting defenses and seizing the moment to catch a ride on an affective wave. Here, however, the therapist can talk—and so can the patient. The goal is to help the patient weave a meaningful narrative: integrating affect and cognition, informed by understanding the contributions of self and other, *always through the lens of empathy toward the self*, a coherent autobiographical tale, a narrative not fractured by defensive exclusion, can unfold.

CHAPTER 12

EXPERIENTIAL–AFFECTIVE STRATEGIES

Experiential–affective interventions can be applied in two clinical contexts: (1) when affect is less accessible, they can be used to bypass defenses and prime affective experiencing; (2) when therapeutic work already has elicited affect, they can be used to deepen affect and work through its psychodynamic concomitants. By focusing on bodily sensations, visual images, olfactory and tactile experiences, as these strategies do, the cognitive–intellectual processes that bolster defenses are bypassed and affective access is enhanced. Furthermore, the adaptive action tendencies associated with the expression of core affects (Darwin, 1872; Greenberg & Safran, 1987) can be more readily awakened when the emotional situation in which the affects arose is lived (or relived) "in thought and fantasy" (Davanloo, 1980, 1986–1988, 1990) with vividness and textured detail (Brennan, 1995; Bucci, 1985). Activating a patient's capacity to experience deep affect gives him a taste of what defense-free functioning is like; this is one of the most effective strategies for enhancing a patient's motivation for difficult therapeutic work (Davanloo, 1986–1988, 1990).

FACILITATING GENUINE AFFECTIVE EXPERIENCE

Direct tracking of affect. Rice and Greenberg (1991) point out that emotion "cannot serve its biologically adaptive function in the complex human environment if emotionally toned experience is not attended to with accuracy and immediacy" (p. 197). Thus the patient's moment-to-moment affective experience is directly tracked and focused on prior to the selection of any particular facilitating intervention (Greenberg, Rice, & Elliott, 1993; Greenberg & Safran, 1987). Tracking and focusing provides a window on the state of the individual at that moment. As the aim is to work with what the patient feels rather than what he thinks, and to transform his emotional experience, the therapist directly tracks, focuses, and "holds" on the patient's affect throughout. The therapist can note and encourage the patient to attend to his emotional state and to experientially register how it changes from one moment to the next. The therapist also *refocuses* the patient on the experiential dimension of the process, when the patient gets off the affective track. Focusing on what he is feeling, and stating it frequently, will shift the *patient's* focus to an awareness of his feelings as well. Even with a highly intellectualized patient, the therapist can bring feelings into the process by asking direct questions about emotional reactions. The patient's difficulty in contacting his emotional reactions to painful events that he is describing can be the result of strong defenses or a deficit in emotional development due to an early childhood lacking a trusted companion to share and to help process emotional experiences. As the therapist is emotionally present herself, she can draw the patient in to examine his own emotional reactions thereby enabling him to pursue unexplored feelings at the core of his pathology.

Translating ordinary language into a language of feelings and motivation (or desire). Another way to cut through defenses and facilitate affective experience is for the therapist to use vivid, dramatic, evocative language and speak in short simple sentences. For example, a patient described an incident of physical abuse matter-of-factly, excusing it on grounds of "everybody did it in that generation." The therapist, going beyond mirroring, asked him to say more about this "nightmare"—a nightmare being a long way from socially validated reality. Another patient described how his mother, without consulting him or his wife, ordered bedroom furniture for them; he allowed as to how his mother was somewhat controlling, though he kept emphasizing that "she meant well." The therapist asked him what it was like to have his mother in bed with him and his wife.

Encouragement to stay with and tolerate deepening emotional experience. Since many patients often have little experience staying with intense affective experience, the depth of the affects generated sometimes can be scary. The therapist's simple and direct encouragement to stay with and tolerate the emotional experience, *and her reassurance of its finite nature,* can help alleviate fear and provide the safe context that is needed.

MIRRORING AND
GOING BEYOND MIRRORING

Mirroring the patient's affect: affective resonance. If the patient is emotional, the therapist *mirrors* the patient's emotions and validates his experience. The therapist does this by reflecting back the patient's emotions, sometimes enhancing, always validating, and letting the patient hear and see, in her voice, eyes, face, and words, the depth and meaning of his own experience. This deepens the patient's own affective experience and makes it "more real." A patient said, "When I'm in pain, and then I look at you, and I see my pain in your eyes, it's like it makes me feel it more deeply, like it's more real."

Mirroring and verbalizing the mirroring not only solidifies and enhances the visceral reality of a patient's emotional experience, but also can serve to increase his awareness of aspects of himself that perhaps were lived but not fully known.

EXAMPLE Clara entered treatment with profound doubts about whether she had it in her to bring to completion a major project she had undertaken. When speaking about the content of her work, however, she slipped into a state where her means of expression were particularly eloquent and graceful. Her love of her work and interest in it were palpable, and listening to her talk was a very pleasurable experience for the therapist. When she began to mirror this to her, Clara felt shy and embarrassed, having difficulty taking it in. With repeated reflections (mirroring *cum* verbalization), Clara eventually came to acknowledge her deep enjoyment of her work and recognize it in herself. Gradually, she came to identify her own sense of what the therapist talked about. More and more, Clara's excluded self experience as reflected by the therapist came to inform her sense of herself, and enhanced both her self-confidence and her sense of her own competence.

Anticipatory mirroring Initially, defenses can be observed by the therapist, who can respond as if they were not there, to see whether the patient will respond less defensively to her assumptions of openness. This is particularly effective with soft defenses, but can be surprisingly effective even with more entrenched defenses. The therapist also can use *anticipatory mirroring* (i.e., responding emotionally to the patient *as if* he were expressing his feelings, were he able to do so). As a consequence of the affective inhibition and distortion characterizing his formative experiences, the patient is an inexperienced "experiencer" and communicator of affect; these capacities, however, lie dormant and can be awakened. The therapist can project what the patient might have felt, or what he might be feeling now, were he able to allow himself to experience emotional responses. By responding to these potential emotions, the therapist can draw the patient "into a more competent set of capacities" (Harris, 1996, p. 167; see also Vygotzky's (1935) zone of proximal development) and thereby facilitate the move toward the patient's getting in touch with his own feelings. This strategy has parallels with how mothers facilitate the development of infants' communications skills by giving meaning to relatively undifferentiated states of affective arousal: the mother empathically enters the infant's experience, names it, and validates it through her response. Mothers of young infants attribute highly specific meanings to their infants' early vocalizations: "yeah, yeah, I know, you wanna look out the window"; such actions play an important a role in structuring the baby's later affective relational experience, as well as linguistic expression. Similarly, the emotional dialogue with the therapist primes the patient's affective capacity, actualizing never before realized potentials for relating.

EXAMPLE A patient was struggling to remember the death of her baby brother, when she was a child. She described how confusing it all seemed and focused on how she couldn't remember what had happened. The therapist acknowledged the confusion of a little girl overwhelmed in the face of an unknown, shocking experience. With pain in her voice, the therapist told the patient that she could imagine her as a little girl, full of pain and in need of someone to comfort her. The patient used the feelings that the therapist imagined she must have had and gained access to a vivid memory of holding the dying infant, including her own physical sensations at the time; these eventually were connected to debilitating physical symptoms the patient experienced chronically in later life, for which she had sought treatment.

Amplifying affect. When only a hint of an emotional experience is present, the therapist *acknowledges* the feeling and *amplifies* it by introducing her own emotional reaction to it. For someone who has experienced the painful isolation of having his feelings ignored or ridiculed, this can be an affecting experience. Amplifying affect also opens the patient to further exploration of his emotional reactions and to unexplored feelings at the core of his pathology. Another method is *upping the ante:* if the patient speaks in terms of irritation, the therapist can reflect it back as anger; similarly, sadness can become grief and an upsetting incident a nightmare. It is important, however, that in upping the ante, the therapist doesn't overshoot: the aim is not to artificially heighten affect but rather to capture the precise nuance of the patient's most undefended affective experience; the patient's visceral experience is the ultimate judge of the proper fine-tuning.

NAMING AND ACKNOWLEDGING AFFECTIVE EXPERIENCE

Whenever a patient has an emotional experience, it is important to acknowledge and name it; it is not unusual for a patient to have tears in his eyes, his hand in a fist, or a tender look on his face without his knowing or acknowledging that he is feeling sad, angry, or loving. Here a simple question, such as "What are the words that go with how you feel?" or a suggestion, such as "Let yourself put these feelings into words" can make a huge difference. The more the patient becomes aware that he is experiencing emotion in the moment, the more he will be able to integrate affect into his cumulative sense of self.

EXAMPLE A highly obsessional patient came in, sat quietly smiling for a little while, and then said "… Anyway," after which he launched into a rote account of his chronic marital problems. Having noted a certain lightness in his manner and his unusually warm greeting, the therapist focused on how he felt in the moment when he first walked in. The patient acknowledged, to his own surprise, that indeed he had felt relaxed and light-hearted. This led to an exploration of a whole new side of his experience, previously dismissed by the patient as insignificant. When they returned to the marital difficulties, it was from a new perspective: the patient was now much more in touch with this resourceful part of himself that he also had kept out of the marital conflict.

For many patients, being emotional means being weak or out of control; naming and acknowledging affect allows working through these associations, lessening shame, anxiety, and fear of affect. With patients who tend to "forget" what happened in the previous session as a way of disavowing their emotional experience, using the videotape to look at an affect-laden segment from a previous session is a useful tool to counteract such defenses and bolster the staying power of affect work (Alpert, 1996).

Undoing reliance on defenses against emotional experience is rarely one-trial learning. These interventions have to be made repeatedly: though it is indeed possible to get past defenses to get to affect, it is important not to underestimate the tenacity of defenses. The technique of naming and acknowledging affects is even more powerful when combined with mirroring emotional responses. As noted earlier, having one's visceral experience amplified and also naming it can be a powerful combination in getting past defenses.

AIMING FOR
SPECIFICITY AND DETAIL

Specificity is the enemy of generalization, vagueness, and denial, as well as other intellectualized defenses. Simply by asking, "Can you give me a specific example?" the patient already is engaged with an other in a situation that is emotionally significant. The specific detail is a window into how the patient perceives, constructs, and operates in his emotional world, and becomes a further source of dynamic information, as it is the patient who spontaneously selects the given scenario.

Every issue or problem the patient brings up can be better understood when described concretely, in specific detail (Davanloo, 1990). If a patient is able to bring in the sights, sounds, and smells of a situation he is describing, he will come closer to reliving the experience and its concomitant emotions. The therapist can help the patient by asking specific questions early on and by trying to picture the scene, people, activity, and drama as it unfolded. If a patient says that she hates her husband's dependency, the therapist can ask her to select one such instance, urging the patient to describe in detail where they were when this happened, how they were sitting, who said what, and so forth. The specific example immediately brings the patient closer to affect, and dynamics come into view in much sharper focus.

In the following vignette, a highly intellectualized patient had been discussing how important her birthday is to her, when a childhood photograph of her on her ninth birthday, with her brand-new bike, came into her mind. Notice how focusing on the details of the purple bicycle seamlessly releases first a flood of emotions, then deep emotional insight.

THERAPIST: So let's look together at this picture of you on your bicycle.

PATIENT: Okay ... *(describes herself at age nine, what she's wearing, etc.)*

THERAPIST: What's inside you, what are you feeling in the very moment when that picture was taken?

PATIENT: *(Silence ... sighs, soft, shy, open)* I don't know, I thought it was the greatest thing in the world, it made me so happy.

THERAPIST: Unh hmm. ... What did the bike look like?

PATIENT: *(ear-to-ear grin, a little shy)* It was purple, with big handle bars, it had a sissy bar and a banana seat with the power flowers all over it.

THERAPIST: Uh huh. [appreciative, mirroring her delight]

PATIENT: You know, I don't know, I just had the thought that *(getting tearful)* that bike was a lot like me ... I liked gaudy things when I was a kid. *(brief laugh, tender)*

THERAPIST: Unh hmm.

PATIENT: I really did. ... My sister used to tease me all the time because I always liked the tackiest and gaudiest, the outfits I would pick out for my mom to buy me

THERAPIST: Unh hmm.

PATIENT: Which she seldom did. She would sometimes buy me a component of the outfit, but the full picture was not going to swing. ... But, um, you know, that bike was kind of me.

THERAPIST: Tell me about it, I really want to see that bike. [eliciting greater detail and specificity, while priming the therapeutic bond: I really want to see that bike]

PATIENT: It was, you know, purple, it was glittery purple, and it had this wild seat and everything, and I just thought it was real neat ... *(crying)* I realize that what's tied into this for me, you know, is how early I started not focusing on my feelings but focusing on everybody else's and my not being good at knowing what was important to me and what I wanted, 'cause I turned that off in pursuit of being accepted.

THERAPIST: Unh hmm.

PATIENT: And I stopped listening to me, the emotional side of me. ... But that bike was me and I didn't care what anybody else thought.

The description of the gaudy purple beloved bike puts the patient in touch with her authentic self, a resonance she finds deeply satisfying. Through a detail viscerally and visually remembered the patient recovers her mother's failure to understand her in her own terms; from there, in graphic, nonintellectualized fashion, the patient becomes aware of how she submerged her individuality to please, to be accepted, and to be acceptable. This vignette captures an often seen dynamic: getting in touch with "having" (in this case, having her wishes for deep understanding be fulfilled, the bicycle being the objective correlative of yearned-for understanding) connects the patient to much more predominant and pervasive experiences of "not having" (i.e, the failure of finding resonant caregiving in her mother). The latter experiences bring about grief and mourning for the survival-dictated betrayal of one's essential self.

In this case, the focus on specificity and detail itself yields therapeutic results, yet this strategy forms the basis of the entire AEDP enterprise. All affective—experiential work is rooted in the specific example. The high level of clarification and detail *lays the groundwork for further affective—experiential exploration*. The more detailed the account, the harder it is for defensive distortion to undo therapeutic gains. The focus on specificity is shared with other theories of affect and emotion, some of which use the idea of specific scripts associated with different emotions (see, e.g., Lazarus, 1991; Nathanson, 1992; Tomkins, 1962, 1963). Specificity is also the technical hallmark of most experiential approaches (e.g., Alpert, 1992; Coughlin Della Selva, 1996; Davanloo, 1990; Fosha & Slowiaczek, 1997; Gendlin, 1991; Greenberg, Rice, & Elliott, 1993; Laikin, Winston, & McCullough, 1991; Magnavita, 1997; Mahrer, 1999; Marke, 1995; McCullough Vaillant, 1997; Osiason, 1995; Sklar, 1992).

Focus on specificity and detail not only combats defense, it helps the *unfolding of experience in the presence of another* (Wachtell, 1995). The therapist's inquiry into the details of experience helps the patient articulate his experience as never before. Defensive exclusion is not the only reason why experience can remain undifferentiated: aspects of experience never before considered become apparent to the patient in the process of locating them when responding to the therapist's questions. Once articulated, these experiences seem as if they were always there, though prior to their evocation through inquiry they were not. This is one sense of Bollas's *unthought known*: through articulation to an other, experience becomes elaborated and known to the self.

FOCUSING ON BODILY ROOTED CORRELATES OF EXPERIENCE

People are not always aware of the extent to which their physical sensations are associated with emotional reactions. Focusing on how the patient's experiences are rooted in the body, the therapist can help the patient to be viscerally grounded when he is speaking (Davanloo, 1990) by asking such questions as "Physically, what do you feel when you say you're 'uptight'?" or "*How* do you experience that reticence?" or "Where in your body do you experience the sadness?" The patient becomes sensitized to sensory, motor, proprioceptive, and visceral aspects of his inner experience. The greater the number of modalities used, the more lasting the affective learning that takes place (Coughlin Della Selva, 1996; Kentgen et al., 1998).

Shifting the focus of attention from what a patient is thinking to how he feels—specifically, his physical sensations and visceral experiences—is another way to circumvent defenses without confronting them head on. The goal is to sensitize patients to all aspects of their inner experience, to make ego-syntonic experiences ego-dystonic (Davanloo, 1886–1888). Memory rooted in physical experience is less ephemeral, and will help fix the experience in the patient's mind.

EXAMPLE A patient's terror of experiencing emotional pain associated with the loss of his father had become generalized into an across-the-board affective constriction. In exploring the anxiety the patient felt in the room at that moment, therapist and patient together kept track of his bodily sensations. When asked to describe his experience of the tight feelings in his chest, the patient said, "it is as though someone is squeezing my heart with their hands." He then had a flash of his father's death from a heart attack. A breakthrough of grief and pain followed. The sobbing was accompanied by the realization that since his father's death, he had made himself emotionally "dead." This brought on another wave of tears. After the waves of grief subsided, the patient felt a tremendous physical relief and relaxation. The therapist then focused in detail on this post-affective breakthrough experience by helping him fix the memory of the powerful visceral relief that followed his painful grief. This made it easier for the patient to risk allowing himself to feel, now knowing that the pain of grief is finite and often followed by the experience of relief, relaxation, and, somewhat surprisingly, well-being.

The focus on bodily-rooted correlates of experience is helpful in (a) triangle of conflict work, helping the patient differentiate defense, anxiety, and affect; (b) self–other–emotion triangle work, helping the patient discern the different physical correlates of "good" versus "bad" self states; and (c) triangle of comparisons work, helping the patient focus on how different his experiences are in affect-facilitating versus affect-disallowing environments. Paying attention to not only psychic experiences, but also how they differ viscerally makes learning to distinguish them easier.

Such visceral focusing operates like experiential biofeedback: the internal experiential sense of the difference between two states—for instance, "bad me" versus "good me"—is extremely powerful. The patient learns to control something previously felt to be completely out of control. By thus being able to reify, objectify, name, and distinguish internal states through visceral experiencing, the first step in the process of transformation already has taken place.

In the following vignette, the visceral exploration of the patient's frighteningly painful grief plays a major role in the unfolding and beginning resolution of the mourning process. The work also illustrates the use of portrayal, the next strategy of intervention to be discussed.

CRYING AT THE GRAVE

The following is an excerpt from a session with a thirty-seven-year-old man who entered treatment for depression and emotional detachment and difficulties sustaining long-term relationships. This session dealt with the patient's reactions to his father's death when he was young boy, at age seven. The father, who was the patient's primary attachment figure, was terminally ill at home, frighteningly emaciated and wasting away before the patient's eyes. The patient avoided his father, with whom he often was alone in the house. His father died in the middle of one night. The patient was rushed out of the house without any explanation and sent to live with relatives for a couple of weeks. He never went to the funeral. He spent large portions of his adult life with little or no recall of his father's death. In this session, as patient and therapist deal with the devastating impact of this death and how it was handled, the therapist suggested that together they look at the last moment when the patient saw his father alive, in an attempt to do it right this time. The patient defended against this and became intensely frustrated with himself and the therapist. This is where we pick up the action.

PATIENT: *(relatively pressured, somewhat abrasive voice; in an agitated state)* **It's like I'm a killer. I feel like a killer, an inhumane cold-blooded killer. I am a killer. I've killed my feelings, I've killed my memories, I've even killed myself.** [patient articulates his experience of defenses and their experiential consequences; profound guilt and self-blame; no self-empathy]

THERAPIST: **But you're coming back to life.** [therapist amplifies patient's vitality despite defenses]

PATIENT: *(somewhat more modulated tone)* **I don't like being a killer, I don't like it at all.**

THERAPIST: **The killer is there for protection. Because underneath that, there is an enormous amount of very vulnerable, very tender, very painful feeling, and all too human feeling. ...** *(tender voice)* **The feelings of a little boy toward his dad who is dying. ... I can see those feelings in your eyes and I certainly feel them. ... Am I right?** [empathic clarification of defenses; explanation; mirroring; explicit empathy; comparing views]

PATIENT: *(less agitated)* **Yeah, you're right** *(long pause, face quivering, starts to cry, then is sobbing)*. [affective breakthrough; state transformation that continues for rest of vignette]

THERAPIST: *(talks quietly as patient is crying)* **... at a time when you were so lonely, so alone** [empathy; amplifying patient's affective experience]

PATIENT: *(wrenching sobs, gasping for breath)*

THERAPIST: **What did the little boy feel? ... Because it isn't the grown-up you who had to face that body ...** [tracking and holding on affect, validating need for defenses]

PATIENT: **No, it's not** *(looking down)*. [relinquishes defense, accepts validation]

THERAPIST: **It is ...** he [meaning the little boy] **who had to deal with it. ... What does he feel? ... What's inside?**

PATIENT: *(patient is overcome with grief)* **Uhn** *(still crying hard; little voice)* **Why does he have to be dead? Why am I left here alone? ... To do it alone? ... Why?** *(bent over, holding himself and mildly rocking)* **... It's so painful ... so fucking painful. ... It's like being ripped open** *(clutching his stomach)*, **like having your guts spilled out and not being able to pick them up. ...** [reliving experience of grief in the moment, in touch with emotional pain, mixed with anxiety; spontaneously describes visceral correlates of experience]

THERAPIST: **Where is the pain?** [eliciting further bodily correlates of emotional pain]

PATIENT: *(comes up for air; crying subsiding)* **It's right here in my chest. It's like being totally torn open, seeing my father die.**

THERAPIST: **Just this wave of feeling that starts right in your stomach.** [mirroring bodily correlates of emotional pain]

PATIENT: *(not crying now, taking big breaths and exhaling)* **It just rips, right straight through me. And I never wanted to feel like that again ...** *(emphatically)* **never ... ever ... ever. ...** *(pause)* **Never. ... It killed me** *(starts to cry again)* **It killed me to see him die. I think I died with him.** *(sobs again, but more connected now; much less anxiety; deep sigh)* [core affective experience; bearing the unbearable; articulates overwhelmingly intense pain as reason for defense]

THERAPIST: **What happened to all those feelings?**

PATIENT: **They got pushed inside.** [experiential account of defense]

THERAPIST: **When you took care of Sammy** [friend who died of AIDS with patient at his bedside], **it's like you took care of your father ... With a tremendous amount of love. ...** *(long pause)* **Where are you now?** [acknowledging patient's capacity to give and feel, validating his positive impact on others; triangle of comparisons linking; implicitly addressing his helplessness before father's illness]

PATIENT: *(quiet tone of voice, uplifted gaze, reflective)* **When you talked about Sammy just now, taking care of him, taking care of my father, I felt that ... I felt *that* took care of something in me ... it took care of something in me** *(tender soft look, soft voice, gentle tears streaming down his face as he makes eye contact with therapist)* [healing affects] **... that I was able to take care of my father in the state that I saw him, as a dying man. ... Somehow. ...** *(deep breathing, sits up straight, deep breath, clear look in his eyes)* [postaffective breakthrough: self-affirmation; acknowledges impact of therapist's giving and its healing impact; beginning of evidence of change, and resolution]

THERAPIST: **What's inside right now?** [tracking affective self experience]

PATIENT: *(soft, tender voice)* **Somehow I feel a little more relieved.** [postaffective breakthrough feelings]

THERAPIST: **So much pain ... so much pain you've been through ...** *(deep sigh)* [validation with painful experience but one step behind patient; mini misattunement; therapist lagging a couple of steps behind patient: therapist still mirroring pain when patient has moved beyond it, to experience of relief from its full experience and expression]

PATIENT: **But at least I could feel it, and I saw it in your eyes too.** [patient corrects therapist misattunement; back on track]

THERAPIST: **How do you feel as you look into my eyes?** [relational affective tracking; reciprocal monitoring]

PATIENT: **Tenderness. The comfort I saw in your eyes. For me. Care for me. For a moment, it made me feel terrific and then I refocused back on the pain. But for that moment, it was good. ...** [seamless ability to acknowledge and experience therapist's care and its healing effects; connection and experience of being cared about allows him to return to

grief feelings, with much less anxiety, as this time he is not alone with overwhelming grief]

THERAPIST: **And the pain?** [affective tracking]

PATIENT: **My dad.**

THERAPIST: **What image this time?**

PATIENT: **Not even an image. ... A feeling. ... Just a feeling. ... Uh
... actually one image did come up.** *(pause)* **I need to go to his
grave.** [natural healing processes being restored as patient is able to engage in
mourning process; spontaneous, adaptive new emotional solution; full experience
of core affect releases adaptive action tendencies]

THERAPIST: **Tell me. ...**

PATIENT: *(moved, but clear voice; thoughtful, determined)* **I think I can
resolve something** *(sits up tall again, blows his nose, clears his throat)* **I
think I need to see his name on the tombstone ... and ... and realize that he is in there ...** [process of self-healing proceeding with its own
spontaneous momentum; undoing of denial; completion of interrupted mourning
allows patient to act with resolve]

THERAPIST: **You felt you need to do that?** [empathic reflection; validation
of beginning resolution of grief process]

PATIENT: **Yeah ... I have an image of myself looking at the grave**
(deep exhale) **yeah ... that's right ... I need to see his name there ...**

THERAPIST: **Do you know what's written on the tombstone?** [encour-
aging even greater specificity in incipient portrayal]

PATIENT: **Just the family name. I don't think there is an inscription.
And my father's name and my uncle's name and my aunt** [recovered
memories: prior to session, patient believed he had never been to cemetery
where his father was buried; it emerged that he was there as a teenager, at the
funeral of his aunt] **... and I have to feel the concreteness of it ... the
finality of it ... and I think** *(starts to tear up again, but maintains eye contact)* **... I think I'd like to cry on his grave actually** *(gentle expression)*
... I think that'll help me a lot. *(deep breath, end of wave of sadness)*
[self-healing proceeding naturally] *(leans toward therapist and looks straight at
her)* **You know, I'm just thinking** *(genuine, very nice, open smile),* **it's
okay to feel like this ... I ... I don't have any trouble once it's out.**
[patient discovers healing aspects of full experience and expression of emotion,
especially once anxiety is no longer in the picture]

This vignette illustrates how bearing previously avoided deep
affects in the presence of a caring other has a therapeutic effect: the
seeds of self-healing are contained within the experience of core affect.
In this example, the first shift occurs in the wake of empathic refram-

ing of defenses and acknowledging, even in the midst of defense-driven numbing, the patient's vitality ("you're coming back to life"). Defenses recede and there is a breakthrough of core affect: the patient viscerally experiences intense grief, of which previously he had been so frightened. Pathological mourning is being transformed into normal mourning. The second shift occurs during an intervention that acknowledges the patient's generative capacity to love and to give, in the context of some triangle of comparisons work, likening a current figure in the patient's life (Sammy) with his father. As the patient reconnects with his deep capacities and no longer experiences himself as bereft and deficient, the feeling of relief begins. He starts to reap the benefits of the deep experiencing that he has allowed. Finally, the shift that gives evidence of on-the-spot, in-the-moment therapeutic effects and benefits occurs as the patient acknowledges the profound impact of feeling the therapist very much with him, and experiencing himself as cared about. Once these shifts occur, the wrenching emotional work bears fruit and a spontaneous process of self-care and self-healing is set in motion. The patient is impelled to continue his affective journey, to face what he needs to face, and to express his feelings directly to the figure with whom the feelings are connected (his wish to cry at the grave of his father, to whom he had never said good-bye).

PORTRAYALS: IMAGINED INTERACTIONS AND THEIR DYNAMIC – EXPERIENTIAL CORRELATES

Portrayal, the pinnacle of experiential-dynamic affect work, builds on technical work described thus far. Once a specific example is located, the patient is asked to find the moment of strongest affect within it (Mahrer, 1996) and to then allow the characters to come to life and interact. The scenes to be portrayed can be real or imagined, dreaded (and thus avoided), or wished for (though never had). At each juncture of the portrayal, the patient is asked to focus on his internal reactions, and note and experience how he is feeling. The goal of a portrayal is to help the patient experience the affect and its concomitant unconscious processes in as many experiential modalities as possible (Coughlin Della

Selva, 1996); it often stimulates more specific memories. By going through imagery, portrayals automatically access a different level of experience.

To illustrate how portrayal might be used, consider an example of a patient who realizes with fresh awareness how angry he is at his mother. The therapist asks the patient to locate a particular interaction with his mother when he felt intensely angry at her, and then zoom in on the moment associated with the strongest affect. The therapist then asks the patient to *portray* in great detail how he experiences his anger: to imagine how he would express his anger at his mother, *in thought and fantasy*, unhampered by moral or reality constraints on actual behavior; how his mother would respond; how each would look in response to one another's words and actions. The patient also is asked to focus on his visceral and emotional experience at each juncture of the portrayal. To explore murderous feelings, for example—making it clear, of course, that this is an exploration of his inner life and not a rehearsal for action—the patient is asked how he imagines acting on his impulses, how the other would look as a result of his actions, and what he, the patient, would feel afterward. As in all in-depth explorations of affect, portrayals can have many healing aspects: desensitization, disinhibition, and dynamic revelation. Whether the patient feels profoundly sad, guilty, or triumphant sheds light on his experiences and the dynamics underlying his pathology.

Key to understanding the technique is understanding the mechanism of change portrayal aims to set in motion. Turning passive into active, in the presence of an affirming other, promotes mastery and undoes pathology. The more the patient is active agent, as opposed to passive recipient, the less the damage.

Portrayals facilitate and intensify the working through of core affects and their associated dynamics, as image-based information processing is much more closely associated with emotion than word-based strategies (Brennan, 1995; Bucci, 1985). Similarly, given that many (if not most) core affects have an implicit motoric action tendency associated with their full and complete expression (Darwin, 1872; Ekman, 1983; Greenberg & Safran, 1987; Izard, 1990; Lazarus, 1991), a fuller affective experience can be obtained if the actions associated with the affects are lived (or relived) "in thought and fantasy" (Davanloo, 1986–1988) rather than described.

Elaborating specific details, whether real or imagined, is very important: it increases the patient's capacity for full emotional experience. To have the patient declare murderous impulses is not sufficient;

the details of the murderous act must be portrayed. It then becomes crucial that the impact of the aggressive act be confronted—that the patient envisions what the person looks like as a result of the confrontation or attack or murder. As the next two examples illustrate, we never know which detail is going to open up a realm of unconscious experience, the source of highly important dynamic information.

EXAMPLE Mira came to the session extremely shaken up after an incident where another child came very close to choking her one-year-old daughter. She was unable to experience any aggression toward the child aggressor. The therapist asked her to portray what her reactions would be to the death of her daughter, had she been killed. Initially horrified, deep grief broke through as Mira pictured just holding the child's body and not being able to let go, unable to say good-bye to her. Again, the therapist chose to bypass this road block—that is, the patient's inability to say good-bye to and let go of her daughter—and kept pressing forward, next asking the patient where she would want to bury her daughter. The patient, surprising herself, immediately responded "next to my mother-in-law," who had died some years back. This unearthed the importance of that relationship for the patient. Sobbing, she remembered how nurturing her mother-in-law had been to her, and how grateful she had felt. It opened up a fresh wave of grief about what was lacking and had always been lacking in her relationship with her own mother. In this example, what started out as an attempt to explore the patient's capacity to experience her aggressive impulses led to a deepening of her mourning of past emotional deprivations, a renewed appreciation of nurturing relationships, and a deeper understanding of the multidetermined emotional significance of being a good mother.

EXAMPLE Another dramatic example was presented by Davanloo (1990, pp. 183–84). The patient was very angry at the therapist. He asked her to portray her anger and what she wanted to do to him. The patient imagined kicking him in the stomach. "So what happens to my stomach?" he asked, clearly expecting her to say something about its being bruised or bloodied. Instead, in a trancelike state, the patient answered much to the surprise of both the therapist and herself, "The baby comes out," after which she broke down sobbing. What came to the fore was that the patient was reliving a very early experience of emotionally losing her mother with the birth of her baby sibling, who became a very sickly child: this was the core loss responsible for the patient's chronic lifelong depression. The portrayal allowed the patient to access unconscious, primary process material that captured the intensity of her experience, which began when she was a girl of two. Note also that this occurred in the first evaluation session.

Completion of portrayal. A portrayal should be taken to its natural conclusion. If the portrayal deals with mourning, the patient should say good-bye, deal with the body of the deceased, and imagine the funeral. If the portrayal is of murderous rage, it should not stop with the attack. The patient needs to look at the body of the object of rage, acknowledge the damage, and explore his feelings about it. To stop before its conclusion is (a) another manifestation of defense and (b) prevents the patient from reaping the full benefit of the adaptive action tendencies released by the completion of the affect sequence. Sometimes it can be a clinical decision to accept the level of the work, as with Mira in the previous example, if the patient feels unable to go further; this is particularly crucial with patients who are dealing with traumatic issues and for whom it is paramount that they feel in control of their personal experience (e.g., Herman, 1982). If only soft defenses are present, it is very important to continue to conclusion: at every step of the way, there are images, visceral sensations, fantasies, and words accompanying action. Since clearly not all can be simultaneously explored without disrupting the flow of the material, the clinician should be aware of these realms of activation and select the most appropriate for the patient in that moment.

Types of portrayals. Portrayals can serve different functions, and there are many different kinds. Here are some examples:

Affective portrayal to complete interrupted affect sequences. Here the goal is to help the patient complete an affective experience that was interrupted or is incomplete (Greenberg & Safran, 1987; Greenberg et al., 1995). Portrayals can be effectively used to advance grief work that is frozen or has reached pathological proportions (Volkan, 1981). One of the principal ways in which affect sequences are completed through portrayals is to have the patient imagine the lost other. If, for example, the patient is dealing with the death of a lover, the therapist might ask the patient to imagine how he and his lover would say good-bye. She would ask the patient to imagine the burial and funeral, as well as elicit memories of emotional times together. *The dialogue is always in the present tense, and always with first-person pronouns.* If the patient says, "I always wanted him to know that I loved him," the therapist might reply, "tell him now, and let yourself tell him directly." The goal is for the patient to either get to where he is able to imagine saying directly to his lover, *"I love you,"* or else gain a deep understanding of why something so seemingly simple is so difficult for him. The latter would lead to another round of therapeutic work. Concretizing fears of loss and exploring them through portrayals of final good-byes is very useful for working with issues of separation and individuation (which often are associated with death in the unconscious), and in some cases—*though by no means all*—with issues triggered by the upcoming termination of therapy.

Internal dialogue portrayals (to help with issues of shame, guilt, ambivalence, and dissociation). Internal dialogue portrayal is used to help the patient deal with experiences of inner conflict and dissociation in an effort to concretize different aspects of the self, giving each a voice so the patient is able to explore the phenomena in much greater detail. Similar to the two-chair technique (Greenberg et al., 1995) used by Gestalt therapists, we have the patient speak to himself with the aim of changing a critical voice to a positive one (to encourage tolerance of positive feelings, and to see what those dynamics are about), or speak to himself in a critical voice to trace its genetic roots. With dissociative dynamics, the portrayal assists integrative goals (as illustrated in the next chapter).

Impulse, affect, and interpersonal desensitization portrayals. Like anger, rage, and murderous feelings, sexual feelings that are difficult for the patient to deal with must also be desensitized. The patient is asked, for instance, what he would like to do, how he imagines the other person's body, what sensations he experiences as he imagines different aspects of the scenario, what parts of the other's body he is most attracted to, and how he would respond if the other reciprocated or rejected his advances. These explorations, accompanied by moment-to-moment attunement to waves of affect, anxiety, and defense, and appropriate interventions, can go a long way toward eventually stripping sexuality of its shameful and guilty associations. This portrayal also can be a powerful technique when an unresolved libidinal fixation—to a parent, for instance, or an unavailable other, such as the therapist—holds back the person from being able to have intimate, committed adult relationships. Portraying the sexual fantasy with the forbidden object and exposing the deep dark secret to the light of day, however excruciating it may be in the process, can be enormously liberating upon completion. This happens in part through having these experiences with a nonjudgmental, nonshaming other; it also happens through the deep unconscious responses that come to the fore as a result of visceral exploration. The specificity and immediacy will derepress memories and bring into focus anxieties, shames, and guilts interfering with the patient's capacity for pleasurable sexual enjoyment and deepening intimacy and closeness. With each successive portrayal, the patient becomes desensitized to the experience of the particular affect, so that the threshold at which it can be fully experienced and processed is lowered. As a result, through practice, the patient acquires increasing fluency, familiarity, and relative ease with the emotion, which facilitates mastery and furthers desensitization. The working-through process can proceed.

Reparative portrayals. The function of a reparative portrayal is to enable the patient to have a healing, wished-for experience of a kind not attained in actuality. By working to enhance the felt reality—that is, the experiential, visceral quality of these fantasies—they come to have a physically rooted actuality of their own, thus adding to the patient's experiential repertoire.

AFFECT RESTRUCTURING: EXPERIENCE AND EXPRESSION OF AFFECT; FEELING AND DEALING

Optimally, the adaptive action tendencies released by the full and complete experiencing of core affect represent the organismic path to affect restructuring. In addition, the "cognitive linkages [that] must be developed to provide *balance, guidance, and control*" (McCullough Vaillant, 1997, p. 281), discussed in chapter 11, focus on the integration of cognition and affect, and on the development of perspective, and meaning.

In less than optimal circumstances, however, or with patients whose psychic organization is more fragile or whose interpersonal skills are rudimentary, specific work aimed at fostering the adaptive translation of the emotional work of the session into real life can be highly beneficial.

Appropriateness of expression. Throughout the affect work (and pointedly so during portrayal work), the therapist underlines that the affective scenarios being explored have only to do with *thought and fantasy,* not enactment. Affect work is liberating and removes inhibitions.

Post affect work focuses on appropriate expression: there is a distinction between (a) intense experience and direct expression, which are at a premium within the therapy session, and (b) appropriateness, modulation, and self- and other-attunement, which need inform action when the patient seeks to translate therapeutic epiphanies into his day-to-day life with others. With many patients, just going over this distinction is sufficient; with patients with compromised self-regulatory abilities, however, the more explicit, specific, and elaborated the discussion, the better.

Feeling and dealing: balancing self-expression with the reality of the other. In the optimal management of an interpersonal situation, balance must be achieved between sensitivity to one's own needs, attunement to the needs of the other, and attention to process issues. Taking into account the reality of the other with whom the patient needs to deal is extremely important. Processing and role playing can also clarify these issues for the patient. Facing a spouse's or a parent's communicative limitations can be extremely painful and can actually initiate another round of work. One patient, for example, wanted to have an honest discussion with his wife about the strengths and weaknesses of their marriage; each time, she would get "her back up," and go on the attack. Over time, he learned that he had to do a fair amount of work reassuring his wife, framing things carefully, before any conversation could take place. Though initially resentful about how hard he had to work, over time, he came to deeply know how much he valued his marriage, which made it easier (though by no means ever easy) to do what was needed. With time, he also came to realize the ways in which he too was not the easiest of partners.

Translation of therapeutic gains into life outside of session. Often, the patient will do beautiful work within sessions, but not experience a great deal of change in his life. For this express purpose, Mahrer (1999) advocates the use of gradual portrayals, starting with the most outrageous, to access and liberate the inner quality of the experience. Over time, the patient is helped to preserve the visceral aspect of experiencing as he engages in imaging increasingly realistic scenarios, which eventually can inform everyday life.

A REPARATIVE PORTRAYAL:
MOTHERING MOTHER

In this excerpt, which comes from the third session of therapy, the patient's attitude toward the poor mothering she received has already undergone a change. Instead of reflecting poorly on the patient (she was unlovable, a pain, not worthy of being cared for, experiences the patient felt were like a "stain" on her soul), the much more positive sense of herself—the result of the treatment experience—led, interestingly, to a much greater empathy for her mother and for her mother's predicament, which may have resulted in the poor mothering she had experienced. In the presence of a growing self-empathy and compassion for others as a result of postaffective breakthrough, we build on this patient's experience through the use of a reparative portrayal. The patient is encouraged to imagine what it would have been like for the baby (that she once was) to be properly and lovingly mothered by the kind of mother her mother might have been, if only her mother had had more support and understanding herself. The following vignette begins about five minutes into the session. The patient, looking relaxed, has been describing the changes that she has experienced over the past week. She had been feeling much less depressed, was very cognizant of taking good care of herself by managing and reducing the stress in her life as much as possible, and feeling less anger and more sadness toward her mother (who had died many years ago).

PATIENT: **There's less anger and more feeling sad for her and feeling sad for me at the same time, kind of like we were both trapped in the same situation that wasn't either of our making. By and large she was kind of fulfilling these ... it was almost like it was planned out how things would be for her.** [development of self-empathy and self-compassion go hand-in-hand with development of empathy and compassion toward her mother, who in the process becomes more real and three-dimensional]

[Here patient discusses family situation in which her mother was supported by neither her own mother nor by her husband, the patient's father]

PATIENT: **I wish we could have been there for each other. I must have been from very early on not able to relate back to her. We just didn't have the time. The opportunity was missed. As soon as I was able to, I left home** [referring to having gone to college and gotten married very young]. **I mean I really left and then left and then left.** [a bit of defense here]

THERAPIST: **See if you can say that to her.** [shift to portrayal: let's see if we can bypass defense and deepen affective experience; in previous two sessions, portrayals had been somewhat difficult for patient]

PATIENT: To her? ... Well, okay. *(speaking in soft, relaxed voice)* "Mom. I just wish that you were still here and we could have this time together and we could go back and get to know each other and care for each other and that's it really ..." It's just that, you know, you can't redo it. You can't become a baby again. You know she would be seventy-two now. That's not so old. [for the first time, patient seamlessly shifts gears and speaks to her mother, to whom she can now imagine relating as a result of empathy toward her; self-blame is nowhere to be seen; patient expresses wish to be able to "redo" early years]

THERAPIST: When you were speaking to her and you said "Mom," who did you see? Who where you speaking to, what was your image? [here is an opportunity to dynamically and experientially deepen work: patient is, in fantasy, repairing relationship with her mother; let's see at what point she goes in]

PATIENT: I don't know. I just closed my eyes ... *(closes her eyes again)*

THERAPIST: What do you see?

PATIENT: I can see her at different ages. I mean, maybe the image that comes first is when she's younger than I can really remember her. It's an image that comes from some pictures ...

THERAPIST: What does she look like [in those pictures]?

PATIENT: *(dreamy voice)* She was graduating high school. She has on a nice dress and her hair is ... she's really pretty. She was an eighteen-year-old. She looked like a warm person. ... If I let go, I see her holding the baby, fixing the picture, you know, making it a loving scene. I mean why not, you know? [patient imagines her mother as she was before she was even pregnant with the patient: this, along with other evidence, suggests trouble in mother-daughter relationship from the start; patient is truly creating a "new beginning" for herself, as well as a new beginning for her mother]

THERAPIST: Help me see what you see.

PATIENT: She's taking care of me. A newborn, two or three months old ... rocking. You know how you hold a baby like that *(demonstrates holding baby's head on her shoulder, holding her around her back, pressing baby's body against her own)*. ... Putting the baby down to sleep, rocking the crib, the cradle. It's nice. She's singing. ... She never sang. [patient is totally absorbed in experience she is portraying: note present tense, i.e., "she's taking care of me" and "she's singing"; the patient is experientially and symbolically elaborating and experiencing something she's never had before, a loving mother-daughter relationship where she is loved and taken care of tenderly]

THERAPIST: Uh huh ...

PATIENT: She was told not to sing. You know, one of those "your voice isn't good enough" type things in school.

THERAPIST: **What is she singing?** [add another experiential channel of associations: the visual, augmented with the auditory channel]

PATIENT: There's a lullaby in my head. It goes *Uh uh uh uh ba—by, Uh uh uh uh ba—by . ...* Not much of a lullaby, but that's what it was. A good rocking one. ... *Uh uh uh uh ba—by . ...* It's for a non-singer. [patient does not miss a beat: her immersion in experiential portrayal continues and deepens]

THERAPIST: **You're empathic even with that. ... So the baby is being sung to sleep. And she** [i.e., the mother], **how is she feeling?** [adding emotional–fantasy component; elaborating inner life of the mother—a crucial aspect of the baby's feeling loved]

PATIENT: Hmmm, this is my fantasy, so let's say she's sitting by the window looking out at the park ...

THERAPIST: **Okay ...**

PATIENT: Rocking the baby, maybe sitting in a rocking chair herself, so she's feeling peaceful too. [in her fantasy, patient intuitively makes sure mother is taken care of herself: the feeling state patient imagines the mother is in is calm, peaceful, and serene, much like her own state during this work; this is a content woman, with plenty of resources to care for a baby]

THERAPIST: **This a long way from the woman who sat on the floor not even looking over at the baby in the basket on the floor.** [therapist contrasts mother of fantasy with patient's actual mother at the time, when patient was an infant]

PATIENT: Yeah!

THERAPIST: **What's the baby feeling in your fantasy?** [continuing with elaboration of the portrayal; experientially filling in more details]

PATIENT: In my fantasy, ... cared for and warm and fed. Just totally relaxed. Feeling totally ... just no stress ... just love and being cared for. Being able to just drift off to sleep. [filling in more texture of the portrayal: the baby's inner experience; patient is given opportunities to articulate affect as she is experiencing it]

THERAPIST: **So when you look at the little girl, you say you have a sense of understanding, no blame. Because in some ways, you are forgiving your mother, but it's also forgiving yourself. Because there has been this dark piece of your soul** [where self-blame lies, i.e., this is an understood reference to an ongoing negative self experience]. **... So what do you say to yourself, to yourself as a little baby?** [beginning of integration work; interpretation; one last internal dialogue portrayal]

PATIENT: *(very tender, warm, and loving voice and manner)* "You're loved ... you're a good person. I love you. You didn't do anything wrong."

[self-blame has been transformed into self-love, self-forgiveness, based on deep empathy; empathy replaces judgment]

THERAPIST: **The little girl you're talking to is how old?** [another psychodynamic fixing: since in this level of affect-driven experience there is much more fluidity than in cognition-driven mentation, it is important to see if the images change, as they most certainly do in this case]

PATIENT: **Five. ... It must have been very hard for me at five because my sister was just born and my mother was so happy with her. It must have felt really personal then. In whatever way, it was clear that I was the one that couldn't bring her happiness. And Sara** [her sister] **could.** [we now have a complete psychodynamic formulation based completely on sequence and depth of experiential material patient was dealing with]

The patient presented with an acute depression superimposed on a more chronic depressive state, the current depression triggered by a rejection. The clinical evidence prior to this session strongly suggested maternal deprivation: her mother had never bonded with her, the mother's first baby. The resulting deep feelings of being fundamentally unlovable—feelings that the patient always had to wage battle against— were at the core of the chronic depression that plagued the patient throughout her life.

The preceding sessions were marked by powerful affective break-throughs: the patient was able to process some of her feelings of shame and worthlessness, and truly take in the therapist's deep affirmation: a state of feeling soothed and peaceful ensued, a state that the patient had been in for some days prior to this third session. She reported taking uncharacteristically good care of herself.

In this reparative portrayal, the patient deepened the self-healing process through healing her mother in her mind. The patient imagined her mother young and as yet unscarred: this is a mother who could mother her and whose mothering she could take in and thereby feel soothed and loved and peaceful. The portrayal fleshed out the dynamics of the core state the patient had been in for days and further illuminated its origins in yearned-for experiences of love, acceptance, and tender care. The state of deep experiencing the portrayal brought about gave the patient access to deeper unconscious material: with the fluidity and freedom from reality constraints that characterizes unconscious material, in the last exchange, the little girl in the patient's mind seamlessly shifts from being an infant to being five years old, a highly significant age, five being the patient's age when the second wave of emotional damage occurred.

The psychodynamic formulation became more thorough. The new material made clear that, for the patient, the maternal deprivation was the injury: the insult occurred—as this reparative portrayal so clearly reveals—when the patient's sister Sara was born, when the patient was *five years old*. Her mother bonded with, adored, and treasured the new baby girl. This one-two combination led the patient to believe that the fault lay not with her mother, who showed herself capable after all of being a loving mother, but rather with the patient herself. Something intrinsically horrible about her must have made the mother not want to be with her from the very beginning. The developmental sequence of emotional events became translated into a psychic structure based on shame, self-blame, and a profound sense of inadequacy, leading to chronic depression and loss of the capacity to bear strong affects alone.

The reparative portrayal led to two important psychic achievements: it enhanced the explanatory power of the psychodynamic formulation, and through the core affects it released, deepened the patient's capacity to love and take care of herself; and it allowed her to feel fully worthy of that love and care, despite her mother's tragic failure to provide these for her.

CHAPTER 13

BELLY TO BELLY, CHEST TO CHEST

*A Case Illustrating
the Ongoing Unfolding
of Core Affective Experience*

Aimee is a twenty-four-year-old woman who came to treatment complaining of long-standing difficulties with depression, and with an eating disorder. She also was struggling with serious marital and sexual difficulties; professional indecision; anxiety; generalized feelings of confusion, doubt, lack of confidence; and pronounced low self-esteem. No aspect of her life was free of difficulty, no aspect a source of reliable satisfaction. At the time of the initial evaluation, she was particularly tormented by conflict about having children: feeling internal and external pressure to have children while feeling not ready to do so, she was overwhelmed by the idea, and questioned whether she had it in her to be a good mother. These difficulties occurred within a personality structure with strong obsessive-compulsive coloring. Since age eighteen, she had been in three prior therapies.

Aimee's defenses included isolation of affect, rationalization and intellectualization, as well as regressive defenses such as numbing, fragmentation, weepiness, and tantrums. Anxiety was a major part of the picture, manifested in confusion and loss of cognitive clarity.

The patient's relationship with her father is pertinent to the following session: she strongly suspected that there had been some sexual abuse by her father around the time she was nine. She did not have any specific memories, although she was aware of a gap in her memory of that time, and a major shift in her functioning. Prior to this period, she had been an exuberant ice-skater; much more subdued after age nine, she gave up figure skating shortly thereafter, and she also stopped playing the recorder. Clearly recalled, however, were innumerable episodes of her father's highly sexual taunts, innuendoes, and lewd conversational gambits toward the patient during adolescence, many of which took place at the dinner table. Physical abuse by the father—chasing her around the house, up the stairs, and beating her—also was part of the picture.

Where the father was controlling, overbearing, grandiose, manipulative, omnipotent, and physically abusive, all the while normalizing his behavior, the mother was taciturn and withdrawn, never challenging her husband's control. Aimee's mother suffered at least two episodes of what sounded very much like major depression, without receiving treatment.

The following vignette is from the twelfth session of psychotherapy. This session begins with Aimee relating some positive changes, all however accompanied by an increase in the intensity of her directly experienced anxiety. The locus of her anxiety, as well as other symptoms, is in her stomach. The patient began the session by recounting a specific incident: she and Edward, her husband, are having dinner at her parents' house, the house where she grew up. We pick up the action about twenty-five minutes into the session. Aimee's father, ignoring her, and "male bonding" with Edward—whom he actually deeply despises, considering him not good enough for his daughter—"sympathizes" with his son-in-law for what he assumes to be the paucity of sex in his life, at the same time completely ignoring the fact that Aimee and Edward were involved in a conversation. Aimee's mother might as well have been absent. It should be noted that in prior sessions, guilt and anxiety prevented the patient from fully experiencing her anger at her father: in reaction to angry feelings, she would start to cry, lose her point of view and her opinion, and become generally confused.

Segment 1

THE FIRST PORTRAYAL:

DESENSITIZATION OF AGGRESSIVE IMPULSES

PATIENT: ... Then he told Edward, "Did you know that pandas only have sex once every five years?" Is that supposed to make Edward feel good? I got up and walked out of the room. [avoidant defense] I guess that's one area I'm just not past with him.

THERAPIST: So let's look at this: Here you are, having a conversation with your husband and not only does your father butt in, he butts in in this very suggestive, intrusive way. What do you feel towards

him? [it is clear that an exploration of patient's aggressive impulses is in the works; it is important to set scene, lay foundation, make things clear so that difficult exploration will be on solid ground; therapist is deliberately using affectively charged language]

PATIENT: I was feeling really angry towards him but I was also feeling … again like that queasiness [mixture of anger, anxiety, and disgust] and I was feeling really angry—

THERAPIST: You were feeling really angry? And queasy? You were in touch with both?

PATIENT: *(speaking fast, with pressure, but also with animation)* Yeah. I think so. At first, I was really queasy, but then I was annoyed that he was such a jerk. Everything is about sex with him. Everything is about sex, there is some connection to it in everything he does. Okay, we're all sexual beings and everything, but everything isn't all about sex. You know, I feel like—he got me so angry like [I wanted to say]— "shut up," like—"leave me alone about it, don't talk to me about it. [beginning of spontaneous portrayal] Don't you see that it gets me upset, don't you see that I walk out of the room, don't you see that I make a face, that I'll make a comment that I don't want to hear it, I'll tell you, don't tell the stupid joke and whatever" and—It doesn't matter. It's about him. [patient, having done this kind of work in previous sessions, spontaneously launches into a portrayal, i.e., what she imagines saying to her father in her mind in order to express her anger]

THERAPIST: Uh huh. Now if, in your mind—clearly we are not talking reality, but in your mind, if you didn't walk out [undoing avoidant defense], but you just stay and let go of these massive rage feelings inside, what do you imagine yourself doing to him? [amplification of feelings: upping ante from "anger" to "massive rage"; deepening of portrayal]

PATIENT: I was thinking about that and I—

THERAPIST: Right then and there? [therapist marks that patient is spontaneously doing this work on her own in the very situation that is triggering intense anger]

PATIENT: No, when I walked out.

THERAPIST: Uh huh.

PATIENT: *(with intensity and animation; demonstrating her actions with gestures)* I was digging my nails into him and telling him to just shut up— "just shut up." [note how absorbed patient is in process; launches in without qualifiers; marker of communications suffused with previously unconscious material]

THERAPIST: Digging your nails—how? what did you see? [getting more specificity and detail]

PATIENT: *(intense, almost shaking)* Just like shaking him and like putting my nails in … you know … in a way I was like—I mean like—this is going to sound like ridiculous ... but like I want to desexualize him. You know like—

THERAPIST: It's not going to sound ridiculous. Well—what? Allow yourself to put into words what the feeling is. [offering support; naming affective experience; patient clearly uses a distancing word "desexualize"; given highly sensitive nature of material and overall forward-moving direction of process, therapist doesn't address this particular tactical defense]

PATIENT: *(intense and intent)* I want to ... castrate him. [patient undoes her own defense] It's like—"no more for you," you know, and like, [I want to] take that piece of his brain out, take out whatever is making him connect everything to sex ... cut out his tongue. ... It's so upsetting to me. *(pause; shifts focus of concentration from inner experience to therapist)*

THERAPIST: Aimee, it's so positive that you are allowing yourself to be so in touch with these feelings and that they are not just reserved for a therapy session, but that you do work on your own in the moment as it's happening—I just think that it's extraordinary! [acknowledgment of patient's therapeutic progress and accomplishments; solidifying foundation before doing more deep work] However, let's stay with what we're doing because clearly this is some very difficult stuff to admit. You want to cut out his brain and his tongue and [get rid of] what he thinks and what he does. ... But ultimately it is all about cutting out that some-thing in him that makes him stick sex into everything. It's like his genitals, his penis—It's always in your face, no pun intended. Maybe pun intended. [given patient's history of eating disorder, and localization of anxiety in her stomach in the form of queasiness, therapist is deliberately using some oral imagery, as hypothesis testing, waiting for confirming or disconfirming evidence]

PATIENT: *(Facial expression of disgust, repulsion)* And that's what's sicken-ing. Yuk. [another wave of anxiety and disgust]

The therapy is taking. The patient is clearly aware of and in touch with her angry feelings as they are happening. Aimee is doing work out-side of the session, which is a positive sign: in the past, an episode such as the one she is recounting would have led to eating problems, increased depression, and provoking a fight with her husband. The therapeutic alliance is high, and the patient spontaneously launches herself into por-trayal work that through intense imagery rapidly accesses the exact nature of her angry feelings and sadistic impulses. In the law of the uncon-scious—an eye for an eye—Aimee, disgusted and enraged by her father's lewdness, imagines removing that which gives offense: his tongue (for speaking dirty), a piece of his brain (for connecting everything to sex), and his genitals. The therapist's test amplification of oral imagery leads to another wave of anxiety and disgust. More work is necessary. The por-trayal is incomplete: the patient has spoken about wanting to castrate the father but that act has not yet been portrayed, nor its consequences.

Segment 2
CONTINUING WITH THE PORTRAYAL

THERAPIST: **When I said that, what did you see? What image did you have?** [next round of portrayal work]

PATIENT: **Just my father.**

THERAPIST: **Just how?**

PATIENT: **I saw him actually sitting at the head of the dining room table.**

THERAPIST: **Mm hmm.**

PATIENT: **And that's where—that's where it happens ... that's where the most vulgar aspect of him comes out and that's so sick. And then I'm thinking about Edward, when he gets too—well, too overbearing or sexual or touchy feely for me, I think, who are we talking about here?** [patient makes a spontaneous defense interpretation in context of triangle of comparisons work, seeing her anger at her husband as displacement of her anger at her father]

THERAPIST: **What do you mean, Who are we talking about here? Who are you reacting to, do you mean?** [clarification]

PATIENT: **Yeah.**

THERAPIST: **Go ahead.**

PATIENT: **I feel like, it's not about Edward. It's about this.** [patient makes spontaneous link between current difficulties with her husband and core difficulties with her father; triangle of conflict and triangle of comparison work is an opportunity to do important work with insight yielded by deep affect, and simultaneously, have a breath-catching moment before next round of affect work]

THERAPIST: **So, in that moment, if you really go on the offensive, if you get it all out, "you're not going to do this to me, take this," and you take your revenge on him—you started out first with this image of digging your nails into him but then you had this image of castration—castration and cutting out the piece of his brain that's always connecting everything to sex, and it's poisoning or contaminating everything for you. How do you do it?** [reorienting, regrounding, going for completion of portrayal]

PATIENT: **That's the hard part** [aversive affects associated with primary affective experience]

THERAPIST: **That's the hard part because now you have to deal with his body—not just his head but now you have to deal with his body.** [empathic elaboration and validation of aversive affects]

PATIENT: *(serious, again absorbed)* **I think it's like ... there's this big meat** cleaver in my hands and it's just like chop—you know, no more penis. *(voice breaking)* But I can't deal with that.

THERAPIST: What do you mean, you can't deal with that?

PATIENT: *(again, look of disgust)* Thinking of actually doing that, not actually, but even ... I don't want to even think about his penis.

THERAPIST: You can't let yourself because what happens if you do?

PATIENT: Yuk. *(total disgust)*

THERAPIST: Yuk is what, Aimee?

PATIENT: *(more anxiety, tearful)* Yuk. Yuk, like "get away from me." I just want him to be desexualized. [note her move toward more intellectualized language; striving for greater safety]

THERAPIST: Right, but it's not going to happen in this fantasy, in this feeling, unless you deal with it, right now. [encouraging her to continue with hard affect work]

PATIENT: *(very shaky voice)* It's just like ... chop it off.

THERAPIST: Aimee, what's happening to you physically? I know you're struggling. Put it out. [shifting focus to her visceral experience; explicit empathy and encouragement to persist]

PATIENT: *(very deep crying, struggling to talk)* It's just so painful. All this pain comes out. I don't know where it's coming from. [breakthrough of core affect of emotional pain]

THERAPIST: It's okay. Let it come. Let it come. [reassurance; being with her; going forward. Therapist's going forward conveys message to patient that it is okay to continue with intense experience, that therapist is not frightened and backing off]

Here the therapist is very supportive and encouraging, but ups the ante in the portrayal of the enactment of the patient's anger at her father by suggesting that she not avoid imagining what she wanted to do to her father's penis, an image the patient spontaneously introduced. The patient viscerally experiences a surge of anxiety, which turns out to be related to the emergence of yet another previously inaccessible wave of deep feeling. The therapist's reassurance and emotional being with her, "It's okay. Let it come. Let it come," helps allay the patient's anxiety and lays the groundwork for a breakthrough of the core affect of emotional pain that follows in the wake of reassurance. This sequence illustrates what is meant by the full experience of core affect (here, anger), leading to yet another layer of unconscious material, which leads to yet another wave of deep affective experience (here, pain).

Segment 3
WORKING WITH EMOTIONAL PAIN

PATIENT: **Why is it so painful to me?**

THERAPIST: **Just let the pain come and let the tears out. They've been inside for a long time. Who's the pain for?** [support; encouraging patient to stay with feeling; starting next round of deep affective processing, this time to explore core affect of pain, which has arisen spontaneously]

PATIENT: *(very poignant, very simply)* **For me.** [beginning of process of mourning the self and its affective marker, emotional pain]

THERAPIST: *(tender voice)* **I know.** [affirmation, empathy, support] **Let that hand go.** *(mirroring her gestures and speaking about her right hand, which is in a tight fist)*

PATIENT: *(opens her hand)*

THERAPIST: **What's that hand doing? Just let yourself connect the hand with what your—** [inviting unconscious to speak through the language of the body]

PATIENT: **It's mutilating him** *(cutting motion)*, **pushing him away.** *(shoving motion)* [invitation accepted]

THERAPIST: **Pushing him away?**

PATIENT: *(very poignant tone)* **I wish I knew why it's so important to push him away.**

THERAPIST: **What are you doing with your other hand? Your other hand is also starting to go ... your left hand.** [further focusing on bodily rooted correlates of affective experience]

PATIENT: *(vulnerable)* **I don't know. It's sort of like protecting me.** *(left arm wraps around herself, holding herself)*

THERAPIST: *(soft tone)* **That was my image. My image was that the left hand was for you and the right hand was for him.** [empathic elaboration]

PATIENT: **I was just thinking—I don't think this is such an issue for Lisa.** [sister]

THERAPIST: **You don't think it's such an issue for Lisa?**

PATIENT: **I know she has a problem with sexuality and it's affected her but I don't think it's like this.** [patient clearly dealing with extremely painful question of whether she was sexually abused; she again very responsibly attempts to link experiential work with different patterns of experience, in this case, for her and her sister] *(clutching her head)*

THERAPIST: **What's happening with your head?**

PATIENT: *(crying deeply, and quietly)* I don't know. [another wave of pain]

THERAPIST: **Just put into words all these things that are coming up—these feelings.** [labeling visceral experience of affect]

PATIENT: **There's so much.**

THERAPIST: *(soft, tender voice)* **It's okay. You're not by yourself this time. You're not alone.** [being with patient; note how reassurance, presence, emotional contact ushers in next layer of deep emotional work]

Segment 4
UNDOING DISSOCIATION THROUGH

REPARATIVE PORTRAYAL

PATIENT: **I keep seeing this little girl.**

THERAPIST: **This little girl. ... Who?**

PATIENT: *(very absorbed in what she is seeing)* **She's sad. Lonely. She's just trying to be everything other people wanted her to be.** [flowing elaboration of portrayal: little girl is clearly herself]

THERAPIST: **How do you see her?**

PATIENT: **Just standing.**

THERAPIST: **Describe her to me. I want to see her as you're seeing her. How old is she?** [getting more detail, while also deepening contact with therapist; therapist wants patient to be aware that she is telling her story to a receptive other who wants to hear]

PATIENT: **She's nine.**

THERAPIST: **Nine?**

PATIENT: **Or eight.** [note precision of age]

THERAPIST: **Mmm hmm.**

PATIENT: **She has two little barrettes in her hair like her mother used to put them in. She has blond hair and she's wearing little green gym shorts and a T-shirt. She's just forlorn.** [specificity of imagery is further evidence of core affect]

THERAPIST: **Mm hmm. And what do you want to say to her or do with her?** [this is now an internal dialogue portrayal]

PATIENT: *(speaking through tears)* **I want to hug her.**

THERAPIST: **Go ahead, hug her. Let yourself hug her. Again, let the hands go, let your arms go. Let yourself be ... so at least it makes a physical. ... How do you hug her to you?** [encouraging patient to allow her body to become involved in portrayal] **Like that?** *(enact a hold)*

PATIENT: Yeah. My mother kept saying how Gina [her niece] is how I used to be when I was three and I keep thinking, what happened? She's this totally energetic curious problem solver—imaginative, endless energy—boundless. She's just delicious—and it's not what I see in my head. She's totally different. [the nine-year-old in the portrayal is totally different from how the three-year-old used to be and from how Gina is now; spontaneous linking of aspects of the self–other–emotion triangle with aspects of the triangle of comparisons]

THERAPIST: So something happened to this little delicious girl. ... This three-year-old, this little boundless, curious, energetic, lively, life-force little girl—by eight or nine becomes this forlorn, lost, lonely, alone little girl. What do you say to her, Aimee, as you hug her? Let yourself hug her. [continuing portrayal by urging dialogue between the two parts of herself]

PATIENT: I just picture taking her out again. [note absence of defense]

THERAPIST: Taking her out again? What do you mean?

PATIENT: Last time when I took the little girl out to someplace else. [referring to a portrayal of a previous session] That's just what I see. She's going to be okay, I'll just take her away.

THERAPIST: Could you please describe to me how you physically hold her? [priming bodily rooted correlates of experience of integration; again note rooting affective work in patient-therapist relationship: therapist urges patient to speak to her directly]

PATIENT: Just like this. *(demonstrates)*

THERAPIST: Belly to belly, chest to chest? [linking words with her actions]

PATIENT: Yeah, except you know, she's shorter.

THERAPIST: So you're standing up as you're hugging her?

PATIENT: Like her head is over here. *(points to her chest, right by her heart)*

THERAPIST: How is she feeling?

PATIENT: *(starts to cry; different crying than earlier; beginning of healing affects)* She's relieved that someone is there for her. Everything comes out while you're crying. [confirms these are tears of relief] Nothing was ever allowed to be felt in my house. Because mommy and daddy will go away. And that's what I thought. That my sister doesn't like me any-more. She's going to go away. She's not going to be my friend. Just like my parents. [identifies another source of anxiety motivating defenses against feeling and experience: fear of abandonment; note directness of language; she is speaking in nine-year-old girl language. Integrative processing and creation of new autobiographical narrative]

THERAPIST: You're totally abandoned, completely on your own. [thera-pist is a step behind]

PATIENT: They're not available.

THERAPIST: And what do you feel as you're holding her and she's sobbing and sobbing and sobbing, like you are doing with me? [exploring experience of the other aspect of herself represented in internal dialogue portrayal; therapist introduces parallel between patient in the here and now and the little girl on one hand, and therapist and patient on the other]

PATIENT: *(eyes clearing, calm, gaze uplifted)* Sad. But I feel like ... it's like I can give her something now ... like starting again. ... That things will be okay. It will be okay. [having worked through concomitants of deep emotional pain, found its source, and done some reparative work, this is the aftermath of deep emotional experiencing; patient now has access to adaptive action tendencies; she is feeling resourceful, confident that she can help the little girl: note uplifted gaze, marker for healing affects]

THERAPIST: What else came to your mind right then?

PATIENT: We'll work things out.

THERAPIST: Hmm? [therapist not sure which "we" patient is referring to]

PATIENT: We'll work things out. Just like now. It will be okay.

One of the consequences of trauma is the fragmentation of the self into a part that feels and is split off from the main personality and a part that thinks and functions, albeit in an anemic way that leaves the individual prone to being easily overwhelmed (Ferenczi, 1931, 1933; Winnicott, 1949, 1960). Through reparative portrayal and the core affect it both leads to and helps process, Aimee is able to bring the two parts of herself together—the forlorn little girl and the anxious, resourceless adult. Her hugging the little girl is an experiential–visceral version of the integration needed to undo dissociation. The feeling part needs to feel not alone; the functioning part needs the deep resources of affective contact to feel that she is not running on empty. Through the affect work, the patient gains a powerful sense of her resources. Through her embrace of the little girl, she undoes the intergenerational transmission of affect-processing pathology: she no longer abandons the feeling part of herself as her mother abandoned her when she was a sad and frightened young child. Aimee starts to find her strength as a generative adult, capable of taking care of a needy child.

Segment 5
COMING TOGETHER

THERAPIST: You and her—the two of you will work things out. You're together.

PATIENT: Things will be okay for me. [statement of quiet faith in herself] My work and our work. What? [refocuses on therapist, notices tears in therapist's eyes]

THERAPIST: It's so painful. And so moving. [therapist a step behind patient, still resonating with emotional pain, also with healing affects; but patient has moved on]

PATIENT: *(with quiet strength)* I'm not afraid now that I'll cry and fall apart. I can cry and feel okay. There's two kinds of crying. [patient is referring to difference between tears of anxiety and tears of core affect] I'm not falling apart. I'm going to be okay. If I fall apart I wouldn't be serving any purpose here and I know I'm here serving a purpose. [addressing her own fears; asserting newfound meaning]

THERAPIST: What do you mean?

PATIENT: Everyone has a task in life and nobody wants me to fall apart because—and God doesn't want me to fall apart and he's not going to let me, and I'm not going to let me, and nobody is gonna let me because then I wouldn't be able to do what I'm meant to do. [statement of faith in self and trust in others]

THERAPIST: And right now what are you in touch with about what you're meant to do?

PATIENT: *(uplifted gaze)* Sort of like goodness and sort of like strength. I have goodness to give and I have love to give to others and I have to be well so I can give that. And I can give to myself. So that I can work at that. I have to take care of myself. I also owe Edward that. In my relationship to him, I think I'm reacting to a lot of other things that don't have to do with him and me. And I want to work those things out, so they aren't in the way with him and me. [very aware of fear that was paralyzing her; touches it, connection through opposition; in touch with her generative capacities and talents; asserts importance of working through difficulties to be more fully in her marriage]

THERAPIST: Those being?

PATIENT: Those things aren't in the way with him and me. I think also that we can bring children into the world and bring them up hopefully in a way that is healthy. [deepest evidence of healing power of this wave of work: her torment about having children is changing: she is beginning to be in touch with her generative capacities, and have some confidence that she can be a better mother than her mother was to her] ... I feel like lighter. [postaffective breakthrough feelings, vitality affect]

THERAPIST: I just feel like I've shared in one of the most beautiful moments that I've ever experienced with somebody. [therapist shares her affective experience of the work]

PATIENT: It feels good. [beautiful simplicity of healing affects]

THERAPIST: Mmmmm. To see you find your strength and your center. [affirmation]

PATIENT: Yeah, that's exactly what it feels like.

THERAPIST: To hear you put everything together in time in a deep deep deep deep deep deep place inside of you, a place where you know things—it's amazing. Just amazing. [affirmation; therapist expresses her experience of awe and appreciation for magnitude of patient's work]

PATIENT: *(deep, simple smile)* It feels good.

THERAPIST: What?

Segment 6
META-PROCESSING OF

AFFECTIVE–RELATIONAL EXPERIENCE

PATIENT: I really feel like I got some strength from what we did today.

THERAPIST: Describe to me what the sense of strength feels like right now. [fixing the experience through its experiential elaboration]

PATIENT: Like there's something inside me. [opposite of feeling of emptiness] That there are people who care about me—outside ... and that I can do it. And it might take a very long time. And it might be forever, but step by step—I can do it. I really feel that way. [self-affirmation]

THERAPIST: Hmm?

PATIENT: I really feel that way and I feel like I saw a step. I saw a step from twelve weeks ago till now. I saw ten steps. [hope based on sense of progress]

THERAPIST: So, what happens if you let yourself really really look at me now? [before session ends, it is important to process relational reverberations of deep affective processing that just took place]

PATIENT: I feel happy. Really happy. I feel like it feels good for you and I'm happy about it. I can't believe that with what we started with that I'm here. [her own deep feeling of happiness; note simple certainty with which she states that she knows how good therapist feels about the work— evidence of secure attachment: confidence that her welfare is pleasurable for therapist; she feels cared about]

THERAPIST: I always want to hear you put it into words so put it into words for me. Just what it's like.

PATIENT: I don't know how long it was but from fifteen or twenty minutes ago I'm in a totally different place ... at least for now. [viscerally experienced difference between pre- and postaffective breakthrough states]

THERAPIST: **And this feeling of shared happiness right now?** [refocusing on relational experience of state of happiness shared by patient and therapist]

PATIENT: It feels really good. It feels like someone really cares. I feel like you really care. It's like my mother can't feel for other people, she can only feel for herself. You can feel for other people and you really understand me. And I think you also think that from what I started with, that I moved. [articulates deep receptive affective experience; reflective self function development at work: her feeling that therapist feels she has made progress only deepens her own sense of her own progress]

THERAPIST: You're not in a different world, it's a different universe.

PATIENT: Yeah. I feel like I'm getting someplace.

THERAPIST: It's been a long time for you.

PATIENT: Yeah. I feel like you give me a lot of guidance. And you're not—a lot of helping me understand me. [promoting patient's development of her reflective self function] I don't know if that's guidance but it's like pushing and being with me and I really appreciate that. I think that you do have—like you could look at this and look at a session three weeks ago and you could connect something. That there's someplace where this is going and that you see an end. That you see an end to our therapy, not an end to working on it. [in her own words, patient articulates her experience of aspects of therapist's stance]

THERAPIST: **Mmm hmm.**

PATIENT: I think that you really want me to get better.

THERAPIST: Explain something to me. In the last half an hour or twenty minutes or however long it's been, my sense is that we got or you got to this place inside of you and you did it and I said reltively little. Tell me how that ... experience, where that fits in with you and me. In other words, I have such a sense of what you, you yourself have been able to do, and I also know that I was very much with you. That's how I felt and I just want to hear you put into words your experience of it.

PATIENT: I feel like, even though you said very little, I felt like from all the times in the past what just seemed like gentle pushing, like a connecting. ... It's just what I needed. I needed you here to ... I don't know what it is ... even just knowing that you are here with me, and that what I'm feeling is valid and that it's not totally crazy what I'm thinking. It's just that you care. ...

THERAPIST: Thank you.

PATIENT: It's just like totally safe here, you know. Like with Dr. X [previous therapist], my father was paying the bill and he recommended her to me. Like you insisted that I pay you with my own check, he doesn't even know your last name. It's safe.

THERAPIST: And it's yours.

PATIENT: Yeah. It's mine.

THERAPIST: What I think about is that little eight- or nine-year-old girl who's really not a live-wire anymore, who's sad and who's forlorn, and she's very alone and very scared.

PATIENT: It's like I'm here for her and you're here for me. We get me helping her and you helping me. Is that what you were thinking?

THERAPIST: That's what I was thinking. And I wanted to know what it felt like.

PATIENT: I feel empowered to help her because I see how you're able to help me. Does that make sense?

THERAPIST: It makes sense and it makes me very happy.

PATIENT: It's like a chain. And as I get better I can more help her.

THERAPIST: And you can take her in. She's been alone out there for a long time.

PATIENT: If you can feel and help in a way with understanding ... It's like the intellectual and the feeling part of it, they can work together. And they can work together to make good. It's great. Thank you. Very much. I'm so happy.

In this last episode, the work of the session is completed by bringing to the foreground what has been in the background: the relationship between the patient and the therapist. Her saying, "I feel lighter" is a signal that the deep unconscious wave she's been riding is over for now and that shifting to examining the therapeutic relationship will not be an interruption or an interference with the emergence of more deep material. There is an exploration of her experience of the therapeutic relationship and her sense of the role of the therapist in the process in which she is engaged. The patient articulates her own sense of what allows deep change to take place, and her own theories about the mechanisms of change. In the process, the bond is further strengthened as a result of sharing the experience and sharing in the articulation of what about that experience renders it meaningful.

So the journey ends, by virtue of the project's nearing a conclusion; and so with a therapy. If the therapy has gone well, termination marks a point of shifting relational arrangements, a moment when the good-bye cues memory and orients attention.

The vision of psychic health that informs the affective model of change has two aspects: feeling deeply and being at ease. The capacity to feel deeply and to feel at ease, open, and relaxed with oneself and with others emerge directly from the two aspects of core affective experience discussed throughout, core affect and the core state. When barriers to their experience no longer are defining aspects of the individual's psychic functioning, these capacities become part of the fabric of his being, and he can engage inner and outer worlds without damaging restrictions.

Much of relief from symptoms, correction of character distortions, and so on—an enormous amount in some patients, a moderate amount in others—comes naturally as barriers against feeling and relating are lifted. Yet even in the best of outcomes, depression, anxiety, unease, relational reticence, occasional bouts of self-doubt or shame, mistrust, aloofness, despair, and hopelessness make their reappearance, for life is very tough. (The necessity for two versions of the representational schemas—for functioning at best and at worst—prevails even in relative health: what is different is the baseline, and what is relative is their ratio to one another.) The index of mental health as defined here is not the outright disappearance of these distressing phenomena, but rather the individual's capacity to optimally manage them, which means including them within the sphere of mastery created by the application of the reflective self function. Being able to acknowledge these experiences, accept them, and investigate them in terms of their meaning and what they reveal about the conditions with which one has to deal, and being able to communicate about them to oneself and to trusted others is the deepest undoing of pathology. As has been articulated throughout, the essence of pathology is that it results from that which must be borne alone and is too feared to openly admit to. Once this dynamic is removed and the directional arrow of communication—to self and other—is reversed, the path toward healing transformation is set. And that's good enough.

In the psychoanalytic world, Winnicott's work on the capacity to be alone (1958) in the presence of another is rightly held in great respect. A related theme through Winnicott's writings asserts the importance of having areas of private experience that remain uncom-municated (e.g., 1963a). This theme has resonated in the work of some current writers (Slochower, 1999; Stein, 1999) in a somewhat romanti-cized manner; I therefore wish to reframe this aspect of health as fol-lows: from the capacity to be alone in the presence of another grows the capacity to be oneself in the presence of another. What is involved in the notion of being oneself in the presence of another involves the confidence that communication—with oneself and with the other—will not threaten the integrity of the self, but rather will only enhance and enrich, and thus strengthen and affirm, the authenticity of the self.

The capacity to feel deeply and the capacity to be at ease with one-self and others, respectively rooted in core affect and the core state, are the vehicles that nourish an essential transformational process: they facilitate the ongoing unfolding of the essential self.

TECHNIQUE AND TABOO IN THE EXPERIENTIAL STDPs[1]

To fully understand AEDP, it is important to place it in the context in which it arose: the realm of short-term dynamic psychotherapies (STDP), and more specifically, the experiential STDPs.

Short-term dynamic psychotherapy bridges the gap between two otherwise nonoverlapping domains: the pragmatic, result-oriented world of short-term treatment and the timeless realm of deep, comprehensive psychoanalytic understanding. Each STDP model has struggled with the problem of how to conduct a truly psychodynamic treatment within a condensed time frame, with ambitiously defined psychoanalytic goals applicable to a wide range of patients. Short-term dynamic psychotherapy has a rich history of experimentation: it begins (as everything therapeutic seems to) with Freud, continues with the work of Ferenczi (1920, 1925), Ferenczi and Rank (1925), and later, with that of Alexander and French (1946). This rich history is covered thoroughly by Crits-Cristoph and Barber (1991), Gustafson (1986) and Messer and Warren (1995), all of whom also deal with many current STDPs not discussed here. My focus is on those models that directly preceded and influenced the development of AEDP.

The common thread linking the STDP approaches under discussion—Malan's brief psychotherapy (1963, 1976; Malan & Osimo, 1992), Davanloo's intensive short-term dynamic psychotherapy (1980, 1986–88, 1990; Coughlin Della Selva, 1996; Fosha, 1992b; Laikin, Winston, & McCullough, 1991; Magnavita, 1997; Malan, 1986), accelerated empathic therapy (Alpert, 1992, 1996; B. Foote, 1992; J. Foote, 1992; Fosha, 1992a, 1992b; Sklar, 1993, 1994) and, of course, accelerated experiential-dynamic psychotherapy (Fosha, 1995, in press; Fosha &

---

[1] This is adapted from Fosha, "Technique and taboo in three short-term dynamic psychotherapies," *Journal of Psychotherapy Practice and Research*, 1995, 4, 297–318. Portions of that article reprinted here with the permission of the *Journal of Psycotherapy Practice and Research*.

Osiason, 1996; Fosha & Slowiaczek, 1997)—is that all consider the experiential component, that is, *the experience of previously unbearable affect in the here and now of the patient-therapist relationship*, as the key agent of therapeutic change.

Wachtel (1993) writes about the centrality of the concept of anxiety in all psychodynamic understandings of psychopathology; it triggers defensive operations, which in turn restrict emotional experience. These STDPs are united in the search for the most effective, efficient, and comprehensive therapeutic methods for maximizing affective experience and minimizing the impact of defensiveness and anxiety. Each model has been innovative in trying to solve and overcome the problems encountered by its predecessor. The developmental process that leads from one model to the next is neither linear nor additive; in the attempt to solve a problem, choices are made that shape and affect all factors within the system. Interestingly, as invariably happens in paradigm shifts (Hanson, 1958; Kuhn, 1970), the techniques used to solve particular problems end up yielding new (i.e., technique-specific) phenomena, new "data" requiring new conceptualizations that lead to the next set of questions—and so on (Fosha, 1992b).

The history of the development of experiential short-term dynamic psychotherapies is a story of progressive taboo breaking; with each step, a different psychoanalytic taboo must be confronted and broken; with each round, greater and greater confidence in the robustness of unconscious phenomena is gained. The freedom to engage in technical experimentation pays off; the result is progressive access to and experience with different kinds of deep affective phenomena. The theme of technique and taboo is explored by closely examining the different answers generated in the quest for the technique that will maximize affective experience, and thus simultaneously accelerate treatment; but first, the notion of taboo.

TABOOS, TABOO BREAKING, AND THE ROBUSTNESS OF UNCONSCIOUS PROCESSES

Webster's dictionary (1961) tells us that taboos are "sacred interdictions laid upon the use of certain things or words or the performance of certain actions, commonly imposed by chiefs or priests. ... Similar restrictions [are] imposed by social convention." At its inception, psycho-analysis dramatically broke taboos in both its content and style of communicative interaction, differentiating itself from ordinary, polite social discourse (Cuddihy, 1974).

Psychoanalysis boldly declared itself interested solely in that realm of the individual's most private experience, where the demands of logic, reality, morality, social convention, and adult mature functioning hold no sway, and where the stuff of primary process, drives, impulses, and infantile wishes reigns supreme. To foster an environment in which the patient may risk such self-exposure, techniques developed to free the analyst's responses of personal bias, self-interest, condemnation, rejection, and criticism, and to ensure that the patient not be taken advantage of or be unduly influenced while in such a vulnerable position. Neutrality, nondirectiveness, and abstinence became the technical aspects of the analytic stance while the patient was encouraged to free associate to gain access to that private realm. (The centrality that nondirectiveness assumed perhaps reflected Freud's concern that his innovations be seen as altogether distinct from hypnosis and suggestion.) These innovations were not followed by many others that matched them in boldness: growing awareness of more complex phenomena (e.g., resistance, negative therapeutic reaction) stimulated conceptual advances rather than major technical developments. The length of analysis grew (Malan, 1963, pp. 6–9). Radical at first, these techniques became codified and later sanctified; and thus the culture of psycho-analysis, like all cultures, came to generate its own taboos.

The content of the taboo became the proscription of all therapeutic activities not considered strictly "analytic," irrespective of their effectiveness in achieving the quintessential psychoanalytic aim (i.e., gaining access to previously unconscious and repressed emotional experience in order to free patients from neurotic suffering). Allegiance to these technical taboos has contributed to the growing length of standard analytic treatment. Each of the experiential STDPs had to break through taboos laid down by the psychoanalytic culture in order to make its technical innovations.

Taboos usually rest on implicit assumptions. Only when such assumptions are made explicit can their merits be examined. So much of classic analytic stance and technique—the therapist's passivity and neutrality, the limits on both content and frequency of her verbal activity, the lack of eye contact between patient and therapist—seems to suggest a fear of exerting undue influence, a fear that the patient's unconscious experience is worrisomely vulnerable to outside interference and tampering. If the assumption is that the patient's experience can be so easily contaminated, it follows then that a sterile setting is required to ensure the integrity of that unconscious material.

In contradistinction, the implicit assumption of experiential STDP techniques is that unconscious processes are robust and by no means so easily contaminated. After all, this is what defenses and resistance are for, and they are formidable forces. The recalcitrance of patients' characteristic ways of being and their intransigence to change are much greater concerns than the plasticity of their core experience and its vulnerability to outside influence. In the (implicit) view of short-term dynamic psychotherapists, the problem is not that the "unconscious" is so easy to derail, but rather, that classical technique offers a limited technical repertoire for effectively dealing with its ruses (i.e., defense and resistance phenomena). Rather than being concerned about being unduly influential, here the concern is about not being influential enough to effect substantive therapeutic change. In this sense, short-term psychotherapy is a tribute to the power of the unconscious: the unconscious knows how to say "no."

The taboo on emotional engagement also comes from the era of the hegemony of the drives and fears of the analyst's venality. Unless strictly checked, the impulses of the analyst (Freud, 1912a, 1912b, 1915) might wreak havoc (on both patient and analyst). This is a consequence of a theory that believes that all aspects of human functioning can be reduced to essential (asocial, untamed) instincts. The result, as is invariable with taboos, is the need for "prohibited, forbidden, or secret aspects of technique, very often furtive gestures of human acknowledgment or responsivity" (Jacobson, 1994, p. 17). With STDP therapists not so worried about being libidinally riotous, the gestures of human acknowledgment or responsivity can come out in the open, their therapeutic potential capable of being investigated. Actively opposing taboos on activity and emotional engagement, short-term dynamic therapists have been freer to experiment: their expanded repertoire includes new techniques to both enhance the impact of unconscious forces pressing for self-expression, and counteract the impact of forces that fuel resistance to change.

The change from traditional analytic techniques to experiential STDP techniques primarily has been a process of *turning passive into active*, as it applies to the *therapist's* activity. Much of STDP technique brings out what used to be kept inside the therapist—inside her mind, inside her heart, inside her gut—and offers it up for use in the transitional space between patient and therapist, where both members of the therapeutic dyad have access to it.

Consider, for example, the issue of videotaping psychotherapy sessions (which all experiential STDPs do). Not at all reluctant to use powerful technology for fear that it might hopelessly contaminate treatment, these STDPs take the position that whatever reactions the patient might have to videotape can be dealt with through active interventions designed to deal with any resistance, whether intrapsychic or iatrogenic in its origin. Thus patient and therapist can reap the benefits of a rich resource, trusting the robustness of the therapeutic process and the versatility of therapeutic tools.

THE EXPERIENTIAL STDPS

Malan's brief psychotherapy, Davanloo's intensive short-term dynamic psychotherapy, and accelerated empathic therapy constitute AEDP's family of origin. The discussion begins with some conceptual and technical innovations that are the foundation for the technical explorations of all the experiential STDPs; though they are integral aspects of brief psychotherapy (BP), they have become a common ground for all experiential STDPs. A comparison follows of each model's stance, technique, main pathway of change, and the taboos broken to achieve them. Some comments on AEDP in relation to its three predecessors close the discussion.

Brief Psychotherapy: Precursor of Experiential STDPs

Brief psychotherapy (Malan, 1963, 1976, 1979) arose in response to the growing length of psychoanalysis and psychoanalytic psychotherapy: "however favorably long-term psychotherapy—and particularly psychoanalysis—may influence the lives of selected individuals, in comparison with the amount of neurotic unhappiness in the world its contribution can never be anything but negligible" (Malan, 1963, p. 3). The aim was to develop a method that would retain the depth of psychoanalytic work, but have a much wider application. The clinical method that emerged breaks taboos on activity, selectiveness, and focusing, while remaining psychoanalytic (i.e., interpretive, in its technical essence). As Malan likes to say, BP is profoundly psychoanalytic, only more so.

The innovations BP introduced constitute the foundation for all the experiential STDPs. The systematic, moment-to-moment conceptualization of the clinical material in terms of the triangles of conflict and the triangle of person (later renamed the triangle of comparisons), and their use in guiding clinical work, is the hallmark of Malan's contribution.

BP FEATURES: COMMON GROUND
OF THE EXPERIENTIAL STDPS

Schematized psychodynamic constructs. Basic psychodynamic theory understands psychopathology in terms of how core emotional experiences, anxiety, and defense mechanisms are intrapsychically structured, and how, in turn, that intrapsychic experience plays an active role in structuring relational patterns. Two schematic representations of the complex relationship among these different aspects of psychic functioning—the *triangle of conflict* and the *triangle of person*—have proved useful in condensing an elaborate theory. From disparate sources, David Malan (1963, 1976, 1979) brought these schemas together, demonstrated how all psychodynamic clinical work can be conceptualized in their terms, and showed how indispensable they are to the therapist trying to do deep dynamic work in a short period of time. The dynamic relationship among core emotional experiences, anxiety and defense, and the congruence of current, past, and therapeutic relational patterns are the core elements of a psychodynamic understanding of clinical phenomena, psychopathological and therapeutic. The specifics of how these constructs are translated into clinical action differentiates the therapeutics of each school of psychodynamic psychotherapy. Being able, on the spot, to capture the essence of these complex relationships through reliance on the schemas of the triangles of conflict and person allows STDP practitioners to rapidly assess clinical material and perform comprehensive in-depth psychodynamic therapeutic work in a condensed time frame.

Rapid structuring of clinical material in the terms of the triangles of conflict and person. The STDP therapist uses the categories of the triangles of conflict and person to guide her listening and her interventions in the initial evaluation and throughout the treatment. With the two triangles in mind, the therapist listens to the material, noting the moment-to-moment shifts in the quality of the patient-therapist rapport and in the depth and intensity of the patient's unconscious communications in response to interventions. Instead of merely noting these mentally and storing them for future use, the STDP therapist, in a manner that Malan describes as "fearless," immediately and explicitly starts to address the defense and anxiety patterns evident in the patient's life as well as in the transference.

Trial therapy. The initial evaluation in STDP is called *trial therapy*, as the therapist enters the relationship with the patient ready for active dynamic interaction from the get-go. The idea is not to wait for material to unfold but actively to foster the kind of therapeutic interaction the treatment defines as optimal. From the first moment, as the patient begins to tell the therapist his story (or not tell it, for that matter), the therapist has access to two potent sources of dynamic information: the content of the story, manifest and latent, and the interactive process between herself and the patient. Taking whatever the patient offers, the therapist uses it as the starting point for a dynamic interaction. She can perform moment-to-moment microanalysis and thereby functionally categorize the emerging clinical material as defense, anxiety, or genuine emotional experience; then, specific interventions aimed at work with that category can be immediately and systematically introduced. In the initial evaluation, Malan calls these *trial interpretations* (Malan, 1963, 1976). The patient's capacity to engage and make use of these interventions is a major selection criterion.

Patient capacity for dynamic interaction as major selection criterion. The patient's capacity to interact dynamically and be able to respond to trial interpretations starting with the first interview (the trial therapy) is a highly important selection criterion in the BP evaluation, as it is indicative of the patient's capacity to make use of the therapy being offered. In the absence of exclusion criteria (Malan, 1976, pp. 67–68), severity of functional disturbance, chronicity of the problem, or the point in development at which the problem is thought to have arisen in the patient's genetic past do not play an automatic role in determining suitability (or lack thereof) for BP. Showing a capacity to do the work, however (i.e., respond to trial interpretations), augurs well and is heavily weighted in the balance with other diagnostic factors. It should be noted that the sought-for response from the patient need not be positive or freely communicated; the patient might very well respond with anxiety or defensiveness; the issue here is the patient's meaningful engagement in the process.

Active engagement of the patient as partner in the treatment endeavor. At the end of the trial therapy, patient and therapist discuss what their work will involve and what their goals are. Encouragement of the patient to participate actively in the treatment and interventions that aim to bring this about are common features of short-term work in general and BP in particular.

Setting termination date at the beginning of the treatment. The final factor that contributes to the decrease in the length of STDP treatment is raising the issue of termination from the beginning. As Malan, paraphrasing Samuel Johnson, quips: "being under the sentence of termination doth most marvelously concentrate the material." Though handled differently by different models, the patient's knowledge—both conscious and unconscious—that his contact with the therapist is finite condenses and intensifies the process. This is such a powerful factor that Mann (1973) makes the passage of time and the individual's futile battle to forestall it the deep focus of every patient's treatment. Freud too was aware of this: when the Wolf Man (1918) was stuck, he used setting a termination date as a tactic to restore the flow of material and recharge the analytic situation.

Use of explicit criteria for assessment of fluctuations in depth of unconscious communication and rapport. Malan (1979) draws attention to fluctuations in *rapport* and in *depth of unconscious communication* as the criteria by which to assess the impact of the therapist's interventions and the patient's capacity to respond to them. These are Malan's criteria for assessing the quality of affective experience, intrapsychically and relationally. "Rapport can be defined as the degree of emotional contact between patient and therapist" (1979, pp. 19–20); "[it] is the universal indicator by which the therapist may be constantly guided" (p. 75). Both in the initial evaluation and throughout the therapy, the therapist monitors the patient's response to each intervention, paying particular attention to qualitative shifts in the depth of the unconscious communication and fluctuations in rapport. Local fluctuations in communication or rapport become grist for the mill: each round provides additional dynamically meaningful information. This allows the therapist to refine interventions according to the patient's responses. "The essential nature of this feedback consists of changes in the level of rapport, so that the capacity to judge this is one of the therapist's most essential qualities" (1979, p. 75). Therapists can be trained to use these specific criteria reliably. Elaborating on his notion of rapport, Malan (1979) writes, "a change from an apparently very ordinary and emotionally composed account of a previous incident, to an intense and heartfelt declaration of ... a feeling of great significance for him ... [amounts to] a dramatic *deepening of rapport*" (pp. 19–20).

Here Malan in essence is talking about affective deepening, and specifically, affective deepening in the context of the patient-therapist connection. Similarly, writing on the features of *unconscious communications*, he notes:

> [I]t is worth summarizing the characteristics of a particular kind of communication by which the therapist should be immediately alerted: (1) the patient—often with an abrupt change of subject—speaks with evident interest and spontaneity about something whose relevance is not immediately obvious. (2) On more careful thought, a clear parallel can be seen with some other subject whose relevance and emotional significance is much greater (1979, p. 23).

This ongoing assessment is a crucial activity in both the evaluation process and actual treatment in BP. By making the implicit explicit, Malan makes possible a rapid assessment of the nature and degree of unconscious engagement in response to interventions, and thus the patient's ability to engage in a dynamic communicative interaction.

Using the focus to guide selective therapeutic responding. The active, dynamic exploration of the patient's past, present, and now also transferential conflicts, informed by the use of the triangles of conflict and person, guided by shifts in the level of rapport and depth of unconscious communication, can quite rapidly lead to a formulation of the patient's central problem. This psychodynamic formulation, known as the *focus*, is completed by the end of the initial evaluation and is used to guide BP treatment. The focus contributes to the acceleration of the treatment by helping the therapist selectively attend to the material, guiding her responses accordingly. What guides selectivity is whether the manifest material the patient presents can be translated, using the constructs of the two triangles, into the focal core conflicts. At the end of the trial therapy, therapist and patient together discuss the focus of their work.

The use of interpretations in BP. The "strategic aim" of BP is "to bring into consciousness and enable the patient to experience his emotional conflicts" (Malan, 1976, p. 259). The BP therapist achieves that goal through clarification and interpretation of all categories of triangle of conflict experience, addressing how they become manifest in all triangle of relationship categories. As "the ultimate aim" of BP is "to bring into consciousness" what was previously unconscious, the main interventions are *interpretations*. Throughout the treatment, the therapist tries to link up the patient's characteristic lifelong patterns with what is happening in the here and now of their treatment relationship. The therapist takes every opportunity to make *T-C-P interpretations*, pointing out the congruence in the patient's patterns of dealing with emotional conflict in transferential, current, and past relationships, with particular attention paid to the T-P link. T-C-P interpretations are particularly effective when they elicit an affective rather than a defensive response in the patient (McCullough et al., 1991). Of all the various aspects of BP treatment studied by Malan and his colleagues, the technique most strongly correlated with positive outcome was the interpretation of the T-C-P link:

> [T]he more radical the technique in terms of transference, depth of interpretation, and the link to childhood, the more radical are the therapeutic effects. ... It needs to be said again and again that the successful use of psychoanalytic methods is a tribute to psychoanalysis, not an attack on it; especially when, as here, it is shown that the more psychoanalytic the technique, the more successful the therapy. (Malan, 1976, pp. 353, 352)

With the development of BP, Malan broke the taboo on activity and directiveness; he showed that it is possible to conduct deep analytic work while being active and selectively focused. Never one to mince words, Malan (1980) begins a paper thus:

> It needs to be stated categorically that in the early part of this century Freud unwittingly took a wrong turning which led to disastrous consequences for the future of psychotherapy. This was to react to increasing resistance with increased passivity—eventually adopting the technique of free association on the part of the patient, and the role of "passive sounding board," free-floating attention, and infinite patience on the part of the therapist. (p. 13)

In BP, the pace and rhythm of therapeutic activity change and treatment is shortened. Any dynamic intervention—whether it deals with defense, anxiety, or core feelings, or whether it addresses events in the present, past, or transference—can be made from the first session on.

Malan's contribution is enormous. Though radical when first introduced, high level of therapist activity, selective focusing, active engagement of the patient as a partner in the treatment process, active focus on the patient-therapist relationship, and active use of the termination date as a treatment parameter all have become standard procedures for the experiential STDPs. The constructs of the triangles of conflict and person are the conceptual tools that allow the moment-to-moment tracking of the patient's experience and thus set the groundwork for later experiential-dynamic techniques.

BP techniques reliably, effectively, and systematically lead to their purported goal: insight. Yet the hope is that insight will lead to the deep experiencing essential for transformation to occur. Over and over, Malan reveals himself as an experientialist at heart: "The aim of every moment of every session is to put the patient in touch with as much of his true feelings as he can bear" (1979, p. 74). This inclination also informs his emphasis on the moment-to-moment analysis of shifts in the session. Though Malan values the experiential and pushes the envelope of interpretation on timing, rhythm, and activity, BP technique remains exclusively interpretive; and interpretive techniques do not reliably lead to visceral experience. As in traditional psychoanalytic psychotherapies, the experience of deep feeling, profoundly welcomed, is serendipitous, not reliably brought about by interpretive techniques.

Malan explores the limits of interpretation and finds them: resistance phenomena that will not respond to interpretation, most pronounced in the character disorders. These are patients who "never respond [to interpretations] with anything but purely intellectual insight, and of course no one is surprised when they show no improvement" (Malan, 1986, p. 63). He further writes:

> The only possible conclusions then are first, that purely interpretive therapy, whether long-term or short-term, has been carried to the limit and has been found inadequate; and second, that unless we are prepared to accept this fatalistically, we need some more powerful kinds of interventions which can be used over and above interpretation. (P. 63)

Malan finds the powerful methods "which can be used over and above interpretation" in Davanloo's techniques, where resistance is not interpreted but rather challenged. Malan finds in Davanloo's technique that which will quench his experiential thirst: "he systematically works with the resistance and eventually brings the patient to a point above the threshold, where there is sufficient true experience of the underlying feelings [for] genuine therapy [to] begin" (p. 106).

Enter Habib Davanloo. Like Reich (1954) before him, Davanloo sees no point to doing psychotherapeutic work as long as there is character armor in the way. As he was fond of saying, "you don't limit yourself to squinting through a peephole when you can walk in through the front door" (Davanloo, 1986–1988). Like Reich, he views working with secondary-process productions, even when colored with some unconscious derivatives, not sufficient to produce genuine therapeutic change. To counteract the pervasive character armor, Davanloo reasons that what is necessary is to access an equally strong visceral experience: only a powerful *experience* can compete with the rigid, entrenched ego-syntonic character defenses. Aimed at highly resistant patients, Davanloo's technique launches an attack on the defenses. The goal is to bring about access to genuine affective experience and then enhance its depth, intensity, and duration. In intensive short-term dynamic psychotherapy (ISTDP), deep rapport and depth of unconscious communication are not merely noted, appreciated, and made most of (as they are in BP), but rather become the goal of active, specific, explicit technique.

Intensive Short-Term
Dynamic Psychotherapy:
Beyond Interpretation

To understand Davanloo, it is necessary to understand his metapsychology. The confrontational techniques of ISTDP (Davanloo 1980, 1986–88, 1990) flow directly from a conceptualization of psychopathology and psychotherapy wherein the superego plays a central role (Fosha, 1992b). All defensive activities and their consequences (i.e., symptom patterns, emotional inhibition, personality restriction, etc.) are understood as reflecting the punitiveness toward the self of a harsh superego for unconscious impulses, particularly aggressive, sadistic, murderous impulses. The ISTDP therapist sets out to do battle with the superego *mano a mano*: the therapy involves a confrontation between superego forces and therapeutic forces (the therapist and the patient's ego, the latter too weakened to do battle alone, but driving the process forward through the unconscious therapeutic alliance). The aimed-for breakthrough that allows the patient to viscerally experience previously forbidden impulses represents a therapeutic triumph over the superego and helps the patient integrate those experiences within the ego's sphere of activity, thereby strengthening the ego. Undoing the effects of the superego allows the ego to have access to the enriching lively quality of the impulses, while giving impulses the modulation benefits of the secondary process, reality testing influence of the ego.

ISTDP raises the ante exponentially in its technique. As in Malan's BP, there is a reliance on the schemas of the triangles of conflict and person, a high level of therapist activity, active engagement of the patient in the treatment endeavor, and use of the patient's response to interventions as the most important selection criterion; but there are some major and defining technical shifts. These can best be understood by focusing on Davanloo's approach to *defense work*, perhaps his most original contribution and the hallmark of his work.

Already in BP, much attention was paid to defense work. Through interpretation, defenses were identified and their operation within the psyche was clarified with the patient. Davanloo (1980, 1986–88, 1990) extends and transforms this process in three profound ways: he redefines and expands the category of defense phenomena; he originates a radical technique for working with defenses; and he makes the aim of defense work not insight into their operation but rather their elimination, as evidenced by the achievement of rapid experiential access to formerly unconscious impulses. The goal of ISTDP therefore is that the experiential quality of a patient's access to his feelings should be intense and visceral. Davanloo makes sure the body inhabits the psychotherapeutic space.

Redefinition of the defensive domain. In ISTDP, the notion of defense is expanded beyond formal defenses such as denial, projection, and reaction formation. The domain is enlarged to include the verbal mannerisms Davanloo calls *tactical defenses* and, most important, nonverbal behavior. Nonverbal behaviors, such as avoidance of eye contact, tone and volume of voice, and body movements or their absence become the focus of therapeutic scrutiny, as illustrated in the following transcript segment:

THERAPIST: Do you notice that you avoid my eyes?

PATIENT: But then I look away so that I can, ah, think for myself ...

THERAPIST: And how do you feel when you look into my eyes?

PATIENT: Fine, I ...

THERAPIST: Fine means what, I mean, fine is another vague ... you smile now.

PATIENT: Is that okay, I mean I smile?

THERAPIST: Uh hmm. Now your eyes go toward the ceiling. (Davanloo, 1990, p. 12)

Habits of speech such as frequent "sort ofs," "maybes," and "I don't knows" similarly are examined. The therapist's focus on the patient's nonverbal communication, which contains within it the expression of unconscious character patterns, is extremely effective: it is intimate and bypasses the verbal system; it is also well outside the realm of ordinary discourse and immediately raises the therapeutic temperature.

Powerful noninterpretive techniques for defense work: Challenge and pressure. Here the technique of dealing with defenses advances far beyond their identification and clarification. The *clarification, description,* and *elucidation of the high psychic cost of continuing to rely on such defensive strategies* (McCullough, 1991) is the first step in a three-step approach aimed at the breakdown of defenses and the breakthrough of the affect underlying them. As the patient realizes how profound his reliance on defensive mechanisms is, he becomes increasingly aware of how restricted he has been by them. The patient's resolve to change, however, is put to the test: the second and third steps of the process, *challenge* and *pressure*, involve patient and therapist in an intense confrontational encounter that Davanloo (1990) aptly calls a *head-on collision with the forces of the resistance*. The patient's habitual reliance on defensive maneuvers, after being labeled and described, is *challenged* through a variety of vigorous nonanalytic measures such as confrontation, interruption, and toxic labeling of defenses with the goal of making them ego-dystonic (i.e., as unpalatable, alien, and untenable to the patient as possible). The following is an example of how Davanloo challenges a patient who says she doesn't know what she feels. Davanloo takes the patient's statement that she doesn't know what she feels as a defense, relabels it as being "crippled," and uses the term over and over, much to the patient's annoyance. The patient is challenged to fully consider the impact of such strategies, which she can no longer keep out of her awareness; the emotional intensity of the interaction is high.

PATIENT: I find it difficult to verbalize [how I experience my feelings].

THERAPIST: But I am talking about how you feel.

PATIENT: Yeah, but to say how I feel. You see if I say I'm angry …

THERAPIST: But you are crippled almost, here, here.

PATIENT: Yeah.

THERAPIST: But yeah is not enough, and you smile as well.

PATIENT: *(laughs)* It is because I recognize it. But uh …

THERAPIST: A woman in the age of thirty so paralyzed to talk about her emotions and feelings in such circumstances of the kind you describe.

PATIENT: I don't know why, uh, I never …

THERAPIST: Here right now we are not looking at *why* you are crippled. We are looking *that* you are crippled, that you are paralyzed. First we have to identify that you are crippled and paralyzed.

PATIENT: Okay *(softly)*. (Davanloo, 1990, p. 61)

The patient is challenged to communicate straightforwardly and once and for all declare her true feelings, without hiding behind defenses. The last step involves putting *pressure* on the patient to make good her declaration of good intentions through such interventions as that in the example that follows. In response to the application of pressure, the ISTDP therapist looks for evidence of deepening unconscious communication that the patient's motivation for change is getting stronger than the forces fueling resistance. We continue:

THERAPIST: **Then we have to see what you are going to do about it. You must have a lot of feelings about such a disastrous situation. ...**

PATIENT: **There is still a lot. Yeah.**

THERAPIST: **But "yeah" is not enough. Let us see how you really feel.**

PATIENT: **How I felt then or how I feel now towards them?**

THERAPIST: **Then or now, because obviously they are the ulcers of your life.** (Davanloo, 1990, p. 61)

Implicit in the technique of challenge and pressure is the belief that radical change is possible not only soon, but right here and now. The aim of this aggressive technique vis-à-vis defenses is to create in the patient what Davanloo calls an *intrapsychic crisis*, a term initially used by Lindemann (1944) to describe the psychic fluidity observed in the aftermath of a shocking traumatic event, such as the sudden death of a loved one. Lindemann commented that the fluidity brought on by the crisis was a rare opportunity to effect substantive change rapidly, the crisis having temporarily softened usually rigid characterologic patterns. In the absence of an external crisis, ISTDP seeks to produce an intrapsychic crisis in order to achieve rapid and substantive change: the therapist's highly charged interventions evoke a clash of intense, conflicting feelings in the patient. On one hand, the patient experiences anger, resentment toward the therapist in response to the massive challenge to the patient's habitual ways of operating; these negative feelings further fuel the unconscious forces of resistance. On the other hand, the patient experiences deeply positive feelings as well, engendered by a perception of the therapist as profoundly committed to helping the patient end his psychic suffering; such feelings as gratitude, sadness, and longing further fuel the forces powering the unconscious therapeutic alliance and desire for help. Both sets of "complex transference feelings" intensify until they reach a level at which the defenses can no longer contain them: there is a breakthrough of previously buried affects and impulses and their unconscious concomitants.

The fact that these complex feelings, mainly in the transference, are so clearly related to the distant past makes the following universally-found observation less surprising: the patient's *experience* of them constitutes the triggering mechanism which will eventually lead to unlocking the whole of his unconscious. (Davanloo, 1990, p. 114, italics added)

Experiential redefinition of the goal of technique. It is of paramount importance in ISTDP not only for the patient to become profoundly aware of buried impulses and feelings, but also as fully as possible to experience them viscerally and express them directly in the transference.

> The therapist aims to bring the patient's most painful feelings to the surface and to enable him to experience them directly. This is possible in proportion to the degree to which there has been direct experience of complex feelings in the transference. Where transference experience has been intense, there will be a major breakthrough. (Davanloo, 1990, p. 117)

Through defense work, the ISTDP therapist thus strives to achieve the affectively charged breakthrough of previously buried impulses and feelings.

Insight is formally and unequivocally replaced by visceral experience as the sought-for catalytic agent. The actual here-and-now experience and expression of previously unconscious feelings and impulses within the transference relationship is the aim of Davanloo's technique; it is the experiential core of what he views as the quintessential corrective emotional experience. Interpretation, for Davanloo no longer a technique used to reach the unconscious layers of the psyche, becomes a technique of summary, cognitive-affective linking, and consolidation that is used only after the visceral work of the session is accomplished (Malan, 1986). The psychodynamically informed working-through process can take place only after the breakthrough to a level of visceral experiencing is accomplished.

Therapeutic goals. The ISTDP therapist's behavior from the first evaluation on aims to foster the patient's experience and expression of buried affects and impulses. Davanloo, taking a page from Malan's book, calls the initial session *trial therapy* and uses it simultaneously for diagnostic and therapeutic purposes. The goal of the trial therapy is to gain access to unconscious material through an affective breakthrough in the transference from the first contact with the patient. If that succeeds, the patient's motivation for treatment increases astronomically, unleashing a powerful force aiding acceleration. The rest of the treatment involves repeated workings through, reaching deeper unconscious layers, and thus building on the work of the initial trial therapy. In ISTDP, as in BP, the patient's capacity to have such an experience in the initial session is the best indication of suitability for the therapy; again, a dynamic criterion takes precedence over factors such as severity of functional impairment and chronicity of symptoms (Davanloo, 1980).

In having the therapist ally vigorously with the ego and do furious battle against the forces of the superego by aggressively attacking defenses, Davanloo broke taboos demanding neutrality and abstinence of the therapist. He also broke another taboo, this one almost a social taboo: going beyond Reich's already radical work on character defenses (Reich, 1949), Davanloo developed a series of techniques expressly designed to disrupt the smooth functioning of entrenched defense patterns. These techniques require that the therapist behave "badly"—that she interrupt, chastise, and speak of the patient's self-destructive functioning in terms so harsh at times as to border on the offensive. Davanloo strongly believes that it is the task of the therapist to help the patient get to the impulses as efficaciously and as rapidly as possible, and that the ends more than justify the means. Davanloo also broke the taboo against the therapist's assumption of a harsh, challenging stance, pointing out that being "nice" is not synonymous with being helpful and effective. If the patient's pathology at times requires relentlessness and ruthlessness (as in Davanloo's opinion it often does), it behooves the therapist to drop the niceties and do what is required of her. The surgeon must not hesitate to use the knife decisively, even if blood is to be spilled.

Davanloo's ISTDP contributions are profound:

▼ He was the first to pioneer a profoundly experiential psychodynamic treatment that also made highly efficient use of time.

▼ Drastically, dramatically, and unambiguously, he changed the aim of psychodynamic technique from insight to a visceral *corrective emotional experience* of previously intolerable feelings and impulses.

▼ He explored the phenomenology of visceral experience and the microdynamics of different experiential realms, especially anger-rage and mourning.

▼ He showed how the phenomenology of core affects and impulses differs from the phenomenology of those same affects and impulses when they are being expressed through layers of anxiety and defense. His distinction between defensive-regressive affects, such as weeping and temper tantrums, and genuine core affects, such as sadness or rage (Davanloo, 1986–88, 1990) is highly original; it is also extremely helpful in precisely orienting the therapist, and eventually the patient as well.

Yet there are major problems with ISTDP's theory and technique. To begin with, ISTDP makes such unusual demands of the therapist that only a few can feel sufficiently comfortable with it to master it and truly make it their own. The level of native aggression required of the ISTDP therapist is a personality trait encountered more frequently in trial lawyers or politicians than in those drawn to psychotherapy as a calling. Second, many patients are similarly overwhelmed and find it difficult to respond to ISTDP. Finally, the conceptualization of all psychopathology as motivated by self-destructive aims (stemming from an excessively harsh superego) actually applies to only a limited number of patients; consequently, interventions stemming from such a conceptualization do not resonate with many patients' experience, as they fail to capture its authentic essence. Self-punishment is indeed a powerful producer of psychopathology, *but only in a select group of patients*. These problems seriously limit ISTDP's applicability.

Accelerated Empathic Therapy (AET): Corrective Emotional Experience Without Transference Repetition

From the beginning, seeking to be much more user-friendly, AET (Alpert, 1992) arose in direct response to the difficulties both patients (Luborsky & Mark, 1991) and therapists (Barber & Crits-Cristoph, 1991) encountered in ISTDP. Preserving the goals of ISTDP (i.e., intensely experiential work with highly resistant patients), AET sought to develop a more widely applicable technique. While ISTDP shortens treatment through confrontational techniques aimed at working more effectively with defenses and resistance, AET does so through a stance and techniques aimed at helping the patient feel safe in a relationship with an emotionally engaged therapist, thereby minimizing the need for defenses (Alpert, 1992). In the process, AET breaks some taboos of its own.

In AET, the focus switches from what the patient is doing wrong to what the patient is doing right. Its pioneering relational techniques (Alpert, 1992) flow from a radical stance of explicit empathy, care, and compassion, a 180-degree shift away from challenge, pressure, and relentless confrontation. In AET, acceleration of treatment is achieved via interventions designed to maximize the likelihood that the patient will experience the therapist's empathic emotional involvement (Alpert, 1992, 1996; B. Foote, 1992; J. Foote, 1992; Fosha, 1992a, 1992b; Sklar, 1992, 1993, 1994).

Rather than rage and sadistic impulses, the emotional pain secondary to loss is conceptualized in AET as the fundamental pathogenically avoided core experience; rather than self-punishment fueled by guilt, the driving motivational force privileged by AET is optimal self-preservation. Whereas anger is the prototypical breakthrough experience for ISTDP, grief plays the same role in AET; anger, rage, and other negative emotions are regarded primarily as defenses against the direct experience of emotional pain.

> AET postulates that neurotic and characterologic pathology is the product of defensive attempts by patients to protect themselves from grief, the pain and loneliness caused by loss. The task of the AET therapist is to help the patient bear the grief. *The therapist and patient together build a reality-based, yet compassionate and sharing environment to facilitate the bearing of grief.* ... A compassionate environment which encourages such interaction creates a strong alliance and unlocks buried affects and associated memories. (Alpert, 1992, p. 133, italics added)

Corrective emotional experience without repetition compulsion: AET's divergence from traditional psychodynamics, BP, and ISTDP. Most psychodynamic models, including BP and ISTDP, assume that the repetition scenario is inevitable and that the therapy process should make use of resistance-generating repetition in order to, this time, achieve the different ending (Alexander & French, 1946). AET seeks to eliminate iatrogenic contributions to the lengthening of treatment; from the beginning, the AET therapist's aim is to engage the patient's hopeful (if cautious) readiness for change, and avoid the repetition–resistance pathway by leading with a corrective emotional experience (Fosha, 1992b). If, from the initial moments of the initial session, the patient feels understood by a therapist who is emotionally present, the drive for self-expression and connection can gain ascendancy before the forces of defense and resistance have a chance to gather momentum and kick in.

The relational factor is of paramount importance in AET. The emphasis on the corrective emotional experience of showing care, compassion, and the willingness to share and bear the patient's emotional pain reflects a basic notion of defense reduction through emotional engagement. AET techniques are distinguished by the active and explicit use of the therapist's emotional responses to the patient. The focus is on three technical aspects: showing care, compassion, and empathy; decreasing the patient–therapist distance; and focusing on pain and loss.

Forging a patient-therapist bond: Showing care, compassion, and empathy. AET techniques (Alpert, 1992, 1996; Sklar, 1993, 1994) aim at the rapid development of a therapeutic relationship based on compassion and emotional sharing of painful feelings. The therapist listens to the patient material from an empathic perspective. From the beginning and throughout the treatment, she starts to *interact empathically* and *show compassion*. Whether the patient responds to these expressive interventions emotionally or with increased anxiety and defensiveness, his reactions are explored in an empathic, supportive, and direct fashion. There is a *reframing and appreciation of defenses*. Rather than challenging the patient's resistance, as in ISTDP, in AET the patient's need for defenses is met with *explicit empathy* (J. Foote, 1992) and is *validated* as having been absolutely necessary in the circumstances in which the defenses arose. Rather then pressuring the patient to change and abandon defensive efforts, the patient is *acknowledged for the good work already done*, and is encouraged to *remove the pressure* he puts on himself to do more, with the assumption that when he no longer needs his defenses, he will no longer rely on them.

> When the therapist takes the pressure off the patient and expresses appreciation of the work done by the patient, both patient and therapist are encouraged. Additionally, deep feelings emerge as the patient experiences the therapist's appreciation. Analogously, if the therapist can receive what the patient offers, and process the moment, rather than insisting they follow the path determined by a preconceived formulation, the therapist as well as the patient will enjoy the work. If the therapist can share an understanding of the tremendous anxiety the patient carries with him into therapy, the pressure on the patient will be decreased. (Alpert, 1992, p. 147)

Reducing patient-therapist distance. Whereas BP and ISTDP encourage active patient participation in treatment decisions, the more radical aim of AET techniques is to reduce patient-therapist distance. Just as the therapist monitors her own reactions as well as those of the patient, the patient is encouraged to monitor the therapist's verbal and nonverbal responses in addition to his own, and verbalize his observations and reactions as part of the ongoing therapeutic processing; Alpert (1992) calls this *reciprocal monitoring*. The patient is invited to share his assessment of the therapeutic process and his interpretation of process events right along with the therapist. Patient and therapist thus constantly *compare views*. The patient also has the option to *take home the videotape of the session* (Alpert, 1996) to review and process the therapeutic interaction at his own pace. The patient is encouraged to become involved in activities traditionally reserved for the therapist (e.g., reciprocal monitoring, comparing views, having access to the videotape); the therapist is encouraged to explore the therapeutic use of responses traditionally assigned exclusively to the patient's realm (e.g., expression of feelings, self-disclosure). The therapist reveals herself and her feelings with the patient; thus, *self-disclosure* (Alpert, 1992, 1996) is used to short-circuit the patient's defensiveness and to demonstrate the therapist's willingness to share difficult, intense affective experiences with the patient.

For Alpert, "omnipotence is an immense problem for the therapist ... [who] also has reasons for avoiding being seen as a real, and hence flawed, person. ... The omnipotent defense of the caregiver often covers profound fear, emptiness, and pain" (1992, p. 147). *Avoiding omnipotence* becomes very important in AET and often is fostered by the therapist's disclosure of her own uncertainties and confusions about the therapeutic process. Increasing the patient's sense of mastery and self-respect, increasing the perception of the therapist as "real," decreasing the perception of the therapist as omnipotent—a less lopsided experience of the therapeutic relationship—all with concomitant rises in self-esteem, are the aimed-for consequences in the patient's responses to these types of intervention (Alpert, 1992, 1996; Sklar, 1993, 1994).

Facilitation of the mourning process. As AET considers loss and grief as primary pathogenic factors, mourning becomes the primary mechanism for resolution. The techniques discussed here become harnessed in the attempt to facilitate both access to and deep experience of the mourning process.

> The patient is encouraged to stay with the hurt, the disappointment, the loss and to experience as fully as possible those feelings that heretofore have been unbearable: the black hole, the abyss, falling apart, losing oneself, total isolation, reminiscent of the unbearable anxieties Winnicott refers [to] in the experience of trauma. Defenses are understood as the best coping mechanism the patient previously had available to handle unbearable disappointments and losses. The therapist empathizes with the patient's experience and this process of sharing diminishes the pain, reduces the anxiety, and brings reality into focus. As the patient feels more able to experience these buried feelings with the therapist, he is confronted with another agony: fuller recognition that significant people in his life were unable to tolerate these feelings and he was forced to find ways to cope with them alone. (Sklar, 1994, p. 8)

AET conceptualizes defenses and the resulting psychopathology as attempts to protect against the overwhelming pain associated with loss. Thus the mourning process becomes the main pathway to healing. Through care, compassion, empathy, and willingness to share his pain, the therapist helps the patient feel the grief associated with the primary pathogenic losses in his life. In addition to actual losses, losses include those resulting from deprivations, disappointments, and missed opportunities. The grief and the mourning process that ensues as a result of its being fully experienced lead the patient on the road to recovery.

AET breaks the taboo demanding an emotionally distant therapist. AET's stance of explicit care and compassion is as distant from the traditional stance of neutrality and abstinence as is Davanloo's confrontational challenge and pressure; AET is also its diametrical opposite. Building on work that regards countertransference as an essential tool of therapeutic work (Ehrenberg, 1992; Gill, 1982; Little, 1951, 1990; Mitchell, 1993; Racker, 1968; Searles, 1979; Winnicott, 1947), in AET the therapist's feelings and reactions are used explicitly in therapeutic interventions: AET's bold explorations of self-disclosure show this to be a powerful therapeutic technique. Having demonstrated how the therapist's sharing of her own feelings fosters the patient's experience and expression of *his* feelings, AET provides yet another route to helping patients rapidly gain access to previously buried painful feelings and memories.

ISTDP made invaluable contributions by elaborating the phenomenological realm of impulse experience; AET's contribution is its elaboration of the phenomenology of relational affective experiences. Traditional psychoanalytic psychotherapists are familiar with phenomena that stem from the patient's responses to a treatment relationship built on frustration: without a therapist who is openly compassionate and loving, it is impossible to fully appreciate just how difficult it can be for many patients to take in love, care, and appreciation. AET's experiential and dynamic elaboration of the phenomena associated with feeling alone in the face of loss and the demonstration of the deep conflicts stirred up by caring and giving interactions are groundbreaking contributions.

With AET's strengths come invariably its limitations. Though much more accessible for therapists than ISTDP's confrontational requirements, and though applicable to a much wider group of patients, AET remains a one-stance, one-etiology, one-pathway-to-change treatment model.

▼ AET, like ISTDP, prescribes a particular way of emotionally behaving with the patient: just as natural aggression is an advantage in ISTDP work, tears that flow easily are a plus in AET. Yet just as not every therapist can feel authentic by relentlessly challenging a patient, not every therapist leads naturally with tears in response to clinical material.

▼ AET continues to assume a single etiology for all suffering. Though the formulation of psychopathology as a result of defenses against the experience of loss has a much wider explanatory power than the formulation of psychopathology as a result of self-punishment for murderous impulses, it too is not *invariably* the only or even the most parsimonious formulation. Similarly, while the experience of the grief attendant on separation or loss, leading to a mourning process, is a major pathway to emotional healing, it is neither the only nor invariably the most efficient pathway for any given patient. For some patients, dealing with anger and rage primarily as defenses against a deeper level of emotional pain is not what heals; for them, healing lies in being able to *fully* experience anger, thus asserting the inalienable rights of the self by being angry when those rights are violated, thereby gaining strength and self-respect.

▼ Therapeutic responses that seek to make explicit use of the therapist's countertransference can at times be powerful, but at other times either prove insufficient or are not what is required.

▼ Finally, though AET makes its greatest contribution in the relational realm, its psychodynamic model remains intrapsychically focused. The realm of the "we" (Emde, 1988) where so much of its therapeutic work takes place, is not conceptually articulated.

Accelerated Experiential-Dynamic Psychotherapy (AEDP): Theory, Affect Facilitation, Authenticity

While preserving the radical experiential aspect of both ISTDP and AET, and many aspects of the stance of AET, AEDP attempts to solve some of these problems. Fundamentally guided by the quest to conceptually account for the transformational power of the direct experience, the affective model of change gradually developed in fits and starts and most nonlinearly; it informs the clinical practice of AEDP (Fosha, in press; Fosha & Osiason, 1996; Fosha & Slowiaczek, 1997).

In its ethos, theory, stance, and technique, AEDP lives and breathes multiplicity: there is no one path, there is no one core affect, there is no one core dynamic in psychopathogenesis that can account for the phenomena encountered in the treatment of a wide range of patients by a wide range of therapists. There are different paths to different cores, and different mechanisms of change are responsible for healing. The common underlying factor is the visceral experience of affect in the context of an emotionally engaged dyadic relationship as a path to transformation.

The affective model of change: An affect-centered model of relational psychodynamics. The affective model of change, the conceptual framework underlying AEDP, hopes to do explanatory justice to the transformational power of core affect phenomena elicited by its therapeutic stance and its strategies of intervention. AEDP's concepts are rooted in the change-oriented work of attachment theorists (Ainsworth et al., 1978; Bowlby, 1973, 1980, 1982; Fonagy et al., 1995; Fonagy, Leigh, Kennedy et al., 1995; Main, 1995, 1999) and clinical developmentalists (Beebe & Lachmann, 1988, 1994; Emde, 1981, 1988; Stern, 1985, 1998; Tronick, 1989, 1998).

Emotion and attachment—natural phenomena hardwired into human nature by evolution—operate to foster the best adaptation of which the individual is capable in a given environment. The affective model of change introduces the concept of *affective competence,* which allows the caregiver to provide an *affect-facilitating environment* within which the self can develop: the attachment relationship protects the individual from danger and thus from the fracturing impact of fear. Through moment-to-moment affective communication, optimally functioning dyads achieve states of mutual coordination and develop the capacity to repair interactive failures. In affect-facilitating environments, the individual feels safe, helped, and deeply understood. When affective experience exceeds the other's affective competence, the individual is alone with frightening experiences. Pathology is rooted in the individual's adaptive efforts to cope with overwhelming affects through the institution of defenses. The therapist seeks to undo the effects of affect-facilitating failures through a stance of emotional affirmation and affective engagement: no longer alone, the patient can now begin to process formerly feared-to-be-unbearable affects. By fostering a therapeutic climate of affective openness and sharing, patient and therapist can evolve a relationship in which mutual affective coordination can be reached without defensive exclusion of vital aspects of the self. Feeling supported and understood, the patient can access core affect, reap its rewards, and thereby reach an increasingly authentic sense of self. To translate this understanding into moment-to-moment clinical work, AEDP introduces a third representational schema, the self–other–emotion triangle, showing affective experiences to be rooted in the matrix of self–other interactions.

Healing-centered rather than pathology-centered model. AEDP's understanding of development, psychopathology, and the phenomena of psychotherapy is shaped by a focus on how change takes place, rather than on how pathology is maintained. Adaptation—intrinsic to affect and attachment theory—is at the heart of the model: core affective experiences tap and harness the organism's adaptive potential for meaningful information-processing and healing. In AEDP, adaptive strivings, healing forces, and the deep motivation for change are recognized, privileged, facilitated, and enhanced.

The potential for nonpathological response is represented in the additional schemas AEDP introduces to structure the clinical material. There are two versions of each of the three representational schemas: one represents the individual's most pathological functioning (in conditions invariably experienced as unsafe), while the other represents the individual's functioning at his best (in conditions experienced as safe).

Expanded realm of core affective phenomena. AEDP goes beyond impulses, grief, and emotional pain to a broader definition of core affective experience: *The domain of affective phenomena is expanded to include self and relational affective experiences, as well as the core state,* each with characteristic microdynamics and phenomenology.

AEDP is equally at home exploring loss, pain, and the difficulties of accepting love and compassion (the phenomenological and experiential realm elaborated by AET) as it is in exploring anger, rage, and grief (the phenomenological and experiential realm elaborated by ISTDP). AEDP also formally adds and elaborates another experiential realm: that of the *meta-therapeutic processes* and their characteristic *healing affects.* These are the experiences that arise in response to feeling effective, feeling helped, and changing for the better: they include joy, vitality, pride, gratitude, and feeling moved. Continuing where AET left off (i.e., the elaboration of dynamics that make it difficult for the patient to accept the therapist's compassion), AEDP explores and elaborates the dynamics of patient difficulties accepting all types of positive experiences, be they self or relational experiences.

Therapeutic stance. It is telling that the E in AEDP stands for *experiential,* whereas the E in AET stands for *empathic.* While AET considers empathy to be a form of interaction and a curative one—(Alpert, 1992), AEDP goes beyond explicit empathy: the stance changes from a *sole focus on empathy* to one that struggles with the *simultaneous maintenance of empathy and authenticity* (Osiasen, 1997, Slavin & Kriegman, 1998). In AEDP, the focus is on the facilitation of the patient's affective experiencing—however that is accomplished. AEDP defines empathy as a certain way of understanding the patient—which informs being with him—but allows for a variety of options for how to behave with the patient. Considered crucial is the dyadic processing of therapeutic experiences that led to the patient's experience of core affect.

Being empathic and striving for affect facilitation, as the AEDP therapist aims to do, can appear paradoxical (see also Rice & Greenberg, 1991). Out of the paradox that results from radical acceptance of the patient as he is now and focused efforts to help him to become as deeply himself as he can comes good productive tension that moves the treatment along. Moment-to-moment attunement to affective fluctuations determines which aspect of the stance is more prominent.

Like its three experiential STDP family members, AEDP features a high level of therapeutic activity and selective focusing, engagement of the patient as active partner in treatment, focus on the here and now of the patient-therapist interaction, and belief in the power of the experiential element to minimize defenses, allay fear, and maximize affective access. From BP, AEDP adopts the techniques of rapid identification and clarification of the moment-to-moment clinical material in terms of basic psychodynamic constructs. AEDP integrates the powerful ISTDP techniques for affective enhancement *sans* its adversarial-confrontational stance. From AET, AEDP adopts systematic interventions that facilitate the rapid development of a trusting patient-therapist relationship based on an emotionally engaged and empathic therapeutic stance. As in AET, the AEDP therapist strives for corrective, affect-facilitating relationships from the get-go, and aims to bypass defenses and facilitate access to a deep experience of core affects. A deepening of the work gets done through acknowledgment of mutual accomplishment and the exploration of the resulting transformations.

AEDP breaks the taboo on positive experience, a fortiori positive therapeutic experiences, challenging the prevailing ethos that getting better is more illusory than suffering, that negative experience is intrinsically truer than positive experience, that feeling bad is more authentic than feeling good, that anger is truer than love, and that resistance is pervasive whereas change is deceptive. Through its stance, techniques, and conceptual tool innovations (the two versions of the representational schemas), AEDP seeks to make conceptual and clinical space for positive experiences: for health as well as pathology, for joy as well as suffering, for relaxation and ease as well as tension and anxiety, and most important, for positive therapeutic experiences as well as resistant and frustrating ones.

AEDP also breaks the taboo demanding therapeutic modesty: the acknowledgment of therapeutic gains as a result of patient and therapist working hard together is an extremely important venue of therapeutic work. So is the exploration of positive feelings that develop between patient and therapist as a result of having a relationship in which the patient feels understood, loved, and helped. As a result of breaking these taboos, AEDP elaborates the phenomenological realm of healing relationships and their characteristic core affective phenomena.

CONCLUSION

In contrast to traditional long-term psychodynamic psychotherapy, short-term dynamic psychotherapy has at times been viewed as limited to treating specifically focused problems with the aim of restoring baseline functioning. The experiential STDPs described in this appendix show that deep psychodynamic work and time-conscious treatment are completely compatible. BP, ISTDP, AET, and AEDP represent four time-condensed psychodynamic pathways to the realm of genuine affective experience, where psychodynamic working through of previously unconscious material can occur. They provide evidence of the robustness of unconscious phenomena, showing that their ready elicitation does not depend on passive, nondirective techniques, but may be accomplished through active techniques, which also significantly shorten the duration of treatment.

BP, ISTDP, and AET have been discussed here as being on a developmental line viewed from the perspective of AEDP. It is important to state explicitly that they are all vital approaches that are alive and well and growing. Furthermore, the process of mutual influence continues and as a result, the sharp boundaries separating different approaches are being creatively blurred (Coughlin Della Selva, 1996; Laikin, Winston, & McCullough, 1991; Magnavita, 1997, 1999; McCullough Vaillant, 1997).

Throughout, I have focused on the psychoanalytic taboos broken by the experiential STDPs. Yet it is an important object lesson that even though psychoanalysis broke many taboos, it also generated its own. One way to avoid new taboos that will inhibit creative development is to recognize that no approach has the answer to all clinical problems faced by all patient-therapist dyads.

All four experiential STDPs break yet another psychoanalytic taboo: this last is part of the current social-constructivist psychoanalytic zeitgeist that holds that no psychic experience should be "privileged" over any other, all experiences gaining meaning only from within the patient-therapist interaction. The four experiential STDPs described here "privilege" affect and intense visceral experiencing, and do so explicitly and unapologetically.

REFERENCES

Ainsworth, M. D. S., Blehar, M. C., Waters, E., & Wall, S. (1978). *Patterns of attachment: A psychological study of the strange situation.* Hillsdale, NJ: Lawrence Erlbaum.

Alexander, F., & French, T. M. (1946). *Psychoanalytic therapy: Principles and application.* New York: Ronald Press. Reprint. Lincoln, NE: University of Nebraska Press, 1980.

Alpert, M. C. (1992). Accelerated empathic therapy: A new short-term dynamic psychotherapy. *International Journal of Short-Term Psychotherapy, 7*(3), 133–156.

Alpert, M. C. (1996). Videotaping psychotherapy. *Journal of Psychotherapy Practice and Research, 5*(2), 93–105.

Bacal, H. A. (1995). The essence of Kohut's work and the progress of self psychology. *Psychoanalytic Dialogues, 5,* 353–366.

Barber, J. P. & Crits-Cristoph, P. (1991). Comparison of the brief dynamic therapies. In P. Crits-Cristoph & J. P. Barber (Eds.), *Handbook of short-term dynamic psychotherapy* (pp. 323–355). New York: Basic Books.

Bates, J. E., Maslin, C. A., & Frankel, K. A. (1985). Attachment security, mother-child interaction, and temperament as predictors of behavior-problem ratings at age three years. In I. Bretherton & E. Waters (Eds.), *Growing points of attachment theory and research. Monographs of the Society for Research in Child Development, 50*(1–2), serial no. 209, 167–193.

Beebe, B., Jaffe, J., & Lachmann, F. M. (1992). A dyadic systems view of communication. In N. Skolnick & S. Warshaw (Eds.), *Relational perspectives in psychoanalysis* (pp. 61–81). Hillsdale, NJ: Analytic Press.

Beebe, B., & Lachmann, F. M. (1988). The contribution of mother-infant mutual influence to the origins of self- and object representations. *Psychoanalytic Psychology, 5,* 305–337.

Beebe, B., & Lachmann, F. M. (1994). Representation and internalization in infancy: Three principles of salience. *Psychoanalytic Psychology, 11*(2), 127–165.

Beebe, B., Lachmann, F. M., & Jaffe, J. (1997). Mother-infant interaction structures and pre-symbolic self and object representations. *Psychoanalytic Dialogues, 7,* 133–182.

Benjamin, L. (1997). Interpersonal psychotherapy of personality disorders. Workshop given at the Thirteenth Annual Conference of the Society for the Exploration of Psychotherapy Integration (SEPI): Embracing new approaches. Toronto, 24 April.

Blake, W. (1987). Augeries of innocence. In A. Ostriker (Ed.), *William Blake: The complete poems* (pp. 506–510). New York: Penguin Books.

Bohart, A. C., & Tallman, K. (1999). *How clients make therapy work: The process of active self-healing.* Washington, DC: American Psychological Association.

Bollas, C. (1987). *The shadow of the object: Psychoanalysis of the unthought known.* New York: Columbia University Press.

Bollas, C. (1989). *Forces of destiny: Psychoanalysis and human idiom*. London: Free Association Books.

Bowlby, J. (1973). *Attachment and loss: Vol. 2. Separation*. New York: Basic Books.

Bowlby, J. (1977). The making and breaking of affectional bonds: Aetiology and psychopathology in the light of attachment theory. *British Journal of Psychiatry, 130,* 201–210.

Bowlby, J. (1980). *Attachment and loss: Vol. 3. Loss, sadness, and depression*. New York: Basic Books.

Bowlby, J. (1982). *Attachment and loss: Vol. 1. Attachment* (2d ed.). New York: Basic Books.

Bowlby, J. (1988). *A secure base: Parent-child attachment and healthy human development*. New York: Basic Books.

Bowlby, J. (1991). Post-script. In C. M. Parkes, J. Stevenson-Hinde, & P. Marris (Eds.), *Attachment across the life cycle* (pp. 293–297). London: Routledge.

Braithwaite, R. L., & Gordon, E. W. (1991). *Success against the odds*. Cambridge, MA: Harvard University Press.

Brennan, T. (1995). Splitting word and flesh. Paper presented at The psychoanalytic century: An international interdisciplinary conference celebrating the centennial of Breuer and Freud's "Studies on Hysteria." New York University Postdoctoral Program, NY.

Brenner, C. (1974). On the nature and development of affects: A unified theory. *Psychoanalytic Quarterly, 53,* 550–584.

Brodkey, H. (1996). This wild darkness. *The New Yorker,* 5 February, pp. 52–54

Bucci, W. (1985). Dual coding: A cognitive model for psychoanalytic research. *Journal of the American Psychoanalytic Association, 33,* 571–608.

Casement, P. J. (1985). *On learning from the patient*. London: Tavistock.

Cassidy, J. (1994). Emotion regulation: Influence of attachment relationships. *Monographs of the Society for Research in Child Development, 69*(240), 228–249.

Coates, S. W. (1998). Having a mind of one's own and holding the other in mind: Commentary on paper by Peter Fonagy and Mary Target. *Psychoanalytic Dialogues, 8,* 115–148.

Coen, S. J. (1996). Love between therapist and patient. *American Journal of Psychotherapy, 50,* 14–27.

Costello, P. C. (2000). *Attachment, communication and affect: Implications for psychotherapy*. Manuscript.

Coughlin Della Selva, P. (1996). *Intensive short-term dynamic psychotherapy*. New York: Wiley.

Crits-Christoph, P., & Barber, J. P. (Eds.). (1991). *Handbook of short-term dynamic psychotherapy*. New York: Basic Books.

Csikszentmihalyi, M. (1990). *Flow: The psychology of optimal experience*. New York: HarperCollins.

Cuddihy, J. M. (1987). *The ordeal of civility: Freud, Marx, Lèvi-Strauss, and the Jewish struggle with modernity*. New York: Basic Books.

Damasio, A. R. (1994). *Descartes' error: Emotion, reason and the human brain.* New York: Grosset/Putnam.

Damasio, A. R. (1999). *The feeling of what happens: Body and emotion in the making of consciousness.* New York: Harcourt Brace.

Darwin, C. (1872/1965). *The expression of emotion in man and animals.* Chicago: University of Chicago Press.

Davanloo, H. (Ed.). (1978). *Basic principles and techniques in short-term dynamic psychotherapy.* New York: Spectrum.

Davanloo, H. (Ed.). (1980). *Short-term dynamic psychotherapy.* New York: Jason Aronson.

Davanloo H. (1986–1988). Core training program. The International Institute of Short-Term Dynamic Psychotherapy. Montreal.

Davanloo, H. (1990). *Unlocking the unconscious: Selected papers of Habib Davanloo.* New York: Wiley.

Davies, J. M., (1996). Dissociation, repression and reality testing in the counter-transference: The controversy over memory and false memory in the psychoanalytic treatment of adult survivors of childhood sexual abuse. *Psychoanalytic Dialogues, 6,* 189–218.

Dozier, M., Stovall, K. C., & Albus, K. E. (1999). Attachment and psychopathology in adulthood. In J. Cassidy & P. R. Shaver (Eds.), *Handbook of attachment: Theory, research and clinical applications* (pp. 497–519). New York: Guilford.

Eagle, M. N. (1995). The developmental perspectives of attachment and psychoanalytic theory. In S. Goldberg, R. Muir, & J. Kerr (Eds.), *Attachment theory: Social, developmental and clinical perspectives* (pp. 407–472). Hillsdale, NJ: Analytic Press.

Eagle, M. N. (1996). Attachment research and psychoanalytic theory. In J. M. Masling & R. F. Bornstein (Eds.), *Psychoanalytic perspectives on developmental psychology* (pp. 105–149). Washington, DC: American Psychological Association.

Ehrenberg, D. (1992). *The intimate edge: Extending the reach of psychoanalytic interaction.* New York: W. W. Norton.

Ekman, P. (1983). Autonomic nervous system activity distinguishes among emotions. *Science, 221,* 1208–1210.

Ekman, P. (1984). Expression and the nature of emotion. In K. R. Scherer & P. Ekman (Eds.), *Approaches to emotion* (pp. 319–343). Hillsdale, NJ: Lawrence Erlbaum.

Ekman, P., & Davidson, R. J. (Eds.). (1994). *The nature of emotion: Fundamental questions.* New York: Oxford University Press.

Ekman, P., & Friesen, W. V. (1969). The repertoire of non-verbal behavior: Categories, origins, usage, and coding. *Semiotica, 1,* 49–98.

Emde, R. N. (1980). Toward a psychoanalytic theory of affect. Part 1. The organizational model and its propositions. In S. Greenspan & G. Pollack (Eds.), *The course of life: Psychoanalytic contributions toward understanding personality and development.* Bethesda, MD: Mental Health Study Center, NIMH.

Emde, R. N. (1981). Changing models of infancy and the nature of early development: Remodeling the foundation. *Journal of the American Psychoanalytic Association, 29,* 179–219.

Emde, R. N. (1983). The pre-representational self and its affective core. *Psychoanalytic Study of the Child, 38,* 165–192.

Emde, R. N. (1988). Development terminable and interminable. *International Journal of Psycho-Analysis, 69,* 23–42.

Emde, R. N., Klingman, D. H., Reich, J. H., & Wade, J. D. (1978). Emotional expression in infancy: I. Initial studies of social signaling and an emergent model. In M. Lewis & L. Rosenblum, (Eds.), *The development of affect.* New York: Plenum Press.

Epstein, M. (1995). *Thoughts without a thinker: Psychotherapy from a Buddhist perspective.* New York: Basic Books.

Erickson, M. F., Sroufe, L. A., & Egeland, B. (1985). The relationship between quality of attachment and behavior problems in a preschool high-risk sample. *Monographs of the Society for Research in Child Development, 50,* 147–166.

Ezriel, H. (1952). Notes on psychoanalytic group therapy: Interpretation and research. *Psychiatry, 15,* 119–126.

Ferenczi, S. (1920/1980). The further development of an active therapy in psycho-analysis. In M. Balint (Ed.), E. Mosbacher (Trans.), *Further contributions to the theory and technique of psycho-analysis* (pp. 198–216). New York: Brunner/Mazel.

Ferenczi, S. (1925/1980). Contra-indications to the "active" psycho-analytic technique. In M. Balint (Ed.), E. Mosbacher (Trans.), *Further contributions to the theory and technique of psycho-analysis* (pp. 217–229). New York: Brunner/Mazel.

Ferenczi, S. (1931/1980). Child analysis in the analysis of adults. In M. Balint (Ed.), E. Mosbacher (Trans.), *Final contributions to the problems and methods of psychoanalysis* (pp. 126–142). New York: Brunner/Mazel.

Ferenczi, S. (1933/1980). Confusion of tongues between adults and the child. In M. Balint (Ed.), E. Mosbacher (Trans.), *Final contributions to the problems and methods of* psychoanalysis (pp. 156–167). New York: Brunner/Mazel.

Ferenczi, S., & Rank, O. (1925/1987). The development of psycho-analysis. In G. H. Pollack (Ed.), C. Newton (Trans.), *Classics in psychoanalysis monograph series,* monograph 4. Madison, CT: International Universities Press.

Flegenheimer, W. (1982). *Techniques of brief psychotherapy.* New York: Jason Aronson.

Flem, L. (1997). *Casanova: The man who really loved women.* New York: Farrar, Straus & Giroux.

Fonagy, P. (1997). Multiple voices vs. meta-cognition: An attachment theory perspective. *Journal of Psychotherapy Integration, 7,* 181–194.

Fonagy, P., Leigh, T., Kennedy, R., Matoon, G., Steele, H., Target, M., Steele, M., & Higgitt, A. (1995). Attachment, borderline states and the representation of emotions and cognitions in self and other. In D. Cicchetti, S. L. Toth et al. (Eds.), *Emotion, cognition and representation* (pp. 371–414). Rochester, NY: University of Rochester Press.

Fonagy, P., Steele, M., Steele, H., Higgitt, A., & Target, M. (1994). The theory and practice of resilience. *Journal of Child Psychology and Psychiatry, 35,* 231–257.

Fonagy, P., Steele, M., Steele, H., Leigh, T., Kennedy, R., Matoon, G., & Target, M. (1995). Attachment, the reflective self, and borderline states. In S. Goldberg, R. Muir, & J. Kerr (Eds.), *Attachment theory: Social, developmental and clinical perspectives* (pp. 233–278). Hillsdale, NJ: Analytic Press.

Fonagy, P., Steele, M., Steele, H., Moran, G. S., & Higgitt, A. (1991). The capacity for understanding mental states: The reflective self in parent and child and its significance for security of attachment. *Infant Mental Health Journal, 12,* 201–218.

Fonagy, P., & Target, M. (1998). Mentalization and the changing aims of child psychoanalysis. *Psychoanalytic Dialogues, 8,* 87–114.

Foote, B. (1992). Accelerated empathic therapy: The first self-psychological brief therapy? *International Journal of Short-Term Psychotherapy, 7*(3), 177–192.

Foote, J. (1992). Explicit empathy and the stance of therapeutic neutrality. *International Journal of Short-Term Psychotherapy, 7*(3), 193–198.

Fosha, D. (1988). Restructuring in the treatment of depressive disorders with Davanloo's intensive short-term dynamic psychotherapy. *International Journal of Short-Term Psychotherapy, 3*(3), 189–212.

Fosha, D. (1990). Undoing the patient's omnipotence. Paper presented at the conference on short-term dynamic therapy: A developing therapy. The Graduate Center of the City University of New York, NY.

Fosha, D. (Ed.). (1992a). Accelerated Empathic Therapy (AET): History, development and theory. *International Journal of Short-Term Psychotherapy, 7*(3).

Fosha, D. (1992b). The interrelatedness of theory, technique and therapeutic stance: A comparative look at intensive short-term dynamic psychotherapy and accelerated empathic therapy. *International Journal of Short-Term Psychotherapy, 7*(3), 157–176.

Fosha, D. (1995). Technique and taboo in three short-term dynamic psychotherapies. *Journal of Psychotherapy Practice and Research, 4,* 297–318.

Fosha, D. (in press). Meta-therapeutic processes and the affects of transformation: Affirmation and the healing affects. *Journal of Psycotherapy Integration.*

Fosha, D., & Osiason, J. (1996). Affect, "truth" and videotapes: Accelerated experiential/dynamic therapy. Presented at the spring meeting of Division 39 (Psychoanalysis) of the American Psychological Association, New York, NY.

Fosha, D., & Slowiaczek, M. L. (1997). Techniques for accelerating dynamic psychotherapy. *American Journal of Psychotherapy, 51,* 229–251.

Frank, J. D. (1971). Therapeutic factors in psychotherapy. *American Journal of Psychotherapy, 25,* 350–361.

Frank, J. D. (1974). Psychotherapy: The restoration of morale. *American Journal of Psychiatry, 131,* 271–274.

Frank, J. D. (1982). Therapeutic components shared by all psychotherapies. In J. H. Harvey & M. M. Parks (Eds.), *Psychotherapy research and behavior change.* Washington, DC: American Psychological Association.

Freud, A. (1937/1966). *The ego and the mechanisms of defense* (C. Baines, Trans.). New York: International Universities Press.

Freud, S. (1912a/1958). The dynamics of transference. In J. Strachey (Ed. and Trans.), *The standard edition of the complete psychological works of Sigmund Freud* (Vol. 12, pp. 97–108). London: Hogarth Press.

Freud, S. (1912b/1958). Recommendations to physicians practicing psychoanalysis. In J. Strachey (Ed. and Trans.), *The standard edition of the complete psychological works of Sigmund Freud* (Vol. 12, pp. 109–120). London: Hogarth Press.

Freud, S. (1915/1958). Observations on transference-love. In J. Strachey (Ed. and Trans.), *The standard edition of the complete psychological works of Sigmund Freud* (Vol. 12, pp. 157–173). London: Hogarth Press.

Freud, S. (1917/1958). Mourning and melancholia. In J. Strachey (Ed. and Trans.), *The standard edition of the complete psychological works of Sigmund Freud* (Vol. 14, pp. 243–258). London: Hogarth Press.

Freud, S. (1923/1958). Beyond the pleasure principle. In J. Strachey (Ed. and Trans.), *The standard edition of the complete psychological works of Sigmund Freud* (Vol. 18, pp. 7–64). London: Hogarth Press.

Freud, S. (1926/1959). Inhibitions, symptoms and anxiety. In J. Strachey (Ed. and Trans.), *The standard edition of the complete psychological works of Sigmund Freud* (Vol. 20, pp. 75–175). London: Hogarth Press.

Frijda, N. H. (1986). *The emotions.* Cambridge: Cambridge University Press.

Frijda, N. H. (1988). The laws of emotion. *American Psychologist, 43,* 349–358.

Garfield, A. S. (1995). *Unbearable affect: A guide to the psychotherapy of psychosis.* New York: Wiley.

Gendlin, E. (1991). On emotion in therapy. In J. D. Safran & L. S. Greenberg, (Eds.), *Emotion, psychotherapy & change* (pp. 255–279). New York: Guilford.

George, C., & Solomon, J. (1999). Attachment and caregiving: The caregiving behavioral system. In J. Cassidy & P. R. Shaver (Eds.), *Handbook of attachment: Theory, research and clinical applications* (pp. 649–670). New York: Guilford.

Ghent, E. (1995). Interaction in the psychoanalytic situation. *Psychoanalytic Dialogues, 5,* 479–491.

Gianino, A., & Tronick, E. Z. (1988). The mutual regulation model: The infant's self and interactive regulation. Coping and defense capacities. In T. Field, P. McCabe, & N. Schneiderman (Eds.), *Stress and coping* (pp. 47–68). Hillsdale, NJ: Lawrence Erlbaum.

Gill, M. (1982). *Analysis of transference: Vol 1. Theory and technique.* New York: International Universities Press.

Gluck, L. (1995). Circe's power. *The New Yorker,* 10 April, p. 90.

Gold, J. R. (1994). When the patient does the integrating: Lessons for theory and practice. *Journal of Psychotherapy Integration, 4,* 133–154.

Gold, J. R. (1996). *Key concepts in psychotherapy integration.* New York: Plenum Press.

Goleman, D. (1995). *Emotional intelligence: Why it can matter more than IQ.* New York: Bantam Books.

Greenberg, L. S., Elliott, R., & Lietaer, G. (1994). Research on humanistic and experiential psychotherapies. In A. E. Bergin & S. L. Garfield (Eds.), *Handbook of psychotherapy and behavior change* (4th ed., pp. 509–539). New York: Wiley.

Greenberg, L. S., Rice, L. N., & Elliott, R. (1993). *Facilitating emotional change: The moment-by-moment process.* New York: Guilford.

Greenberg, L. S., & Safran, J. D. (1987). *Emotion in psychotherapy.* New York: Guilford.

Guntrip, H. (1961). *Personality structure and human interaction.* London: Hogarth Press.

Guntrip, H. (1969). *Schizoid phenomena, object relations and the self.* New York: International Universities Press.

Gustafson, J. D. (1986). *The complex secret of brief psychotherapy.* New York: W. W. Norton.

Guterson, D. (1995). *Snow falling on cedars.* New York: Vintage.

Hanson, N. R. (1958). *Patterns of discovery.* Cambridge: Cambridge University Press.

Harris, A. (1996). False memory? False memory syndrome? The so-called false-memory syndrome? *Psychoanalytic Dialogues, 6,* 155–187.

Hart, J. (1991). *Damage.* New York: Columbine Fawcett.

Heatwole, H. (1988). *Guide to Shenandoah National Park and Skyline Drive.* Shenandoah Natural History Association, Bulletin no. 9, Luray, VA.

Herman, J. L. (1982). *Trauma and recovery.* New York: Basic Books.

Hesse, E. (1999). The adult attachment interview: Historical and current perspectives. In J. Cassidy & P. R. Shaver (Eds.), *Handbook of attachment: Theory, research and clinical applications* (pp. 395–433). New York: Guilford.

Høeg, P. (1993). *Smilla's sense of snow.* (T. Nunnally, Trans.). New York: Dell.

Izard, C. E. (1977). *Human emotions.* New York: Plenum.

Izard, C. E. (1990). Facial expressions and the regulation of emotion. *Journal of Personality and Social Psychology, 58,* 487–498.

Jacobson, J. G. (1994). Signal affects and our psychoanalytic confusion of tongues. *Journal of the American Psychoanalytic Association, 42,* 15–42.

James, W. (1902/1985). *The varieties of religious experience: A study in human nature.* Penguin Books.

Joffe, W. G., & Sandler, J. (1965). Pain, depression and individuation. *Psychoanalytic Study of the Child, 20,* 394–424.

Jordan, J. V. (1991). Empathy and self boundaries. In J. V. Jordan, A. G. Kaplan, J. B. Miller, I. P. Stiver, & J. L. Surrey (Eds.), *Women's growth in connection: Writings from the Stone Center.* New York: Guilford.

Kelly, V. C. (1996). Affect and the redefinition of intimacy. In D. L. Nathanson (Ed.), *Knowing feeling: Affect, script and psychotherapy* (pp. 55–104). New York: W. W. Norton.

Kentgen, L., Allen, R., Kose, G., & Fong, R. (1998). The effects of rerepresentation on future performance. *British Journal of Developmental Psychology, 16,* 505–517.

Kiersky, S., & Beebe, B. (1994). The reconstruction of early nonverbal relatedness in the treatment of difficult patients: A special form of empathy. *Psychoanalytic Dialogues, 4*(3), 389–408.

Kihlstrom, J. (1987). The cognitive unconscious. *Science, 237,* 1445–1452.

Kissen, M. (1995). *Affect, object, and character structure.* New York: International Universities Press.

Klinnert, M. D., Campos, J. J., Sorce, J. F., Emde, R. N., & Svejda, M. (1983). Emotions as behavior regulators: Social referencing in infancy. In R. Plutchik & H. Kellerman (Eds.), *Emotion: Theory, research and experience: Vol. 2.* New York: Academic Press.

Kohut, H. (1977). *The restoration of the self.* New York: International Universities Press.

Kohut, H. (1984). *How does psychoanalysis cure?* Chicago: University of Chicago Press.

Kuhn, T. (1970). *The structure of scientific revolutions* (Rev. ed.). Chicago: University of Chicago Press.

Lachmann, F. M., & Beebe, B. (1992). Reformulations of early development and transference: Implications for psychic structure formation. In J. W. Barron, M. N. Eagle, & D. Wolitzy (Eds.), *Interface of psychoanalysis and psychology* (pp. 133–153). Washington, DC: American Psychological Association.

Lachmann, F. M., & Beebe, B. (1996). Three principles of salience in the organization of the patient-analyst interaction. *Psychoanalytic Psychology, 13,* 1–22.

Lachmann, F. M., & Lichtenberg, J. (1992). Model scenes: Implications for psychoanalytic treatment. *Journal of the American Psychoanalytic Association, 40,* 117–137.

Laikin, M. (1999). Personal communication.

Laikin, M., Winston, A., & McCullough, L. (1991). Intensive short-term dynamic psychotherapy. In P. Crits-Christoph & J. P. Barber (Eds.), *Handbook of short-term dynamic psychotherapy* (pp. 80–109). New York: Basic Books.

Lamb, M. E. (1987). Predictive implications of individual differences in attachment. *Journal of Consulting and Clinical Psychology, 55,* 817–824.

Lazarus, R. S. (1991). *Emotion and adaptation.* New York: Oxford University Press.

LeDoux, J. (1996). *The emotional brain: The mysterious underpinnings of emotional life.* New York: Simon & Schuster.

Levine, L. V., Tuber, S. B., Slade, A., & Ward, M. J. (1991). Mother's mental representations and their relationship to mother-infant attachment. *Bulletin of the Menninger Clinic, 55,* 454–469.

Lindemann, E. (1944). Symptomatology and management of acute grief. *American Journal of Psychiatry, 101,* 141–148.

Lindon, J. (1994). Gratification and provision in psychoanalysis. *Psychoanalytic Dialogues, 4,* 549–582.

Little, M. (1951). Countertransference and the patient's response to it. *International Journal of Psychoanalysis, 32,* 32–40.

Little, M. (1990). *Psychotic anxieties and containment*. Northvale, NJ: Jason Aronson.

Lubin-Fosha, M. S. (1991). Personal communication.

Luborsky, L. & Mark, D. (1991). Short-term supportive-expressive psychoanalytic psychotherapy. In P. Crits-Christoph & J. P. Barber (Eds.), *Handbook of short-term dynamic psychotherapy* (pp. 110–136). New York: Basic Books.

Lyons-Ruth, K., & Jacobvitz, D. (1999). Attachment disorganization: Unresolved loss, relational violence, and lapses in behavioral and attentional strategies. In J. Cassidy & P. R. Shaver (Eds.), *Handbook of attachment: Theory, research and clinical applications* (pp. 520–554). New York: Guilford.

Magnavita, J. J. (1993). The evolution of short-term dynamic psychotherapy: Treatment of the future? *Professional Psychology: Research and Practice, 24,* 360–365.

Magnavita, J. J. (1997). *Restructuring personality disorders: A short-term dynamic approach*. New York: Guilford.

Magnavita, J. J. (1999). *Relational therapy for personality disorders*. New York: Wiley.

Mahler, M. S., Pine, F., & Bergman, A. (1975). *The psychological birth of the human infant*. New York: Basic Books.

Mahrer, A. R. (1996). *The complete guide to experiential psychotherapy*. New York: Wiley.

Mahrer, A. R. (1999). How can impressive in-session changes become impressive postsession changes? In L. S. Greenberg, J. C. Watson, & G. Lietaer (Eds.), *Handbook of experiential psychotherapy* (pp. 201–223). New York: Guilford.

Main, M. (1995). Recent studies in attachment: Overview with selected implications for clinical work. In S. Goldberg, R. Muir, & J. Kerr (Eds.), *Attachment theory: Social, developmental and clinical perspectives* (pp. 407–472). Hillsdale, NJ: Analytic Press.

Main, M. (1999). Epilogue. Attachment theory: Eighteen points with suggestions for future studies. In J. Cassidy & P. R. Shaver (Eds.), *Handbook of attachment: Theory, research and clinical applications* (pp. 845–888). New York: Guilford.

Main, M., & Goldwyn, R. (1990). Adult attachment rating and classification system. In M. Main (Ed.), *A typology of human attachment organization assessed in discourse, drawings and interviews*. New York: Cambridge University Press.

Main, M., & Hesse, E. (1990). The insecure disorganized/disoriented attachment pattern in infancy: Precursors and sequelae. In M. T. Greenberg, D. Cichetti, & E. M. Cummings (Eds.), *Attachment in the preschool years: Theory, research and intervention* (pp. 161–182). Chicago: University of Chicago Press.

Malan, D. H. (1963). *A study of brief psychotherapy*. New York: Plenum Press.

Malan, D. H. (1976). *The frontier of brief psychotherapy*. New York: Plenum Press.

Malan, D. H. (1979). *Individual psychotherapy and the science of psychodynamics*. London: Butterworth.

Malan, D. H. (1980). The most important development in psychotherapy since the discovery of the unconscious. In H. Davanloo (Ed.), *Short-term dynamic psychotherapy* (pp. 13–23). New York: Jason Aronson.

Malan, D. H. (1986). Beyond interpretation: Initial evaluation and technique in short-term dynamic psychotherapy. Parts I & II. *International Journal of Short-Term Psychotherapy, 1*(2), 59–106.

Malan, D. M., & Osimo, F. (1992). *Psychodynamics, training, and outcome in brief psychotherapy*. London: Butterworth-Heinemann.

Mann, J. (1973). *Time-limited psychotherapy.* Cambridge, MA: Harvard University Press.

Mann, J., & Goldman, R. (1982). *A casebook in time-limited psychotherapy*. New York: McGraw-Hill.

Marke, J. (1993). Cognitive and affective aspects of dissociative experiences: Implications for the STDP of early trauma. Paper presented at the conference on short-term dynamic therapy: Healing the wounds of childhood. The Graduate Center of the City University of New York, NY.

Marke, J. (1995). *A manual of short-term dynamic psychotherapy*. Manuscript.

McCullough, L. (1991). Intensive short-term dynamic psychotherapy: Change mechanisms from a cross-theoretical perspective. In R. Curtis and G. Stricker (Eds.), *How people change: Inside and outside of therapy.* New York: Plenum Press.

McCullough, L., Winston, A., Farber, B., Porter, F., Pollack, J., Laikin, M., Vingiano, W., & Trujillo, M. (1991). The relationship of patient-therapist interaction to outcome in brief psychotherapy. *Psychotherapy, 28,* 525–533.

McCullough Vaillant, L. (1997). *Changing character: Short-term anxiety-regulating psychotherapy for restructuring defenses, affects, and attachment.* New York: Basic Books.

McGuire, K. N. (1991). Affect in focusing and experiential psychotherapy. In J. D. Safran & L. S. Greenberg (Eds.), *Emotion, psychotherapy & change* (pp. 227–254). New York: Guilford.

Menninger, K. (1958). *Theory of psychoanalytic technique.* New York: Basic Books.

Messer, S. B., & Warren, C. S. (1995). *Models of brief dynamic psychotherapy: A comparative approach.* New York: Guilford.

Miller, A. (1981). *Prisoners of childhood: The drama of the gifted child and the search for the true self.* R. Ward (Trans.). New York: Basic Books.

Mitchell, S. A. (1988). *Relational concepts in psychoanalysis: An integration.* Cambridge, MA: Harvard University Press.

Mitchell, S. A. (1993). *Hope and dread in psychoanalysis.* New York: Basic Books.

Molnos, A. (1986). The process of short-term dynamic psychotherapy and the four triangles. *International Journal of Short-Term Psychotherapy, 1,* 112–125.

Nathanson, D. L. (1992). *Shame and pride: Affect, sex and the birth of the self.* New York: W. W. Norton.

Nathanson, D. L. (1996). About emotion. In D. L. Nathanson (Ed.), *Knowing feeling: Affect, script and psychotherapy* (pp. 1–21). New York: W. W. Norton.

Okin, R. (1986). Interpretation in short-term dynamic psychotherapy. *International Journal of Short-Term Psychotherapy, 1,* 271–280.

Orlinsky, D. E., Grawe, K., & Parks, B. K. (1994). Process and outcome in psychotherapy–*Noch einmal*. In A. E. Bergin & S. L. Garfield (Eds.), *Handbook of psychotherapy and behavior change* (4th ed., pp. 270–378). New York: Wiley.

Osiason, J. (1995). Accelerated empathic therapy: A model of short-term dynamic psychotherapy. Paper presented at the symposium on short-term models of psychotherapy. The IV Congress of Psychology, Athens, Greece.

Osiason, J. (1997). Personal communication.

Pao, P. N. (1979). *Schizophrenic disorders: Theory and treatment from a psychodynamic point of view.* New York: International Universities Press.

Perls, F. S. (1969). *Gestalt therapy verbatim.* Lafayette, CA: Real People Press.

Person, E. S. (1988). *Dreams of love and fateful encounters: The power of romantic passion.* New York: W. W. Norton.

Phillips, A. (1997). Making it new enough: Commentary on paper by Neil Altman. *Psychoanalytic Dialogues, 7,* 741–752.

Preston Girard, J. (1994). *The late man.* New York: Signet/Onyx Books.

Racker, H. (1968). *Transference and counter-transference.* London: The Hogarth Press.

Radke-Yarrow, M., Zahn-Waxler, C., & Chapman, M. (1983). Children's prosocial dispositions and behaviour. In P. M. Mussen (Ed.), *Handbook of child psychology: Vol. 4* (4th ed.), E. M. Hetherington (Ed.). New York: Wiley.

Reich, W. (1954). *Character analysis* (3d ed.). V. R. Carfagno (Trans.). Reprint. New York: Farrar, Straus & Giroux, 1972.

Rice, L. N., & Greenberg, L. S. (1991). Two affective change events in client-centered therapy. In J. D. Safran & L. S. Greenberg (Eds.), *Emotion, psychotherapy & change.* New York: Guilford.

Rogers, C. R. (1957). The necessary and sufficient conditions of therapeutic personality change. *Journal of Consulting Psychology, 21,* 95–103.

Rogers, C. R. (1961). *On becoming a person.* Boston: Houghton Mifflin.

Safran, J. D., & Greenberg, L. S. (Eds.). (1991). *Emotion, psychotherapy & change.* New York: Guilford.

Safran, J. D. & Muran, J. C. (1996). The resolution of ruptures in the therapeutic alliance. *Journal of Consulting and Clinical Psychology, 64,* 447–458.

Safran, J. D., Muran, J. C. & Samstag, L. (1994). Resolving therapeutic alliance ruptures: a task analytic investigation. In A. O. Horvath & L. S. Greenberg (Eds.), *The working alliance: Theory, research, and practice* (pp. 225–255). New York: Wiley.

Safran, J. D., & Segal, Z. V. (1990). *Interpersonal process in cognitive therapy.* New York: Basic Books.

Sandler, J. (1960). The background of safety. *International Journal of Psychoanalysis, 1,* 352–356.

Sandler, J., & Joffe, W. G. (1965). Notes on childhood depression. *International Journal of Psychoanalysis, 46,* 88–96.

Schore, A. N. (1994). *Affect regulation and the origin of the self: The neurobiology of emotional development.* Hillsdale, NJ: Lawrence Erlbaum.

Searles, H. (1958/1965). Positive feelings in the relationship between the schizophrenic and his mother. *Collected papers in schizophrenia and related subjects.* New York: International Universities Press.

Searles, H. F. (1979). *Countertransference and related papers*. New York: International Universities Press.

Seligman, S. (1998). Child psychoanalysis, adult psychoanalysis, and developmental psychology: An introduction. *Psychoanalytic Dialogues, 8,* 79–86.

Shane, M. S., Shane, E., & Gales, M. (1997). *Intimate attachments: Toward a new self psychology*. New York: Guilford.

Sifneos, P. E. (1987). *Short-term dynamic psychotherapy: Evaluation and technique* (2d ed.). New York: Plenum Press.

Sklar, I. (1992). Issues of loss and accelerated empathic therapy. Paper presented at the conference on brief therapy approaches: The sequelae of trauma. STDP Institute, Denville, NJ.

Sklar, I. (1993). The use of eye contact in AET: Working with separation and loss. Grand Rounds, Saint Clare's Medical Center, Denville, NJ.

Sklar, I. (1994). The corrective emotional experience in AET. Paper presented at the conference on empathic interactions on STDP. The Graduate Center of the City University of New York, NY.

Slavin, M. O., & Kriegman, D. (1998). Why the analyst needs to change: Toward a theory of conflict, negotiation, and mutual influence in the therapeutic process. *Psychoanalytic Dialogues, 8*(2), 247–284.

Slochower, J. (1999). Interior experience within analytic process. *Psychoanalytic Dialogues, 9,* 789–809.

Spezzano, C. (1993). Affect in psychoanalysis: A clinical synthesis. Hillsdale, NJ: Analytic Press.

Sroufe, L. A. (1995). *Emotional development: The organization of emotional life in the early years*. Cambridge: Cambridge University Press.

Steele, H., Steele, M., & Fonagy, P. (1996). Associations among attachment classifications of mothers, fathers and their infants: Evidence for a relationship-specific perspective. *Child Development, 67,* 541–555.

Stein, R. (1999). From holding receptacle to interior space—the protection and facilitation of subjectivity: Commentary on paper by Joyce Slochower. *Psychoanalytic Dialogues, 9,* 811–823.

Stern, D. N. (1985). *The interpersonal world of the infant: A view from psychoanalysis and developmental psychology*. New York: Basic Books.

Stern, D. N. (1994). One way to build a clinically relevant baby. *Infant Mental Health Journal, 15,* 9–25.

Stern, D. N. (1998). The process of therapeutic change involving implicit knowledge: Some implications of developmental observations for adult psychotherapy. *Infant Mental Health Journal, 19*(3), 300–308.

Stern, D. N., Sander, L. W., Nahum, J. P., Harrison, A. M., Lyons-Ruth, K., Morgan, A. C., Bruschweiler-Stern, N., & Tronick, E. Z. (1998). Non-interpretive mechanisms in psychoanalytic psychotherapy: The "something more" than interpretation. *International Journal of Psychoanalysis, 79,* 903–921.

Strupp, H. H., & Binder, J. L. (1984). *Psychotherapy in a new key: A guide to time-limited dynamic psychotherapy*. New York: Basic Books.

Sullivan, H. S. (1953). *The interpersonal theory of psychiatry*. New York: W. W. Norton.

Sullivan, H. S. (1956). *Clinical studies in psychiatry*. New York: W. W. Norton.

Suttie, I. D. (1935/1988). *The origins of love and hate*. London: Free Association Books.

Terr, L. (1990). *Too scared to cry*. New York: Basic Books.

Tomkins, S. S. (1962). *Affect, imagery, and consciousness: Vol. 1. The positive affects*. New York: Springer.

Tomkins, S. S. (1963). *Affect, imagery, and consciousness: Vol. 2. The negative affects*. New York: Springer.

Tomkins, S. S. (1970). Affect as amplification: Some modifications in a theory. In R. Plutchik & H. Kellerman (Eds.), *Emotions: Theory, research and experience* (pp. 141–164). New York: Academic Press.

Tronick, E. Z. (1989). Emotions and emotional communication in infants. *American Psychologist, 44*(2), 112–119.

Tronick, E. Z. (1998). Dyadically expanded states of consciousness and the process of therapeutic change. *Infant Mental Health Journal, 19*(3), 290–299.

Tronick E. Z., Als, H., Adamson, L., Wise, S., & Brazelton, T. B. (1978). The infant's response to entrapment between contradictory messages in face-to-face interaction. *Journal of Child Psychiatry, 17,* 1–13.

Truax C. B., & Carkhuff, R. R. (1967). *Toward effective counseling and psychotherapy: Training and practice*. Chicago: Aldine.

Urban, J., Carlson, E., Egeland, B., & Sroufe, L. A. (1991). Patterns of individual adaptation across childhood. *Development and Psychopathology, 3,* 445–560.

Vaillant, G. (1993). *Wisdom of the ego*. Cambridge, MA: Harvard University Press.

van den Boom, D. (1990). Preventive intervention and the quality of mother-infant interaction and infant exploration in irritable infants. In W. Koops (Ed.), *Developmental psychology behind the dykes* (pp. 249–270). Amsterdam: Eburon.

Volkan, V. (1981). *Linking objects and linking phenomena: A study of the forms, symptoms, metapsychology and therapy of complicated mourning*. New York: International Universities Press.

Vygotsky, L. S. (1935/1978). *Mind and society: The development of higher psychological processes*. M. Cole, V. John-Steiner, S. Scribner, & E. Souberman (Eds.). Cambridge, MA: Harvard University Press.

Wachtel, P. L. (1993). *Therapeutic communication: Principles and practice*. New York: Guilford.

Wachtel, P. L. (1999). Personal communication.

Webster's new collegiate dictionary. (1961). Springfield, MA: G. C. Merriam.

Weiss, J. (1952). Crying at the happy ending. *Psychoanalytic Review, 39*(4), 338.

Weiss, J., Sampson, H., & The Mount Zion Psychotherapy Research Group (1986). *The psychoanalytic process: Theory, clinical observations & empirical research*. New York: Guilford.

White, E. B. (1952). *Charlotte's web*. New York: Harper & Row.

White, R. W. (1959). Motivation reconsidered: The concept of competence. *Psychological Review, 66,* 297–333.

White, R. W. (1960). Competence and the psychosexual stages of development. In M. R. Jones (Ed.), *Nebraska symposium on motivation* (pp. 97–141). Lincoln: University of Nebraska Press.

Winnicott, D. W. (1947/1975) Hate in the countertransference. In *Through paediatrics to psycho-analysis* (pp. 194–203). New York: Basic Books.

Winnicott, D. W. (1949/1975). Mind and its relation to the psyche-soma. In *Through paediatrics to psycho-analysis* (pp. 243–254). New York: Basic Books.

Winnicott, D. W. (1960/1965). Ego distortion in terms of true and false self. In *The maturational process and the facilitating environment* (pp. 140–152). New York: International Universities Press.

Winnicott, D. W. (1962/1965). Ego integration in child development. In *The maturational process and the facilitating environment* (pp. 56–63). New York: International Universities Press.

Winnicott, D. W. (1963a/1965). Communicating and not communicating leading to a study of certain opposites. In *The maturational process and the facilitating environment* (pp. 179–192). New York: International Universities Press.

Winnicott, D. W. (1963b/1965). The development of the capacity for concern. In *The maturational process and the facilitating environment* (pp. 73–82). New York: International Universities Press.

Winnicott, D. W. (1963c/1965). From dependence towards independence in the development of the individual. In *The maturational process and the facilitating environment* (pp. 83–92). New York: International Universities Press.

Winnicott, D. W. (1965). *The maturational process and the facilitating environment*. New York: International Universities Press.

Winnicott, D. W. (1972). The basis for self in body. *International Journal of Child Psychotherapy, 1,* 7–16.

Winnicott, D. W. (1974). *Playing and reality*. London: Pelican.

Winnicott, D. W. (1975). *Through paediatrics to psycho-analysis*. New York: Basic Books.

Winston, A., Laikin, M., Pollack, J., et al. (1994). Short-term psychotherapy of personality disorders. *American Journal of Psychiatry, 151,* 190–194.

Yeats, W. B. (1921/1956). The second coming. In *The collected poems of W. B. Yeats* (pp. 184–185). New York: Macmillan.

Zahn-Waxler, C., & Radke-Yarrow, M. (1982). The development of altruism: Alternative research strategies. In N. Eisenberg (Ed.), *The development of prosocial bevavior*. New York: Academic Press.

Zajonc, R. B. (1985). Emotion and facial efference: A theory reclaimed. *Science, 228,* 15–22.

INDEX

Accelerated empathic therapy (AET), 339; AEDP and, 335, 337–338; facilitation of mourning process and, 333–334; focus of, 330; limitations of, 334–335; patient-therapist distance and, 332; patient-therapist relation and, 331–332; repetition compulsion and, 331

Accelerated experiential-dynamic psychotherapy (AEDP), 2; AET and, 337–338, 339; affective competence and, 70; affective experience and, 69, 154; affective model of change and, 336; autobiographical narrative and, 270; clinical vignette of a first session, 190–212; versus confrontation, 251; defense and, 40; the exploratory system and, 36–38; feelings and, 144; intergenerational pathology and, 55; moment-to-moment assessment of clinical material and, 103; the patient's resources and, 234; psychopathogenesis and, 335; relational experience and, 90, 149; the reparative drive and, 67; repetition and, 134; restructuring strategies of intervention and, 245; self–other–emotion triangle and, 129; specificity and, 278; spontaneous emotional response and, 88; strategies of intervention, 215–216, 218; T–C–P and, 133; versus traditional psychoanalysis, 4; triangle of comparisons and, 131; visceral experience and, 20, 24

Acceleration and trial therapy, 328

Accomplishment, achievement, 161; acknowledging, 225; validating, 224

Acknowledgement, 176, 177, 224–225; clinical vignette of, 235–237; in clinical vignette of reflective self function, 98; clinical vignette of triangle of expressive response and, 261; of competence, 231; of error, 230; of impact, 231; of mastery, 162; the therapist's modesty and, 178–179

Acknowledging affective experience, 275–276; experiential-affective strategies of intervention and, 217(table)

Active helpfulness, 51

Adaptation: AEDP and, 336, 337; affect facilitation and, 68; death rituals and, 73; emotion and, 14–15; psychopathology and, 87; restructuring strategies of intervention and, 245

Adaptive action tendency, 15; appraisal and, 24; in clinical vignette of grief and visceral exploration, 283; compassion and, 141; core affective experience and, 113; healing and, 21; motivation and, 26; new self and, 134; self-actualization and, 27

Adaptive experience: adaptive expression and, 158

Adaptive relational tendency: AEDP and, 149; the other and, 27–29

Adaptive self action tendencies, 147; adaptive self experience and, 158

Admiration v. shame, 255

AEDP. *See* Accelerated experiential-dynamic psychotherapy

AET. *See* Accelerated Empathic Therapy

Affect, 13–14; attachment and, 45–46; attachment experience and, 46; attention and, 24; the body and, 25; expression of, 289–290; facilitation of, 59–60; holding environment and, 22; negative, 63, 64, 66–67, 74; positive, 63–64, 66–67, 70; restructuring, 289; triangle of conflict and, 120; the unconscious and, 21; as the work medium, 19; *See also* Aversive affects; Core affect

Affect facilitation: in AEDP, 338; intense emotion and, 68

Affect-facilitating environment: AEDP and, 88, 336; affective competence and, 68; in clinical vignette of reflective self function, 92; defensive exclusion and, 59; and failure of, 40; soft defenses and, 117; *See also* Environment

Affective communication: coordinated states and, 151; the therapist's emotional experience and, 70

Affective competence, 6, 29; AEDP and, 70, 336; the caregiver and, 49–50; the child and, 59–61; defense and, 85; dyadic interaction and, 7; the good-enough caregiver and, 68; the internal working model and, 42; reflective self function and, 58; reparation and, 66; the secure–autonomous caregiver and, 52; triangle of expressive response and, 119

Affective experience, 272, 339; AEDP and, 154, 336, 337; AEDP strategies of intervention and, 218; the AEDP therapist and, 69; affective sharing as, 150; attachment and, 45; as the central agent of change, 61; in clinical vignette of core affective experience, 308; core state and, 138, 142; defense mechanisms and, 83; development of psychopathology and, 71–72; emotion and, 25; examples of negative, 76; examples of negative response to, 75; examples of positive, 76; facilitation of, 103; holding environment and, 22; processing of, 23; reflective self function and, 48, 58; relational strategies of intervention and, 216(table); reliance on defenses and, 86; restructuring strategies of intervention and, 217(table); safety and, 74; self–other–emotion triangle and, 118; therapeutic presence and, 29; therapist's expression of, 230; tracking of, 271; unbearable, 80, 82

Affective markers: in clinical vignette of core affective experience, 303; to evaluate interaction, 64; motivational vectors and, 63; mourning and, 162; See also Green-signal affects; Red-signal affects; Signal affects

Affective model of change, the, 17, 215; attachment theory and, 33, 42; core affect and, 21; Davanloo and, 1–2; defense and, 19; empathy and, 151; in the first year of life, 61; focus of, 4; as a model of relational psychodynamics in AEDP, 336; patient's awareness of

emotional environment and, 265; patient-therapist interaction and, 54; patient-therapist relationship and, 64; psychic health and, 311; relationship and, 27; response and, 56; restructuring strategies of intervention and, 245; visceral experience and, 24

Affective resonance, 111(table); in clinical vignette of reflective self function, 93, 94; mirroring as, 273; therapeutic presence and, 29

Affective sharing: in clinical vignette of reflective self function, 95; process of, 149; as relational experience, 149

Affective state: self–other–emotion triangle and, 122(figure), 124–125

Affective–relational experience: in clinical vignette of core affective experience, 308; meta-processing of, 238; relational strategies of intervention and, 216(table)

Affects of transformation: meta-therapeutic process and, 161–163

Affirmation, 225; AEDP and, 336; in clinical vignette of a first session, 197; in clinical vignette of core affective experience, 308; in clinical vignette of defense against empathy, 228, 229; clinical vignette of reparative portrayal and, 294; in clinical vignette of triangle of expressive response, 261; intervention and, 222–223; receiving, 162, 171, 176; relational strategies of intervention and, 216(table); self-blame and, 248; See also Receiving affirmation

Aggression (psychotherapeutic): Davanloo and, 2; ISTDP and, 330; therapists and, 334

Aloneness, 84; in clinical vignette of a first session, 197; in clinical vignette of reflective self function, 97; communication and, 28, 30; defense and, 85; psychopathology and, 5, 37; the Strange Situation paradigm and, 41n; transformation of, 155; the unbearable and, 82

Alpert, Michael C., 331; on therapist omnipotence, 333

"Amazing Grace" (Newman); 171–172, 173

Amplifying affect, 274–275
Analysis. *See* Psychoanalysis
Anger, 120, 156; adaptive action
    tendencies and, 140; adaptive
    experience and, 158; AET and, 335; in
    clinical vignette of a first session, 195,
    196, 199–200, 205–206, 207, 208; in
    clinical vignette of core affective
    experience, 299, 300, 301, 302; core
    affective experience and, 26; in
    example of portrayal, 286; ISTDP and,
    331
Anxiety, 81, 252–254, 333; attachment
    and, 35, 39–40, 43–44, 108; attachment
    theory and, 37; autobiographical
    narrative and, 269; awareness of
    emotional environment and, 265; brief
    psychotherapy and, 318; the caregiver
    and, 47; clinical vignette of, 253; in
    clinical vignette of a first session, 197,
    198, 199, 209, 212; in clinical vignette
    of core affective experience, 297, 298,
    299, 300, 302, 307; in clinical vignette
    of insufficient adaptive action
    tendencies, 221–222; in clinical
    vignette of reflective self function, 91;
    in clinical vignette of triangle of
    expressive response, 259, 261; core
    affect and, 233; falling and, 154; as red-
    signal affect, 114; removing pressure
    and, 251; restructuring strategies of
    intervention and, 216(table); secure
    attachment and, 41; solitude and, 83;
    STDP and, 314, 319; the therapeutic
    relationship and, 48; triangle of conflict
    and, 104, 105(figure); triangle of
    defensive response and, 109; as
    unbearable experience, 81, 166
Appraisal, 24; receptive experience and,
    152
Appreciation, 178, 334; Alpert on, 332;
    versus anxiety or shame, 255
Attachment: AEDP and, 336; affect and,
    4–5, 45–46; affective competence and,
    49; anxiety abatement and, 108;
    avoidant, 43, 90; the avoidant child
    and, 118; defense and, 47;
    disorganized/disoriented, 44; infancy
    and, 53; the internal working model
    and, 39–40; patterns in children, 41;

patterns of, 52; personality and, 19;
    preoccupied, 118; principles of
    affective salience and, 74; reflective self
    function and, 57–58; resistant, 43;
    security of, 29; sensitive response and,
    54; *See also* Insecure attachment;
    Secure attachment
Attachment theory, 3; affective model of
    change and, 33, 42; anxiety and, 37;
    child-caregiver bond and, 34
Attention, emotion and, 23–24
Attunement, 258; in clinical vignette of
    acknowledgement, 235; portrayal and,
    288; relational strategies of
    intervention and, 216(table);
    transformation and, 232; vitality affects
    and, 142; *See also* Little-step-by-little-
    step process
Auguries of Innocence (Blake), 136, 161
Auster, Paul, 153
Authentic self, the, 138; clinical vignette
    of specificity and, 278; interaction and,
    31; *See also* True self
Authenticity: AEDP and, 337; affective
    resonance and, 22; the affirmation
    process and, 172; little-step-by-little-
    step process and, 151; of the self, 312
Aversive affects, 110, 114, 120; categories
    of, 111(table); in clinical vignette of
    core affective experience, 301;
    emotional engagement and, 151;
    response and, 154; of shame, 256;
    triangle of defensive response and, 113;
    triangle of expressive response and,
    119; *See also* Affect; Core affect
Avoidant defense: in clinical vignette of
    core affective experience, 298; in
    clinical vignette of reflective self
    function, 92
Awareness (patient's): affective model of
    change and, 56; of defensive strategies,
    326; of emotional environment, 265;
    emotional experience and, 239;
    negative v. positive self states and,
    262–263; of the physical correlates of
    defense, 248

Barber, Jacques D., 188
Beebe, Beatrice, 63, 149
Benjamin, L., copy processes and, 85

Biological, the: categorical emotions and, 139; core affective experience and, 26; emotion and, 22; emotion theory and, 16; happiness and, 143; the need to feel understood and, 57; response and, 38; *See also* Physical; Physiological; Visceral experience

Blake, William, 136, 161

Body landscape, the: background feeling and, 142; visceral experience and, 25

Body, the: categorical emotions and, 139, 140; in clinical vignette of a first session, 198; in clinical vignette of core affective experience, 303, 304; core affect and, 16, 17; core emotions and, 20; core state and, 143; Davanloo and, 325; emotion and, 16, 18; example of shame of, 257; experiential-affective strategies of intervention and, 271; the feared-to-be-unbearable and, 80; focusing on, 279–280; portrayal and, 288; the self and, 146; visceral experience and, 24–25; *See also* Physical; Physiological; Visceral experience

Bonding: of caregiver and child, 35; of patient and therapist in AET, 331

Bowlby, John, 28, 35, 46; behavioral systems of attachment and, 34; on emotion, 33; on the patient-therapist relationship, 37

Brief psychotherapy (BP), 332, 338, 339; Malan and, 317–318; versus psychoanalysis, 317; use of interpretations in, 321–323, 325; *See also* Malan

Brodley, Harold, 166

Care: versus grief, 333; versus neutrality, 334; patient-therapist bond and, 331; versus pressure, 330

Caregiver, the: affective competence and, 49–50; aloneness and, 83; anxiety and, 47; attachment and, 34–35, 40, 43–44; availability of, 39–40; copy processes and, 85; emotion and, 53; emotional environment and, 72; emotional experience and, 59; errors of commission and, 79; errors of omission and, 78; holding environment and, 63;

insecure–dismissing, 52; insecure–preoccupied, 52; intergenerational pathology and, 73; the internal working model and, 51; omnipotence of, 333; openness to communication and, 60; reflective self function and, 45, 54–55, 57; secure–autonomous, 52; as self, 71; the Strange Situation paradigm and, 41n; transformational model of mutual influence and, 124; unresolved–disorganized, 53; *See also* Father; Good-enough caregiver; Mother; Parent

Caregiving: attachment and, 57; response and, 38

Caregiving behavioral system, 34, 35

Casanova, Giovanni Jacopo, 174–175

Cases. *See* Clinical vignettes

Categorical emotions, 8, 16, 23, 144; core state and, 138; of particular interest to AEDP, 141; the self and, 15; transformation and, 139; true self state and, 148; as type of core affective experience, 20; vitality affects and, 142; *See also* Core emotions

Challenge (Davanloo technique), 325–327, 329; versus AET, 330; clinical vignette of, 326

Character disorders, 104; Malan and, 323

Child, the: affective competence and, 49, 52, 59–61; affective experience and, 72; aloneness and, 82–83; attachment and, 35–36, 38, 40, 55, 56; avoidant, 43, 53, 117–118; the coordinated state and, 63; errors of commission and, 79; errors of omission and, 78; good-enough caregiving and, 72; high reflective self function in the caregiver and, 57; intergenerational pathology and, 73; psychoanalytic theory and, 178; relational experience and, 148–149; resistant, 43, 52; the responsive mother and, 50–51, 54; the Strange Situation paradigm and, 41n; theory of mind and, 44–45; *See also* Father; Mother; Parent

Child–caregiver dyad, the: the principles of affective salience and, 74

Circe's Power (Gluck), 29

Clinical cases. *See* Clinical vignettes

Clinical material, 7; in AEDP, 337, 338; categorizing of, 187, 246; flow of, 119; Malan and, 318; the reparative drive and, 67; STDP and, 318

Clinical method: brief psychotherapy v. psychoanalysis, 317; *See also* AEDP; AET; Brief psychotherapy; ISTDP; Psychoanalysis; STDP; Technique; Therapeutic process

Clinical phenomena: core state and, 138; experience and, 5

Clinical vignettes: of acknowledgement, 235–237; of anxiety, 253; of Davanloo challenge, 326; of Davanloo pressure, 327; of defense against empathy, 228–229; of grief and visceral exploration, 281–284; of insufficient adaptive action tendencies, 221–222; of mourning, 168; of nonverbal behavior, 325; of receiving affirmation and healing affects, 179–185; of reparative portrayal, 291–295; of self reflective function, 90–100; of shame, 255–256; of specificity, 277; of therapist self-disclosure, 239–242; of triangle of expressive response, 258–261

Clinical work: in AEDP, 336; Davanloo and, 2; Malan and, 318; *See also* AEDP; AET; Brief psychotherapy; Initial contact; ISTDP; Psychoanalysis; STDP; Therapeutic

Closeness (relational): in clinical vignette of a first session, 198; in clinical vignette of reflective self function, 95; in clinical vignette of triangle of expressive response, 261; communication and, 28; defense and, 40; example of, 246; the first session and, 189; reflective self function and, 45; relational experience and, 149; relational strategies of intervention and, 216(table); sense of competence and, 234; through little-step-by-little-step attunement, 232; triangle of expressive response and, 109

Coates, Susan W., 44

Cognition: autobiographical narrative and, 270; in clinical vignette of a first

session, 207; in clinical vignette of therapist self-disclosure, 240; the sense of being taken over and, 82

Communication: AEDP and, 336; affect facilitation and, 59–60; affective sharing and, 150; aloneness and, 30; clinical developmentalists and, 18; in clinical vignette of a first session, 192–211; confidence and, 312; core state and, 21; defensive, 120; defensive exclusion and, 40; emotion and, 25, 28; emotional truth and, 160; of empathic understanding, 226; processing of core affective experience and, 23; strategies of intervention and, 215; the therapist's emotional experience and, 70; transformation and, 6, 311; triangle of conflict and, 121; triangle of expressive response and, 121; unconscious, 191; *See also* Intervention; Nonverbal communication; Response; Unconscious communication

Compassion: AEDP and, 144; in AET, 332; affirmation and, 223; in clinical vignette of a first session, 193; in clinical vignette of reparative portrayal, 291; versus confrontation, 330; example of, 145; versus grief, 333; versus neutrality, 334

Compromised self–distorted other–blocked emotion triangle, 130; versus effective self–realistic other–core emotion triangle, 130; and self at worst, 127, 128(figure); self–other–emotion triangle and, 125–126

Confidence: in clinical vignette, 185; communication and, 312; healing affects and, 177; the secure–autonomous caregiver and, 52

Confrontation: versus AEDP, 251; versus AET, 330; Davanloo and, 326; ISTDP and, 324

Connection (patient-therapist): and acknowledgement of, 235; AET and, 331; in clinical vignette, 182; in clinical vignette of reflective self function, 96, 99; intensity of, 233; Malan and, 321; therapy and, 219; *See also*

Communication; Therapist-patient relationship

Contact: core state as, 138; Davanloo and, 2; the essential self and, 233; the first interview and, 191; mirroring and, 234; relational experience and, 149

Control: adaptive experience and, 158; autobiographical narrative and, 269; core emotion and, 117; negative self labels and, 263; portrayal and, 287; the sense of being taken over and, 82; the unbearable and, 81; *See also* Anger; Rage

Coordinated state, the: affective communication and, 151; affective interaction and, 63; affective sharing and, 150; the mother-child dyad and, 149; negative affect and, 64; versus reparation, 66; reparation and, 65–66; *See also* In-syncness

Core affect, 26, 120; adaptation and, 14–15; adaptive expression and, 158; AEDP and, 336, 338; appraisal and, 24; autobiographical narrative and, 269; as central agent of change, 19; in clinical vignette of a first session, 199, 205, 206, 208; in clinical vignette of core affective experience, 302, 304, 306, 307; in clinical vignette of grief and visceral exploration, 283, 284; in clinical vignette of receiving affirmation and healing affects, 179–185; clinical vignette of reparative portrayal and, 295; in clinical vignette of therapist self-disclosure, 239; communication and, 6; defense and, 233; experience and, 15–17; experiential-affective strategies of intervention and, 218, 271; feeling of inner spaciousness and, 121; the first interview and, 191; healing and, 72; mutuality and, 263; new self and, 134; the other and, 29; pathology and, 113; psychic health and, 311; the therapist and, 159; transformation and, 137; the true self and, 31–32; the unbearable and, 117; visceral experience and, 24

Core affective experience, 8, 137; adaptive action and, 113; categories of, 111(table), 112(table); clinical vignette

of, 297–310; in clinical vignette of reflective self function, 91; communication and, 28; emotion and, 15–16, 23; emotional truth and, 160; external reality and, 26; genuine, 158; matching and, 64; psychic health and, 311; self–other–emotion triangle and, 154; therapeutic constructs and, 31; triangle of comparisons and, 132(figure); triangle of conflict and, 104–106; triangle of defensive response and, 119; types of, 20; various ways to access, 215; visceral experience and, 24

Core affective phenomena: AEDP and, 336, 337, 339; as emerging dyadic phenomena, 148; reparation and, 127; self at best and, 129(figure); self at worst and, 128(figure); transformation and, 137

Core emotions: adaptive experience and, 158; in clinical vignette of a first session, 202; nonverbal communication and, 215; self at best and, 129(figure); as type of core affective experience, 20; varieties of, 138–140; *See also* Categorical emotions

Core experience: AET and, 331; attachment and, 36

Core state, 8, 20–21; AEDP and, 337; affective sharing and, 150; the body and, 143; in clinical vignette of a first session, 202; in clinical vignette of shame, 256; conversation and, 233; emotional truth and, 160; experiential-affective strategies of intervention and, 218; feelings and, 144; little-step-by-little-step process and, 150; psychic health and, 311; self state and, 148; vitality affects and, 142

Corrective emotional experience, 106, 329, 330

Costello, P. C., 35

Coughlin Della Selva, Patricia, 84

Countertransference in AET, 334; as a limitation, 335

Crits-Cristoph, Paul, 188

Crying, 173–175

Current relationships (C): in clinical vignette of a first session, 201, 206; triangle of comparisons and, 130–133

Damage (Hart), 153

Damasio, Antonio R., 25

Danger, 114; AEDP and, 336

Darwin, Charles, 18, 140; response and, 28

Davanloo, Habib, 1–3, 323; ISTDP and, 324–329

Dealing but not feeling, 43; the insecure–dismissing caregiver and, 52; *See also* Feeling but not dealing

Death: emotional truth and, 27; joy and, 166; portrayal and, 287

Deep affect: in clinical vignette of grief and visceral exploration, 283; experiential-affective strategies of intervention and, 271

Deep experiencing: in clinical vignette of grief and visceral exploration, 284; the unconscious and, 21

Defense: adaptation and, 87; anticipatory mirroring and, 273; attachment and, 39–41; autobiographical narrative and, 269; avoidant, 298; awareness of emotional environment and, 265; benefits of, 250; bonding and, 19; in clinical vignette of a first session, 193–197, 207, 212; in clinical vignette of grief and visceral exploration, 281–282, 284; in clinical vignette of insufficient adaptive action tendencies, 221–222; in clinical vignette of receiving affirmation and healing affects, 179–183; in clinical vignette of reflective self function, 91–95, 100; core effect and, 233; costs of, 249–250; Davanloo and, 323, 324–329; development of psychopathology and, 71; emotional experience and, 272; against emotional knowledge, 220; emotional pain and, 115; empathy and, 227; against empathy (clinical vignette), 228–229; end-of-session processing and, 238; environment and, 33; in example of reparation, 128–129; the exploratory system and, 37; ISTDP and, 324, 328; portrayal and, 287; psychopathology and, 5; regressive, 43, 118, 297; reparation and, 66; response and, 155; safety and, 47; self at worst and, 127, 128(figure); STDP and, 318,

319; strategies of, 83–84, 86; taxonomy of, 84; the therapeutic relationship and, 48; the therapist's modesty as, 178–179; tracking and, 4; triangle of comparisons and, 132(figure); triangle of conflict and, 104–106; triangle of defensive response and, 119; versus triangle of expressive response, 134; triangle of expressive response and, 119; undoing reliance on, 276; *See also* Entrenched defense; Soft defense

Defense mechanisms, 115–116; affective experience and, 83; brief psychotherapy and, 318

Defensive affects, 115, 120; features of, 159; regressive, 156

Defensive exclusion, 40, 43; affect-facilitating environment and, 59; in clinical vignette of a first session, 195; fear and, 114; versus reflective self function, 45, 47, 54, 60; restriction of learning and, 116; safety and, 74; specificity and, 278

Defensive response: AEDP and, 247; restructuring strategies of intervention and, 216(table)

Defensive self-reliance, 177; in clinical vignette, 182, 183

Depression: clinical vignette of a first session and, 208; clinical vignette of core affective experience and, 297, 298; clinical vignette of receiving affirmation and healing affects, 179–185; clinical vignette of reflective self function and, 90–100; clinical vignette of reparative portrayal and, 294; in example of portrayal, 287

Desensitization, 288–289; in clinical vignette of core affective experience, 298

Despair: in clinical vignette of a first session, 196, 197, 210; clinical vignette of reflective self function and, 90–100

Detail. *See* Specificity

Development of the self: affective mastery and, 165; emotion and, 30; optimal, 61–62; the other and, 39–40

Developmentalists, clinical, 3; relationship and, 18

Dialogue, 28; in portrayal, 287

Disgust in clinical vignette of core affective experience, 299, 300

Disorganized/disoriented attachment, 44; reflective self function and, 48; the unresolved–disorganized caregiver and, 53

Disruption (relational), 59; reparation of, 69–70

Distance (patient/therapist): in AET, 331, 332; reflective self function and, 45

Distancing (defense), 116; in clinical vignette of core affective experience, 300

Dyadic interaction, 125; between caregiver and child, 61; the coordinated state and, 63; the first session and, 189; between infant and mother, 62; internalization and, 7

Dyadic relationship, the: affect and, 17; affective model of change and, 21; James and, 18

Dynamic information, 187–188, 190; portrayal and, 286; STDP and, 319

Eagle, Morris N., 44, 46

Eating disorder in clinical vignette of core affective experience, 297, 300

Education: versus anxiety, 254; in clinical vignette of a first session, 207

Effective self–realistic other–core emotion triangle: versus compromised self–distorted other–blocked emotion triangle, 130; and self at best, 127, 129(figure); self–other–emotion triangle and, 125

Ego, the, 30; Davanloo and, 329; ISTDP and, 324

Ego-dystonic defense: appreciative reframing and, 248; in clinical vignette of a first session, 194; Davanloo and, 326; mourning and, 249

Ego-syntonic, the: appreciative reframing and, 248; in clinical vignette of a first session, 202; costs of defense and, 249; Davanloo and, 323

Emergent dyadic phenomena, 124, 148

Emotion: adaptation and, 14–15, 27; AEDP and, 336, 338; AET and, 330–332; affect facilitation and, 68; affective competence and, 42; affective mastery and, 165; attachment and, 4–5, 33; attention and, 23–24; the biological and, 22; the body and, 16, 18, 25, 26, 143; child-mother interaction and, 50; communication and, 6, 28; core affective experience and, 23; Davanloo and, 2; defense and, 104; development and, 30; versus emotionality, 158–159; errors of commission and, 79; experience and, 5, 158, 238; failure in handling and, 74; and full experience of, 27; healing and, 72; the infant and, 62; James and, 19; James on, 137; mastery and, 21; portrayal and, 289; the preoccupied individual and, 118; repeating relationship patterns and, 264; the secure–autonomous caregiver and, 52; self at worst and, 128(figure); self–other–emotion triangle and, 124; suppression of, 43; the unbearable and, 80; See also Categorical emotions; Core emotions; Feelings

Emotional conflict, 321–322

Emotional engagement: AET and, 331; aversive affects and, 151; STDP v. traditional psychoanalysis, 316

Emotional environment: affect and, 14; aloneness and, 84; defense and, 85, 87; experience and, 142; failure of, 84; green-signal affects and, 258; interactive errors and, 77; love and, 144; negative response and, 80; optimal development of the self and, 72; patient's awareness of, 265; self–other–emotion triangle and, 118; signal affects and, 114; triangle of conflict and, 107, 109; See also Environment; Environmental failure

Emotional experience, 13, 271–276; AET and, 331; affective interaction and, 61; aloneness and, 84; in clinical example of the pathogenic past, 268; clinical vignette of a first session and, 212; clinical vignette of therapist self-disclosure and, 243; corrective, 329, 330; Davanloo and, 328; defensive affects, 156; empathy and, 59; environmental failure and, 73; intensity v. duration, 73–74; intimacy and, 58;

portrayal and, 285; self–other–emotion triangle and, 126; STDP and, 314, 319; the therapist's, 70; triangle of comparisons and, 188; triangle of conflict and, 105(figure); validating, 256

Emotional expression: aversive affects and, 113; regulation and, 14

Emotional functioning: self at best v. self at worst, 127

Emotional intensity: in clinical vignette of therapist self-disclosure, 240; Davanloo and, 326

Emotional pain: AET and, 331; attachment theory and, 33; in clinical vignette, 181; in clinical vignette of a first session, 193; in clinical vignette of core affective experience, 302, 303; in clinical vignette of reflective self function, 99; fear of, 141; the first interview and, 191; Freud and, 81; healing affects and, 172; as mourning, 166–167; mourning and, 162; as red-signal affect, 115; videotape and, 167

Emotional truth, 27; versus intellectualization, 160

Emotionality versus emotion, 158–159

Empathic elaboration, 226; in clinical vignette of a first session, 200; in clinical vignette of reflective self function, 91; See also Communication; Expression

Empathic response, 226; relational strategies of intervention and, 216(table); See also Intervention; Response

Empathic understanding: intervention and, 226; self-blame and, 249

Empathy, 144–146; adaptive self experience and, 158; in AEDP, 337; attachment and, 36; versus challenge, 330; in clinical vignette of a first session, 197, 204; in clinical vignette of core affective experience, 302; in clinical vignette of reparative portrayal, 294; in clinical vignette of therapist self-disclosure, 239, 241; in clinical vignette of triangle of expressive response, 260; defense against (clinical vignette), 228–229; defense and, 227;

versus grief, 333; little-step-by-little-step process and, 151; mourning and, 249; the patient and, 178; versus pressure, 332; receptive experience and, 151–153; reflective self function and, 57–59; relational experience and, 149; therapeutic presence and, 29

Encouragement: affirmation and, 223; in clinical vignette of core affective experience, 302; versus pressure, 251; versus shame, 255

Engagement: AEDP and, 336, 338; Davanloo and, 2

Entrenched defense, 247; anticipatory mirroring and, 273; Davanloo and, 329

Environment, 5–6; AEDP techniques and, 69; as affective state, 125; Alpert on, 331; appraisal and, 24, 152; attachment and, 34, 36; attachment theory and, 33–34; compassionate, 331; examples of hard-to-handle positive experiences and, 76; failure of, 41, 47, 154; negative v. positive self states and, 263; primary depressive reaction and, 81; reflective self function and, 56–57; relational strategies and, 218; relationship patterns and, 265; See also Emotional environment; Holding environment

Environmental failure: defense and, 115; development of psychopathology and, 71; emotional experience and, 73; errors of omission and, 78; understanding and, 60

Essential self, the, 32; contact and, 233; the ongoing unfolding of, 312; See also Authentic self; Self; True self

Evolution, 336; categorical emotions and, 139

Experience: acknowledging, 239; AEDP and, 56, 338; AET and, 330, 335; affect and, 14; of authenticity, 32; autobiographical narrative and, 268; co-constructed through interaction, 61; continuous, 142–143; Davanloo and, 323; dyadic emotional interaction, 125; emotion and, 158, 238; emotional environment and, 142; end-of-session processing and, 238; of feelings, the unconscious and, 328; of mastery, 165; negative, 258, 338; ownership of the

Intellectualization: in clinical vignette of a first session, 196; versus emotional truth, 160

Intensive short-term dynamic therapy (ISTDP): AEDP and, 335, 338; AET and, 330–332, 334; Davanloo and, 324–329; STDP and, 339; *See also* Davanloo

Interaction, 86; affect and, 14; affective salience and, 73–74; affective state and, 125; Alpert on, 331; analysis and, 54; the authentic self and, 31; between child and mother, 50; core state and, 142; Davanloo and, 2, 326; imagined, 284; between infant and mother, 142; intense emotion and, 68; the patient in AET and, 332; positive mother-infant matching and, 64; reflective understanding, 58; repeating relationship patterns and, 264; self at best v. self at worst, 127; self–other–emotion triangle and, 121, 122(figure); Seligman on, 58; tracking and, 220; triangle of expressive response and, 109; *See also* Communication; Intervention; Response; Therapeutic relationship

Interactive errors, 63, 67, 76; of commission, 77, 78–79; of omission, 77–78; Triangle of defensive response and, 109

Interactive repair, 65; Triangle of defensive response and, 109

Internal dialogue, 288; in clinical vignette of core affective experience, 304, 306; in clinical vignette of reparative portrayal, 293

Internal working model, the, 47; AEDP and, 88; attachment and, 39–40; avoidant attachment and, 90; insecure attachment and, 53; principles of affective salience and, 74; reflection and, 57; reflective self function and, 55; reparation and, 66; secure attachment and, 51

Internalization: of defenses, 85; of dyadic interaction, 7; the first interview and, 191; reflective self function and, 45

Interpersonal, the: core affect and, 23, 26; defense and, 47; relationship patterns and, 264–265; and self–other–emotion patterns of, 263; *See also* Relationships

Interpretation: brief psychotherapy and, 321–322, 323, 325; Davanloo and, 328; Malan and, 323; the patient in AET and, 332

Intervention, 7, 109, 155; in AEDP, 336, 338; AET and, 330, 332, 334; anxiety and, 252; attachment status and, 54; autobiographical narrative and, 270; brief psychotherapy and, 319, 321, 322; in clinical vignette of a first session, 190–211; collaborative interpretation of patient's experience and, 245; costs of defense and, 250; Davanloo and, 2; empathic understanding and, 226; ISTDP and, 330; Malan and, 320; self-disclosure as, 231; STDP and, 318; strategies of, 213, 215–216, 218; structuring tools for, 103; the therapist and, 6; tracking and, 271; the unit of, 214; visceral experience and, 24; *See also* Communication; Response; Therapeutic process

Intimacy: affective resonance and, 22; affective sharing and, 150; in clinical vignette of reflective self function, 98; communication and, 28; emotional experience and, 58; the first session and, 189; relational experience and, 148–149; relational strategies of intervention and, 216(table); the therapeutic relationship and, 219; through little-step-by-little-step attunement, 232; triangle of expressive response and, 109

Intrapsychic, the, 7, 188; appraisal and, 24; brief psychotherapy and, 318; core affect and, 23, 26; defense and, 47; the first session and, 189; as a limitation in AET, 335

Isolation, 141; in clinical vignette of reflective self function, 92–93

ISTDP. *See* Intensive short-term dynamic therapy

James, William: affect and, 19; on emotion, 137; healing affects and, 173; the religious and, 18

Joffe, W. G., 166
Joy, 165; versus fear, 166; healing affects and, 172, 173; tears of, 175

Kihlstrom, J, 125

Labeling defenses, 247–248; toxic, 326
Lachmann, Frank M., 63, 149; model scenes and, 126
Language: in clinical vignette of core affective experience, 305; ordinary, 272; therapeutic, 269; *See also* Communication
Lichtenberg, J., 126
Lindemann, E., 327
Little-step-by-little-step process, 142; intimacy and, 150–151; relational strategies of intervention and, 216(table); sharing and, 232; *See also* Attunement
Loss: AET and, 331, 333–334, 335; in clinical vignette of a first session, 201, 208; emotional truth and, 27; in example of portrayal, 287; pathology and, 168; relinquishing defense and, 250; self–other–emotion triangle and, 121; the unresolved–disorganized caregiver and, 53
Love: AEDP and, 144; core affective experience and, 26; versus falling, 153–154; the patient and, 178

Malan, David H., 65; brief psychotherapy and, 317–323, 324; *See also* Brief psychotherapy
Marriage: in clinical example of the pathogenic past, 268; feeling and dealing and, 290
Mastery: acknowledging, 162; AET and, 333; affective, 165; autobiographical narrative and, 269; awareness of emotional environment and, 265; in clinical vignette of therapist self-disclosure, 242; healing and, 21; mental health and, 311; negative self labels and, 263
Matching (imitating), 61, 63–64; receptive experience and, 153; as relational experience, 149, 150; *See also* In-syncness

Meaning: versus anxiety, 254; appraisal and, 24; autobiographical narrative and, 269; in clinical vignette of a first session, 197; emotional truth and, 160
Meaninglessness in clinical vignette of a first session, 197, 210
Meta-processing: of affective–relational experience, 238; in clinical vignette of core affective experience, 308; relational strategies of intervention and, 216(table)
Meta-therapeutic process: AEDP and, 337; in clinical vignette, 182, 184, 185; example of, 164–165; the therapist and, 176, 178–179; transformation and, 161–163; *See also* Therapeutic process
Mind, the: the body and, 25; the feared-to-be-unbearable and, 80; Winnicott and, 60
Mirroring: as affective resonance, 273; versus anxiety, 253; in clinical vignette of a first session, 192, 193, 194, 204; in clinical vignette of grief and visceral exploration, 281; in clinical vignette of reflective self function, 99, 100; in clinical vignette of specificity, 277; in clinical vignette of triangle of expressive response, 260; deepening contact and, 234; emotion and, 214; experiential-affective strategies of intervention and, 217(table); naming and, 276; Tronick on, 62
Modesty (therapist's), 221; AEDP and, 338; meta-therapeutic process and, 178–179
Moment-to-moment shift, 7; in child-mother interaction and, 50; Malan and, 323; STDP and, 318; the unit of intervention and, 214
Moment-to-moment therapeutic process: clinical vignette of a first session, 190–212; *See also* Focusing; Tracking
Moment-to-moment therapeutic relationship (T): in clinical vignette of a first session, 201; triangle of comparisons and, 130–133
Moon Palace (Auster), 153
Mother, the: affective competence and, 60; attachment and, 35; in clinical example of the pathogenic past,

266–268; clinical vignette of core affective experience and, 298; in clinical vignette of reparative portrayal, 291–295; the coordinated state and, 63; isomorphism and, 40; regulation of emotional experience and, 62; reparation and, 65–66

Motivation: adaptive action tendencies and, 26; AET and, 331; appraisal and, 24; emotion and, 28; and function served by communication of the patient, 120; language and, 272; negative affect and, 63; trial therapy and, 328

Mourning, 166–169; AET and, 333–334, 335; clinical vignette of visceral exploration and, 281–284; ego-dystonic defense and, 249; emotional truth and, 27; example of new self and, 135; portrayal and, 287

Mourning the self, 162; in clinical vignette, 181; emotional pain and, 166

Mutuality: empathy and, 227; matching and, 64; resonance and, 62; self-empathy and, 263; sense of competence and, 234

Naming affective experience, 275–276; experiential-affective strategies of intervention and, 217(table)

Narrative (autobiographical), 268–270; in clinical vignette of core affective experience, 305

Negative affect, 63, 64; failure in handling and, 74; and reparation of, 66–67

Negative response: defense and, 116; vulnerability and, 114

Neutrality (analytic stance), 38, 315; the reparative drive and, 68

New self, 134–135

Nonverbal communication, 84; Davanloo and, 325; reciprocal monitoring of, 234; strategies of intervention and, 215

Not feeling and not dealing, 44; the unresolved–disorganized caregiver and, 53

Odyssey, The (Homer), 166

Openness: in AEDP, 336; AEDP interventions and, 245; affective

sharing and, 150; in clinical vignette, 185; in clinical vignette of a first session, 209; in clinical vignette of insufficient adaptive action tendencies, 222; in clinical vignette of reflective self function, 97; in clinical vignette of shame, 256; core state as, 138; healing affects and, 173; intensity of relational connection and, 233; little-step-by-little-step process and, 151

Other, the: affect and, 22; core emotion and, 262; feeling and dealing and, 290; secure attachment and, 39; security and, 40; self–other–emotion triangle and, 123, 262; See also Relationship; True other

Pain. See Emotional pain

Parent, the: attachment and, 35–38; attachment status and, 56; emotionally unresponsive, 53; good-enough caregiving and, 72; intergenerational pathology and, 73; reflective self function and, 54, 56; relational experience and, 149; secure attachment and, 57; self-righteousness of, 231; the Strange Situation paradigm and, 41n; See also Caregiver

Passivity (analytic stance), 315; Malan on, 322

Past relationships (P): in clinical vignette of a first session, 199, 201; the first interview and, 191; triangle of comparisons and, 130–133

Past, the: affective model of change and, 54; memories of relational experience and, 165

Pathogenic, the: clinical example of, 266–268; repetition and, 266; T–C–P and, 133

Pathology, 105(figure); adaptive experience and, 158; AEDP and, 336–337, 338; Alpert on, 331; awareness of emotional environment and, 265; communication and, 311; versus Davanloo challenge, 329; development of, 71; dyadic interaction and, 7; intergenerational, 55, 73, 249; loss and, 168; reflective self function and, 47; the reparative drive and, 67;

repetitions of relation patterns and, 264; response to affective experiences and, 75; traditional psychoanalysis and, 4; triangle of comparisons and, 266; *See also* Psychopathology

Patient, the: the AEDP therapist and, 69; AEDP therapy and, 70; affect and, 13; affective mastery and, 165; affirmation and, 223, 225; aloneness and, 82; anxiety and, 252–254; and awareness of nondefended states, 249; defense and, 247–252; emotional experience and, 272–276; empathy and, 144–145, 152, 227; example of new self and, 135; example of reparation and, 128–129; experience and, 5; fragility of, 2; and function served by communication of, 120; holding and, 156; intervention and, 155, 213–216, 218; meta-therapeutic process and, 161–163, 176, 178; negative v. positive self states and, 262–263; portrayal and, 284–290; presence of the therapist and, 30, 89–90; psychological expertise of, 237; relational experience and, 149; and relationship patterns of, 263–265; the reparative drive and, 68; and self at worst, 127; self-empathy and, 224; sharing and, 232–233; therapist self-disclosure and, 230–232; vulnerability and, 147; *See also* AEDP; AET; Brief psychotherapy; Clinical vignettes; ISTDP; STDP; Therapeutic relationship

Patient-therapist interaction. *See* Therapist-patient interaction

Patient-therapist rapport: focus in brief psychotherapy and, 321; Malan and, 320; STDP and, 318

Patient-therapist relationship. *See* Therapist-patient relationship

Peak experience: matching and, 64; resonance and, 150; the true other and, 169–170

Perls, Fritz, 148; on phobia, 165

Person, Ethel Spector, 18, 23

Personality: affective experience and, 72; attachment and, 35; authentic, 148; in clinical vignette of core affective experience, 306; feeling of inferiority and, 146; the insecure internal working model and, 41; James and, 19; obsessive-compulsive, 297; psychic structure and, 55; transformational model of mutual influence and, 124

Phenomenology: AEDP and, 337; of affective experiences, 46; categorical emotions and, 139; Davanloo and, 329; of healing affects, 172–174, 176; of rage, 140; of relational affective experiences in AET, 334

Physical, the: anxiety and, 252; focusing on, 279; healing affects and, 172

Physiological, the: anxiety and, 253; categorical emotions and, 140; core emotions and, 20; core state and, 143; healing affects and, 172; intersubjectivity and, 149; *See also* Body

Portrayal, 284; affective type, 287; in clinical vignette of core affective experience, 298–301, 304–306; completion of, 287; desensitization type, 288–289; examples of, 286–287; experiential-affective strategies of intervention and, 217(table); expression and, 289–290; internal dialogue type, 288; reparative type, 289; reparative type (clinical vignette of), 291–295; technique and, 285

Positive affect, 63–64; reparation and, 66–67, 70

Positive affective experience: examples of hard-to-handle, 76; fear of, 177

Presence (the therapist's), 29–30, 89–90

Pressure: versus anxiety, 255; removing, 250–252

Pressure (Davanloo technique), 325–327; versus AET, 330

Primary affective reactions: categories of, 111(table), 112(table)

Principle of ongoing regulations, the, 73, 74

Psychic space: affect facilitation and, 59–60; visceral experience and, 25

Psychic structure, 55–56; depression, 295; transformational model of mutual influence and, 124

Psychoanalysis: versus brief psychotherapy, 317; child development and, 178; deep feeling and, 323; developmental theory and, 3; Malan on, 322; versus STDP, 339; technical aspects of, 315; traditional, 4, 54; transference and, 220

Psychodynamic formulation, 187–188; brief psychotherapy and, 321; clinical vignette of a first session and, 208, 211; in clinical vignette of reparative portrayal, 294, 295; See also Focusing

Psychopathology: adaptation model of, 87; AET and, 333, 335; anxiety and, 37, 47, 114; autobiographical narrative and, 269; aversive affects and, 113; avoidant attachment and, 90; brief psychotherapy and, 318; defense and, 5; development of, 71–72, 86; genesis of, 105(figure); the insecure internal working model and, 41; ISTDP and, 324, 330; response and, 155; STDP and, 314; transgression and, 212; See also Pathology

Psychotherapy, 339; ISTDP and, 324, 330; Malan on, 322

Rage, 85, 331; AET and, 335; in clinical vignette of a first session, 200, 205, 206, 209, 212; in clinical vignette of core affective experience, 299; fantasy and, 158; phenomenology of, 140; portrayal and, 287

Reaction formation in clinical vignette of a first session, 195, 196

Reality: core affective experience and, 26; denial of painful and, 167; grief and, 166; of the other, 290; visceral, 273

Receiving affirmation, 162, 171; clinical vignette of, 179–185; dynamics of, 176

Receptive affective experience, 172; in clinical vignette of reflective self function, 94; empathy and, 151–153; matching and, 64; relational experience and, 149; self–other–emotion triangle and, 123

Receptive experience, 153; appraisal and, 152

Reciprocal monitoring, 282; in AET, 332

Red-signal affects, 107(figure), 113, 114–115; anxiety, 252, 255; the avoidant child and, 118; categories of, 111(table); in clinical vignette of

acknowledgement, 236; core emotions and, 140; end-of-session processing and, 238; features of, 159; psychopathology and, 155; restructuring strategies of intervention and, 216(table); self at worst and, 128(figure); See also Affective markers; Green-signal affects; Signal affects

Reflection: in clinical vignette of reflective self function, 100; experience and, 56; ownership of the process of transformation and, 177; in the therapeutic relationship, 90

Reflective self function: AEDP and, 238; affective competence and, 49, 58, 60; the caregiver and, 54–55; clinical vignette of, 90–100; in clinical vignette of core affective experience, 309; versus defensive exclusion, 45, 47, 60; green-signal affects and, 258; high, 56, 57, 59; versus intergenerational transmission of trauma, 56; the internal working model and, 51; mental health and, 311; meta-therapeutic process and, 162; presence of the therapist and, 89–90; reparation and, 66; restructuring strategies of intervention and, 245; self-identity and, 262; theory of mind and, 44

Reflective work, meta-therapeutic process and, 162–163

Reframing: in AET, 332; versus anxiety, 254

Regressive defense, 43, 118; clinical vignette of core affective experience and, 297

Regulation: communication and, 23; emotional expression and, 14; holding environment and, 22; the infant and, 80; See also Handling

Reich, Wilhelm, 323

Relational affective experience, 15; core state and, 138; phenomenology of in AET, 334

Relational defenses, 84; the avoidant child and, 118; in clinical vignette of defense against empathy, 228; in clinical vignette of reflective self function, 93

Relational experience: core state and, 138; emerging dyadic phenomena and, 148;

empathy and, 152; negative v. positive, 262; optimal development of the self and, 72; of particular interest to AEDP, 149; relational strategies of intervention and, 216(table); relationship patterns and, 264; reliance on defenses and, 86; restructuring strategies of intervention and, 217(table); *See also* Relationships; Therapeutic relationship

Relational process, the: Affect and, 4; *See also* Therapeutic relationship

Relational strategies of intervention, 215, 219; versus defense, 218; table of, 216(table)

Relationships: AEDP strategies of intervention and, 215–216; affect and, 13; affective competence and, 49; affective model of change and, 27; attachment and, 39–41; the avoidant child and, 118; child-parent, 53; clinical developmentalists and, 18; compromised affective competence and, 52; core affect and, 17; current, 265; defense and, 47; developmental processes and, 58; past, 264; principles of affective salience and, 74; psychoanalytic processes and, 58; reflective self function and, 55–56; reparation and, 7; sexual, 288; therapeutic, 48; triangle of comparisons and, 263; *See also* Dyadic relationship; Therapeutic relationship; Therapist-patient relationship

Relaxation: affective sharing and, 150; receptive experience and, 153

Reparation, 106; versus coordinated states, 66; dyadic interaction and, 7; example of, 128–129; between infant and mother, 65–66; versus in-syncness, 65; negative affect and, 63; self at best and, 127; triangle of expressive response and, 119

Reparative drive, the, 67–68

Reparative portrayal, 289; clinical vignette of, 291–295; in clinical vignette of core affective experience, 304, 306

Repetition: AET and, 331; analytic theory and, 38; exceptions to relationship patterns and, 264; relationship patterns

and, 264; versus resilience, 107; triangle of comparisons and, 266

Repetition compulsion, 106; AET and, 331

Resilience: affective competence and, 60; defense and, 41; reflective self function and, 45, 55, 56; versus repetition, 107; safety and, 37

Resistance: AET and, 331; confrontational techniques v. AET, 330; Davanloo and, 323; ISTDP and, 327; Malan and, 323; presence of the therapist and, 30; versus triangle of expressive response, 134; the Wizard of Oz effect and, 250

Resonance: in clinical vignette of a first session, 200; clinical vignette of specificity and, 278; clinical vignette of triangle of expressive response and, 261; matching and, 64; mutuality and, 62; peak experience and, 150; as relational experience, 149; as silence, 210; structuring tools for, 103

Response: affective competence and, 49; affective model of change and, 56; affirmation and, 225; attachment and, 35–36, 39–41; aversive affects and, 154; awareness of emotional environment and, 265; in caregiving, 38; core affect and, 233; Darwin and, 28; disorganized/disoriented attachment and, 44; dyadic interaction and, 7; empathy and, 227; failure in handling and, 74–75; ISTDP and, 324; Malan and, 320, 323; the mother and, 50–51, 54; negative, 80, 114; to patient's emotions, 274; in portrayal, 289; reflective self function and, 45; regulation of experience and, 62; the reparative drive and, 68; STDP and, 318; the true other and, 170; *See also* Communication; Intervention

Responsibility: relationship patterns and, 265; self-empathy and, 158

Restructuring strategies (of intervention), 245; empathy and, 218; entrenched defenses and, 247; table of, 216–217

Risk-taking: patient-therapist relationship and, 37; vulnerability and, 147

"Rock 'n' Roll Nigger" (Smith), 226

correlates of experience, 280; new self and, 134; relational dynamics and, 118; relational experience and, 262; restructuring strategies of intervention and, 217(table); self experience and, 262; triangle of comparisons and, 132(figure); triangle of conflict and, 131

Self-punishment, 331; AET and, 335; ISTDP and, 330

Seligman, Stephen, 57; on interaction, 58

Sense of self, the: adaptive experience and, 158; AEDP and, 336; awareness of emotional environment and, 265; repeating relationship patterns and, 264; and self at worst, 127

Sexual, the: abuse, 297–298; portrayal and, 288; shame and, 257

Shakespeare, William, 140

Shame, 113; clinical vignette of, 255–256; clinical vignette of reparative portrayal and, 295; core affect and, 233; example of, 257; as red-signal affect, 114; restructuring strategies of intervention and, 217(table)

Shane, Estelle, 134

Shane, Morton S., 134

Sharing: in AEDP, 336; in AET, 332; versus anxiety, 333; in clinical vignette of core affective experience, 308; in clinical vignette of reflective self function, 99

Short-term dynamic psychotherapy (STDP), 338–340; brief psychotherapy and, 317–318; Davanloo and, 2–3; the first session and, 189; history of, 313; Malan and, 322; rapid restructuring of clinical material and, 318; schematized psychodynamic constructs and, 318; termination of treatment and, 320; versus traditional analytic techniques, 315–316; trial therapy and, 318; videotape and, 317

Signal affects, 117, 121; self-expression and, 114; triangle of comparisons and, 132(figure); triangle of conflict and, 104–106; See also Affective markers; Green-signal affects; Red-signal affects

Smilla's Sense of Snow (Høag), 80, 87, 106

Smith, Patti, 226

Soft defense, 247; affect-facilitating environment and, 117; anticipatory mirroring and, 273; categories of, 112(table); in clinical vignette of shame, 256; self at best and, 129(figure)

Solitude, 83

Specificity, 276–278; clinical vignette of, 277; in clinical vignette of core affective experience, 299, 304; detail in portrayals, 285–286; experiential-affective strategies of intervention and, 217(table); initial interview and, 189

Speech, habits of, 325

Spontaneous portrayal: in clinical vignette of core affective experience, 299; in clinical vignette of reflective self function, 94

STDP. See Short-term dynamic psychotherapy

Subcortical, the: appraisal and, 24; emotion and, 22

Superego, the, 330; Davanloo and, 329; ISTDP and, 324

Support. See Affirmation

Suppression: of core affect, 262; the first interview and, 191

Tactical defenses, 84–85, 115; in clinical vignette, 181; in clinical vignette of triangle of expressive response, 259; Davanloo and, 325

T–C–P (moment-to-moment therapeutic–current–past relationships): brief psychotherapy and, 321–322; example of, 133; triangle of comparisons and, 130–133

Tears, 174; in clinical vignette of core affective experience, 307; healing affects and, 172–173, 175–176; therapists and, 334

Technique (therapeutic): in AEDP, 338; Davanloo and, 327–329; emotional experience and, 239; environment and, 69; moment-to-moment assessment of clinical material and, 103; in portrayal, 285; problems with ISDP theory, 330; STDP and, 313–317; T–C–P and, 322; theory and, 215; in traditional psychoanalysis, 315; See also AEDP; AET; Brief psychotherapy; Davanloo; ISTDP; Malan; Psychoanalysis; STDP

The body: AEDP and, 215; experiential-affective strategies of intervention and, 217(table)

Theory of mind, 44–45

Therapeutic experience, the: meta-therapeutic process and, 163–164

Therapeutic process, the, 27; autobiographical narrative and, 270; experiential processing and, 247; feeling understood and, 64; optimal, 67; the patient in AET and, 332; reflective self function and, 56; self state and, 147; See also AEDP; AET; Brief psychotherapy; Initial contact; ISTDP; Meta-therapeutic process; Psychoanalysis; STDP; Technique

Therapeutic relationship, the, 109, 219–221; in AET, 332; affect and, 17; analytic theory and, 38; anxiety abatement and, 108; clinical vignette of core affective experience and, 310; presence of the therapist and, 90; T–C–P and, 131, 133; visceral experience and, 20, 138; See also Patient

Therapeutic response, 109; as a limitation in AET, 335

Therapeutic technique. See Technique

Therapeutic work: AEDP strategies of intervention and, 215; autobiographical narrative and, 269; countertransference in AET and, 334; experiential-affective strategies of intervention and, 271; little-step-by-little-step process and, 151; mourning and, 166; negative v. positive affect and, 67; presence of the therapist and, 89; reparation and, 66; transformation and, 137; See also AEDP; AET; Brief psychotherapy; ISTDP; Psychoanalysis; STDP; Technique

Therapist, the: achievements of the patient and, 224; affective model of change and, 6; affirmation and, 223, 225; appraisal and, 152; collaborative work with the patient, 234; core affect and, 159; emotional experience and, 70; empathy and, 152–153, 227; example of reparation and, 128–129; the good-enough caregiver and, 68; holding and, 156; ill-placed modesty and, 221; intervention and, 213–218; Malan on, 322; meta-therapeutic process and, 161–163, 176, 178–179; presence of, 29–30, 38, 89–90; relational experience and, 149; relationship patterns and, 264–265; the reparative drive and, 68; response and, 155; working with anxiety, 252–254; working with shame, 255–257; See also AEDP; AET; Brief psychotherapy; Clinical vignettes; ISTDP; STDP

Therapist-patient interaction, 187–189; affective model of change and, 54; STDP and, 319, 340; transformational model of mutual influence and, 124; See also Clinical vignettes; Communication; Initial contact; Interaction; Intervention; Response

Therapist-patient relationship: AEDP and, 339; in AET, 330, 334; affective model of change and, 64; analytic theory and, 38; clinical vignette of a first session, 192–211; Malan and STDP and, 322; response and, 37; safety and, 48; STDP and, 319

Therapy, the therapeutic, 108; affective competence and, 70; autobiographical narrative and, 269; clinical vignette of a first session, 188–212; connection and, 219; Davanloo and, 1–3; emotional experience and, 239; experience and, 5; expression and, 290; intergenerational pathology and, 55; ISTDP and, 324; Malan on, 322; the patient's gratitude and, 178; repetition and, 134; self state and, 147; the work of, 38; See also AEDP; AET; Brief psychotherapy; Clinical vignettes; ISTDP; Psychoanalysis; STDP

Tomkins, Silvan S., 24

Tracking, 219; the AEDP process, 190; in clinical vignette of grief and visceral exploration, 281, 282; of emotional experience, 271–272; of fluctuations in openness v. defensiveness, 246–247; of green-signal affects, 257–258; Malan and STDP and, 322; relational strategies of intervention and,

216(table); of relationship patterns, 264; restructuring strategies of intervention and, 216(table), 217(table); structuring tools for, 103; *See also* Affective markers; Signal affects

Transference: AEDP v. psychoanalysis, 220; analytic theory and, 38; interaction and, 54; ISTDP and, 327–328; Malan on, 322; tracking and, 4

Transformation, 215; AEDP and, 336; Affect and, 4; affective salience and, 73–74; categorical emotions and, 139; communication and, 6; core affect and, 15, 17, 137; core and, 138; emotion and, 19–20; experience and, 5; feelings and, 144; holding environment and, 22; little-step-by-little-step process and, 232; meta-therapeutic process and, 161–163; ownership of, 177; positive therapeutic experience and, 179; processing of core affective experience and, 23; receiving affirmation and, 171; religious faith and, 18; the therapeutic process and, 27; visceral experience and, 20

Trauma, 333; in clinical vignette of core affective experience, 306; disorganized/disoriented attachment and, 44; portrayal and, 287; reflective self function and, 45, 55, 56; relationship patterns and, 265; secure attachment and, 41; the unresolved–disorganized caregiver and, 53

Treatment. *See* Therapy

Trial therapy (initial evaluation): brief psychotherapy and, 321; ISTDP and, 328; STDP and, 319

Triangle of comparisons, 7, 103–104, 136; in clinical example of the pathogenic past, 267; in clinical vignette of a first session, 199; in clinical vignette of core affective experience, 301; in clinical vignette of grief and visceral exploration, 282; emotional experiences and, 188; the first interview and, 191; and focus on bodily-rooted correlates of experience, 280; Malan and, 318; patterns of self–other–emotion and, 263;

repetition and, 266; restructuring strategies of intervention and, 217(table); T–C–P and, 130–133

Triangle of conflict, 7, 103–106, 107, 136; affective experience and, 154; affects and, 120; autobiographical narrative and, 269; categorical emotions and, 139; categories of, 110–112; in clinical vignette of acknowledgement, 237; in clinical vignette of a first session, 195, 198; in clinical vignette of core affective experience, 301; core emotions and, 140; emotional truth and, 160; the first interview and, 191; focus in brief psychotherapy and, 321; and focus on bodily-rooted correlates of experience, 280; ISTDP and, 324; Malan and STDP and, 318, 322; moment-to-moment clinical material and, 246–247; in moment-to-moment translation of patient material, 187; relationship patterns and, 263; self–other–emotion triangle and, 118; therapeutic response and, 109; triangle of comparisons and, 132(figure)

Triangle of defensive response, 106–107; averse affects and, 113; categories of experience leading to, 111(table); clinical vignette of acknowledgement and, 237; in clinical vignette of a first session, 195; in clinical vignette of insufficient adaptive action tendencies, 221; entrenched defenses and, 247; insecure attachment and, 117; self at worst and, 128(figure); versus triangle of expressive response, 119

Triangle of expressive response, 107, 108–109; affect-facilitating environment and, 117; categories of experience leading to, 112(table); clinical vignette of, 258–261; in clinical vignette of insufficient adaptive action tendencies, 221; example of, 110; facilitating affects and, 113; soft defenses and, 247; versus transference repetition, 134; versus triangle of defensive response, 119

Triangle of person, 103; focus in brief psychotherapy and, 321; Malan and STDP and, 318, 322

Tronick, Edward Z., 61; the coordinated state and, 63; on mirroring, 62

True other, the, 8, 169–170; idealization and, 170; *See also* Other

True self experience, 147–148

True self, the, 8; authentic personality of, 148; as clarity, 121; in clinical vignette of defense against empathy, 228; in clinical vignette of reflective self function, 91; in clinical vignette of triangle of expressive response, 259; core affect and, 31–32; the true other and, 169–170; *See also* Authentic self; Essential self

Trust: affirmation and, 223; in clinical vignette of a first session, 207; as green-signal affect, 258; healing and, 6; intervention and, 213; between patient and therapist, 36

Unbearable, the, 80–82; in clinical vignette of reflective self function, 96; emotional isolation and, 141; errors of commission and, 79

Unconscious communication: in clinical vignette of a first session, 193, 204; Davanloo and, 327; Malan and, 320–321; STDP and, 318

Unconscious, the, 339; affect and, 21; classical analytic technique v. STDP, 315–316; in clinical vignette of a first session, 201; in clinical vignette of core affective experience, 299, 303, 310; clinical vignette of reparative portrayal and, 294; Davanloo and, 325, 327–328; patient's response to interventions and, 191; portrayal and, 284, 286, 289

Understanding: autobiographical narrative and, 269, 270; environmental failure and, 60; experience and, 57; reflective, 58; *See also* Feeling understood

Validating, 223–224; in clinical vignette of grief and visceral exploration, 281; in clinical vignette of therapist self-disclosure, 239; emotional experience, 256

Varieties of Religious Experience (James), 137

Videotape: the patient and, 332; the patient in AET and, 332; STDP and, 317; the therapist and, 167

Vignettes. *See* Clinical vignettes

Visceral experience: in AEDP, 336; affect and, 20, 21; the body and, 24–25; in clinical vignette of acknowledgement, 237; clinical vignette of a first session and, 212; in clinical vignette of core affective experience, 302, 304, 309; in clinical vignette of reflective self function, 93; in clinical vignette of shame, 256; in clinical vignette of triangle of expressive response, 260; Davanloo and, 2, 323, 329; focusing on, 279–280; interpretive techniques and, 323; ISTDP and, 328; naming and, 276; within the therapeutic relationship, 138; transformation and, 137; upping the ante and, 275

Visceral, the, 273; in portrayal, 289

Vitality affect: in clinical vignette of reflective self function, 93; core state and, 138, 142

Vulnerability: in clinical vignette of reflective self function, 91; errors of commission and, 79; healing affects and, 173; negative response and, 114; self state and, 147

"We," the, 148; as a limitation in AET, 335

Winnicott, Donald Woods, 311; the mind and, 60

Wolf Man case, the, 320

Yeats, William Butler, 71